The M & E Handbook Series

Company Law

KU-758-180

M C Oliver

revised by Enid A Marshall, MA, LLB, PHD

Tenth edition

Pitman Publishing
128 Long Acre, London WC2E 9AN

A Longman Group Company

First published in Great Britain 1966
Second edition 1967
Third edition 1971
Fourth edition 1973
Fifth edition 1976
Sixth edition 1977
Seventh edition 1979
Eighth edition 1981
Ninth edition 1982
Tenth edition 1987
Reprinted 1988

© Longman Group UK Ltd 1987

British Library Cataloguing in Publication Data

Oliver, M. C.
Company law. – 10th ed. – (M & E
handbooks, ISSN 0265-8828).
1. Corporation law – Great Britain
I. Title II. Marshall, Enid A.
344.106′66   KD2079

ISBN 0 7121 0698 7

Founding Editor: P. W. D. Redmond

Printed and bound in Great Britain by
Richard Clay Ltd, Bungay, Suffolk

Contents

Preface to the tenth edition

'Company law is not difficult', stated Lady Oliver in her preface to the first edition in 1966. 'It merely requires *Work*. Precision is essential and gossip useless'. By 1982, however, when the preface to the ninth edition was written, Lady Oliver had to admit that 'since this book was first published in 1966 there has been an uninterrupted flow of company law legislation' and had to refer to company law as 'an immensely technical subject'.

With the long-overdue consolidation of company law in 1985, one might have thought that the ideal time had arrived for the publication of another edition. But it was not to be, for already in 1985 many amendments were made to the brand new consolidated provisions by the Insolvency Act 1985. Swiftly, and mercifully, a further, this time partial, consolidation followed in 1986, making it necessary for the revisor to accommodate in the new text the company law provisions of the Insolvency Act 1986 and the Company Directors Disqualification Act 1986. Substantial amendments have since been made in parts of the subject by the Financial Services Act 1986.

Given that company law is now an immense, and no longer a particularly easy, subject, there is all the more need to supply a tenth edition of Lady Oliver's distinguished Handbook, which filled so well the role of being a small introductory work designed primarily for beginners with no previous legal training and for the examination requirements of company secretaries, accountants and students of business management. The aim still is, as in the first edition, 'to be as simple as possible, in the hope that readers will pursue the subject in more advanced books'.

Thanks to Jackie Thomas for preparing the Table of Statutes and to David Palfreman who supplied part of the Appendix on examination technique.

Enid A. Marshall   February 1987

Table of cases

Table of statutes

1

The basic principles of company law

1. The subject-matter of this book. The aim of this book is to give an elementary account of the law which applies to registered companies, i.e. to companies registered under the Companies Act 1985.

Students may approach their study of company law with the notion that it consists of a dull mass of complex rules and restrictions, coupled with even more complex exceptions, all to be searched for in a bulky volume of legislation of which the Companies Act 1985 is the principal part. There is only a vestige of truth in that notion. Company law is much more interesting than that.

It is true to say that there are very many detailed statutory provisions applicable to registered companies, and that their bulk is constantly on the increase. Against this, however, one must balance the following factors:

(a) the basis of common law and equity on which the legislation has been superimposed;

(b) the fact that the subject is a modern one;

(c) the circumstance that the latest consolidation is as recent as 1985-86; and

(d) the recognition that the more complex the statutory provisions are, the greater is the likelihood that they will not feature in ordinary examination questions at an elementary level.

A little more must be said about each of these encouraging factors.

2. The basis of common law and equity. There has never been a codification of company law in this country. There have been several *consolidating* Acts, each in its turn gathering into a single Act all the pre-existing statutory provisions with the result that the earlier provisions are repealed and re-enacted in a more convenient and compact form in a new Act.

The rules of common law and of equity continue as the base on which all the statutory provisions are superimposed, and where no statutory provision exists to cover the situation, the rules of common law and equity are applicable.

Despite the great mass of legislation, therefore, company law is still partly to be found in, and enlivened by, decided cases.

3. A modern subject. By legal standards company law is a modern subject. The system of registration for companies had its origins in an Act of 1844. The principle of limited liability, which was introduced in 1855, was then combined with the registration system in the Joint Stock Companies Act 1856.

Six years later, there was passed the first of a series of consolidating Acts – the Companies Act 1862.

Since that date the pattern has been for amendments to company law to be made by separate new Acts passed as the need for them became evident, and then, when the consolidating Act plus its often numerous amendments became too cumbersome, to have a new consolidating Act passed so as to accommodate all the existing legislation once more in a single Act.

Such consolidating Acts were passed in 1908, 1929 and 1948. The current consolidation is that of 1985–86.

4. The consolidation of 1985–86. By 1985 a new consolidating Companies Act had been long overdue, to replace the 1948 Act which had been heavily amended by Acts of 1967, 1972, 1976, 1980 and 1981 in particular. As a result of all these amending Acts, it had become increasingly difficult to find what the present statutory provisions were.

However, the consolidation which was at last accomplished in 1985 did not precisely follow the pattern of earlier consolidating Acts (*see* 3). It consisted, for the first time, not of a single Act but of four Acts:

(*a*) the Companies Act 1985;
(*b*) the Company Securities (Insider Dealing) Act 1985;

(c) the Business Names Act 1985; and

(d) the Companies Consolidation (Consequential Provisions) Act 1985.

The last is of a transitional nature, and need not be further mentioned. The first is the principal Act and throughout this book references to sections are references to sections of that Act unless the context indicates otherwise. The provisions of the second and third Acts, each of which has a restricted subject-matter, will be dealt with at appropriate points in later chapters.

However, these four Acts of 1985 are not the end of the story of our present consolidation. In the very same year Parliament was already passing an Act – the Insolvency Act 1985 – substantially amending the law relating to disqualification of company directors and the law relating to insolvency generally, including insolvent companies. The position reached called for a further consolidation of the *affected parts* of the 1985 consolidation, and this took the form of two Acts of 1986:

(a) the Company Directors Disqualification Act 1986; and

(b) the Insolvency Act 1986.

The first of these latest consolidating Acts is dealt with principally in the chapter on directors (Chapter 16). The second is a much longer Act and must be looked at for several chapters, particularly those concerned with the winding up of companies (Chapters 28–31).

While the Companies Act 1985 remains the principal Act, it must be remembered that not a few sections of it were amended or repealed by the Insolvency Act 1985, and the corresponding new provision is to be found in the two consolidating Acts of 1986.

A further major amending Act has since been passed: the Financial Services Act 1986, making substantial alterations on the provisions of the consolidating Acts dealing with prospectuses, insider dealing and takeover offers.

In all, therefore, the student now approaching his study of company law is faced with six consolidating Acts of 1985–86 and their subsequent amendments. He does, however, enjoy an immense advantage over his counterpart of a few years ago. A student of 1983, for instance, had to look to no fewer than 11 Acts, i.e. to the then principal Act (the Companies Act 1948) and 10 later Acts which amended it. Even a student of 1985, after the passing of the Insolvency

Act 1985, had the task of consulting two Acts at the same time – the Companies Act 1985 and the Insolvency Act 1985.

Although the consolidation of 1985, so long awaited, was quickly broken into by the passing of the Insolvency Act 1985, a notable welcome feature in the most recent phase of company law development is the speed with which a new consolidation of the relevant part of company law was achieved by the passing of the two consolidating Acts of 1986. It can confidently be expected that in the next one or two years a further consolidation will take place, removing the present need to consult amending Acts (such as the Financial Services Act 1986) superimposed on the existing consolidated provisions. On the other hand, it must be admitted that company law is a fast-moving subject and further amendments are never far away.

5. Complex statutory provisions and examination questions. Many of the readers of this book will be studying for examinations on company law, usually at a comparatively elementary level (though it may not seem elementary to them).

Be comforted! No self-respecting examiner would set questions calling for a knowledge of complex statutory provisions. The rote learning required for success in such questions is out-moded and frowned upon. Even experts in company law would shy from giving an answer without close scrutiny of the actual wording and context of the statutory provision, and the only examination question which could justifiably be set on complex provisions would be an open-book examination taken by advanced students of company law who are beyond the scope of this book.

Complicated provisions have been enacted mainly because *in practice* they were found to be necessary or desirable. The student of this book should first grasp the *principles* and the *general objects* of company law.

As regards principles, two are fundamental:

(*a*) the concept of *legal personality*; and
(*b*) the theory of *limited liability*.

As regards the general objects, much of the detail will fall into place once the student appreciates the fact that most of the statutory rules are intended for one of two purposes:

(a) the *protection of creditors* (e.g. the rules preventing reduction of capital without proper safeguards); and

(b) the *protection of investors* (e.g. the rules concerning offers of shares to the public and concerning the accounts).

6. EEC legislation. Much of the reform of company law in recent years has resulted from this country's membership of the EEC.

Legislation emanating from the EEC institutions may take the form of:

(a) regulations, which are directly enforceable in member states; or

(b) directives, which require the member state to alter its law so as to comply with the directive, although it has a discretion as to the means by which it achieves that end; or

(c) decisions.

The binding force of EEC law in the United Kingdom was established by the European Communities Act 1972.

Section 9 of that Act made changes in this country's company law in compliance with the First Directive of the EEC Council of Ministers. Especially noteworthy was the modification of the *ultra vires* doctrine. Similarly, the Companies Act 1980 implemented the Second Directive and the Companies Act 1981 implemented the Fourth Directive.

Directives and regulations are issued first in draft, and it is clear from the number in draft form awaiting implementation that EEC law is to continue to be a fruitful source of amendments to company law for as long as the United Kingdom remains a member of the EEC.

7. The starting-point. Every subject should have a starting-point which a beginner with no previous knowledge can understand. Here it is suggested that the easiest way of beginning to study company law is to imagine that you yourself are about to 'go into business', i.e. that you have a little money saved or lent to you and are about to start a small business.

The first legal question which arises is: in which legal form shall the business operate? In order to decide this question it is necessary to examine the legal forms of a business and understand the differences between them. There are three:

(a) You may be a *sole trader*.

(b) You may form a *partnership* with one or more other persons.

(c) You may form a *limited company* by registration under the Companies Act.

Each of these must now be considered in turn.

8. A sole trader. A sole trader is so called because *he alone* bears the responsibility for running the business, and *he alone* takes the profits.

He may of course be helped by his wife and family, or he may employ other people to work for him, but this does not alter the fact that the management is entirely in his hands. A man in this position has not formed any kind of 'association' in law.

9. A partnership. In a partnership the members 'associate', i.e. they form collectively an association in which they all participate, as a rule, in management and in sharing the profits. The basic rules governing such an association are to be found in the Partnership Act 1890.

(a) *Number of partners.* Obviously there must be at least two members in a partnership, but there may be more. There is, however, in most cases a maximum number. Section 716 Companies Act 1985 states that this maximum is 20, but exempts from this provision partnerships of solicitors, accountants, members of a recognized stock exchange and other partnerships specified in regulations made by the Secretary of State for Trade and Industry. If a partnership not covered by any of the exemptions has a membership of more than 20, the members must *incorporate* themselves by registering as a company under the Companies Act.

(b) *Liability of partners.* In a partnership the legal position of the members is not very different from that of a sole trader. If the firm gets into financial difficulties, all the partners may find that their creditors are seeking to make them bankrupt, and since all the partners are liable for the debts of the firm, they are not protected against the possibility of total bankruptcy. At the same time, just because they are liable for the firm's debts, they may find that tradesmen are willing to give them credit on the grounds, for example, that one of the partners is known to be a very wealthy man.

(c) *Legal position of partners.* The members of a partnership may sue and be sued collectively by using the name of the firm, but this is a matter of legal procedure only, and does not alter the fact that the action is being brought by or against the *partners*. All the partners are *agents* for each other, i.e. each one can bind the others when he makes contracts on behalf of the firm. It follows that each partner is a *principal*. They are therefore all in a *fiduciary relation* with each other, i.e. they must not only tell each other the truth in conducting the business, but they must disclose the whole truth. For instance, no partner may make a secret profit. The word 'fiduciary' comes from the Latin *fides*, meaning trust or confidence.

(*d*) *Rights of partners.* Usually the rights of the partners are regulated by a contract drawn up between them and put in writing, called the 'articles' of partnership or the 'partnership deed'. The partners may make what arrangements they like in this contract, but when they have not made any provision at all the position is regulated by the Partnership Act 1890. A partnership need not be created formally, however, and may arise through an oral agreement or even by conduct.

10. A limited partnership. There is a special type of partnership which is very rare but should be mentioned. It is called a *limited partnership* and is regulated by the Limited Partnerships Act 1907. Here it is possible for all the partners except one to be 'limited partners'. A limited partner puts into the firm a certain amount of money, e.g. £500, and then he is not responsible for the debts of the firm above that figure. This means that he can lose his £500, but cannot be made bankrupt or made to pay more than this sum. The £500 is the 'limit' of his liability. He cannot, however, take part in the management of the firm.

There must always be at least one partner whose liability for the firm's debts is not limited in this way, and he is called a 'general partner'. He manages the business, bears the risk, but normally gets the bulk of the profits. Limited partnerships are very rare because in the same year in which they were introduced the Companies Act 1907 made it possible to form a *private company*, which is a much more convenient way of running a small business. The ordinary type of partnership described in **9** above, however, is very common and will be referred to later when a comparison will be drawn between it and the limited company (*see* **4:5**).

11. The meaning of the word 'company'. Partnerships often describe themselves as 'Smith, Brown and Co.', but this is misleading because they are not companies in the strict sense of the word. The difficulty is caused by the fact that the word 'company' has a variable meaning and can be used in many ways. The meaning depends on the context. When a partnership describes itself in this way the partners are simply indicating that there are other persons in their association besides Smith and Brown. They are *not* indicating that their business is a company registered under the Companies Act.

12. A limited company formed by registration under the Companies Act. If you choose this form for your business you are *incorporating* it, i.e. you are forming a corporation. You are also going to acquire *limited liability*. The actual process of incorporation by registration forms the subject-matter of Chapters 2–4 and there is much detail to be learnt about it, but before this process is described it is essential to clarify the two legal concepts which have already been mentioned as being the basis of company law, i.e. legal personality and limited liability (*see* **13–16** below).

13. The concept of legal personality. A *human* person is a man, woman or child and usually recognizable as such, but a *legal* person is not quite the same thing. In the first place, a legal person is not always human. In the second place, in some societies (though not in ours today) a human person is not necessarily a legal person.

A legal person can be described as any person, human or otherwise, who has rights and duties at law, i.e. who can seek the aid of the court and against whom the aid of the court can be sought by others. It is clear that in a modern civilized community all human persons fall into this category, but slaves, when slavery was lawful, did not: they were regarded as property, not persons, and they could be owned and dealt with as property. Today it is almost universally true that no-one may own another person. In a modern state all human persons, whatever their sex or age, can enforce their rights in the court and can be made liable for breach of their legal duties by the court.

A human person is, therefore, a legal person all his life, i.e. from birth to death. But it is important to remember that for some purposes he has pre-natal rights and the courts protect him even before he is born, while for other purposes his rights remain enforceable after death for specified periods. Students learn more about this when they study criminal law and the law of tort, but it is outside the proper scope of this book.

Although all human persons are legal persons, not all legal persons are human. The non-human legal persons are called *corporations*, a word derived from the Latin '*corpus*' (body). A corporation is a legal person created by a process other than natural birth. It is therefore sometimes called an *artificial* legal person, but it should not be called 'fictitious', because it really exists. For instance, if a man has a carnation in his button-hole it may be a real one or an artificial one, but it can hardly be said to be fictitious if it is there.

14. Types of corporation. There are many types of corporations and they can be classified in various ways, e.g.:

(*a*) *sole* (where one human being constitutes the corporation and has a dual personality, one corporate and the other human or natural. The Crown is an example of this type of corporation);

(*b*) *aggregate* (where the corporation consists of two or more persons).

Another classification is into:

(*a*) *lay* (e.g. Imperial Chemical Industries or the Institute of Chartered Secretaries and Administrators);

(*b*) *ecclesiastical* (e.g. the Archbishop of Canterbury).

A third classification is into:

(*a*) *trading* (e.g. Imperial Chemical Industries);

(*b*) *non-trading* (e.g. the Institute of Chartered Secretaries and Administrators).

Thus the particular type of corporation which we are about to study is a lay trading corporation aggregate.

For our purposes, however, by far the most useful classification is based on the method of formation. Corporations may exist as a result of:

(*a*) *common law*, e.g. the Crown or a bishop;

(*b*) *prescription*, i.e. the corporation has existed so long that the law presumes that it had a charter which was lost;

(*c*) *royal charter*;

(*d*) *statute*;

(*e*) *registration under the Companies Act.*

The corporation we are studying is formed in this last way.

NOTE: Students are often confused by being told that a corporation can be statutory, i.e. formed by statute, and that this is a different method of formation from registration under the Act. They feel that both these types of corporation are 'statutory'. The difference, however, is that a statutory corporation is directly created by a particular Act of Parliament which is passed for that specific purpose. The Companies Act, on the other hand, does not itself create any corporations at all. It merely lays down a *process* by which any two or more persons who so desire can themselves create a corporation by complying with the rules for registration which the Act prescribes.

15. The nature of the corporate person. The corporate legal person is very different from the natural or human legal person. It has neither body, mind nor soul. In the *Case of Sutton's Hospital* (1612), it was said that it 'is invisible, immortal, and rests only in intendment and consideration of the law'. Corporations 'cannot commit treason, nor be outlawed, nor excommunicated, for they have no souls'. A corporation is not subject to 'death of the natural body'.

It is not surprising, therefore, that a variety of legal problems, of which space does not permit treatment here, have arisen as to its criminal and tortious liability. There were at one time procedural difficulties in prosecuting it, and there were bound to be practical difficulties in punishing it. These have been largely overcome.

Less progress, however, seems to have been made on the spiritual plane. In *Rolloswin Investments Ltd* v. *Chromolit Portugal etc.* (1970), Mocatta J. declared: 'A limited company is incapable of public worship or repairing to a church or exercising itself in the duties of piety and true religion, either publicly or privately, on any day of the week'. More recently, in *Re Armvent Ltd* (1975), Templeman J. said: 'The company has no soul and no feelings', and he was accordingly 'not horrified' at the prospect of winding it up.

All corporations, then, however they came into existence, have *perpetual succession*, i.e. they were not born and so cannot die. They have been created by a process of law and can only be destroyed by a process of law and until so destroyed will continue to exist. They will exist even if all their human members are dead, for every corporation is a *separate* legal person from those legal persons who compose it.

In the latter part of this book the methods of destruction or dissolution are dealt with.

16. Limited liability. Students sometimes confuse the idea of limited liability with the principle outlined above concerning the independent legal personality of a corporation. It is true that in a large number of corporations the members have limited liability, but this is not necessarily so. Later we shall see that the Act itself provides for the creation of an unlimited company – i.e. a company where the members have unlimited liability.

The meaning of liability must be understood: it means the *extent to which a person can be made to account at law*. He is either fully liable, i.e. he can be made to pay the full amount of the debts owed, or he is liable only to a limited extent, i.e. he can be made to pay towards those debts only up to a certain limit, but not beyond it. In our company we shall see that the member's liability for the debts of the company is normally limited to the amount unpaid on his shares. Thus, if he buys 100 £1 shares 'at par', i.e. at £1 per share, and pays up 50p on each share, he has paid up £50 and can be made to pay another £50, but he cannot be made to pay more than £100 in all. This is so even if the debts of the company amount to many thousands of pounds.

Notice that it is only the *members'* liability for the *company's* debts which is limited. The company itself, the artificial legal person, is always fully liable and so has unlimited liability. It follows that so long as there are assets available to pay the debts, it must pay them. It will be seen later (*see* **18**) that these debts must be paid in a strict order laid down by the law and certain classes of creditor receive preferential treatment.

Of course a company, like a human person, may not have enough assets to pay its debts. It will then be dissolved by liquidation, while a human person in such a case would be made bankrupt. This condition of insolvency is in no way related to limited liability. Insolvency is a simple matter of *fact*: a person cannot pay his debts because he has not enough money. Liability is a matter of *law*: a person is liable to pay his debts to a limited or unlimited extent regardless of whether he has enough money. Thus, *ability* to pay one's debts must never be confused with *liability* to pay them.

17. Implications of the creation of a registered company. Now that we have considered the concepts of legal personality and limited liability, we must turn to the implications of the creation of this artificial legal person in the form of a registered company. This involves the study of the most famous of all company law cases:

Salomon v. *Salomon & Co. Ltd* (1897). The case, however, can only be thoroughly understood if a student already knows the order of distribution of a company's assets when it goes into liquidation. This is therefore given below and should be carefully studied and thoroughly learnt.

18. The order of distribution of a company's assets in liquidation. On liquidation the usual important distinction between capital and revenue ceases and these merge to become, collectively, the company's *assets* which the liquidator must assemble and distribute in the following order:

(*a*) Secured creditors with *fixed* charges usually take payment out of their security. If their security is inadequate, they rank as unsecured creditors for the balance of their debts.

(*b*) The costs of liquidation (including the liquidator's remuneration).

(*c*) Preferential creditors. (The 6th Schedule Insolvency Act 1986 lists them, and will be studied later: *see* 31:**2**.)

(*d*) Secured creditors with *floating* charges.

(*e*) Unsecured creditors.

(*f*) Debts due to members *as members*, e.g. dividends declared but not yet paid, and interest on calls paid in advance: s. 74(2)(*f*) Insolvency Act 1986.

(*g*) Repayment of capital to members *pari passu* (i.e. proportionately in relation to their shareholdings) unless the articles or terms of issue provide otherwise. (Often they give priority to the preference shareholders, but this is a modification by contract of the basic rule.)

(*h*) Surplus assets divisible among the members *pari passu*, unless the articles or terms of issue provide otherwise.

From this order it is apparent that the law protects the creditors of the company at the expense of the members. Even a debt due to a member in his capacity of member is deferred below the claims of the unsecured creditors by s. 74(2)(*f*) Insolvency Act 1986.

Moreover, the normal rule by which secured creditors rank before unsecured ones is reversed by s. 175(2) Insolvency Act 1986, which provides that preferential debts (which are unsecured) rank *before* secured creditors with floating charges. Floating charges are often over the whole of the company's assets generally, so if s. 175(2) did not make this provision there would be a much greater risk to the preferential creditors who include, of course, the Revenue.

A secured creditor part of whose debt is preferential and who realizes his security for less than the amount owing to him may appropriate the proceeds of sale to that part of his debt which is non-preferential, thus leaving his preferential claim outstanding: *Re William Hall (Contractors)* (1967).

Debenture-holders, being simply creditors, fall into (*a*), (*d*) or (*e*) according to whether they have a fixed charge, a floating charge, or are 'naked', i.e. unsecured and have no charge at all.

Finally, under s. 107 Insolvency Act 1986, the assets of a company must be applied to its liabilities *pari passu*, subject to the claims of its preferential creditors. Thus unsecured creditors all rank equally and if the assets are insufficient to discharge their debts in full, they will each receive a proportionate amount. Even a *judgement* creditor has no priority although he has brought a successful action for his debt. If, therefore, a contract is made which would result in a distribution of the company's property in a manner contrary to s. 107, the court will refuse to give effect to it, even though it was made for good business reasons and without any thought for the effect of insolvency on the arrangement agreed under it: *British Eagle International Air Lines* v. *Compagnie Nationale Air France* (1975).

NOTE: Students often ask whether a floating charge which has *crystallized* (21: 7) and so become fixed is promoted, as it were, from (*d*) to (*a*) on crystallization. This is not the case. One of the events which causes crystallization is liquidation, and if the holders of floating charges which had crystallized were in the same position as the holders of fixed charges, there would be no need to put the holders of floating charges into a separate category as shown above.

19. *Salomon* v. *Salomon & Co. Ltd.* The facts of this leading case were as follows:

Salomon ran a boot business which he decided to incorporate. He formed a registered company by the process of registration, and then sold his business to the company. The only members of the company were Salomon, his wife, and his children, who by luck or judgment were just sufficient in number to form a registered company. (The minimum number of subscribers required to form a public company was seven until the Companies Act 1980 reduced it to two, and it was not possible to form a private company with the smaller minimum number of members until 1907.) All the members knew of and approved the entire arrangement.

Salomon's wife and children each held one share in this company, and the remainder were held by Salomon himself. In payment for the business these shares were allotted to Salomon fully paid up, but part of the purchase-price was left outstanding as a debt due to Salomon from the company. He was careful to see that it was secured by a floating charge over the company's assets.

When at length the company went into liquidation, these assets were insufficient to pay all the debts. The unsecured trade creditors claimed that they were entitled to such assets as existed, on the grounds that the whole transaction was a sham, and that the secured debentures originally issued to Salomon were therefore invalid. They regarded the company as in essence the same person as Salomon himself, since he controlled it.

The House of Lords either had to agree that this was so, thereby rejecting the whole principle of incorporation and the theory of the corporate legal personality, or had to hold that once a corporation has been formed, it is an entirely different legal person from the members who compose and control it. They chose the latter course, and accordingly the company was treated as a different legal person from Salomon. It followed that since the debentures originally issued to him were secured by a floating charge, the holder had priority over the unsecured trade creditors, who in consequence received nothing.

This famous case established beyond all doubt the existence of the 'veil of incorporation', i.e. the legal personality of the corporation through which the identity of the members cannot be perceived.

20. Application of *Salomon* v. *Salomon & Co. Ltd.* It is a consequence of the principle of *Salomon* v. *Salomon & Co. Ltd* that the property of the company belongs to the company and not to the individual members of the company.

Thus in *Macaura* v. *Northern Assurance Co. Ltd* (1925) Macaura, having sold timber to a company in which he and his nominees were the sole shareholders, insured the timber against fire by policies taken out in his own name. Macaura was also a creditor of the company. Most of the timber was destroyed by fire. HELD: Neither as a shareholder nor as a creditor did Macaura have any insurable interest in the timber, since it was an asset owned by the company. Lord Wrenbury said: 'The corporator even if he holds all the shares is not the corporation'.

Similarly, in a Privy Council case *Lee* v. *Lee's Air Farming Ltd* (1961) Lee was, apart from a solicitor who held one share, the sole shareholder and the governing director of a company. He was employed at a salary as chief pilot and was killed in an aircrash while piloting the company's aircraft. The question in the case was whether he was a 'worker' for the purposes of a Workers' Compensation Act. HELD: Since the company was a person distinct from its shareholders, Lee was a servant of the company and so a 'worker', even though he was the controlling shareholder and sole director.

Several other instances of the application of *Salomon* v. *Salomon & Co. Ltd* will be discovered in later chapters.

21. Lifting the veil of incorporation. The principle of the separate legal personality of the company is not, however, without its exceptions. Both at common law and under the provisions of the Act there are instances of the veil being 'lifted', so that the identity of the members can be seen, not through a glass darkly, but face to face. A few of the instances are given in the next two paragraphs. Others will be seen at appropriate points in later chapters.

22. Cases illustrating lifting of the veil. The following are a few instances of cases where the court has decided that in the interests of justice and equity the veil of incorporation should be lifted.

In *Gilford Motor Co. Ltd* v. *Horne* (1933) a managing director's contract of employment included a covenant in restraint of trade by which he undertook that, on the termination of his employment, he would not solicit the company's customers. However, on the termination of his employment, he formed a new company consisting virtually of himself and sent out circulars to his former employer's customers. HELD: The new company was a mere channel, a mere cloak or sham for the purpose of enabling the former managing director to commit a breach of the covenant. An injunction was therefore granted against him and the new company to restrain any further breach of the covenant.

In *Jones* v. *Lipman* (1962) there had been a written agreement for the sale of land by Lipman to Jones. Lipman asked to be released from the contract, and on Jones' refusal transferred the land to a company in which he himself and his solicitor's clerk were the sole shareholders and sole directors. HELD: Jones was entitled to specific performance. Russell J. said: 'The defendant company is the creature of the first defendant, a device and a sham, a mask which he holds before his face in an attempt to avoid recognition by the eye of equity'.

There are several cases where the court has lifted the veil to identify the relationship within a group of companies. Thus, in *Smith, Stone & Knight Ltd* v. *Birmingham Corporation* (1939) a subsidiary company was held to be an agent of its holding company, while conversely in *Wm Cory & Son Ltd* v. *Dorman Long & Co. Ltd* (1936) a parent company was held to be the agent of its subsidiary, and in *D.H.N. Food Distributors Ltd* v. *Tower Hamlets London Borough Council* (1976), where two subsidiary companies were wholly owned by the holding company and had no separate business operations, the court held it just to treat the group as a single entity.

A particularly striking instance of lifting the veil is *Re Bugle Press Ltd* (1961) which arose out of a 'take-over bid' (*see* 32:**10**). Two out of the three shareholders in a company formed themselves into a new company which made a take-over bid for all the shares of the first company. These two shareholders accepted the bid, but the third rejected it. As, however, he held only one-tenth of the shares, the new company became entitled to acquire his shares compulsorily under s. 209 Companies Act 1948 (now s. 428 Companies Act 1985). HELD: The compulsory acquisition would not be allowed because the section was being abused for the purpose of enabling the majority shareholders in the first company to evict the minority shareholder. The court was thus lifting the veil so as to reveal that the new company was in reality the same in identity as the majority shareholders of the first company. Harman L.J. said that the new company was 'nothing but a little hut built round' the two majority shareholders and that the whole scheme was a 'hollow sham'.

23. Provisions of the Act illustrating lifting of the veil. Some of the sections of the Act which have the effect of lifting the veil of incorporation are as follows:

(a) Section 24 (*see* 2:**34**). Under this section the members, if they fall below two in number, can lose the protective shield of the company as regards its debts.

(b) Section 349(4) (*see* 2:**10**). Under this subsection an officer of the company or any person on its behalf who omits to place the company's name on a negotiable instrument which he signs on behalf of the company may be personally liable to the holder for the specified amount.

(c) Section 433 (*see* 22:**4**). This concerns the power of an inspector appointed by the Department of Trade and Industry to investigate the affairs of any company within the same group as the company primarily under investigation.

(d) Section 442 (*see* 22:**8**). This concerns the power of the Department of Trade and Industry to investigate membership.

(e) Section 283(4) (*see* 16:**3**). The device of the corporation cannot be used to evade s. 283(2).

(f) Section 324 and the 13th Schedule (*see* 16:**16**). Here a person is deemed interested in shares or debentures if he has a certain degree of control over the company which holds them.

(g) Section 229 (*see* 18:**7**). This section requires group accounts to be laid before the general meeting of the holding company, disregarding the separate corporate personalities of the companies in the group and emphasizing their economic unity.

(h) Section 346 and the 13th Schedule (*see* 16:**30**). Under this provision a director is identified with a body corporate controlled by him.

(i) Section 203 (*see* 12:**15**). Here again a person is deemed interested in shares if he has a certain degree of control over the company which holds them.

An instance from the Insolvency Act 1986 is:

(j) Section 214 Insolvency Act 1986 (*see* 2:**34**). By this provision a director guilty of wrongful trading may be declared by the court to be liable to make such contribution to the company's assets as the court thinks proper.

If these examples are examined closely, it will be seen that the expression is used in more than one way. In its strict sense, it is applied to cases where the personality of the corporation is penetrated to reveal the *members* of the company as individuals, e.g. in *Re Bugle Press*

Ltd or under s. 24. In these cases it is as though one were looking at the bricks rather than the building. The emphasis is on the composition, not the structure. In a wider sense, however, the expression covers in a loose and academically unsatisfactory way cases where the personality of the corporation is swept aside in order to reach the *officers* of the company, e.g. under s. 349(4). Here it is not a matter of the law substituting composition for structure, since the officers do not compose the corporation, but rather enabling an injured outsider to pursue his remedy against the persons responsible for his injury, whether they are members or not. If there is any rationale behind these cases, it may be that the *corporation* ought not to be made liable for wrongful acts done by *individuals* purporting to act on its behalf or in its name.

24. The arrangement of this book. It is appropriate to conclude this first chapter by taking a bird's eye view of the individual topics which are dealt with in the succeeding chapters and noting in passing some of the essential terminology of our subject.

25. Registration. As is already known, a registered company comes into existence through a process of registration. This involves the filing with the registrar of companies of certain documents, of which, at the beginning of the company's life, the most important are the company's memorandum of association and articles of association. The certificate of incorporation, issued by the registrar in response to compliance with the registration procedure laid down in the Act, is the company's birth certificate.

This material – the memorandum of association, the articles of association and registration – is discussed in Chapters 2–4.

Throughout company law, there are many further requirements for registration with the registrar, including the filing of resolutions, accounts and reports.

The object of all the registration requirements is to secure publicity for important matters concerning the company. The information filed with the registrar may be consulted by any member of the public who is interested in any way in the company – it may be as a prospective creditor or prospective investor.

26. Setting the company going. Although, with the issue of the company's certificate of incorporation, the company is formally in existence as a legal person, there are normally many arrangements to be made before the company can be said to be a 'going concern'.

The company may require to obtain a further certificate in order to be entitled to trade and enter into contracts. Chapter 5 deals with this.

The persons who take steps to set the company going are called 'promoters'. They are in a fiduciary relationship to the company and must make full disclosure of any profit which they obtain from their position. Although the persons who sign the memorandum of association (and so become the company's first members) are not normally promoters, the Act has provisions aimed at ensuring that these persons also do not obtain for themselves an undisclosed profit. Chapter 6 deals with these matters.

27. Raising capital. The company, if it is to trade on a large scale, will normally wish to raise capital, directly or indirectly, from the public. Offers of listed and unlisted shares to the public are the subject matter of Chapter 7.

Those who offer shares to the public will want the offer to be successful. They will, however, realize that it is possible that not all the shares offered in the prospectus will in fact be taken up, and to safeguard themselves against such a failure they will arrange for the shares to be 'underwritten', i.e. to be taken up by a financial house, in return for a commission, in so far as the public does not take up the offer. The provisions of the Act which regulate the paying of underwriting commission are given in Chapter 8.

Where a person applies to the company for shares and receives from the company the shares applied for, the company is said to 'allot' the shares. The 'allottee' is then the first holder of these shares. He may later choose to sell his shares to another person, who will be a 'transferee' (not an allottee, because the term 'allottee' is used only of a person who obtains his shares *from the company*). The price paid for shares allotted is paid to the company. The provisions of the Act on allotment and payment for shares are in Chapters 9 and 10.

Finally in this group of chapters is Chapter 11 on capital itself. It deals with what the company may do with its capital, once obtained, e.g. the procedure by which it may alter its amount or structure.

28. Shareholders and members. Capital is divided into shares and the persons who hold the shares are, obviously enough, referred to as 'shareholders'. In the ordinary type of company the word 'shareholders' is synonymous with 'members'. There are, however, some companies (in particular companies limited by guarantee) where the company has no share capital, and so has no shareholders, but does have members.

In the normal trading company with which we are concerned in this book, Chapters 12–14 are on closely related topics. Chapter 12 deals with shares (how they may be transferred, used as security for a loan, etc.), Chapter 13 with membership (how one becomes a member, who may be members, etc.) and Chapter 14 with the register of members, which must be kept by the company – another instance of the emphasis placed on publicity as a protection for prospective investors and creditors.

29. Operation of the company. It has been seen how the company is formed by registration, and, by the raising of capital divisible into shares held by the members, is in a position to operate as a legal person.

As the company is an *artificial* legal person, however, its operations must be initiated by resolutions passed at meetings of the members or by the board of directors. The Act requires the company to hold certain meetings of its members (*see* Chapter 15), but these are, on all but rare occasions, sparsely attended, and in practice the day-to-day management of the company is in the hands of the directors or other persons to whom the directors have delegated their own power. Chapters 16 and 17 are concerned with the directors, the secretary, and meetings of the board of directors.

30. Accounts and related matters. The Act requires the company to have annual accounts and to give to such accounts a degree of publicity which varies according to the size of the company. The provisions are described in Chapter 18.

There are also requirements for the accounts to be audited (*see* Chapter 19), and some restrictions placed by the common law and by the Act on the distribution of dividends to the shareholders (*see* Chapter 20).

31. Debentures. A debenture is a document by which a company acknowledges that a loan has been made to it. The company may or may not give to the lender security over some or the whole of its property, so that the creditor may have recourse to that property in the event of the company's failing to make due repayment of the loan.

Although, from the point of view of investors, shares and debentures are similar in that they both provide a home for a sum of money, with the prospect of increased capital value and the payment of an annual return on the money invested, they are in law radically different from one another. Shareholders are the members who comprise the company itself, whereas debenture-holders are creditors of the company, i.e. are outsiders. Also, the return received by shareholders in the form of a dividend, is due only where there are available profits, whereas the interest paid on debentures is, like the loan itself, a debt due by the company, even when the company is making a loss.

Chapter 21 is devoted to debentures and the related matters of charges (including floating charges) and receivers.

32. Investigations and inspections. The Department of Trade and Industry has certain powers of investigation and inspection over registered companies. These are dealt with in Chapter 22.

33. Majority rule and minority protection. A principle which will have been noted at several points in earlier chapters is known as 'the rule in *Foss* v. *Harbottle*', and is to the effect that an individual shareholder is not permitted to bring an action against any person who has injured the company if the majority of the shareholders are opposed to that step, i.e. the company as a separate legal person can act only through its majority shareholders.

There are, however, exceptions to the rule in *Foss* v. *Harbottle*, because the common law and the Act both recognize that there are certain circumstances where the minority shareholders require to have protection from the majority.

The rule in *Foss* v. *Harbottle* and the exceptions to it are explained in Chapter 23.

34. Insider dealing. The Company Securities (Insider Dealing) Act 1985 is part of the criminal law. It is aimed at preventing a person who has some inside information about a company from abusing his position by dealing in the company's shares or debentures in such a way as to make a private gain. Chapter 24 outlines this somewhat complex topic.

35. Private companies. Throughout the text there are many references to exemptions and privileges available to private companies. It may be found convenient to have the principal distinguishing provisions gathered together in a separate chapter, and this is done in Chapter 25.

36. Administration orders. Where a company is likely to be unable to pay its debts but has not yet gone into liquidation, the court may make an administration order directing that the company's affairs be managed by an 'administrator' appointed by the court. The procedure is aimed at rescuing the company from liquidation, or at least ensuring a more advantageous sale of the company's assets than would otherwise be possible in a liquidation. The provisions, which are in the Insolvency Act 1986, are outlined in Chapter 27.

37. Dissolution and winding up. A company's life is brought to an end by dissolution. There are several modes of dissolution, as explained in Chapter 26, but of these the one on which there are copious statutory provisions, now in the Insolvency Act 1986, is winding up or liquidation.

Some of the more important aspects of winding up are outlined in Chapters 28–31, entitled 'Contributories', 'Voluntary winding up', 'Winding up by the court' and 'Provisions of general application in winding up', respectively.

38. Arrangements and reconstructions. Finally Chapter 32 gives a brief account of schemes of arrangement and reconstruction of which a company may avail itself.

Progress test 1

1. Name the six consolidation Acts which are now applicable to registered companies. (**4**)
2. Which of the following are legal persons:

(a) Bloggins, Grindinghalt & Co., Solicitors? (**9**)
(b) a dog? (**13**)
(c) a child? (**13**)

(*d*) a soldier? (**13**)

3. What is the maximum number of persons who may lawfully form a partnership? Are there any cases where this maximum does not apply? (**9**)

4. If more persons than this maximum wish to form a business association, what should they do? (**9**)

5. What type of association is not a legal person, though the liability of its members is limited? (**10**)

6. What type of association is a legal person with the liability of its members unlimited? (**16**)

7. In what order of priority are the company's assets distributed in a winding up? (**18**)

8. What is the leading case on the principle of a company's separate personality? (**19**)

9. What case illustrates the point that a shareholder has no insurable interest in the company's property? (**20**)

10. What are the general grounds on which the court will lift the veil of incorporation? (**22**)

11. Why is it inadvisable for one person to continue as sole shareholder, when his co-shareholder has given up his membership? (**23**)

12. What is the role of promoters and what is their relationship towards the company? (**26**)

13. What is the function of company directors? (**29**)

14. In what respects do debentures differ from shares? (**31**)

15. What is the leading case on 'majority rule'? (**33**)

2
The memorandum of association

1. Who may form a registered company? Section 1(1) tells us who may form a company under the Companies Act and by what process. It states that any two or more persons may form a company and that these persons must be associated for a lawful purpose. No company may have an illegal object. These same two persons must subscribe their names to, i.e. sign, a document called a *memorandum of association*. They must also comply with the requirements of the Companies Act 1985 in respect of registration.

If they fulfil these conditions they can form an incorporated company, i.e. a corporation registered under the Act with or without limited liability. This means that the members' liability for the company's debts may be limited or unlimited (*see* **3**).

2. Public and private companies. A company may be a public company or a private company. The Act gives a statutory definition of a public company and defines a private company as any company which is not a public company. While the number of public companies in England and Wales (approximately 6,000) is small compared with that of private companies (approximately 816,000), it includes many large companies well-known to the ordinary person.

Section 1(3) defines a public company as a company which is *either*:

(*a*) limited by shares; *or*
(*b*) limited by guarantee with a share capital (*see* **30**);

provided that in either case:

(*a*) its memorandum states that it is to be a public company; and

(b) the statutory provisions governing the registration of a public company have been complied with.

A public company, accordingly, is always a limited company. It follows that an unlimited company is necessarily a private company.

It should also be noted that s. 1(4) prohibits a company limited by guarantee from having a share capital unless it did so before 22 December 1980 (i.e. the date when the Companies Act 1980 came into force). Companies limited by guarantee *with* a share capital are therefore of diminishing importance and will cease to exist in time.

3. Limited and unlimited companies. Section 1(2) enlarges on the subject of liability. A company may be:

(a) *limited by shares* (i.e. the liability of the members is limited by the memorandum to the amount unpaid on their shares); *or*

(b) *limited by guarantee* (i.e. the liability of the members is limited by the memorandum to the amount which the members have undertaken or guaranteed to contribute to the assets of the company on winding up); *or*

(c) *unlimited* (i.e. there is no limit to the liability of the members. Here, although the association is a corporation and not a partnership, the extent of the members' liability is the same as that of partners. Unlike partners, however, they are not directly liable to the creditors, but are only directly liable to the company).

4. The contents of the memorandum. The contents of the memorandum are prescribed in the main by s. 2. The document must contain:

(a) The name of the company (*see* **7–13**).

If the company is a public company, s. 25(1) requires its name to end with the words 'public limited company' and by s. 1(3) the memorandum must state that the company is to be a public company (*see* **2**).

If the company is a private company, the last word of its name must be 'limited': s. 25(2).

(b) The domicile of the company, i.e. whether the registered office is to be in England and Wales, Scotland or Wales (*see* **14–15**).

(c) The objects of the company (*see* **17–28**).

(*d*) The limitation of the liability of the members, if the company is limited by shares or guarantee (*see* **29-34**).

(*e*) Unless the company is an unlimited company, the amount of share capital, divided into shares of a fixed amount (*see* **35**).

These six clauses are usually referred to as the *compulsory clauses* and each of them is considered separately later in this chapter. Other clauses, however, are often included.

Where the memorandum states that the registered office is to be in Wales, s. 25(2) permits it to state a private company's name with 'cyfyngedig' as the last word, instead of 'limited'. Similarly, under s. 25(1), the name of a Welsh public company may end with the words 'cymni cyfyngedig cyhoeddus', instead of 'public limited company'.

Furthermore, none of these expressions is required to be given in full. Section 27 permits abbreviations to be used in all cases, as follows:

for 'limited', 'ltd';
for 'public limited company', 'plc';
for 'cyfyngedig', 'cyf.';
for 'cwmni cyfyngedig cyhoeddus', 'ccc'.

5. The form of the memorandum. By s. 2(6) the memorandum must be signed by each subscriber in the presence of at least one witness. Anyone may be a witness so long as he is old enough to understand what he is doing.

Section 2(5) requires each subscriber to take at least one share and for there to be shown against his name the number of shares he takes.

Model forms of memorandum for the different types of companies are to be found in the Companies (Tables A-F) Regulations 1985. The model form for a public company limited by shares is in Table F of the Schedule to these Regulations, while Table B gives the model for a private company limited by shares. The models must be followed as closely as circumstances admit: s. 3(1). In both forms, after the compulsory clauses, appears what is known as the *association clause* by which the subscribers bind themselves together to form a company, but no mention of this clause is made in the Act itself.

6. Alteration of the memorandum. Section 2(7) of the Act deals with the legal rules relating to alteration of the memorandum. It is an important provision governing the *whole document* and states that a company may not alter the clauses in its memorandum except in the cases, in the mode and to the extent for which the Act expressly provides.

The result of this provision is that each clause of the memorandum must be separately studied, for the rules regarding alteration of the clauses are not all the same.

Section 18(2) provides that where a company is required to send to the registrar any document relating to an alteration in its memorandum, it must also send to him a printed copy of the memorandum as altered. Alterations of objects under s. 4 are exempted from this provision since s. 6(1) already contains a requirement for a printed copy of the memorandum as altered to be sent to the registrar (*see* **27**).

Section 711 requires the registrar to publish his receipt of any such document in the *Gazette* and gives the term 'official notification' to publication in this manner. If an alteration of the memorandum has not been officially notified by the registrar at the material time and if the company cannot show that it was known at that time to the person concerned, the company cannot rely on the alteration against that person: s. 42.

7. The choice of a name for the company. Regarding the choice of a name, s. 26, which prohibits the registration of certain names, must be complied with. There is also some important case-law on this topic.

Section 26(1) prohibits a company from being registered by a name:

(*a*) which includes the words 'limited', 'unlimited' or 'public limited company', or their abbreviations, anywhere except at the end of the name;

(*b*) which is the same as any name appearing in the index of names kept by the registrar under s. 714; *or*

(*c*) the use of which would in the opinion of the Secretary of State constitute a criminal offence or be offensive.

As indicated in (*b*), s. 714 requires the registrar to keep an index of company names. However, in determining whether any name is the same as another appearing in the index, s. 26(3) lists certain words or printing characteristics which are to be disregarded. These are as follows:

(a) the word 'the' when it is the first word of the name;

(b) the words 'company', 'and company', 'company limited', 'and company limited', 'limited', 'unlimited', and 'public limited company' when they are the last word or words of the name;

(c) abbreviations of any of the words in (b) above when they appear at the end of the name; and

(d) type and case of letters, spaces between letters, accents and punctuation marks.

The subsection ends by providing, in a phrase which has already become immortal: 'and "and" and "&" are to be taken as the same'. Presumably this means that one cannot rely on an ampersand to constitute a difference.

If, despite these rules, a company is registered by a name so similar to that of another that the public are likely to be deceived, the court will grant an injunction restraining it from using that name.

Thus in *Ewing* v. *Buttercup Margarine Co. Ltd* (1917) the plaintiff, who carried on business under the name of the Buttercup Dairy Co., obtained an injunction against the defendant on the grounds that the public might think that the two businesses were connected.

The same considerations will apply where a company chooses an invented word, rather than a real one, as part of its name.

In *Exxon Corporation* v. *Exxon Insurance Consultants International Ltd* (1981), the plaintiffs, after a long period of research to find a suitable name, invented the word 'Exxon' as part of it. The defendant company later used the same word as part of its name although it had no connection with the plaintiffs' business. The plaintiffs sought an injunction to restrain the defendant from using the word 'Exxon' on the grounds that its use was an infringement of their copyright, the word being an 'original literary work' within s. 2(1) Copyright Act 1956. They also sought an injunction to restrain the defendant from passing off its goods as the plaintiffs' goods by using a similar name. HELD: The plaintiffs were entitled to an injunction restraining the defendant from passing off its goods as the plaintiffs' goods by the use of the word 'Exxon'. However, they were not entitled to an injunction restraining infringement of copyright since the word 'Exxon' was not an 'original literary work'. A 'literary work', said Stephenson L.J., is 'something ...

intended to afford either information and instruction or pleasure in the form of literary enjoyment', and the word 'Exxon' did not do either of these things.

The courts view much more favourably the use of a purely descriptive word with a definite meaning and in common use. If the names of two companies contain such a word, a very trifling distinction between them will suffice to make them acceptable.

Thus in *Aerators Ltd* v. *Tollitt* (1902) the plaintiff was refused an injunction restraining the defendant from using the name of *Automatic Aerators Patents Ltd* and Farwell J. said: 'If the name is simply a word in ordinary use representing a machine or an article of commerce, the probability of deception is out of all proportion less than it would be in the case of an invented or fancy word.'

8. Names requiring the approval of the Secretary of State.

Section 26(2) requires the company to obtain the approval of the Secretary of State before it is registered by any name which:

(*a*) in his opinion would be likely to give the impression that the company is connected with the government or any local authority; or

(*b*) includes any word specified in regulations made under s. 29.

Where a company carries on business under a name which is not its corporate name, s. 2 Business Names Act 1985 provides that these rules apply to its business name as well.

The regulations mentioned in (*b*) are to be found in S.I. 1981, No. 1685, entitled 'The Company and Business Names Regulations 1981'. This statutory instrument was made under authority of the Companies Act 1981, but now has effect as if made under s. 29 Companies Act 1985 and ss. 3, 6 Business Names Act 1985. It contains in its Schedule a long list of words for the use or registration of which the approval of the Secretary of State is required, together with the names of the 'relevant bodies' whose objections in each case must first be sought.

Where a company proposes to adopt a corporate name which contains any of the listed words, the appropriate person must first, under s. 29(2) Companies Act 1985, make a written request to the relevant body to indicate whether it has any objections to the proposal and, if so, why. He must then, by s. 29(3), submit to the registrar a statement that the request has been made and a copy of any response received from the relevant body, together with:

(*a*) in the case of a company seeking to register under the 1985 Act, the statutory declaration required by s. 12(3) (*see* 4:**1**);

(*b*) in the case of an existing company, a copy of the special resolution changing the company's name (*see* **12**).

The expression 'the appropriate person' means, in the case of (*a*), the person making the declaration and, in the case of (*b*), a director or secretary of the company: s. 29(2).

Where a company proposes to use a business name which contains any of the listed words, it is required by s. 3(2) Business Names Act 1985 to make a similar request to the relevant body and submit a similar statement to the Secretary of State along with a copy of the relevant body's response.

9. Disclosure of corporate name by company using business name. Section 4(1) Business Names Act 1985 requires any company using a business name to state:

(*a*) its corporate name; and

(*b*) an address in Great Britain at which service of any document relating to its business will be effective;

in legible characters on all business letters, orders for goods or services to be supplied to the business, invoices and receipts issued in the course of the business and written demands for payments of business debts.

Such a company is also required, in any premises where it carries on business and to which customers or suppliers have access, to display a notice containing the same information in a prominent position. Further, under s. 4(2), the company must immediately give the same information in writing to any person with whom business is conducted and who asks for it.

Section 5 Business Names Act 1985 gives a civil remedy to the other party to any business transaction in which a company has infringed the provisions in s. 4(1) or (2). It states that where the defaulting company brings legal proceedings to enforce a right arising out of a contract made in the course of the business, the action will be dismissed if the defendant shows that owing to the company's breach of s. 4(1) or (2):

(*a*) he has been unable to pursue a claim against the company arising out of that contract; *or*

(*b*) he has suffered some financial loss in connection with that contract:

unless the court thinks it just and equitable to permit the proceedings to continue.

The section makes it clear, however, that if it is the other party who sues the defaulting company, the company will be able to enforce any rights which it may have against the plaintiff, despite the fact that it has infringed s. 4.

10. Publication of the company's name. Once a company has chosen its name, it must comply with ss. 348–350 Companies Act 1985 regarding publication.

(*a*) *Publication of name.* Sections 348–350 make it compulsory to have the name painted or affixed on the *business premises,* engraved on the *seal,* and mentioned on all *business documents and negotiable instruments.*

We have already seen in **4** that the word 'limited' or 'cyfyngedig' must appear in the name of a limited company so as to indicate the true legal position of the members regarding the company's debts. Where the name of a public company contains the words 'cwmni cyfyngedig cyhoeddus', s. 351(3) requires the fact that it is a public limited company to be stated in English also on all business documents and in a notice on the business premises.

Conversely, however, under s. 34, any person who carries on business under a name of which 'limited' or 'cyfyngedig' is the last word, without being incorporated with limited liability, commits an offence. Section 33(1) contains a similar provision, stating that any person who is not a public company and who carries on business under a name which includes, as its last part, the words 'public limited company', or their equivalent in Welsh, commits an offence.

Finally, s. 33(2) makes it an offence for a public company to use a name which may reasonably be expected to give the impression that it is a private company in circumstances where the fact that it is a public company is likely to be material.

(*b*) *Fines for non-compliance.* Other provisions in ss. 348–350 impose fines on the company and the officers for non-compliance with the sections. The fines need not be learned in detail, but a distinction should be noted between 'officer' and 'officer in default' in these provisions. In the case of failure to comply with the provision as to having the name painted or affixed on the business premises, the fine is on the company and every officer who is in default, whereas in the case of failure to comply with the other provisions as to publication the fine is on the company and any officer using the seal or issuing or signing the business document or negotiable instrument.

Section 730(5) states that the expression 'officer in default' means an officer who *knowingly and wilfully* authorizes or permits the default, while s. 744, the main definition section, alphabetically arranged, defines 'officer' as including *director, manager or secretary*.

(*c*) *Personal liability*. Section 349 has an important provision. It not only imposes a fine on the officer for signing a negotiable instrument without the company's name on it, but it states that he will be personally liable to the holder of such a negotiable instrument for the amount thereof unless it is duly paid by the company. This could be a serious matter for an officer of a company, as a negotiable instrument may be for any amount and could involve him in personal liability which far exceeds the amount of the fine. The omission of any part of the name is sufficient to render him personally liable in this way.

Thus in *Hendon* v. *Adelman* (1973), where an ampersand was omitted, and in *Penrose* v. *Martyr* (1858) and *British Airways Board* v. *Parish* (1979), where the word 'limited' was not on the instrument, the officers were in every case held personally liable.

In *Stacey & Co. Ltd* v. *Wallis* (1912), however, it was held not only that the abbreviation 'Ltd' was permissible – a rule now enshrined in s. 27 (*see* **4**) – but also that it did not matter whereabouts on the instrument the company's name appeared, so long as it was correctly stated. Similarly, in *Banque de l'Indochine et de Suez S.A.* v. *Euroseas Group Finance Co. Ltd* (1981) it was held that 'Co.' was an acceptable abbreviation for 'Company'. Further, if the error in the name is caused by the holder of the instrument, he will not be able to enforce the resulting liability against the officer who signed it: *Durham Fancy Goods* v. *Jackson (Michael)* (1968).

Confusion can arise where a company uses a business name. In *Maxform S.p.A.* v. *Mariani and Goodville Ltd* (1980), however, it was held that the word 'name' in what is now s. 349 means the registered corporate name and the fact that the company uses a business name does not prevent the application of the section.

11. Power to dispense with the word 'limited'. There are certain cases where, even in a limited company, the last word of the name need not be 'limited'.

Section 30 provides that where *a private company limited by guarantee* has for its objects the promotion of commerce, art, science, education, religion, charity or any profession and its memorandum or articles comply with certain requirements, it is exempt from the provisions of the Act relating to the use of the word 'limited' as part of its name, the publishing of its name and the sending of lists of members to the registrar of companies.

The requirements are that the company's memorandum or articles:

(*a*) require its profits or other income to be applied in promoting its objects;

(*b*) prohibit the payment of dividends to its members; and

(*c*) require all the assets which would otherwise be available to its members to be transferred, on its winding up, either to another body with *similar* objects or to one which has for its objects the *promotion of charity*.

Where a company is seeking registration a statutory declaration that it is one to which s. 30 applies may be made by a solicitor engaged in its formation or by a person named as a director or secretary in the statement delivered under s. 10(2) (*see* 4:1). This declaration may be delivered to the registrar who may accept it as sufficient evidence of that fact and who may refuse to register a company by a name which does not include 'limited' unless he has received such a declaration. Where a company is already in existence but is seeking to change its name and dispense with the word 'limited', the declaration may be made by a director or the secretary.

A company to which s. 30 applies and which does not have the word 'limited' in its name is prohibited by s. 31 from altering its memorandum or articles so that the section ceases to apply to it. If, however, it appears to the Secretary of State that such a company has carried on any business other than the promotion of the listed objects, or has infringed the provisions of its memorandum or articles stated in (*a*) or (*b*) above, he may direct the company to change its name by a resolution of the directors so that its name ends with 'limited'. This resolution must be filed with the registrar under s. 380 (*see* 15:**41**).

12. Voluntary change of name. Section 28(1) tells us how we can change the company's name. It provides that a company may change its name by special resolution. This is a general permission to any company to change its name at any time and as often as it wishes, but of course the new name must not contravene the statutory rules described above.

Where a company changes its name, s. 28(6) requires the registrar to enter its new name on the register in place of its former name and to issue an altered certificate of incorporation. The change of name takes effect from the date on which the altered certificate is issued, but it does not affect the company's legal position. Thus legal proceedings by or against it may be continued under the new name: s. 28(7).

The fee for registration of a new name in pursuance of a special resolution passed under s. 28(1) is £40: Companies (Fees) Regulations 1980 (S.I. 1980, No. 1749).

13. Compulsory change of name. Under the above rules a company may change its name voluntarily. There are, however, three cases where it can be *directed* to change its name and must comply with the direction:

(*a*) If a company is registered by a name which is either *the same* as one appearing in the index (*see* **7**) at the time of its registration or, in the opinion of the Secretary of State, *too similar* to such a name, the Secretary of State may, within 12 months, gave a *written direction* to the company to change its name within a specified period.

The same rule applies if a company is registered by a name which is the same as, or too similar to, one which should have appeared in the index at the time of its registration, even though it did not: s. 28(2).

(*b*) If it appears to the Secretary of State that a company has provided *misleading information* for the purpose of its registration by a particular name, or has given undertakings or assurances which have not been fulfilled, he may, within five years, give a *written direction* to the company to change its name within a specified period: s. 28(3).

(*c*) Section 32(1) empowers the Department of Trade and Industry to *direct* a company to change its name if, in their opinion, its registered name gives *so misleading an indication of the nature of its activities* as to be likely to cause harm to the public.

Section 32(2) requires the company to comply with such a direction within six weeks unless, under s. 32(3), it applies to the court within three weeks to set the direction aside. The court may set the direction aside or confirm it, in which case it must specify the period within which the company must comply.

14. The distinction between domicile and residence. In the case of a public company the second clause of the memorandum will be, as explained in **4**, a statement that the company is to be a public company. The alteration of the memorandum with regard to this clause is best considered in Chapter 25 on private companies.

We come now, therefore, to the second or, in the case of a public company, the third compulsory clause of the memorandum. This states the country in which the registered office of the company is situated, thus giving the company's domicile. Section 351(1) requires both the domicile and the registration number of the company to be mentioned in all business letters and order forms. The registration number of a company is given on its certificate of incorporation (*see* **4:2**).

Domicile must be distinguished from *residence*. The domicile of a company is the place where it was incorporated or registered, and this domicile adheres to the company throughout its existence. A company can have only one domicile, which cannot be changed.

The test of residence, on the other hand, is not registration but the place where the company does its business, i.e. the place of its management and control. This will usually be the place where the board of directors meets. The main importance of residence is with regard to taxation, for which purpose a company may have more than one residence.

15. The importance of the registered office. Although the domicile of the company cannot be changed, the address of the registered office within that domicile can be changed freely at any time to suit the company's convenience. Section 351(1) requires that address to be mentioned in all business letters and order forms.

Section 287(1) makes it compulsory for a company to have a registered office at all times. Its intended situation must, under s. 10(6), be specified in the statement delivered to the registrar prior to incorporation (*see* 4:**1**), while any subsequent changes in its situation must, under s. 287(2), be notified to the registrar within 14 days.

Section 711(1) requires the registrar to publish in the *Gazette* the receipt by him of notice of any change in the situation of a company's registered office. If the change had not been officially notified by the registrar at the material time and if the company cannot show that it was known at that time to the person concerned, the company cannot rely on it against that person as regards service of any document on the company: s. 42(1).

The importance of the registered office is that it is the address where writs may be served on the company and where communications may be sent. It is also the address at which the following registers and documents must normally be kept:

(*a*) the register of members: s. 353;

(*b*) the register of debenture-holders: s. 190;

(*c*) the register of directors and secretaries: s. 288;

(*d*) the register of directors' interests in shares and debentures: the 13th Schedule, Part IV;

(*e*) the register of charges: s. 407;

(*f*) copies of instruments creating the charges: s. 406;

(*g*) minute books of general meetings: s. 383;

(*h*) the register of interests in shares: s. 211.

This list must be carefully learnt. The order in which the eight items are memorized is not important, but they have been arranged above as far as possible so that they fall into couples in order to facilitate learning them.

There are some exceptions to the requirement that all these items must be kept at the registered office – in particular, the register of members may be kept at the office where the work of making it up is done if that office is not the company's registered office: s. 353(1).

NOTE: All these documents are open to members free, during business hours for at least two hours a day. (*e*) and (*f*) are also open to creditors free, while (*b*) is open to debenture-holders free. (*a*) to (*e*) are open to the public on payment of the prescribed fee, while (*h*) is open to the public free.

16. The statutory books. Often the student is required to state what are the statutory books. This is a list of the registers and documents which every company is required by law to keep. There are eight items here:

(a) the register of members: s. 352;

(b) the register of directors and secretaries: s. 288;

(c) the register of directors' interests in shares and debentures: s. 325;

(d) directors' service contracts: s. 318;

(e) the register of charges: s. 407;

(f) the minute books of general and directors' meetings: s. 382;

(g) the register of interests in shares: s. 211;

(h) the accounting records, which are:

  (i) receipts and expenditure;

  (ii) assets and liabilities;

  (iii) statements of stock held and sales and purchases of goods: s. 221.

NOTE: The two lists are very similar. Most of the statutory books must normally be kept at the registered office since they appear in both lists. But the minute books of directors' meetings and the accounting records may be kept at any convenient place; they do not appear in the first list and therefore there is no obligation to keep them at the registered office. Directors' service contracts must be kept at an appropriate place, defined as the registered office or the place where the register of members is kept (if other than the registered office), or the principal place of business.

On the other hand, while there is no obligation to keep a register of debenture-holders at all, most companies do so in practice, in which case the register must be kept either at the registered office or at the office where the work of making it up is done.

Directors' service contracts are open to members free, during business hours for at least two hours a day. The accounting records are open to the officers of the company at all times, though not to members: s. 222(1).

17. The objects clause. The third or, in the case of a public company, the fourth compulsory clause in the memorandum sets out the objects or *vires* of the company. It is of great importance because it determines the *capacity* of the company wherever the *doctrine of ultra vires* applies. We must now see where this doctrine is applicable, what are its effects, and what changes in the law have been made by statute, i.e. Act of Parliament.

18. Application of the doctrine of *ultra vires*. This doctrine has never applied to chartered corporations, but only to statutory and registered ones. A chartered corporation will of course have objects or *vires*, which will be set out in its charter, but it nevertheless has at law the full capacity of a human person, so that even if it acts outside those objects the transaction will be valid. However, if it persistently violates its charter, there is a procedure by which the charter can be forfeited, called *scire facias*.

Statutory and registered corporations, on the other hand, are in an entirely different position. The statutory corporation has its *vires* set out in the Act of Parliament creating it, while a registered corporation has its *vires* stated in the objects clause. The doctrine of *ultra vires* applies to them both, so that if either of them acts outside the *vires* the transaction is *void*. The *vires* limit their contractual capacity. It is obvious that it is of great importance to know whether any particular transaction is *intra* (within) or *ultra* (outside or beyond) *vires*, for on this depends its validity.

19. Construction of the objects clause. The court will always construe the objects clause reasonably. The clause usually ends, as may be seen from the model forms of memorandum mentioned in 5, with a general permission to do anything 'incidental or conducive' to the stated objects, but this adds nothing to the general rule of law. Moreover, in recent years the courts have construed objects clauses in an increasingly liberal manner. Thus in *Re New Finance and Mortgage Co. Ltd* (1975) Goulding J. gave a very wide construction to the words 'merchants generally', holding that they covered 'all purely commercial occupations'.

Usually there are several objects set out in the clause. If this is done, the first object is regarded as the *main object* or *substratum* of the company, and if it fails the company may be wound up by the court under s. 122(1)(*g*) Insolvency Act 1986: *Re German Date Coffee Co.* (1882). To avoid this result the memorandum may provide by what is called an 'independent objects' clause at the end that *all* the objects shall be regarded as main or substantive ones, so that the failure of any one of them will not prevent the company from carrying on with the others. This was done successfully in *Cotman* v. *Brougham* (1918), where there were 30 objects and also in *Anglo-Overseas Agencies* v. *Green* (1960). The decision in *Introductions Ltd* v. *National Provincial Bank Ltd* (1970), however, shows that there are limits to the success of this device. It was there held that, despite an independent objects clause, a power to borrow could not stand by itself, but was necessarily for some purpose. This purpose must be legitimate and *intra vires* for the borrowing to be valid. Moreover, Harman L.J. indicated that this was not the only power about which he would take a similar view (*see* 21:3). This distinction between objects and powers has recently been emphasized by Browne-Wilkinson L.J. in *Rolled Steel Products (Holdings) Ltd* v. *British Steel Corporation* (1986).

20. The effect of *ultra vires* transactions. When an act is *ultra vires* and void, it can never subsequently be ratified and validated, even if every shareholder consents to it: *Ashbury Carriage Co. Ltd* v. *Riche* (1875). All that can be done is for the company to alter its objects clause for the future, and such an alteration will never have a retrospective effect. It is therefore essential to study carefully the legal position both of the company and of the persons who deal with it under an *ultra vires* transaction.

Section 9(1) European Communities Act 1972, implementing the First EEC Directive of 1968, made an important change here. These provisions are now in s. 35 Companies Act 1985 and, for a proper understanding of their effect, it is necessary to consider the position both before and after the 1972 Act.

21. Effect of *ultra vires* contract on other party before the European Communities Act 1972. Where the contract was *executory*, a person who had agreed to supply goods or perform services for the company under an *ultra vires* contract had no action for breach if the company repudiated the contract before he had performed it.

Where the contract had been *executed by the other party*, i.e. where he had performed his bargain, he did not have any action for the price of goods supplied by him, nor for services rendered by him. *At common law*, however, he was sometimes able to 'follow' goods supplied to the company and recover them. He could do this only if he could identify the goods and if they had not been consumed by the company. He based his claim on the fact that the *title* to the goods was still his, since no property can pass under a void contract.

Even where the goods had ceased to be identifiable, he might *in equity* be able to 'trace' them under the equitable doctrine of restitution. By means of a tracing order he might obtain an equitable charge on a *mixed mass of assets* out of which, or the proceeds of which, he could satisfy his claim. The property, at least in equity, remained his: *Sinclair* v. *Brougham* (1914).

22. Effect of *ultra vires* contract on company before European Communities Act 1972. Although an *ultra vires* contract was void, it seems that any property obtained by a company under such a transaction could be protected by it against damage by other persons, even though it should not have acquired the property in the first place. Thus a company which, acting *ultra vires*, built a factory was nevertheless entitled to sue a person who threw stones through the windows.

Furthermore, we must examine the legal position from another point of view. It might not be the *supplier* who wished to enforce the *ultra vires* contract, or who had performed it and demanded payment. It might instead be the *company* who sued the other party for breach of contract. Here it seemed logical to argue that since the contract was void, the company was in no better a position to enforce it than the supplier, and that even if the company had performed its part of the bargain it would not be able to bring a successful action for payment.

Nevertheless, this was not universally accepted as the correct view and textbooks differed on the question, so that it was helpful to have the position clarified by the judgment of Mocatta J. in *Bell Houses* v. *City Wall Properties* (1966), even though his decision was reversed in the Court of Appeal on the construction of the particular objects clause in question. Mocatta J. said:

'A defendant when sued on a contract by a company is entitled to take the point *by way of defence* that the contract was *ultra vires*. The contract is void and in the eyes of the law non-existent. There is no ground for distinguishing between executory and executed contracts.'

23. Criticism of the doctrine of *ultra vires*. From **21** above it will be seen that the former state of the law concerning the third party was obviously not a satisfactory one, especially since he had no means of telling whether a transaction was *intra vires* or *ultra vires* without actually reading and understanding the objects clause of the memorandum. Moreover, *he was always deemed to have done this whether he had in fact done it or not*, i.e. he was said to have *constructive* knowledge of the contents of the memorandum in all cases where he did not have *actual* knowledge of them.

Thus, in legal theory a supplier to a company was formerly not safe unless he took the trouble to read the objects clause and see whether his particular transaction was within it. In practice, however, the business world is peopled by individuals who seldom concern themselves with such hazards until they are involved in them, and hardship could, and did, result.

24. Modification of doctrine of *ultra vires*. Section 35 Companies Act 1985 provides that in favour of a person dealing with a company in good faith, any transaction decided on by the directors is deemed to be within the company's capacity (i.e. *intra vires*), and the directors' power to bind the company is deemed free of limitations under the memorandum or articles. Such a person need not inquire into the company's capacity or the directors' powers, and is presumed to have acted in good faith unless the contrary is proved.

This provision seems to lack the customary precision of English legislation. It certainly destroys the doctrine of constructive notice in these circumstances, but how much further does it go? What, for instance, is the precise meaning of the word 'transaction'? What constitutes proof of bad faith? What is the position if the third party is given, or already has in his possession, a copy of the memorandum but does not trouble to read it?

The valuable judgment of Lawson J. in *International Sales & Agencies Ltd* v. *Marcus* (1982) now provides guidance on several of these mysteries. Where a director of a company, acting purely from a sense of moral obligation, used the company's money to discharge a personal debt of his deceased friend, who formerly had been also a director as well as the major shareholder in the company, Lawson J. held that s. 9(1) European Communities Act had no application to the principles of constructive trust which governed the facts before him. The subsection related, he said, only to *legal obligations* of the company under transactions with third parties. Thus it would seem to follow that the word 'transaction' excludes a gratuitous payment. Further, he opined that the court was entitled to look at the First Directive as an aid to the interpretation of the subsection and he then proceeded to apply the test of lack of good faith propounded by it. A third party would accordingly be taken to have acted in bad faith if the company could *either*:

(*a*) prove that he had *actual knowledge* that the transaction was *ultra vires* the company; *or*

(*b*) show that, in view of all the circumstances, he *could not have been unaware* that he was a party to an *ultra vires* transaction.

This seems to come very close to the 'reasonable man' test so often employed in English law.

Some questions, however, still remain unanswered. What is the position if the contract is still entirely executory? Can this cosseted third party take the point *by way of defence* that the contract was *ultra vires*? If so, the law still seems unduly severe towards companies, for a man is not necessarily either nice or honest merely because he does not carry on his business in corporate form. We must await with interest further judicial decisions on these matters.

It seems unfortunate that the opportunity was not taken in 1972 to eradicate the doctrine completely from English law. Originally it was said to have two purposes, namely, to protect both investors and creditors by preventing the unrestricted use of the company's assets for any transaction in which the directors, as its agents, cared to engage. Today, however, under modern economic conditions, it can be equally dangerous for a company to have only one type of activity, and objects clauses have thus become increasingly wide so as to enable it to engage in the maximum range of commercial operations which could be of benefit to it. The doctrine from the point of view of businessmen is no more than an outdated irritant, and because it is deeply rooted in English company law they can only look encouragingly at a legislature which in 1972 took the first slightly uncertain step in the right direction. A recent hopeful sign, however, was the appointment by the Department of Trade and Industry in December 1985 of Dr Dan Prentice of Oxford University to carry out a study of the legal and commercial implications of abolishing the doctrine.

25. Gratuitous payments by companies. One further matter connected with the doctrine of *ultra vires* must be considered: namely, how far a company may make gratuitous payments out of its assets for various purposes.

Charitable donations seem never to have been challenged in the courts, being regarded as permissible on the grounds that they preserve goodwill. As regards *educational* donations, the court may hold that these are incidental or conducive to the attainment of the company's objects as in *Evans* v. *Brunner, Mond and Co. Ltd* (1921), where a donation for scientific research by chemical manufacturers was held *intra vires*.

In *Parke* v. *Daily News* (1961), however, a gratuitous payment to the employees of a company who had become redundant on an amalgamation was held *ultra vires*, and the court decided that *ex gratia* payments out of the assets are only *intra vires* and valid if they are:

(a) *bona fide*;

(b) reasonably incidental to the carrying on of the company's business; and

(c) made for the benefit and prosperity of the company.

Thus in *Re W. and M. Roith* (1967), the controlling director of a company, after many years' service without any contract, was given a service agreement providing for payment of a pension to his executors on trust for his wife. He died in office two months later and the pension was paid for several years. Then the company went into liquidation. The executors claimed the capitalized value of the pension, but the liquidator rejected their claim. HELD: The payment of the pension was not reasonably incidental to the carrying on of the company's business, nor undertaken *bona fide* for the benefit and prosperity of the company, and the claim was therefore rightly rejected.

Some doubt was thrown on these rules by the decision in *Charterbridge Corporation Ltd* v. *Lloyds Bank Ltd* (1969). In that case Pennycuick J. held that where a company is carrying out the purposes expressed in its memorandum, and does an act within the scope of an express power in the memorandum, the *state of mind* of the parties concerned is immaterial on the issue of *ultra vires*. If this is so, then for an act to be *intra vires* the only one of the three conditions mentioned above which needs to be satisfied is (b). Motive becomes a relevant factor in determining whether any act is a *bona fide* exercise of the directors' power to do it, but is irrelevant in determining whether or not they have that power.

The decision of Pennycuick J. in the *Charterbridge* case was followed in *Re Halt Garage (1964) Ltd* (1982) and expressly approved by the Court of Appeal in *Re Horsley & Weight Ltd* (1982). There it was held that provided an act is expressly authorized by the memorandum, the question whether it will benefit or promote the prosperity of the company is irrelevant. A company's objects do not need to be commercial. They can be charitable or philanthropic. All that is required is that they should be legal.

In any event, s. 719(1) resolves the difficulty to a limited extent by stating that the powers of a company include power to provide for its past and present employees and those of any of its subsidiaries on the *cessation or transfer* of the whole or any part of its undertaking or that of the subsidiary in question. Moreover, under s. 719(2) the company may exercise the power even when it is not in its best interests to do so. Section 719(4), however, stipulates that any such provision, if made before the commencement of winding up, may be made out of distributable profits (*see* 20:3–5), while if made after the commencement of winding up, it may, by s. 187(3) Insolvency Act 1986, be made out of the assets available to shareholders.

Section 719(3) Companies Act 1985 imposes certain conditions on the exercise of the power. It must be sanctioned:

(*a*) in a case not falling under (*b*) or (*c*) below, by an *ordinary resolution*; *or*

(*b*) if so authorized by the memorandum or articles, a *directors' resolution*; *or*

(*c*) if the memorandum or articles require the sanction of a resolution for which a higher majority is necessary, a *resolution of that kind*.

Furthermore, any other requirement of the memorandum or articles must also be observed.

If, before winding up has commenced, the company has decided to make a payment in accordance with these conditions, the fact that it later goes into liquidation will not affect the position. Section 187(1) Insolvency Act 1986 expressly authorizes the liquidator to make the payment in these circumstances, although if the company is being wound up by the court his power to do so is subject to the control of the court: s. 187(4) Insolvency Act 1986.

If winding up has already commenced, s. 187(2) Insolvency Act 1986 governs the position. It authorizes the liquidator, after providing for the costs of winding up and discharging the company's liabilities, to exercise the company's power to make a payment. The conditions stated in s. 719(3) Companies Act 1985 above, however, again apply with the exception of (*b*) which can have no application to a company in liquidation since on winding up the powers of directors cease (*see* 29:**3**(*d*) and 30:**9**(*f*)).

It should be noted that if there should be any conflict between the rules governing the power to make a payment to employees under s. 187(1) or s. 187(2) Insolvency Act 1986 and the normal rules relating to distribution of assets in liquidation (*see* 1:**18**), s. 187(5) Insolvency Act 1986 makes it clear that the former prevail.

Finally, the 7th Schedule to the Companies Act 1985 requires the directors' report to contain particulars of money given by the company for *political* or *charitable* purposes if, in a financial year, the total sum given exceeds £200 in amount.

In each case the report must state the *amount* of money given. In the case of money given for *political* purposes, it must also state:

(*a*) the name of each person to whom more than £200 has been given and the amount given;

(*b*) if more than £200 has been given by way of donation or subscription to a political party, the identity of the party and the amount given.

These provisions of the 7th Schedule, like the other accounting requirements in the Act, may be altered by statutory instrument from time to time: s. 256(1).

26. Alteration of the objects clause. So far, as regards this clause of the memorandum, only the doctrine of *ultra vires* has been considered. It is now important to see how the clause can be altered where this is desired.

Section 4 enables the company to alter the objects at any time by *special resolution* in order to:

(*a*) carry on its business more economically or efficiently; *or*

(*b*) attain its main purpose by new or improved means; *or*

(*c*) enlarge or change the local area of operations; *or*

(*d*) carry on some business which may be conveniently combined with its own; *or*

(*e*) restrict or abandon any of its objects; *or*

(*f*) sell or dispose of all or any of its undertaking; *or*

(*g*) amalgamate with another company.

NOTE: The *first four* of the above *increase* the scope of the company's activities, while the *last three* do not. The list should be carefully learnt.

27. Objections to alterations. Once the special resolution is passed, the company must wait for a period of 21 days to see whether or not any application to the court is made to cancel the alteration: s. 5(3). If the 21 days elapse without such an application having been made, s. 6(1)(a) requires the company, within a further period of 15 days, to deliver to the registrar a printed copy of the memorandum as altered.

It may be, however, that during the permitted period of 21 days specified in s. 5(3) an application to the court for cancellation of the alteration is made. Section 5(2) states that such an application can be made only by:

(a) the holders of at least 15 per cent of the issued share capital, or any class thereof, or, if the company is not limited by shares, 15 per cent of the members; *or*

(b) the holders of at least 15 per cent of any debentures secured by a floating charge and issued before 1 December 1947: s. 5(8).

NOTE: One person may hold the requisite 15 per cent and so be able to apply to the court on his own.

If an application to the court for cancellation of the alteration is made, s. 4 states that the alteration is then ineffective unless confirmed by the court, but this is the *only time* when the consent of the court is required. Under s. 5(4) the court may make such order as it thinks fit, or may adjourn the proceedings in order that an arrangement may be made for the purchase of the shareholdings or other interests of the dissentient persons. The court order may provide for the purchase by the company of the shares of any members and for the resulting reduction of capital (*see* 13:22). It can also make any alterations to the memorandum or articles which are thereby rendered necessary and prohibit the company from making subsequent alterations to these documents. The company may then make such alterations only with the leave of the court: s. 5(5) and (6).

As soon as an application is made, s. 6(1)(b) requires the company to notify the registrar. Then when the court order is made, the company must deliver to the registrar within 15 days an office copy of the order and, if it confirms the alteration, a printed copy of the altered memorandum.

28. Unauthorized alterations. The above provisions of ss. 4–6 clearly state within what limits the objects clause can be altered, and how and by whom an objection to an alteration within these limits can be made. They do not, however, cover the case where an alteration is made which is *outside the permitted limits*. Yet it is obviously possible for a company to pass a special resolution altering its objects quite beyond these limits, and one might think that such an alteration, in view of s. 2(7), would be totally ineffective.

Nevertheless, s. 6(4) states that the validity of an alteration of the objects clause cannot be questioned on the grounds that it was not authorized by s. 4 except within 21 days. Thus presumably any member could object to an unauthorized alteration, provided he did so within 21 days, but after that period has elapsed the alteration cannot be challenged. From the viewpoint of an outsider dealing with the company, such a provision is essential, for if the *vires* of a company could be questioned at any time on the grounds that they were the result of an unauthorized alteration of the objects clause, the outsider could never be sure whether his particular transaction was *intra* or *ultra vires*.

29. The liability clause. The fourth or, in the case of a public company, the fifth compulsory clause of the memorandum states that the liability of the members is limited if in fact this is the case.

In the normal trading company, as we have seen, the members' liability will be limited to the amount, if any, unpaid on their shares. But in a company limited by guarantee, it will be limited to the amount which the members have agreed to contribute to the assets in the event of liquidation. This amount will be the sum specified in the fifth or, in the case of a public company, the sixth clause of the memorandum of such a company.

30. Companies limited by guarantee. Some details concerning companies limited by guarantee may be considered here. Such companies have normally been formed for educational or charitable purposes, and may or may not have a share capital. If there is a share capital, then a member has a double liability, for he is liable not only up to the amount unpaid on his *shares*, but also up to the amount of the *guarantee* whatever it may be.

Model forms of memorandum for companies limited by guarantee with a share capital are found in Table D of the Schedule to the Companies (Tables A–F) Regulations 1985, but it should be borne in mind that no more companies of this type can be created (*see* **2**).

If there is no share capital, the member is liable only up to the amount of the guarantee which is, as stated above, not payable until liquidation (*see* Table C in the Schedule). Companies limited by guarantee with no share capital normally obtain their funds through subscriptions or endowments.

31. Alteration of liability. Sections 49–52 provide re-registration procedures enabling a limited company to become unlimited and an unlimited company to become limited.

A company cannot however use *both* procedures. Thus once a limited company has re-registered as unlimited under s. 49 it cannot re-convert itself into a limited company under s. 51 or vice versa.

32. Re-registration of limited company as unlimited. Section 49 states that a *limited* company may be re-registered as *unlimited* by application to the registrar. There is a re-registration fee of £5 under the Companies (Fees) Regulations 1980 (S.I. 1980, No. 1749). The application must be framed in the prescribed form, signed by a director or the secretary, and lodged with the registrar together with certain other documents.

Section 49(5) and (6) requires the application to set out such alterations in the memorandum and, if articles have been registered, in the articles as are necessary to conform with the requirements of the Act as regards unlimited companies with share capital or, if the company is not to have a share capital, as are necessary in the circumstances. By s. 49(7) if articles have not been registered, appropriate printed articles must be annexed and their registration requested.

Section 49(8) requires the application to be accompanied by:

(*a*) the *form of assent* to the company's being registered as unlimited, subscribed by *all the members*;

(*b*) a *statutory declaration* by the directors that the persons subscribing the form of assent constitute the whole membership of the company;

(c) a printed copy of the *memorandum* and, if articles have been registered, of the *articles* incorporating the alterations set out in the application.

Section 50(1) requires the registrar to retain the application and other documents, to register the articles if annexed, and to issue to the company an appropriate certificate of incorporation. By s. 50(2) on the issue of this certificate the status of the company is changed from limited to unlimited, and the alterations in the memorandum and, if articles were previously registered, in the articles take effect as if made by resolution of the company.

Section 50(3) states that the certificate of incorporation is conclusive evidence of compliance with the requirements of s. 49 as to re-registration.

It must be remembered, however, that owing to the definition of a public company in s. 1(3) (*see* **2**), the procedure laid down in s. 49 is confined to private companies: s. 49(3).

33. Re-registration of unlimited company as limited. Section 51 states that an *unlimited* company may be registered as *limited* if a *special resolution* is passed to that effect and an application made to the registrar. There is a re-registration fee of £50 under the Companies (Fees) Regulations 1980 (S.I. 1980, No. 1749). The application must be framed in the prescribed form, signed by a director or the secretary, and lodged with the registrar, together with certain other documents on or after the day on which a copy of the resolution is received by him (*see* **15:41**).

Section 51(3) requires the resolution to state whether the company is to be limited by shares or by guarantee and, if limited by shares, what the share capital is to be. It must also provide for such alterations to the memorandum and articles as are necessary to conform with the statutory requirements.

Section 51(5) requires the application to be accompanied by a printed copy of the memorandum and articles as altered.

Section 52(1) requires the registrar to retain the application and other documents, and to issue to the company an appropriate certificate of incorporation. By s. 52(2) on the issue of this certificate the status of the company is changed from unlimited to limited, and the alterations in the memorandum and articles specified in the resolution take effect.

Section 52(3) is similar to s. 50(3) (see **32**).

It must again be stressed that this procedure is confined to *private* companies: s. 51(2).

34. Other statutory provisions regarding liability. There are a number of other statutory provisions regarding liability, some of which are of importance while others are rarely used. They are as follows:

(*a*) Section 16 states that the liability of a member cannot be increased without his written consent.

(*b*) Section 24 states that where a company carries on business for more than six months without having at least two members, any person who, for the whole or any part of the period that it carries on business after those six months:

    (*i*) is a member of the company; and

    (*ii*) knows that it is carrying on business with only one member,

is liable, jointly and severally with the company, for the payment of the company's debts contracted during that period or the relevant part of it. Such a person thus *loses the protection of limited liability*.

The horrifying effect of this section can be avoided by a member quite easily, since under s. 122 Insolvency Act 1986 a reduction of members below the statutory minimum is a ground for winding up by the court, and under s. 124 of that Act this is one of the occasions on which a member can present a winding-up petition and so protect himself.

(*c*) Section 306 states that the memorandum may provide that the *directors* in a limited company shall have *unlimited liability*, but that they must be notified of this before accepting office by the promoters, existing directors or secretary.

If they are not notified, then, though their liability will still be unlimited, the person responsible for the failure to notify them is liable for any damage which they may sustain.

(*d*) Section 307 states that a limited company with authority in its articles may by special resolution alter its memorandum so as to make the liability of a director unlimited.

Section 306 and s. 307 are rarely used in practice. Stock Exchange rules now permit stockbroking firms to become limited companies provided the directors give an undertaking that they will be personally liable without limitation to the Stock Exchange in respect of stock exchange transactions. Such an undertaking, however, does not confer unlimited liability on the directors either to the company or to its creditors and thus does not give rise to the position contemplated by these two sections: *Mitton Butler Priest & Co. Ltd.* v. *Ross* (1976).

(*e*) Section 213 Insolvency Act 1986 deals with *fraudulent trading*. The section states that where, in the course of liquidation, it appears that the company's business has been carried on with intent to defraud creditors or for any fraudulent purpose, the liquidator may apply to the court, which may declare that any persons knowingly parties to the carrying on of the business in that way are to be liable to make such contributions to the company's assets as the court thinks proper.

To be a 'party' within this section, a person must take some *positive steps* in the carrying on of the company's business in a fraudulent manner: *Re Maidstone Buildings Provisions Ltd* (1971). However, a creditor who accepts money knowing that it has been procured by carrying on the business with intent to defraud other creditors for the very purpose of paying him is a 'party' within the section: *Re Gerald Cooper Chemicals Ltd* (1978). 'A man who warms himself with the fire of fraud cannot complain if he is singed,' said Templeman J. of the creditor in question. He further held that even an isolated transaction can be within the section provided that it amounts to a fraud on a creditor perpetrated in the course of carrying on business.

Lastly, in *Re Sarflax Ltd* (1979) it was held that the expression 'carrying on business' had a wider meaning than carrying on trade. It included the collection of assets acquired in the course of business and their distribution in discharge of business liabilities provided there was a 'continuous course of active conduct'. The court further held that the mere preference of one creditor over another did not amount to an 'intention to defraud' within the section.

(*f*) Section 214 Insolvency Act 1986 deals with *wrongful trading by a director*. The provisions were introduced by the Insolvency Act 1985. The provisions apply where:

(*i*) the company has gone into *insolvent liquidation,* i.e. its assets are insufficient for the payment of its debts and other liabilities and the expenses of the winding up; and

(*ii*) the director concerned, at some time before the commencement of the winding up, knew or ought to have concluded that there was no reasonable prospect that the company would avoid going into insolvent liquidation.

In these circumstances the liquidator may apply to the court, which may declare that the director concerned is to be liable to make such contribution to the company's assets as the court thinks proper.

No order is made if the director succeeds in satisfying the court that, on becoming aware of (*ii*) above, he took every step which he ought to have taken with a view to minimizing the potential loss to the company's creditors. The standard applied is that of a reasonably diligent director.

(*g*) Sections 216 and 217 Insolvency Act 1986 deal with the *use of prohibited company names*. They too were introduced by the Insolvency Act 1985.

The provisions apply to a person who has been a director of a company which has gone into *insolvent liquidation* within 12 months of his holding that office. Section 216 prohibits such a person, within the next five years after the commencement of the liquidation, from being a director of, or otherwise taking part in the promotion or management of, a company which has the same name as the first company or a name so similar as to suggest an association with that company. The prohibition may be lifted by leave of the court or in prescribed circumstances.

By s. 217 a person who in contravention of s. 216 becomes a director or otherwise becomes involved in the management of a company is personally liable for that company's debts incurred during his period of office.

The object of these provisions is to remedy the situation in which directors of a company which had failed might mislead the public by immediately becoming directors of another company with a closely similar name.

35. The capital clause. Consideration of this topic will be postponed, since it requires a chapter to itself. Two points, however, should be noted at this stage:

(*a*) The figure given in the capital clause of the memorandum is the *nominal* or *authorized* capital of the company. The Act does not state any *minimum figure* for share capital in the case of a private company. This can, in theory, be of any amount, provided the subscribers to the memorandum take at least one share each. Thus one private company was incorporated with a capital of ½d divided into two shares of ¼d each. Presumably today the minimum capital for a private company would be 1p.

In the case of a public company, however, s. 11 requires the capital clause of the memorandum to state a figure which is *not less than the authorized minimum*. Section 118(1) defines the authorized minimum as £50,000 or such other sum as the Secretary of State may specify by order made by statutory instrument. Presumably the definition is designed to allow the Secretary of State sufficient latitude to take account of inflation.

(*b*) The shares must have a *fixed value* which can also be of any amount. This fixed value is called the *par* or *nominal* value of the share.

Once the share is allotted, the holder will be able to sell it at its current *market* value, which is a fluctuating figure and may be either above or below the par value according to the prosperity and prospects of the company. When the market value is *above* the par value, the share is said to be standing *at a premium*. When the market value is *below* the par value, the share is said to be standing *at a discount*.

Similarly, when shares are first issued by the company, they may be issued at par or at a premium, although not at a discount.

36. Other clauses in the memorandum. The compulsory clauses of the memorandum have now been separately considered in this chapter, but of course the memorandum may have other clauses containing matters which might equally well have been put in the articles instead.

The alteration of any such non-compulsory clauses is governed by s. 17 which states that they may be altered by special resolution, with the same provision for dissentients to apply to the court to cancel the alteration as was made by s. 5 regarding alterations of the objects clause, except that debenture-holders have no right of application.

There are, however, three cases where s. 17 does not apply:

(*a*) If the memorandum expressly, or by reference to the articles, lays down a method of alteration of the particular clause, then that method must be used.

(*b*) If the memorandum prohibits alteration, then the clause can only be altered with the leave of the court under s. 425.

(*c*) Section 17 does not apply to class rights. The nature of class rights and the method of alteration required will be considered later.

Progress test 2

1. What is the minimum number of persons required to form a registered company?　(**1**)

2. Give the definition of a public company found in s. 1 Companies Act 1985.　(**2**)

3. Section 1 Companies Act 1985 states that three types of company may be formed by registration under the Act. What are they?　(**3**)

4. What are the compulsory clauses in the memorandum of assocation?　(**4**)

5. Where does one find:

(*a*) a model memorandum for a public company limited by shares?

(*b*) a model memorandum for a private company limited by shares?　(**5**)

6. What is the association clause?　(**5**)

7. What do you understand by the term 'official notification'?　(**6**)

8. Give the provisions of s. 2(7) Companies Act 1985.　(**6**)

9. Give the statutory restrictions on the choice of a company's name.　(**7, 8**)

10. Give the statutory rules which apply where a company uses a business name.　(**8, 9**)

11. Once the name has been chosen and accepted, where must it appear?　(**10**)

12. Give the provisions of the Companies Act 1985 governing the publication of its name by a public company.　(**4, 10**)

13. Define an officer of a company.　(**10**)

14. If the secretary of a company signs a cheque on its behalf without putting the word 'limited' anywhere on the document, what is the possible effect?　(**10**)

15. What companies may dispense with the use of the word

'limited' as part of their name, even though they are limited companies? (**11**)

16. How may a company change its name? (**12**)

17. Can a company be compelled to change its name? (**13**)

18. What is a company's domicile, and can it be changed? (**14**)

19. Can the address of the registered office within the domicile be changed? (**15**)

20. What documents must normally be kept at the registered office? (**15**)

21. What are the statutory books? (**16**)

22. What remedy had a supplier of goods to a company under an *ultra vires* contract before the European Communities Act 1972 if:

(*a*) the company refused to take delivery of the goods;

(*b*) the company took delivery and the goods were on the premises;

(*c*) the company took delivery and the goods were then consumed? (**21**)

23. What remedy before the European Communities Act 1972 had a company which had made an *ultra vires* contract with an outsider who refused to perform it? (**22**)

24. Discuss the provisions of s. 35 Companies Act 1985 with regard to the doctrine of *ultra vires*. (**24**)

25. How far is it lawful to make gratuitous payments out of a company's assets? (**25**)

26. By what method and within what limits may the objects clause of a company's memorandum be altered? (**26**)

27. Who may apply to the court to cancel an alteration of the objects clause? (**27**)

28. What are the powers of the court on such an application? (**27**)

29. In what circumstances can a limited company convert itself into an unlimited company? And vice versa? Describe the procedures available. (**31–33**)

30. Can the liability of a member be *increased*? (**34**)

31. What constitutes *fraudulent trading* by a company and what is its possible result? (**34**)

32. What constitutes wrongful trading by a director and what is its possible result? (**34**)

33. The number of members in a company became reduced to one on 28 April 1986. The company incurred trade debts on 29 April

1986, 20 September 1986, 27 October 1986 and 28 October 1986. How far is the remaining member liable for these debts?   **(34)**

34. What is the *authorized minimum* of share capital required to be stated in the capital clause of the memorandum of a public company?   **(35)**

35. How can the non-compulsory clauses of the memorandum, if any, be altered?   **(36)**

3

The articles of association

1. The nature of the articles of association. The articles of a company are the regulations for its internal management, corresponding to the partnership deed in a partnership. The management of every company is governed by articles, though not every company need *register* articles with the registrar, as will be seen later.

2. The Companies (Tables A–F) Regulations 1985. Sections 3 and 8 of the Companies Act 1985 authorize the Secretary of State to make, by statutory instrument, regulations specifying forms of memorandum and forms of articles for the different categories of registered companies. The regulations made under these sections of the Act are the Companies (Tables A–F) Regulations 1985 (S.I. 1985, No. 805), and the forms of memorandum and articles are to be found in the Schedule to these regulations.

Section 3, which deals with the forms of memorandum, provides that the forms specified in the Schedule must be adhered to as nearly as circumstances admit.

The forms specified are:

(*a*) Table B for a private company limited by shares;

(*b*) Table C for a company limited by guarantee and not having a share capital;

(*c*) Table D, Part I, for a public company limited by guarantee and having a share capital;

(*d*) Table D, Part II, for a private company limited by guarantee and having a share capital;

(*e*) Table E for an unlimited company having a share capital; and

(*f*) Table F for a public company limited by shares.

The forms in both Parts of Table D are of diminishing importance because, by s. 1(4), it has not been permissible since 22 December 1980 to form any *new* company limited by guarantee with a share capital.

The forms in Tables C and E are necessarily for private companies since a public company, by its definition in s. 1(3), must have a share capital and must be a limited company.

Section 8 deals with forms of articles. The forms of articles specified in the Schedule are:

(*a*) Table A for a company (public or private) limited by shares;

(*b*) Table C for a company limited by guarantee and not having a share capital;

(*c*) Table D, Part III, for a company (public or private) limited by guarantee and having a share capital; and

(*d*) Table E for an unlimited company having a share capital.

Again because of the definition of a public company, the forms of articles in Tables C and E are necessarily for private companies only.

As regards Tables C, D and E, s. 8(4) provides that these forms must be adhered to as closely as circumstances admit. There is no corresponding provision regarding Table A. The articles of a company limited by shares, therefore, do not need to be in any specified form.

The provisions of the Act relating to Table A, however, require further consideration, and constant reference will be made throughout the book to the contents of Table A.

3. The nature of Table A. Table A consists of the regulations for the management of the commonest category of registered company, i.e. a public or private company limited by shares. Many of the clauses in it must eventually be learnt, but at this stage it is best simply to glance at the headings in order to see the type of material normally found in the articles of companies limited by shares. The headings may be grouped as follows:

(*a*) shares (share capital, share certificates, lien on shares, calls on shares and forfeiture, transfer of shares, alteration of share capital, purchase by company of its own shares);

(*b*) meetings (general meetings, notice of general meetings, proceedings at general meetings, votes of members);

(*c*) directors (number of directors, alternate directors, powers of

directors, delegation of directors' powers, appointment and retirement of directors, disqualification and removal of directors,
remuneration and expenses of directors, directors' appointments and
interests, directors' gratuities and pensions, proceedings of directors
(including board meetings);

(*d*) company secretary;

(*e*) minutes;

(*f*) company's seal;

(*g*) financial matters (dividends, accounts, capitalization of
profits);

(*h*) notices;

(*i*) winding up; and

(*j*) indemnity.

4. The obligation to register articles. Section 7(1) states that a
company limited by shares *may* register articles, i.e. may do so if it
wishes, while a company limited by guarantee or an unlimited
company *shall* (i.e. *must*) do so.

Section 7(3) further states that articles must be signed by the
subscribers to the memorandum, i.e. the same persons sign both
documents.

5. The application of Table A. It is clear from s. 7(1) that a
company limited by shares need not register articles, though other
types of companies are required to do so. The section does not,
however, tell us what happens if a company limited by shares does not
register articles.

Section 8 deals with this situation. Section 8(1) merely gives a
general permission for the articles of any company to adopt the Table
A provisions, but s. 8(2) is of great importance. It deals exclusively
with companies limited by shares, and states that Table A applies to
such companies *automatically, unless excluded or modified*.

It is essential to grasp the fact of the automatic application of Table
A. The result of s. 8(2) is that if a company limited by shares does not
register any articles, Table A automatically applies. Moreover, even if
it *does* register articles of its own, Table A will still apply automatically
unless it has been excluded or modified.

The company can easily exclude Table A by express words to that
effect in its articles. Modification can be either *express*, as where the
company's articles state that some clauses of Table A will apply with

certain alterations, or *implied*, as where the company's articles are inconsistent with Table A, in which case they will prevail.

Students often find s. 8(2) a little difficult to understand. Its meaning, as explained above, is quite simple, and it should be read slowly several times until it becomes clear.

6. Companies formed prior to 1985. A question which arises in connection with Table A is whether a company is always governed by the Table A prescribed under authority of s. 8 of the 1985 Act or, if it was formed prior to 1985, by the Table A of the particular Companies Act under which it was registered. Each Act had a Table A of its own, and each differed to some extent from the others, so this can be an important point.

The rule here is that a company is always governed by the Table A of the Act *under which it was registered* with *one exception*: under s. 370(2) the *method of service of notice of company meetings* is regulated in every case by the Table A prescribed by the 1985 Act, no matter when the company was formed, unless the company's own articles stipulate some other method: s. 370(1).

7. Statutory requirements regarding articles. By s. 7(3) articles must be:

(*a*) printed;

(*b*) in numbered paragraphs;

(*c*) signed by the subscribers to the memorandum in the presence of at least one witness.

8. The duties of the subscribers to the memorandum. The duties of the subscribers must at some stage be noted, and since we have already come across three of them, they can now conveniently be listed in full:

(*a*) They must sign the memorandum (*see* 2:5).

(*b*) They must sign the articles.

(*c*) They must take at least one share each (*see* 2:5).

(*d*) They normally appoint the first directors (*see* 16:4).

(*e*) They must sign the statement required by s. 10 on the registration of the company (*see* 4:1).

9. Alteration of the articles. Section 9 states that a company may alter its articles by special resolution. This may be done at any general meeting and as often as required. It should be noted, however, that s. 9 merely lays down a procedure whereby *some only* of the shareholders can validly alter the articles. There is nothing in it to override the basic principle of company law that all the shareholders, acting together, can do anything which is *intra vires* the company. Hence the articles can also be altered by their unanimous agreement: *Cane* v. *Jones* (1980). Section 380, which requires all special resolutions to be filed with the registrar, also requires such unanimous agreements to be filed with him (*see* 15:**41**).

There are certain important rules regarding alteration:

(*a*) Under s. 9, the alteration is subject to the provisions of the memorandum, and if the two documents conflict, the memorandum will prevail.

(*b*) The alteration must be lawful. It must not conflict with the provisions of the Act, nor with the general law.

(*c*) If, in response to an application by the prescribed minority for the cancellation of an alteration of the company's objects clause, the court has made an order under s. 5 prohibiting any alteration to the articles, the company may not alter them without the leave of the court (*see* 2:**27**).

(*d*) If, in response to an application by the prescribed minority for the cancellation of a resolution by a public company to be re-registered as a private company, the court has made an order under s. 54 prohibiting any alteration to the articles, the company may not alter them without the leave of the court (*see* 25:**5**).

(*e*) If, in response to a petition on the ground that the company's affairs are being conducted in a manner unfairly prejudicial to the interests of some part of the members, the court has made an order under s. 461 prohibiting any alteration to the articles, the company may not alter them without the leave of the court (*see* 23:**9**).

(*f*) Under s. 16, the alteration may not increase the liability of any member without his written consent (*see* 2:**34**).

(*g*) If the alteration concerns class rights, s. 127 protects dissentients, i.e. persons who disagree. (Section 127 and class rights are discussed in 11:**14**.)

(*h*) The alteration must be *bona fide* for the benefit of the company as a whole. Provided this condition is satisfied, individual hardship is irrelevant: *Allen* v. *Gold Reefs of West Africa* (1900); *Shuttleworth* v.

Cox Bros & Co. Ltd (1927); *Sidebottom* v. *Kershaw, Leese & Co. Ltd* (1920).

(*i*) If the alteration involves a breach of contract, it will still be valid, but the injured party will have all the normal remedies against the company for the breach.

NOTE: The first seven of these rules have a restrictive effect on the company's statutory power to alter its articles freely by special resolution under s. 9, while the last two rather emphasize its power to alter its articles as it wishes.

Section 18(2) provides that where a company is required to send to the registrar any document relating to an alteration in its articles, it must also send him a printed copy of the articles as altered. Section 711 requires him to publish his receipt of any such document in the *Gazette*. If an alteration has not been officially notified by the registrar at the material time and if the company cannot show that it was known at that time to the person concerned, the company cannot rely on it against that person: s. 42.

10. The legal effect of the articles. Section 14(1) states that the memorandum and articles bind the company and the members as though signed and sealed by each member, and as though they contained covenants (i.e. promises under seal) by each member to observe their provisions.

Section 14(2) states that money payable by the member to the company under the memorandum or articles is a *specialty debt*, i.e. the period of limitation is 12 years and not the normal six. It appears, however, that this is not the case as regards debts owed by the company to the members, e.g. declared dividends (*see* 20:**10**).

The effect of the articles is therefore as follows:

(*a*) The company is bound to the members *in their capacity of members*.

(*b*) The members *in their capacity of members* are bound to the company.

(*c*) The members are contractually bound *to each other*.

(*d*) The company is *not bound to any person*, except to members in their capacity of members.

Each of these will be considered in turn. It should, however, be noted as a preliminary that the precise effect of the statutory provisions has been the subject of considerable controversy and there have been many apparently conflicting decisions by the courts.

11. Company bound to members in their capacity of members. Section 14(1) does *not* state that the memorandum and articles bind the company and the members as though signed and sealed *by the company* and as though they contained covenants *by the company* to observe their provisions. However, case-law indicates that the company is bound.

In *Wood* v. *Odessa Waterworks Co.* (1889), a case decided by Stirling J., a company which had applied its profits to the construction of works instead of paying a dividend to the shareholders passed a resolution proposing to give to the shareholders debenture bonds carrying interest. The company's articles empowered the directors with the sanction of the company to declare a dividend 'to be paid' to shareholders. HELD: What was proposed by the resolution was not in accordance with the articles and therefore the directors were restrained by injunction from acting on the resolution.

A Court of Appeal case to a similar effect was *Salmon* v. *Quin & Axtens Ltd* (1909): By the company's articles the powers of general management were vested in the directors except that no resolution of the directors for acquiring or letting premises was to be valid if Salmon, a managing director, dissented. The directors passed a resolution for acquiring and letting premises, despite Salmon's dissent, and at an extraordinary meeting of shareholders resolutions were passed by a simple majority affirming the directors' action. HELD: Since the company's resolutions were inconsistent with the articles, the company could be restrained from acting upon them. *Wood's* case was approved as accurate subject to the observation that it might well be that the court would not enforce the covenant as between individual shareholders in most cases (*see* **13**).

However, in *Re Compania de Electricidad de la Provincia de Buenos Aires Ltd* (1980) it was held that the limitation period in actions by members against the company for unpaid dividends was six years, since such actions were not actions upon a specialty for the purposes of the Limitation Act 1939 (now the Limitation Act

1980). Under that Act the limitation period would have been 12 years if the contract had been regarded as sealed *by the company*.

12. Members as members bound to company. The memorandum and articles constitute a contract between the company and its members *in respect of their ordinary rights as members*. This was stated by Astbury J. in *Hickman* v. *Kent or Romney Marsh Sheep-Breeders' Association* (1915). The judgment in the case contains a comprehensive review of decided cases.

A clause in the articles of the association provided for disputes between the association and any of its members to be referred to arbitration. Hickman, who was a member as a flock owner, issued a writ against the association and its secretary claiming an injunction to restrain the association from employing that secretary and for other purposes. The defendants asked for the proceedings to be stayed and the matters in dispute to be referred to arbitration. HELD: Hickman's action was a breach of the arbitration clause in the articles and the matters had to be referred to arbitration.

This case was approved by the Court of Appeal in *Beattie* v. *E. & F. Beattie Ltd* (1938), also relating to an arbitration clause in the articles. The essential difference, however, was that here it was a director who was arguing that a member's action against the company and himself should be stayed on the ground that the articles were a contract giving him the right to demand arbitration. HELD: There was no contractual force in the articles as between the company and its directors as such. Sir Wilfred Greene M.R., who gave the leading judgment, said: 'The contractual force given to the articles of association by the section is limited to such provisions of the articles as apply to the relationship of the members in their capacity as members'.

13. Members contractually bound to each other. The memorandum and articles constitute a contract between individual members but the rule in *Foss* v. *Harbottle* (1843) (*see* 1:**33**) normally prevents an individual member from enforcing that contract against another individual member except through the company, or, if it is in liquidation, through the liquidator.

The dissenting speech of Lord Herschell in the House of Lords in *Welton* v. *Saffery* (1897) is often quoted from in this connection. The decision in the case was that as it was *ultra vires* to issue shares at a discount, the holders of such shares were not relieved from liability to calls in the winding up.

Lord Herschell said: 'The articles constitute a contract between each member and the company, and ... there is no contract in terms between the individual members of the company; but the articles do not any the less, in my opinion, regulate their rights *inter se*. Such rights can only be enforced by or against a member through the company, or through the liquidator representing the company; but I think that no member has, as between himself and another member, any right beyond that which the contract with the company gives'.

It is different, however, where the right given to a member by the articles is a personal right. The contract can then be directly enforced by one member against another member without the aid of the company.

In *Rayfield* v. *Hands* (1960), Clause 11 of the articles of a private company provided: 'Every member who intends to transfer shares *shall* inform the directors, who *will* take the said shares equally between them at a fair value'. The plaintiff, a member, informed the defendants, the directors, of his wish to transfer his shares. The directors denied liability to take and pay for them. HELD: (*a*) 'Will' indicated an *obligation* to take the shares. (*b*) The article created a *contractual relationship* between the *plaintiff as a member* and the *defendants as members*.

It is submitted that (*a*) above is correct in that it probably gives effect to the intention behind the clause, although one may well wonder why, if obligation was intended, the word 'shall' was not used again. But (*b*) is more difficult to understand. The defendants in the case were in fact members, but the clause imposed the obligation to buy the shares on the *directors*. If one of them had not been a member, would he too have been bound? Can an article which refers to a person as a director, or employee, or coal-supplier, bind him *as a member* if he also happens to be one? And how far does such an article give a *direct right of action* between one member and another?

The case is difficult to reconcile with other cases on the topic of the legal effect of the articles, but it should be noted that it does not stand entirely alone. Much the same reasoning appears to have been adopted by Plowman J. in *Re Richmond Gate Property Co. Ltd* (1965), a case which concerned a managing director's claim for remuneration, and where in his judgment Plowman J. said: 'The effect of Article 9, coupled with Article 108 of Table A, *coupled with the fact that the applicant was a member of the company*, in my judgement is that a *contract exists between himself and the company*'.

14. Company not bound to members in any other capacity than that of members. This rule is seen clearly in the leading case of *Eley* v. *Positive Life Assurance Co. Ltd* (1876), from which it follows that a person cannot rely on the articles as a contract of employment or supply since they only bind the company to members in respect of their membership rights, and not contractual rights of other kinds. This is so whether he is a member or not.

In *Eley* v. *Positive Life Assurance Co. Ltd* (1876), the articles provided that E should be the company's solicitor *for life*. He was employed by the company and took shares in it, but later the company dismissed him from his employment with it. He sued for breach of contract. HELD: His action failed, for the articles on which he relied were not a contract between the company and any other person, except in respect of their *membership* rights.

However, the terms of a separate contract, e.g. with a director, may by implication be incorporated into the company's contract with him from the terms of the articles.

An example is *Re New British Iron Co. Ltd ex parte Beckwith* (1898). The articles provided that the remuneration of the directors should be £1000 per annum. The directors, who were also members, accepted office, but were not paid. HELD: The directors were entitled to recover the arrears of remuneration on the basis of the separate contract between the company and themselves, of which the articles were evidence.

Further, where a person performs services for the company at its request without any contract, he may sue in *quasi-contract* for a reasonable sum (*quantum meruit*) for the work done. A clause in the articles then may be *evidence* of what the parties thought reasonable, and though unable of itself to create contractual rights of this type, may be of evidential value in a quasi-contractual claim such as was made in *Craven-Ellis* v. *Canons Ltd* (1936).

In *Craven-Ellis* v. *Canons Ltd* (1936), C was appointed the company's managing director by a contract in writing and under the company's seal, by a resolution of the board of directors. The articles imposed a share qualification on the directors, none of whom ever obtained it. C sued for his salary under the contract and, alternatively, for reasonable remuneration (*quantum meruit*) for work done, in quasi-contract. HELD: His claim on the *contract* failed, for under the articles his appointment could not be valid owing to his failure to take up his qualification shares. His claim in *quasi-contract*, however, succeeded, for he had performed services for the company at its request.

Although *Eley* v. *Positive Life Assurance Co. Ltd* has been described above as the leading case, some doubt as to its authority has been created by cases such as *Rayfield* v. *Hands* (*see* **13** above), and the only safe conclusion to draw is that this is an uncertain and controversial area of the subject.

Progress test 3

1. What is Table A? To which companies and when does it apply? (**3** and **5**)

2. If a company limited by shares was formed in 1965 and did not register articles, is it governed by the Table A of the Companies Act 1948 or by the Table A of the Companies (Tables A–F) Regulations 1985? (**6**)

3. What are the statutory requirements regarding the articles? (**7**)

4. What are the duties of the subscribers to the memorandum? (**8**)

5. By what method may a company alter its articles? What rules govern alteration? (**9**)

6. What is the legal effect of the articles? (**10–14**)

4
Registration

1. Documents to be delivered to the registrar on registration. We have now dealt with the memorandum and articles of association and it remains to consider the next step after preparation of these documents.

By ss. 10 and 12 the memorandum and articles, if any, must be delivered to the registrar, who retains and registers them. But this is not enough, and the complete list of documents which must be delivered to him is as follows:

(*a*) the memorandum: s. 10;

(*b*) the articles, if any: s. 10;

(*c*) a statement signed by the subscribers of the memorandum:

   (*i*) containing the names and particulars of the directors and secretary and a consent signed by each of them to act in the relevant capacity; and

   (*ii*) specifying the intended situation of the company's registered office: s. 10 and the 1st Schedule;

(*d*) a statement of capital: s. 47(3) Finance Act 1973;

(*e*) a statutory declaration of compliance signed by a solicitor engaged in the formation of the company, or a person named as director or secretary in the statement delivered under s. 10: s. 12(3).

2. The certificate of incorporation. Once the required documents have been delivered the registrar, under s. 12(1), must satisfy himself that all the requirements of the Act in respect of registration have been complied with. He then, in accordance with s. 13(1), issues a certificate of incorporation (the company's 'birth' certificate) and, under s. 705, allocates to the company its registered number.

Section 13(3) provides that from the date of incorporation

mentioned in the certificate the subscribers of the memorandum become a body corporate by the name contained in the memorandum. This occurs even if the date mentioned in the certificate is *not* in fact the date when it was issued: *Jubilee Cotton Mills* v. *Lewis* (1924). If the company's memorandum states that it is to be a public company, the certificate of incorporation must also contain a statement to that effect: s. 13(6).

Section 13(7) states that the certificate, once issued, is conclusive evidence that the company has been duly registered and, if it contains a statement to that effect, that the company is a public company. Section 711 requires the registrar to publish notice of its issue in the *Gazette*.

The company is now formed, i.e. it is now a 'registered' corporation.

3. Summary of the statutory provisions studied so far. It is at this stage helpful to look at the first two chapters of Part I of the Act and to see that some comprehension of them should now have been achieved. Chapter I (ss. 1–24) is headed 'Company Formation' and Chapter II (ss. 25–34) 'Company Names'. The groups of provisions may be listed:

Sections 1–3 deal with formation and the memorandum in general.
Sections 4–6 deal with alterations of the company's objects.
Sections 7–9 deal with the articles.
Sections 10–21 deal with the procedure for, and the effect of, registration.
Sections 22–24 deal with the company's membership.
Sections 25–34 deal with the company's name.

4. The expenses of formation. These are as follows:

(*a*) a registration fee of £50 under the Companies (Fees) Regulations 1980 (S.I. 1980, No. 1749);

(*b*) stamp duty of £1 per cent on the actual value of assets of any kind contributed by the members less any liabilities assumed or discharged by the company as consideration for them: s. 47(5) and the 19th Schedule Finance Act 1973.

In addition, the cost of professional services and preparing the requisite documents must be defrayed.

5. Differences between a company limited by shares and a partnership. It is sometimes convenient at this stage to set out the differences between a company limited by shares and a partnership. The process of incorporation has been completed and its implications discussed, so that comparisons can now be drawn. There are a large number of differences, but the most important are as follows:

(a) A limited company is an *artificial legal person*.

A partnership is not. It is an association of two or more legal persons, in the same way as a company, but the *association itself* has no legal personality and outsiders deal directly with the members.

(b) In a limited company the *liability* of the members is *limited* to the amount unpaid on their shares.

In a partnership, the *liability* of the partners is *unlimited* except in the case of a limited partnership, and even then there must be at least one general partner with unlimited liability.

(c) A limited company must be *formed by the process of registration* described above.

A partnership may be formed quite *informally*, e.g. orally, or even by conduct, though it is wise to have a written agreement or articles, often called the deed of partnership.

(d) In a *public* limited company the *shares* are usually *freely* transferable.

In a partnership no partner may transfer his share without the *consent* of the others.

(e) In a limited company the members are *not ipso facto agents* of the company.

In a partnership each partner is an *agent* of the others, and each therefore is also a principal. A partnership is thus a collection of principals and agents.

(f) In a limited company the *death or bankruptcy* of a member (or even of all the members) has *no effect* on the existence of the company.

In a partnership death or bankruptcy of a partner causes *dissolution* unless the articles provide otherwise.

(g) A limited company is subject to many *special rules of law*, both statutory and otherwise. The *ultra vires* doctrine is an outstanding instance.

In a partnership the partners are *free* to make any arrangement they like which would be lawful between private persons.

Progress test 4

1. What documents must be delivered to the registrar on registration of a company? (**1**)

2. From what date is a registered company incorporated? (**2**)

3. What is the legal effect of the certificate of incorporation? (**2**)

4. What are the main differences between a company limited by shares and a partnership? (**5**)

5

Commencement of business and contracts

1. Commencement of business. A *private* company can commence business on incorporation. Once it has received its certificate of incorporation, nothing further is required.

A company registered as a *public* company on its *original incorporation*, however, must obtain a *second* certificate, often called a *trading certificate*, before it can commence business or exercise its borrowing powers. In order to obtain its trading certificate, the company must comply with s. 117.

2. Procedure for obtaining trading certificate. In order to obtain its trading certificate the company must apply to the registrar. Section 117(2) and (3) requires the application to be made in the prescribed form and accompanied by a statutory declaration signed by a director or the secretary of the company.

The statutory declaration must state:

(*a*) that the nominal value of the company's allotted share capital is not less than the authorized minimum (*see* **2:35**);

(*b*) the amount paid up on the company's allotted share capital;

(*c*) the amount of the company's preliminary expenses and the persons who paid them; and

(*d*) any amount paid or benefit given to any promoter and his consideration for it.

Section 117(4) states that any shares allotted under a share scheme for employees must be disregarded for the purposes of (*a*) above unless they are paid up at least as to one quarter of their nominal value and the whole of any premium.

ires the registrar to publish in the *Gazette* the
a declaration.

ertificate. If the registrar is satisfied as to (*a*)
received the statutory declaration, s. 117(2) requires
ssue a trading certificate.

Section 117(6) provides that this certificate is conclusive evidence
that the company is entitled to do business and exercise its borrowing
powers.

If the company is not issued with a trading certificate within a year
from incorporation, it may be wound up by the court under s.
122(1)(*b*) Insolvency Act 1986 (*see* 30:**1**).

4. Contracts. In studying the contracts of a company, it is important
first to grasp the situations which may arise.

In the case of a *private* company, there are only two:

  (*a*) contracts made on behalf of the company before incorporation;
  (*b*) contracts made after incorporation.

Owing to s. 117, however, in the case of a *public* company, there are
three:

  (*a*) contracts made on behalf of the company before incorporation;
  (*b*) contracts made after incorporation but before obtaining the
trading certificate;
  (*c*) contracts made after obtaining the trading certificate.

These situations must be dealt with separately.

5. Pre-incorporation contracts. The rules here are the same for
both public and private companies. Clearly no legal person, natural or
artificial, can contract before he or it exists. Therefore a contract made
by a promoter on behalf of the company before incorporation never
binds the company, because the company is not yet formed. It has no
legal existence. Even if the parties act on the contract, it will not bind
the company: *Re Northumberland Avenue Hotel Co.* (1886).

Problems formerly arose, however, with regard to the promoter. It
must be remembered that he was not automatically bound simply
because the company was not yet in existence. He was bound only if
he had shown an intention to be bound, and this intention was
deduced from his conduct and the surrounding circumstances.

Similarly, he could not enforce the contract unless he had sh
an intention, since the right to enforce a contract n
accompanies liability to perform it.

Although the principle was clear enough, the question of wheth
the promoter had shown an intention to be bound often rested on
subtle differences in the words used. Thus in *Kelner* v. *Baxter* (1866),
the directors were held personally liable on a pre-incorporation
contract where they had signed it 'A, B and C, on behalf of the X
Company'. But in *Newborne* v. *Sensolid Ltd* (1954), Newborne was
held unable to enforce the contract (and therefore presumably not
bound by it) because he had signed it 'Leopold Newborne and Co.
Ltd', even though underneath he had added his own name, 'Leopold
Newborne'.

The position is now governed by s. 36(4) which had its origin in the
European Communities Act 1972 and which provides that, unless
otherwise agreed, a pre-incorporation contract has effect as a contract
entered into by *the person purporting to act as agent for the company* and
he is personally liable on it.

In *Phonogram Ltd* v. *Lane* (1982) a company to be called Fragile
Management Ltd was about to be formed to manage a group of
'pop' artists who intended to perform under the name 'Cheap Mean
and Nasty'. The group's manager, Mr Brian Lane, entered into an
arrangement with Phonogram under which, in anticipation of a
subsequent contract between Fragile Management and Phonogram, the latter were to finance the group by providing £12,000,
payable in two instalments of £6000 each. Phonogram duly paid the
first instalment by a cheque made out to Jelly Music Ltd, a
company of which Mr Lane was a director, for purely administrative reasons. The cheque was accompanied by a letter addressed to
Mr Lane and stating that if the contract was not completed within
a certain period, 'you will undertake to repay us the £6000'. A copy
of the letter was enclosed which Mr Lane was asked to sign and
return to Phonogram. He did so, signing 'for and on behalf of
Fragile Management Ltd'.

The contract was never completed and Phonogram accordingly
issued a writ against Mr Lane claiming repayment of the money.
Mr Lane asserted that he was not personally liable to repay it since
he had throughout been acting on behalf of Fragile Management
Ltd, even though it had not yet been incorporated.

HELD: The fine distinctions adopted by the common law were no longer relevant. 'Unless there is a clear exclusion of personal liability, s. [*36(4)*] should be given its full effect. It means that in all cases such as the present, where a person purports to contract on behalf of a company not yet formed, then however he expresses his signature he himself is personally liable on the contract' (*per* Lord Denning M.R.).

6. Contracts made after incorporation but before issue of trading certificate.

This situation can arise, as we have seen, only in the case of a *public* company.

Section 117(8) states that failure to obtain its trading certificate will not affect the validity of any transaction entered into by a company.

If, however, a company contravenes the section by entering into a transaction before its trading certificate has been issued, and then fails to comply with its resulting obligations within 21 days from being called upon to do so, the directors become jointly and severally liable to indemnify the other party to the transaction in respect of any loss which he has suffered through such failure.

7. Contracts made after issue of the trading certificate in the case of a public company and after incorporation in the case of a private company.

These are, of course, valid provided they are *intra vires*, but it must always be remembered that the doctrine of *ultra vires* restricts the contractual capacity of companies, and that the *vires* will always depend on the objects as stated in the memorandum.

There are, however, some statutory provisions relating to form and other matters which must be studied.

8. Form of contracts made by companies.

Section 36(1) states in effect that the contracts of a company may be made in the same form as those of a private person.

At common law the contracts of a corporation were required to be by deed, but today statute has rendered this rule practically obsolete. The result of s. 36(1) is that a registered company never needs to contract by deed unless a deed would also be required in the case of a private individual, e.g. for a lease exceeding three years.

Thus today the company's common seal is required by law only in the case of the following documents:

(a) contracts which would be required to be by deed if entered into by a private person;

(b) deeds;

(c) share certificates: s. 186;

(d) share warrants: s. 188.

Section 37, of less importance, states that a bill of exchange or promissory note will be in order if made, accepted or endorsed in the name of the company by a person acting under its authority.

Section 41 states that a document requiring authentication by a company may be signed by a director, secretary or other authorized officer and need not be under its seal.

9. The official seal. Section 39(1) states that a company whose objects comprise the transaction of business in foreign countries may, if authorized by its articles, have for use in any place outside the United Kingdom an official seal. This is a facsimile (copy) of the common seal, with the addition on its face of the name of the place where it is to be used.

Progress test 5

1. With what statutory requirements must a public company comply in order to commence business or exercise its borrowing powers? (2)

2. Discuss the legal effect of pre-incorporation contracts. (5)

3. What is the legal effect of a contract made by a public company after incorporation but before obtaining its trading certificate? (6)

4. In what form may registered companies contract? (8)

5. On which documents is the company's seal required? (8)

6. What is the official seal of a company? (9)

6

Promoters and subscribers to the memorandum

1. The legal position of a promoter. There is no general statutory definition of a promoter, though he was indirectly described in s. 56(1) as a person 'engaged or interested in the formation of the company', and s. 67(3) gave a definition for the purpose of ss. 67–69 only, which dealt with compensation for mis-statements in a prospectus. That definition was:

> ' "promoter" means a promoter who was party to the preparation of the prospectus, ... but does not include any person by reason of his acting in a professional capacity for persons engaged in procuring the formation of the company.'

These provisions were repealed by the Financial Services Act 1986, which uses the term 'promoter' without any definition. It is clear that in the normal way persons assisting the promoters by 'acting in a professional capacity' do not thereby become promoters themselves. Thus the solicitor or counsel who drafts the articles, or the accountant who values the assets of a business to be purchased, are merely giving professional assistance to the promoters. They will be paid for their services, but they will not be implicated further. Perhaps the true test of whether a person is a promoter is whether he has a *desire* that the company shall be formed, and is prepared to take some steps, which may or may not involve other persons, to implement it.

While the accurate description of a promoter may be difficult, his legal position is quite clear. He is said to be in a *fiduciary* position towards the company, analogous to the relation of an agent with his principal, and, like an agent, he may not make a secret profit. The fiduciary relation requires *full disclosure* of the relevant facts, including any profit made. Students of the law of contract will recall many examples of this relation.

NOTE: It is important to understand that it is not the profit made by the promoter which the law forbids, but the non-disclosure of it. Provided full disclosure is made, as was done in *Salomon* v. *Salomon & Co. Ltd*, the profit is permissible. It must be disclosed to an independent board of directors, if there is one, but if, as is often the case in a private company, the promoter is himself the only director, it must be disclosed to the shareholders. Frequently they will be the promoter's own family, and he will in practice be free to make what arrangements he likes, since their fortunes rise and fall with his.

2. Remedies of the company against a promoter. As regards public companies, s. 103 imposes strict rules on the valuation of non-cash consideration for an allotment of shares (*see* 9:**18–20**). These statutory rules greatly diminish the importance of the remedies evolved by the courts against a promoter for non-disclosure of profit in a public company. In private companies, however, these remedies remain the only sanction and continue to be of significance. In theory, the remedies apply with respect to all companies, public or private.

If any profit made is not disclosed, the company has a remedy against the promoter which varies according to the circumstances. These can be divided into two possible situations:

(*a*) *Where the promoter was not in a fiduciary position when he acquired the property which he is selling to the company, but only when he sold it to the company:*

Here the promoter, as in Salomon's case, has had the property for a considerable period of time. He can hardly be said to be in a fiduciary position towards the company if he bought a business 10 years before its formation, and though the moment at which his fiduciary relation arises may be difficult to determine, it can at least be said that it does not arise until he contemplates, i.e. considers the possibility of, forming a company to take over his business.

The remedy for non-disclosure in such a case is that the company may rescind the contract with the promoter, which of course means that it restores the property to him and recovers its money.

(*b*) *Where the promoter was in a fiduciary position both when he acquired the property, and when he sold it to the company:*

Here the promoter bought the property with a view to selling it to the company, and the company will then have a choice of remedy. It may either:

(*i*) rescind the contract as in (*a*) above: *Erlanger* v. *New Sombrero Phosphate Co.* (1878); *or*

(*ii*) retain the property, paying no more for it than the promoter, thereby depriving him of his profit: *Gluckstein* v. *Barnes* (1900); *or*

(*iii*) where the above remedies would be inappropriate, such as when the property has been altered so as to render rescission impossible, and the promoter has already received his inflated price, the company may sue the promoter for misfeasance (breach of the duty to disclose). The measure of damages will be the amount of the profit made by the promoter: *Re Leeds and Hanley Theatres of Varieties Ltd* (1902).

3. Remuneration of promoters. It is clear that a promoter, if he makes proper disclosure, may expect to be rewarded for his efforts. In practice he is recompensed in *one* of the following ways:

(*a*) He may sell his own property to the company for *cash* at an over-valuation of which proper disclosure has been made.

(*b*) He may sell his own property to the company for *fully paid shares*, again having fully disclosed any over-valuation.

(*c*) He may be given an *option* to take up further shares in the company *at par* (i.e. at their *nominal* value) after their true value has risen and is reflected in their market price.

(*d*) The articles may provide for a fixed sum to be paid to him. Such a provision has no contractual effect and he cannot sue to enforce it (3:**10, 14**), but if it is acted on – and the promoter can in practice probably make sure that it is – the company cannot recover its money.

It must again be borne in mind that in a public company s. 103 will normally operate to prevent any over-valuation.

4. Disqualification of promoters. Section 1 Company Directors Disqualification Act 1986 empowers the court to make a disqualification order against a promoter which can prohibit him from taking part in the promotion of a company for a period of up to 15 years.

This Act is of very wide application and is fully considered in 16:**20**.

5. Valuation of non-cash assets acquired from subscriber. The subscribers to the memorandum are not normally the promoters of the company. Nevertheless, s. 104 provides that where, in a public company, a subscriber sells non-cash assets to the company, those assets must be valued by an independent person in the same way as is prescribed by s. 103 in relation to payment for shares: ss. 108–111 (*see* 9:**18–20** and 10:**1**).

Section 104(1) prohibits a public company from entering into an agreement with a subscriber for the transfer by him, within two years from the date of issue of its trading certificate, of a non-cash asset to the company for a consideration equal to *one-tenth or more of the nominal value of its issued share capital* unless four conditions are satisfied.

These are:

(*a*) The consideration to be received by the company and any consideration other than cash to be given by it must have been *valued*.

(*b*) *A report* on the consideration so received and given must have been made to the company during the six months immediately preceding the agreement.

(*c*) The terms of the agreement must have been approved by an *ordinary resolution* of the company.

(*d*) Not later than the giving of notice of the meeting at which the resolution is proposed, copies of the resolution and the report must have been *circulated to the members* and, if the subscriber in question is not then a member, to him: s. 104(4).

Section 111(2) requires a copy of the resolution, together with the report, to be delivered to the registrar within 15 days of the passing of the resolution, while s. 711(1) requires the registrar to publish in the *Gazette* the receipt by him of the report.

6. Report on non-cash assets acquired from subscriber. Section 109(1) provides that s. 108(1)–(3) and (5) applies to the valuation and report, requiring the valuation to be made by an independent person qualified to be an auditor of the company (the 'valuer'), or some other qualified person chosen by him (*see* 9:**18** and **19**).

Further, s. 110(1) entitles the person making the valuation or report to require from the company's officers any necessary information and explanation.

Under s. 109(2) the report must:

(*a*) state the consideration to be received by the company, describing the asset in question (specifying the amount to be received in cash) and the consideration to be given by the company (specifying the amount to be given in cash);

(*b*) state the method and date of valuation;

(*c*) contain a note as to the matters mentioned in s. 108(6)(*a*)–(*c*) (*see* 9:**19**); and

(*d*) contain a note that on the basis of the valuation the value of the consideration to be received by the company is not less than the value of the consideration to be given by it.

7. Effect of contravention of s. 104. Section 105 provides that where a public company enters into any agreement with a subscriber to its memorandum which contravenes s. 104 and *either*:

(*a*) the subscriber has not received a report; *or*

(*b*) there has been some other contravention of s. 104 or of s. 108(1), (2) or (5) or s. 109 which he knew or ought to have known amounted to a contravention,

the company is entitled to recover from him any consideration which it gave under the agreement or a sum equivalent in value, and the agreement itself is *void*.

Special rules apply, however, where the agreement involves an *allotment of shares* in the company. In such a case, and regardless of whether there has also been a contravention of s. 103, the agreement remains enforceable in so far as it is for the allotment of shares, and the allottee is liable to pay the company the nominal value of the shares plus any premium. In a proper case, however, the court may grant relief from liability under s. 113. Further, s. 115(2) expressly preserves the enforceability of any undertaking given by the subscriber to do work or provide services or do anything else in respect of the allotment.

Progress test 6

1. What do you understand by the term 'promoter'? (**1**)

2. What remedies has a company against a promoter who fails to disclose his profit? (**2**)

3. In what ways may a promoter be remunerated for his services? (**3**)

4. What is the possible effect of a disqualification order made against a promoter? (**4**)

5. What rules apply to the valuation of non-cash assets acquired from subscribers to the memorandum in public companies? (**5**)

6. What are the contents of the report on non-cash assets acquired from a subscriber to the memorandum? (**6**)

7. What effect does contravention of the rules on the valuation and report have on the agreement between the company and the subscriber? (**7**)

7
Offers of shares to the public

1. The raising of capital. A company raises its share capital in the first instance by issuing shares to optimistic persons who hope to benefit by investing their money in a rapidly developing enterprise. It repeats this process as many times as is required in the course of its existence, so that the first issue of shares may well be followed by other later issues as the company's business expands and new capital is needed.

In the raising of capital, there is an important distinction between a public company and a private company. A public company will normally wish to attract applications for its shares, i.e. to raise capital, from the public. This has given rise to many statutory provisions designed to protect the investing public. These provisions are now in Parts IV and V of the Financial Services Act 1986. That Act wholly repealed Part III of the Companies Act 1985 which consolidated the then applicable law relating to prospectuses.

References in this Chapter are to sections of the Financial Services Act 1986 unless the contrary is indicated.

As regards private companies there are only two statutory provisions to note:

(*a*) A private company must not apply for its shares to be listed on the Stock Exchange: s. 143(3).

(*b*) A private company must not issue any advertisement offering its shares, unless the circumstances in which the advertisement is issued are covered by an order made by the Secretary of State for Trade and Industry exempting the company from this provision: s. 170.

This Chapter is therefore, apart from the exception in (*b*) above, confined to public companies.

There are three main methods by which a company may raise capital from the public:

(*a*) *By making a direct invitation to the public.*

(*b*) *By an offer for sale.* Here the company sells all the shares to an *issuing house*, i.e. a company or firm whose business is finance, and which may be involved in many types of financial enterprise, including the handling of new issues.

The issuing house sells the shares to the public at a higher price than it paid for them by publishing a document called an 'offer for sale' with an application form attached.

This method is more common than (*a*) above, as it relieves the company from the administrative work of a new issue, and at the same time ensures that the whole issue is sold, i.e. the issue here is *underwritten firm* (*see* 8:4).

(*c*) *By placing.* Here an issuing house may *either* subscribe for the issue itself and then invite other persons – normally its clients – to purchase from it at a higher price, *or* it may, without itself subscribing, find persons who wish to buy the shares. In the latter situation the issuing house is a mere agent, and will be paid a commission called 'brokerage' for its services.

2. Listed and unlisted securities. Part IV (i.e. ss. 142–57) of the Financial Services Act 1986 deals with the *official listing of securities*. Its leading provision is that no investment shall be admitted to the Official List of the Stock Exchange except in accordance with Part IV of the Act: s. 142(1).

The investments (referred to in the Act as 'securities') to which Part IV applies are specified in detail in the 1st Schedule to the Act, taken along with s. 142. They include shares, stock, debentures and certain other investments. At this stage in the study of company law it will be convenient to refer only to shares.

A company which wishes its shares to be freely marketable will want to have them admitted to the Official List of the Stock Exchange. It will, therefore, require to comply with Part IV of the Act.

The provisions in Part IV had their origin in three EEC directives:

(a) the Admissions Directive (dealing with the conditions for admission to listing);

(b) the Listing Particulars Directive (relating to the drawing up, scrutiny and distribution of listing particulars); and

(c) the Interim Reports Directive (relating to the regular publication of information by listed companies).

Before the 1986 Act these directives had been given effect to in the UK by the Stock Exchange (Listing) Regulations 1984. These Regulations were repealed by the 1986 Act, and the provisions of Part IV of the Act take their place.

Part V (i.e. ss. 158–71) deals with *offers of unlisted securities*. These provisions, by s. 158(1), relate to investments (or 'securities') which are not listed. Again, for what are investments for the purposes of Part V reference must be made to the 1st Schedule, from which, taken along with s. 158, it will be found that shares, stock, debentures and certain other investments are again included.

3. Applications for listing. An application for listing must, by s. 143(1), be made to 'the competent authority' in the way required by the 'listing rules'. These terms are explained in s. 142(6).

'The competent authority' means the Council of the Stock Exchange, except that, by s. 157, the Secretary of State for Trade and Industry may by order transfer the Council's functions in that connection to another body either at the request of the Council or if it appears to him:

(a) that the Council is exercising those functions in a way which is unnecessary for the protection of investors and fails to take into account the proper interests of issuers and proposed issuers of shares; or

(b) that it is necessary to do so for the protection of investors.

'Listing rules', referred to in s. 143 (1) above, are rules made by the competent authority for the purposes of Part IV of the Act.

By s. 142(8) any functions of the competent authority under the provisions may be exercised by any committee, sub-committee, officer or servant of the authority except that listing rules must be made by the authority itself or if made by a committee or sub-committee be confirmed by the authority within 28 days.

Section 143(2) provides that no application for the listing of shares can be made except by or with the consent of the issuer of the shares.

The competent authority may impose other requirements on an applicant in addition to compliance with the listing rules: s. 144(1).

By s. 144(3) the competent authority may refuse an application for listing:

(a) if it considers that, because of any matter relating to the issuer, the admission would be detrimental to the interests of investors; or

(b) in the case of shares already officially listed in another EEC state, if the issuer has failed to comply with his obligations in connection with that listing.

The competent authority must, by s. 144(4), notify the applicant of its decision within six months, but if there is no notification, the application must be taken, by s. 144(5), to have been refused.

4. The content of listing rules. Several provisions of the Act specify particular matters which may be included in listing rules. The competent authority has, however, a general power as regards the making of listing rules for admission, not restricted by the specific matters mentioned: s. 144(2).

By s. 144(2) listing rules may require as a condition of admission to the Official List:

(a) the submission to, and approval by, the authority of a document (called 'listing particulars') in such form and containing such information as may be specified in the rules; and

(b) the publication of that document.

The rules may alternatively provide that in specified cases a document other than listing particulars be published as a condition of admission.

By s. 153 listing rules may make provisions as to the action which may be taken by the competent authority where there is non-compliance with listing rules. Provisions may be included:

(a) authorizing the competent authority to publish the fact that an issuer has contravened any provision of the rules; and

(b) if the rules require an issuer to publish any information, authorizing the authority itself to publish it if the issuer fails to do so.

By s. 155 listing rules may require the payment of fees to the competent authority for applications for listing and for retaining shares in the Official List.

Finally, s. 156 sets out a number of general provisions on listing rules, including the following:

(*a*) Listing rules may make different provision for different cases.

(*b*) Listing rules may authorize the competent authority to dispense with or modify the application of the rules in particular cases.

(*c*) Listing rules must be made in writing, be printed and made available to the public with or without payment. A person must not be taken to have contravened any listing rule if he shows that it had not been made available in this way.

5. Listing particulars. The details of the information required to be stated in listing particulars are as specified in listing rules. The competent authority may also, under s. 144(1), require further information to be stated as a condition of admission to the Official List. In addition, there is imposed, by s. 146 of the Act, a *general duty of disclosure* in listing particulars.

The general duty of disclosure covers all such information as investors and their professional advisers would reasonably require, and reasonably expect to find in listing particulars, for the purpose of making an informed assessment of:

(*a*) the assets and liabilities, financial position, profits and losses, and prospects of the issuer of the shares; and

(*b*) the rights attaching to the shares.

This provision relates only to information which is within the knowledge of any person responsible for the listing particulars or which it would be reasonable for him to obtain by making inquiries.

Further, in deciding what information comes under the general duty of disclosure, regard must be had:

(*a*) to the nature of the shares and of the issuer of them;

(*b*) to the nature of the persons likely to consider acquiring them;

(*c*) to the fact that certain matters may reasonably be expected to be within the knowledge of such professional advisers as the persons mentioned in (*b*) may reasonably be expected to consult; and

(*d*) to any information available to investors or their professional advisers under this or any other Act.

6. Supplementary listing particulars. Section 147 provides that if at any time after the preparation of listing particulars for submission to the competent authority under s. 144 and before the commencement of dealings in the shares there is a *significant change* affecting any matter in the required particulars or a *significant new matter* arises which would have had to be included if it had arisen when the particulars were prepared, the issuer must submit to the competent authority for its approval, and (if approved) publish 'supplementary listing particulars' of the change or of the new matter as the case may be.

Where the issuer is not aware of the change or new matter in question, he is not under any duty to submit or publish supplementary listing particulars unless he is notified of the change or new matter by a person responsible for the listing particulars, but it is the duty of any person responsible for the listing particulars who is aware of the matter to give notice of it to the issuer.

7. Exemptions from disclosure in listing particulars. By s. 148 the competent authority may authorize the omission from listing particulars or supplementary listing particulars of any required information if its disclosure would be:

(*a*) contrary to the public interest; or

(*b*) seriously detrimental to the issuer.

As regards (*a*), the Secretary of State or the Treasury may issue a certificate stating that the disclosure of any information would be contrary to the public interest.

As regards (*b*), no authority can be granted if the non-disclosure would be likely to mislead a person considering the acquisition of the shares as to any facts which it is essential for him to know in order to make an informed assessment.

8. Registration of listing particulars. Section 149 provides that on or before the date on which listing particulars or supplementary listing particulars are published a copy of the particulars must be delivered to the registrar of companies for registration, and a statement that a copy has been delivered to him must be included in the particulars.

If particulars are published without a copy of them having been delivered to the registrar, the issuer and any person who is knowingly a party to the publication is guilty of an offence and liable to a fine.

9. Compensation for false or misleading particulars. Section 150 provides that, with the exemptions stated in s. 151, the *person responsible for* any listing particulars or supplementary listing particulars is liable to pay compensation to any person who has acquired any of the shares in question and suffered loss as a result of any untrue or misleading statement in the particulars or the omission of any of the required particulars or failure to comply with s. 147 as to supplementary listing particulars.

10. Exemption from liability to pay compensation. Section 151 provides for certain exemptions from the liability to pay compensation under s. 150.

By s. 151(1) a person is exempt from liability if he satisfies the court that at the time when the particulars were submitted to the competent authority he *reasonably believed*, after having made reasonable inquiries, that the statement was true and not misleading or that the omission was proper *and*:

(*a*) that he continued in that belief until the shares were acquired; or

(*b*) that they were acquired before it was reasonably practicable to bring a correction to the attention of persons likely to acquire the shares; or

(*c*) that before the shares were acquired he had taken all reasonable steps to secure that a correction was brought to the attention of those persons; or

(*d*) that he continued in that belief until after the commencement of dealings in the shares and that the shares were acquired after such a lapse of time that he ought in the circumstances to be reasonably excused.

Section 151(2) relates to *statements made by experts* and included in the particulars.

The term 'expert' for the purposes of s. 151 includes any engineer, valuer, accountant or other person whose profession, qualifications or experience give authority to a statement made by him.

Section 151(2) provides that a person is exempt from liability for a loss caused by a statement purporting to be made by another person as an expert and included in the particulars with the expert's consent if he satisfies the court that at the time when the particulars were submitted to the competent authority he believed on reasonable grounds that the expert was competent to make the statement and had consented to its inclusion in the form and context in which it appeared *and*:

(*a*) that he continued in that belief until the time when the shares were acquired; or

(*b*) that the shares were acquired before it was reasonably practicable to bring the fact that the expert was not competent or had not consented to the attention of persons likely to acquire the shares; or

(*c*) that before the shares were acquired he had taken all reasonable steps to secure that that fact was brought to the attention of those persons; or

(*d*) that he continued in that belief until after the commencement of dealings in the shares and that the shares were acquired after such a lapse of time that he ought in the circumstances to be reasonably excused.

Section 151(3) provides that a person is exempt from liability if he satisfies the court:

(*a*) that before the shares were acquired a *correction* (or, in the case of an expert's statement, the fact that the expert was not competent or had not consented) had been published in a way calculated to bring it to the attention of persons likely to acquire the shares; or

(*b*) that he took all reasonable steps to secure such publication and reasonably believed that it had taken place before the shares were acquired.

Section 151(4) relates to statements made by an *official person* or contained in a *public official document* and included in the particulars. A person is exempt from liability for any loss resulting from such a statement if he satisfies the court that the statement is accurately and fairly reproduced.

By s. 151(5) a person is exempt from liability if he satisfies the court that the person suffering the loss acquired the shares *with knowledge* that the statement was false or misleading, or of the omitted matter or of the change or new matter, as the case may be.

A further exemption from liability arises in relation to failure to submit *supplementary listing particulars*. Section 151(6) provides that a person is exempt from liability if he satisfies the court that he reasonably believed that the change or new matter in question was not such as to call for supplementary listing particulars.

11. Persons responsible for listing particulars. The liability to pay compensation under s. 150 is imposed on *persons responsible for listing particulars or supplementary listing particulars*. Section 152(1) provides that these persons are:

(*a*) the issuer of the shares;

(*b*) where the issuer is a body corporate, the directors of that body;

(*c*) where the issuer is a body corporate, persons named in the particulars as having agreed to become directors;

(*d*) persons stated in the particulars as having accepted responsibility for any part of the particulars;

(*e*) any other persons who have authorized the contents of any part of the particulars.

As regards (*b*), a person is not responsible for any particulars if they are published without his knowledge or consent and on becoming aware of their publication he immediately gives reasonable public notice that they were published without his knowledge or consent: s. 152(2).

A person who under (*d*) or (*e*) has accepted responsibility for or authorized only *part* of the particulars, is responsible only for that part and only if it is included in the form and context to which he has agreed: s. 152(3).

A further limitation is that neither (*b*) nor (*c*) applies to any director certified by the competent authority as a person to whom the provision should not apply because of his having an interest, or because of other circumstances, making it inappropriate for him to be responsible: s. 152(5).

By s. 152(9) where the issuer pays or is liable to pay compensation under s. 150, no account is taken of that payment or liability in any question as to the amount paid on subscription for the shares or as to the amount paid up on them.

12. Advertisements in connection with listing applications. Section 154 provides that where listing particulars are published in connection with an application for the listing of any shares no advertisement or other information of a kind specified by listing rules can be issued unless the contents of the advertisement or other information have been submitted to the competent authority and that authority has either:

(a) approved those contents; or

(b) authorized the issue of the advertisement or information without such approval.

13. Discontinuance and suspension of listing. Section 145 provides that the competent authority may, in accordance with the listing rules, discontinue the listing of any shares if satisfied that there are special circumstances which prevent normal regular dealings in the shares. The competent authority may also, in accordance with the listing rules, suspend the listing of any shares.

14. Definitions for Part V. It is now time to turn to the provisions of Part V of the Act, which is concerned with offers of *unlisted* securities. As with the provisions in Part IV, attention will be confined to shares, though the provisions also relate to other securities (as defined in the 1st Schedule) as well as to shares.

As a preliminary to the study of Part V, the definitions of three expressions which are used throughout Part V should be noted:

(a) *Advertisement offering shares.* For the purposes of Part V an advertisement is said to offer shares if:

(i) it invites a person to enter into an agreement for subscribing for or otherwise acquiring or underwriting any shares; or

(ii) it contains information calculated to lead directly or indirectly to a person entering into such an agreement: s. 158(4).

(b) *Approved exchange.* The term approved exchange, when used of dealings in any shares, means a recognized investment exchange approved by the Secretary of State for the purposes of Part V. The Secretary of State must give notice of the exchanges which are, for the time being, approved exchanges: s. 158(6).

(c) *Prospectus.* By s. 159(1) a prospectus is a document containing information about shares which are being admitted to dealings on an approved exchange.

15. Offers of shares on admission to approved exchange. The two leading provisions in Part V are in ss. 159 and 160. Section 159 relates to advertisements offering shares which are being admitted to dealings on an approved exchange, and s. 160 relates to other advertisements offering shares.

Section 159(1) provides that, with some exceptions, no person must issue an advertisement offering any shares on the occasion of their admission to dealings on an approved exchange unless:

(a) a prospectus containing information about the shares has been submitted to and approved by the exchange and delivered for registration to the registrar of companies; or

(b) the advertisement is such that no agreement can be entered into in pursuance of it until a prospectus has been submitted, approved and delivered as in (a) above.

The provision does not apply if a prospectus relating to the shares has been delivered for registration in the previous 12 months *and* the approved exchange certifies that it is satisfied that persons likely to consider acquiring the shares will have sufficient information to enable them to decide whether to do so from that prospectus and any information published in connection with the admission of the shares: s. 159(2).

By s. 161 there are further exceptions to the requirements of s. 159(1).

(a) It does not apply to any advertisement offering shares if the offer is conditional on their *admission to listing* under Part IV or if the shares have been listed under Part IV within the previous 12 months and the approved exchange certifies that persons likely to consider acquiring them will have sufficient information to enable them to decide whether to do so: s. 161(1).

(b) It does not apply if other shares issued by the same person (not necessarily shares of the same class as those in the present offer) are *already dealt in* on an approved exchange and the exchange certifies to the same effect as in (a) above: s. 161(3).

(c) It does not apply if, in the case of shares dealt in on an exchange in a *country outside the UK*, the Secretary of State considers that the law of the other country provides investors in the UK with protection at least equivalent to that of Part IV or Part V and makes an order specifying circumstances in which the requirement is not to apply: s. 161(4).

16. Other advertisements offering shares. Other advertisements offering shares, i.e. advertisements where there is no admission of the shares to dealings on an approved exchange, are divided, by s. 160, into 'primary' offers and 'secondary' offers.

By s. 160(2) a primary offer is an advertisement (not issued in connection with admission to dealings on an approved exchange) inviting persons to enter into an agreement for *subscribing for or underwriting* the shares to which it relates or containing information calculated to lead directly or indirectly to their doing so.

By s. 160(3) a secondary offer is an advertisement (not issued in connection with admission to dealings on an approved exchange) inviting persons to enter into an agreement for *acquiring* the shares to which it relates or containing information calculated to lead directly or indirectly to their doing so. The advertisement must in the case of a secondary offer be issued:

(*a*) by a person who has acquired the shares from the issuer directly or indirectly *with a view to issuing the advertisement;* or

(*b*) by a person who is a *controller* of the issuer and who is acting with the consent or participation of the issuer in issuing the advertisement.

The main provision in s. 160 is that (with exceptions) no person must issue an advertisement offering shares which is a primary or secondary offer unless:

(*a*) he has delivered a prospectus to the registrar for registration; or

(*b*) the advertisement is such that no agreement can be entered into in pursuance of it until a prospectus has been delivered to the registrar for registration: s. 160(1).

This provision, however, does not apply to a secondary offer if a prospectus has already been delivered to the registrar in respect of an offer of the same shares made in the previous six months: s. 160(5).

Further exceptions to the requirement of s. 160(1) include:

(*a*) It does not apply to an advertisement issued in circumstances covered by an exemption order made by the Secretary of State. By s. 160(6) the Secretary of State may make such an order for specified classes of advertisements including:

(*i*) those appearing to him to have a private character (e.g. because of a connection between the person issuing them and the persons to whom they are addressed);

(*ii*) those appearing to him to deal with investments only incidentally;

(*iii*) those issued to persons appearing to him to be sufficiently expert to understand any risks involved; and

(*iv*) those of any other class he thinks fit.

(*b*) By s. 161, the exceptions to s. 159(1) in **15** (admission to listing, shares already dealt in and shares dealt in outside the UK) also apply to s. 160(1) (*see* **15**).

17. Contents of prospectus. By s. 162 a prospectus must contain such information and comply with such other requirements as may be prescribed by rules made by the Secretary of State.

Compliance with requirements imposed by the law of a country outside the UK may be treated as compliance with the rules, if the rules so provide: s. 162(2).

If it appears to the Secretary of State that an approved exchange has rules on prospectuses which provide investors with protection at least equivalent to that provided by rules made by himself, he may direct that any prospectus must comply with the rules of the exchange instead of his own rules: s. 162(3).

In addition to information required to be included in a prospectus by s. 162, there is under s. 163 a *general duty of disclosure*. The provisions of s. 163 match those relating to the general duty of disclosure in listing particulars in s. 146 (*see* **5**).

18. Supplementary prospectus. Section 164 requires a supplementary prospectus to be delivered for registration by the person who delivered the prospectus if a *significant change* occurs or a *significant new matter* arises after registration of the prospectus and while an agreement can still be entered into in pursuance of the offer. The provisions correspond to those in s. 147 relating to supplementary listing particulars (*see* **6**), with the substitution of 'the person who delivered the prospectus for registration' for 'the issuer', and of 'person responsible for the prospectus' for 'person responsible for the listing particulars'.

19. Exemptions from disclosure in prospectus. By s. 165, if in the case of any approved exchange the Secretary of State so directs, the exchange has power to authorize the omission from a prospectus or supplementary prospectus of any required information. The provisions are otherwise the same as those relating to exemptions from disclosure in listing particulars (*see* **7**).

20. Compensation for false or misleading prospectus. Section 166 provides that, with the exemptions stated in s. 167, the *person responsible for* a prospectus or supplementary prospectus is liable to pay compensation to any person who has acquired the shares to which the prospectus relates and has suffered loss as a result of any untrue or misleading statement in the prospectus or the omission of any of the required particulars or failure to comply with s. 164 (supplementary prospectus). These provisions correspond to those of s. 150 relating to listing particulars.

21. Exemption from liability to pay compensation. The provisions of s. 167 are to the same general effect as those of s. 151 (*see* **10**).

References in s. 151 to 'the time when the particulars were submitted to the competent authority' become in s. 167 'the time when the prospectus was delivered for registration', and there is in s. 167 no reference to the commencement of dealings in the shares; contrast s. 151(1)(*d*) and s. 151(2)(*d*).

22. Persons responsible for prospectus. Section 168 lists the same persons as being responsible for a prospectus as are listed in s. 152 as being responsible for listing particulars (*see* **11**).

Instead of the reference in s. 152(2) to publication without the person's knowledge or consent there is substituted in s. 168(2) a reference to delivery for registration without the person's knowledge or consent, and instead of certification by the competent authority in s. 152(5) there is substituted in s. 168(5) a reference to certification by an approved exchange.

23. Rules made by the Secretary of State. Section 169(1) provides that the Secretary of State may make rules:

(*a*) regulating the terms on which a person may offer shares by an advertisement under Part V; and

(*b*) otherwise regulating his conduct with a view to ensuring that the persons to whom the offer is addressed are treated equally and fairly.

24. Non-statutory remedies for mis-statements in listing particulars or prospectus. We have now considered the main statutory provisions on listing particulars and prospectus, but there are two other remedies for mis-statements which are available to an injured party under the general law. These are:

(a) damages for fraud; and
(b) rescission of the contract of allotment.

25. Damages for the tort of deceit or fraud. This remedy exists at *common law* for the plaintiff who can prove that he suffered damage by acting on a deceitful statement addressed to him. Thus, as a rule, only allottees taking their shares directly from the company may sue for deceit, though exceptionally a transferee may be able to prove that he was intended to be affected by the statement.

Deceit was defined in *Derry* v. *Peek* (1889), as 'a false statement made *knowingly*, without belief in its truth, or *recklessly*, careless whether it be true or false'. Thus in law something less immoral than a deliberate lie amounts to deceit: the defendant may merely have been reckless, i.e. he did not care whether the statement was true or not. But not caring involves considering the possibility that the statement might be false, and making it just the same, regardless of the consequences to the plaintiff. Thus the defendant is equally liable whether he made the false statement *knowing* that it was untrue, or *thinking that it might be*, for in both cases the possibility of deception was in his mind.

It is clear from this that to succeed in a claim for fraud, the plaintiff has to prove a certain state of mind in the defendant. This may well be 'as much a fact as the state of his digestion', but it is even harder to prove. Consequently the statutory remedy of compensation under s. 150 or s. 166 Financial Services Act 1986 is a much more reliable remedy; to recover compensation under those sections fraud need not be proved, and the mere untruth of the statement is enough. It is then for the defendant to show, if he can, that he reasonably believed that the statement was true, and so escape liability.

The action for damages for fraud may be brought either against the company or against the directors. If, however, the plaintiff sues the *company*, he must rescind his contract to take the shares. He may not sue the company for fraud and at the same time remain a member.

If he sues the *directors*, he need not rescind, though he may of course do so if he wishes.

26. Rescission. This remedy exists in *equity* for the plaintiff who can prove a mis-statement, either innocent or fraudulent.

The rules here are the ordinary rules of misrepresentation familiar to students of contract, so that the plaintiff must prove a mis-statement of fact which had an effect on his mind and induced him to buy the shares. He may then rescind and return the shares, receiving his money back with interest. But it is important to remember that this is an equitable remedy which is basically discretionary and may be lost in certain circumstances. Thus the plaintiff will not be allowed to rescind if:

(*a*) He displays laches, i.e. delays in taking proceedings. Delay defeats equity.

(*b*) He does some act showing a clear manifestation of ownership, e.g. attends meetings or tries to sell the shares.

(*c*) The company goes into liquidation. Here the rights of creditors are involved, and the law always favours creditors at the expense of members.

By s. 2(2) Misrepresentation Act 1967 damages in lieu of rescission may be recovered if the misrepresentation has not been fraudulent.

Progress test 7

1. What is an offer for sale?   (**1**)

2. Which three EEC directives are the origin of Part IV of the Financial Services Act 1986?   (**2**)

3. Outline the statutory provisions relating to applications for listing.   (**3**)

4. What is meant by 'the competent authority' for the purposes of Part IV of the Financial Services Act 1986?   (**3**)

5. Explain the general duty of disclosure in listing particulars which is imposed by s. 146 Financial Services Act 1986.   (**5**)

6. In what circumstances are supplementary listing particulars required?   (**6**)

7. What exemptions may be obtained from disclosure in listing particulars? **(7)**

8. What defences are available where a claim is made for compensation for a loss suffered as a result of a false statement in listing particulars? **(10)**

9. List and comment on the persons who are responsible for listing particulars. **(11)**

10. What is an 'approved exchange' for the purposes of Part V of the Financial Services Act 1986? **(14)**

11. What exceptions are there to the requirement for a prospectus under s. 159(1) Financial Services Act 1986? **(15)**

12. Distinguish between a 'primary offer' and a 'secondary offer' for the purposes of Part V of the Financial Services Act 1986. **(16)**

13. Explain why the statutory remedies of compensation under ss. 150 and 166 Financial Services Act 1986 are more reliable than an action for the tort of deceit or fraud at common law. **(25)**

14. In what circumstances is rescission of the contract of allotment available as a remedy for misrepresentation? **(26)**

8
Underwriting commission and brokerage

1. The meaning and purpose of underwriting. For all companies the raising of capital is a matter of practical importance, since without capital a newly formed company can neither start nor purchase a business. For public companies it is also a legal necessity for, as was seen in 5:**2** and **3**, no trading certificate will be granted unless the company's allotted share capital reaches the authorized minimum. The success of any issue to the public, however, depends on many factors and will always be doubtful to some extent, and therefore to ensure that the shares will be taken up even if the issue is a failure as far as the public are concerned, a company normally arranges for it to be underwritten.

This involves entering into an agreement with an *underwriter*, i.e. a financial house which undertakes to buy as many of the shares as are not taken up by the public. If the issue is a large one, several underwriting agreements may be made with different underwriters, since one alone may not be prepared to bear the risk. Alternatively, the principal underwriters may pass on the risk by entering into a *sub-underwriting agreement*, i.e. arranging for one or more other underwriters to underwrite them, while they underwrite the whole of the company's issue. If the issue is being handled by an issuing house by means of an offer for sale, the issuing house will make the same sort of arrangement.

2. Underwriting commission. The underwriters make their profit by charging a commission on the number of shares underwritten. This commission is still payable even if the issue is a complete success so that all the shares are bought by the public and the underwriters are not compelled to take up any of them. Where the underwriters have entered into a sub-underwriting agreement, the underwriting commission is passed on to the sub-underwriter and is known as *sub-*

underwriting commission, while the principal underwriters retain some part of it, called *overriding commission*, for their services. Thus overriding commission is the difference between underwriting and sub-underwriting commission.

3. Statutory control of underwriting commission. A company which has been in existence for some years and is making, for instance, its third issue of shares to raise capital for expansion may have revenue reserves out of which it can pay the underwriting commission, or funds in its share premium account which, under s. 130, may lawfully be used for this purpose although a capital reserve. But a new company making its first issue will have no reserves of any kind. Any commission paid, therefore, will have to be provided out of the capital obtained from the issue, and this clearly reduces the amount of capital which the company will ultimately derive from that issue. Since the preservation of capital is one of the most important aims of the Act, ss. 97–98 permit the payment of underwriting commission only on certain conditions.

4. Power of company to pay underwriting commission. Section 97(1), as amended by the Financial Services Act 1986, states that it is lawful to pay underwriting commission if:

(*a*) it is authorized by the articles; and

(*b*) it does not exceed 10 per cent of the price at which the shares are issued, or the rate specified in the articles, whichever is the less; and

(*c*) it complies with any rules made by the Secretary of State under s. 169(1) Financial Services Act 1986 (*see* **7:23**).

Table A, Article 4, authorizes the payment of commission.

It will be noted that s. 97 does not mention the word 'underwriter' and that it is very loosely phrased so that it might appear to cover the payment of a commission to anyone who undertakes to buy shares in a company. This was not, of course, what it was intended to do, but misuse of the section has sometimes occurred.

It will also be seen that the section uses the words: 'subscribe (absolutely or conditionally)'. To subscribe *conditionally* is to enter into the kind of agreement described above in **1**, i.e. to undertake to buy as many shares as are not taken up by the public. The underwriter here is agreeing to take up the shares only on a condition, namely, that the public do not do so. To subscribe *absolutely* is to agree to take up the shares, i.e. underwrite them *firm*, and then re-sell them at a higher price to the public. Thus an issuing house making an offer for sale, as described in 7:**1**, is in effect underwriting firm. Either way the company can be sure that the entire issue will be taken up, and that the risk of its failure lies with the underwriters.

NOTE

(1) Section 98(1) states that a company may not pay underwriting commission out of *capital* 'except as permitted by s. 97', i.e. unless it complies with the conditions laid down in s. 97. It does not, however, refer to the payment of commission out of *revenue*, i.e. profits, and this therefore seems to be unrestricted by the section.

(2) Section 98(1) refers not only to *commission*, but also to *discount* or *allowance*. This is because it is possible to pay a commission by allowing a discount: thus it makes no difference whether £1 shares are issued at £1 and the underwriters then receive 5p for each share underwritten, or whether they are issued to the underwriters at 95p. Either way the company is left with 95p for each £1 share issued. Thus s. 98 is the only *statutory* exception to the rule that shares may not be issued at a discount.

(3) Section 98 refers only to shares and does not mention debentures, since they are not capital and can therefore be issued at a discount freely.

5. Brokerage. Brokerage is the sum paid to a person by the company for *placing* shares. Sections 97–98 do not restrict it in any way, and s. 98(3) expressly states that ss. 97–98 in no way affect the payment of 'lawful brokerage'.

Lawful brokerage is reasonable brokerage, but it must be paid to a person carrying on the business of broker, and not to a private person: *Andreae* v. *Zinc Mines of Great Britain* (1918).

Progress test 8

1. Describe what is meant by underwriting commission, sub-underwriting commission, and overriding commission. **(1, 2)**

2. Under what circumstances is it lawful for a company to pay underwriting commission out of capital? **(4)**

3. What rules govern the payment of brokerage? **(5)**

9
Allotment

1. The meaning of allotment. Although allotment is only one of several methods by which a person can become a member of a company, it is one of considerable importance and complexity owing to the large number of statutory provisions which apply to it. When this method of acquiring membership is employed, shares are taken to be allotted when a person acquires the unconditional right to be included in the company's register of members in respect of them: s. 738(1).

2. Basic feature of allotment. In this chapter the rules governing allotment are considered. It will be seen that its basic feature is that the investor acquires the shares from the *company* and not from a previous holder.

3. The contract to take shares. Listing particulars or a prospectus issued by a company or an offer for sale made by an issuing house is not an offer in the contractual sense, but merely an invitation to treat. It is the applicant for the shares who makes the offer, and it is the company which accepts or rejects it. The transaction is governed by the normal rules of contract and no special form is required. In practice, the applicant makes his application in writing on the application form issued to him, but in theory it could be oral.

NOTE: Where the contract is made by post, as it usually is, the ordinary rules of contract again apply to the position. These rules are fully dealt with in textbooks on the law of contract, and they are outside the scope of this book.

There are, however, two points of importance where special rules apply regarding:

(*a*) the persons to whom the shares are offered;
(*b*) variation of the offer to buy shares.

These will now be discussed in turn.

4. The persons to whom the shares are offered. Sections 89–96 deal with *pre-emption rights* for existing shareholders. Under these sections existing shareholders normally have a statutory right to be offered shares in proportion to their present holdings whenever a new issue is made (*see* **10–13**).

Pre-emption rights were introduced by the Companies Act 1980. Before that Act such rights were given only by the company's articles or, in the case of listed companies, by the rules of the stock exchange.

5. Variation of the offer to buy shares. The law of contract requires the acceptance of an offer to be entire. If the acceptance introduces a new term, or varies the offer to the slightest degree, it will amount in law to a counter-offer and itself require acceptance by the original offeror.

This rule could obviously lead to difficulty where the issue of shares is *over-subscribed*, i.e. where the public have applied for more shares than the company is issuing. This is a common occurrence, and the company usually deals with it by 'scaling down' the numbers of shares applied for, or by holding a ballot, or some other method intended to be a fair solution. The law of contract would allow the company either to accept an applicant's offer, or to reject it, but it would not allow any variation of the offer by allotting the applicant a lesser number of shares than the number for which he applied.

In consequence the application form is worded: 'I agree to accept — shares, or such lesser number as may be allotted to me', and the company is then able to accept the offer by allotting the applicant any number of shares not in excess of the number for which he applied. This may, of course, involve sending the applicant back a cheque for the difference between the price of the shares applied for and those ultimately allotted.

6. Conditional applications. An application for shares, like any other offer, may be conditional, i.e. subject to a *condition precedent*. Then if the condition is not fulfilled, no contract for the shares can result.

> Thus in *Simpson's Case* (1869), the applicant for the shares made his offer conditional on his being given a building contract by the company. He was allotted the shares, but was never given the building contract, so that the condition on which he had made his application was never fulfilled. HELD: He was not bound to pay up the amount unpaid on the shares.

This is exactly the result to be expected, of course, from the ordinary law of contract.

7. Applications subject to a condition subsequent. With regard to a *condition subsequent*, however, the ordinary law of contract does *not* apply to applications for shares. In most types of contract the parties may agree that their contractual relationship shall be terminated on the happening of an event: this is one form of discharge by agreement. Such arrangements are often made when a contract is to endure for a considerable period of time, and either or both of the parties fear a change in circumstances which might render it no longer beneficial to them. But in shareholding, as in marriage, it would hardly be in the public interest if the parties to the agreement decided that on the happening of a certain event their contract should be terminated, for the company's creditors could never be certain how many of the present members might suddenly become entitled to have their capital returned to them.

The law, of course, permits an allotment to be set aside for fraud or error, just as it permits a marriage to be destroyed by certain events or conduct, but it will not allow the parties themselves to agree to discharge their contract on the happening of an event which they, but not the law, find sufficient to make termination of their relationship desirable. Their contractual freedom is restricted: they may make, but not break, their agreement.

It follows, therefore, that an applicant who is allotted shares in the company may not set the allotment aside merely because he and the company have agreed that it should become invalid on the happening of an event. Once the applicant becomes a member, he is liable to pay for the shares. Similarly, where he has applied for shares and at the same time made a *collateral agreement* with the company, i.e. another contract *side by side* with his contract to take the shares, he cannot set the allotment aside merely because the company has broken the collateral agreement.

> Thus in *Elkington's Case* (1876), the applicants for £10 shares relied on an agreement which they had made with the company that they should pay 30s. per share in *cash*, and the balance should be set off against goods with which they were to supply the company. The company never ordered the goods. HELD: The applicants were liable to pay the balance due on the shares in cash, since the arrangement concerning the goods merely amounted to a collateral agreement, and not to a condition precedent.

A collateral agreement of this type will of course, if a valid contract in itself, give rise to all the normal remedies for breach if either party should break it. But it in no way affects the validity of the allotment.

Here is yet another example of the law's preference of creditors to members.

8. The statutory provisions on allotment. The statutory provisions on allotment are in ss. 80–116, as amended by the Financial Services Act 1986. Of these sections, ss. 97–98, on underwriting commissions, have already been considered (*see* Chapter 8); other sections are dealt with in this chapter. Important changes in this part of company law were made by the Companies Act 1980. It is essential to notice in each case to which companies the particular section applies.

9. Authority of company required for allotment. Section 80 is the most comprehensive of all the sections on allotment. It applies to *all companies, public and private.* Section 80(1) provides that the directors may not allot *'relevant securities'* of the company unless they are *authorized* to do so by either:

(*a*) a general meeting; *or*

(*b*) the articles.

It should be noted that Table A contains no such authority.

Section 80(2) defines 'relevant securities' as shares in the company *excluding those*:

(*a*) shown in the memorandum as having been taken by the subscribers to it; *or*

(*b*) allotted under a share scheme for employees.

The expression includes, however, a *right to subscribe for*, or *convert any security into*, shares in the company other than those comprised in (*b*) above. Thus it would include a convertible debenture (*see* 21:**1**).

Under s. 80(3) the company's authority to the directors may be general or particular, conditional or unconditional, but in all cases s. 80(4) requires it to state:

(*a*) the maximum amount of relevant securities which may be allotted under it; and

(*b*) the date on which it will expire.

The date of expiration may not be more than five years from whichever of the following dates applies:

(a) where on the company's original incorporation the authority was contained in the articles, the *date of incorporation*;

(b) where this is not the case, the *date of the resolution* giving the authority.

Whether given by the articles or by a resolution, the authority may always be revoked or varied by the company in general meeting.

Section 80(5) permits the authority to be renewed by a resolution of the general meeting as many times as is desired, but never for a period exceeding five years. The resolution must always state the amount of relevant securities to be allotted, or which still remains to be allotted, as well as the date on which the renewed authority will expire.

Section 80(8) permits any resolution mentioned in the section, regardless of whether it gives, varies, revokes or renews the authority, to be an *ordinary* resolution, even if it alters the articles of the company (*see* 3:**9**). It must, however, by s. 380, be filed with the registrar (*see* 15:**41**) who, under s. 711(1), is required, in the case of a *public* company, to publish his receipt of it in the *Gazette*.

Although it can be seen that the rules imposed by s. 80 are stringent, the validity of an allotment is not affected if they are broken: s. 80(10). A director who knowingly and wilfully contravenes the section is, however, liable to a fine: s. 80(9).

10. Pre-emption rights. Section 89(1) and (4) prohibits any company, public or private, from allotting to any person *equity securities* which are to be paid up wholly in cash unless it has first offered to each holder of *relevant shares* or *relevant employee shares*, on terms at least as favourable, a proportion of them equal in nominal value to that already held by him of the total relevant shares or relevant employee shares already issued.

Under s. 94(7) 'holder' includes any person who holds shares on any day within the 28 days immediately preceding the date of the offer.

Further, it is not enough for the company merely to make such an offer: the prohibition on allotment endures until either the period for the acceptance of the offer has expired (*see* **11**) or the company has, in every case, been notified of its acceptance or refusal: s. 89(1).

It is important to note the three technical expressions used in s. 89(1) and printed in italics above. They are defined in s. 94, and it will be seen that the most crucial of the definitions is that of *relevant shares*.

(*a*) *Relevant shares* means shares in the company *excluding*:

(*i*) shares having a limit on their right to participate in distributions of both dividend and capital (*see* 13:**14** for a comparison with the term *equity share capital*); and

(*ii*) shares which are held or are to be allotted in pursuance of a share scheme for employees: s. 94(5).

(*b*) *Relevant employee shares* means shares which would be relevant shares within (*a*) above if they were not held in pursuance of a share scheme for employees: s. 94(4).

(*c*) *Equity security* means a relevant share in the company *excluding those:*

(*i*) shown in the memorandum as having been taken by the subscribers to the memorandum; *or*

(*ii*) issued as bonus shares: s. 94(2).

A reference to allotment of equity securities includes, however, a *right to subscribe for*, or *convert any security into*, relevant shares (*see* **9**): s. 94(3).

It often happens that the company's memorandum or articles contain a clause giving a pre-emption right to holders of a *particular class* of shares in the event of any further issue of shares of that class. Section 89(2) and (3) covers this situation and states that where such a clause exists, the provisions of s. 89(1) apply *only to the balance of the securities which remains unallotted*. Thus such shareholders have 'double' pre-emption rights – the first as holders of a particular class of shares, and the second as members of the company.

11. Procedure for making pre-emption offer. Section 90 deals with the procedure for communicating pre-emption offers to share-holders. Whether made under s. 89(1) or under a clause in the memorandum or articles, s. 90(2) requires the company's offer of the new shares to be in writing and made to the holder either personally or by posting it to his registered address in the UK. If this is impossible because he has no registered address in the UK or is the holder of a share warrant (*see* 12:**26**), it may be published in the *Gazette*.

Section 90(6) requires the offer to state a period of at least 21 days during which it may be accepted. It cannot be revoked before the end of that period.

12. Contravention of rules governing pre-emption rights. Where there is any contravention of s. 89(1) or of a class pre-emption clause in a company's memorandum or articles under s. 89(2) and (3) or of communication provisions in s. 90, then s. 92(1) provides that the company, and every officer who knowingly authorized or permitted the contravention, are jointly and severally liable to compensate any person entitled to receive an offer for any damage suffered or expenses incurred owing to the contravention.

Such a person must, however, commence proceedings within two years: s. 92(2).

13. Exclusion, withdrawal or modification of pre-emption rights. In the case of a *private* company s. 91 permits the above rules to be entirely excluded by the company's memorandum or articles. Even in the case of a *public* company, however, s. 95 permits the company to dispense with or modify the statutory pre-emption rights given by s. 89(1) if it so desires.

Where the directors have been given a *general* authority to exercise the company's power of allotment under s. 14 (*see* **9**), s. 95(1) permits the articles or a special resolution of the company to empower them to allot equity securities either entirely free from any pre-emption rights, or with those rights modified in whatever manner they decide.

Under s. 95(2), of much narrower application, the company may by special resolution withdraw or modify the pre-emption rights as regards any specified allotment. In this case it is immaterial whether the directors' authority to allot the equity securities in question is general or particular.

Whenever the directors' authority to allot is revoked or expires, their power under s. 95(1) or the special resolution under s. 95(2) to dispense with or modify the pre-emption rights terminates with it. In consequence, on the renewal of their authority a special resolution will be required to renew that power or special resolution if the company desires to do so: s. 95(3).

A special resolution passed under s. 95(1), (2) or (3) must, like all special resolutions, be filed with the registrar under s. 380. In the case of a *public* company the registrar is then required, under s. 711, to publish his receipt of it in the *Gazette*.

14. Further rules regarding specified allotments. Further rules apply where the special resolution to withdraw or modify the pre-emption rights relates to a particular specified allotment and therefore falls under s. 95(2).

Section 95(5) provides that no such special resolution, or special resolution for its renewal, can be proposed unless:

(*a*) it is recommended by the directors; and

(*b*) a written statement by the directors has been circulated with the notice of the relevant meeting giving:

(*i*) their reasons for recommending it;

(*ii*) the amount to be paid to the company in respect of the allotment; and

(*iii*) the directors' justification of that amount.

Section 95(6) gives penalties for false or misleading matter in the statement.

15. Minimum amount to be paid before allotment. The three sections considered above (i.e. s. 80 as to authority required for allotment, s. 89 as to pre-emption rights and s. 95 as to disapplication of such rights) all apply to both public and private companies. The sections now to be considered apply to *public companies only*.

Section 101(1) states that a public company may not allot a share unless it is paid up at least as to *one-quarter of its nominal value and the whole of any premium on it*.

If the company makes an allotment which contravenes this rule, s. 101(3) requires the shares in question to be treated *as if the minimum amount had been received*, but s. 101(4) renders the allottee liable to pay that amount, less the value of any consideration applied in payment for the allotment, with interest at the appropriate rate. *Bonus shares* are not affected by these two subsections unless the allottee knew or ought to have known of the contravention: s. 101(5).

None of the above provisions applies to shares allotted under a *share scheme for employees*: s. 101(2).

Section 112(1) extends the liability of the allottee under s. 101(4) to *subsequent holders* unless the subsequent holder is exempted from such liability under s. 112(3). This last-mentioned subsection, taken along with s. 112(1), provides that where a person becomes liable through a contravention of s. 101 to pay an amount in respect of the shares, any subsequent holder also becomes liable, jointly and severally with him, unless *either*:

(*a*) he is a purchaser for value without actual notice of the contravention at the time of the purchase; *or*

(*b*) he derived title to the shares from a person who acquired them after the contravention and was not himself so liable.

There is thus a chain of liability which can be broken only by an innocent purchaser (the *bona fide purchaser for value*).

Finally, if a company contravenes s. 101, the company and any officer of it who is in default is liable to a fine: s. 114.

16. Allotment for non-cash consideration. The Companies Act 1980 introduced special rules to apply in public companies where the consideration to be furnished by the allottee for the allotment is not in cash but in some other form. It is entirely proper for an allottee to furnish consideration for the allotment in a form other than money, but the detailed rules on this topic will be found in Chapter 10.

Section 102(1) prohibits any public company from allotting shares as fully or partly paid up otherwise than in cash if the consideration consists of or includes an undertaking which is to be or may be performed *more than five years after the date of the allotment*.

Where the company makes an allotment which contravenes subsection (1) the allottee, under s. 102(2), becomes liable to pay to the company an amount equal to the nominal value of the shares, together with any premium – i.e. he becomes liable to pay for his shares in *cash*, with interest at the appropriate rate.

The same rule applies, under s. 102(5) and (6), where the terms of the contract for allotment, without any fault on the part of the company, have not been complied with by the allottee within the prescribed period.

In both these cases – i.e. whenever the allottee becomes liable to pay for his shares in cash – any subsequent holder also becomes liable, jointly and severally with the allottee, to pay for the shares in cash unless *either*:

(*a*) he is a purchaser for value without actual notice of the contravention at the time of the purchase; *or*

(*b*) he derived title to the shares from a person who acquired them after the contravention and was not himself so liable: s. 112(5), applying s. 112(1) and (3).

Once again, therefore, as with the extension of s. 101(4) to subsequent holders (*see* **15**), liability in a subsequent holder does not arise if the chain is broken.

Finally, if a company contravenes s. 102, the company and any officer of it who is in default is liable to a fine: s. 114.

17. Exemption from liability under s. 102. Section 113(1) provides that where a person is liable to a company under s. 102 regarding payment for his shares, he may apply to the court for relief from that liability.

The court may then exempt him from liability if it appears just and equitable to do so: s. 113(2).

18. Valuation of non-cash consideration. Section 103 gives detailed rules for the valuation of non-cash consideration in public companies. Section 103(1) prohibits any public company from allotting shares as fully or partly paid up otherwise than in cash unless:

(*a*) the consideration has been valued in accordance with s. 108;

(*b*) a report on its value has been made to the company by a person appointed by the company during the six months immediately preceding the allotment; and

(*c*) a copy of the report has been sent to the proposed allottee.

If a company contravenes s. 103, the company and any officer of it who is in default is liable to a fine: s. 114.

Section 108(1) requires the valuation and report to be made by an *independent person*, i.e. a person qualified to act as the company's auditor. Thus the company's auditor is not precluded from acting in this capacity, if the company desires him to do so. By s. 108(2) the term 'valuer' is applied to the independent person.

If the valuer thinks it reasonable to do so, he may, by s. 108(2), arrange for the valuation to be made by some other person provided such person appears to him to have the requisite knowledge and experience and is *neither* an officer or servant of the company or of any company in the same group *nor* a partner or employee of any such officer or servant. Such other person must then make a report to the valuer which will enable him to make his own report as required by s. 103(1)(*b*).

Whoever carries out the valuation or makes the report under s. 103 is entitled, under s. 110(1), to require any information and explanation which he thinks necessary from the company's officers. Any person who responds by knowingly or recklessly making a statement to him which is misleading, false or deceptive in a material particular is guilty of an offence and liable to penalties under s. 110(2).

Lastly, s. 111(1) requires the company receiving the report to deliver a copy of it to the registrar for registration at the same time that it files its return of allotments for the shares in question (*see* **27**). The registrar must then, under s. 711, publish his receipt of it in the *Gazette*.

19. Contents of valuer's report. Section 108(4) requires the valuer's report to state:

(*a*) the nominal value of the shares to be wholly or partly paid for by the consideration in question;

(*b*) the amount of any premium payable on them;

(*c*) the description of the consideration and the method and date of valuation;

(*d*) the extent to which the nominal value of the shares and any premium are to be treated as paid up:

    (*i*) by the consideration;

    (*ii*) in cash.

Where a valuation is made by some person other than the valuer the latter's report, under s. 108(5), must also state:

(*e*) the fact that the valuation was made by some other person;

(*f*) that other person's name and relevant knowledge and experience; and

(*g*) the description of the consideration valued by him and the method and date of valuation.

Finally, s. 108(6) requires the valuer's report either to contain or to be accompanied by a *note* by him:

(*a*) that it appeared reasonable to him to arrange for the valuation to be made by another person if in fact it was so made;

(*b*) that the method of valuation was reasonable;

(*c*) that it appears to him that there has been no material change in the value of the consideration in question since the valuation; and (*d*) that on the basis of the valuation the value of the consideration, together with any cash to be paid for the shares, is not less than the amount treated as paid up on the shares allotted.

20. Effect of contravention of ss. 103 and 108. Section 103(6) provides that where a public company allots shares in contravention of s. 103(1) and *either*:

(*a*) the allottee has not received a report; *or*

(*b*) there has been some other contravention of s. 103 or s. 108 which the allottee knew or ought to have known amounted to a contravention;

the allottee becomes liable to pay to the company an amount equal to the nominal value of the shares together with any premium, or such proportion of that amount as is treated as paid up by the consideration, with interest at the appropriate rate.

Section 112(1) and (3) applies the now familiar provision previously encountered in relation to s. 101 and s. 102 (*see* **15** and **16**) to the effect that whenever the allottee becomes liable through a contravention of the section to pay an amount under it in respect of the shares, any subsequent holder also becomes liable, jointly and severally with the allottee, to pay the amount in question unless *either*:

(*a*) he is a purchaser for value without actual notice of the contravention at the time of the purchase; *or*

(*b*) he derived title to the shares from a person who acquired them after the contravention and was not himself so liable.

Thus once again a subsequent holder or purchaser is not liable if a previous holder or purchaser was not liable. Further, s. 113 again applies to any person liable under s. 103 (*see* **17**).

21. Cases where valuation of non-cash consideration is not required. Section 103(3) and (5) gives two cases where no valuation is required even though a public company is allotting shares for non-cash consideration. These are:

(*a*) Where the company makes an *arrangement* for an allotment of its shares on terms that all or part of the consideration for them is to be provided by the transfer to it, or the cancellation, of shares in another company (whether or not shares in that other company are *issued* to it).

For this exception to apply, however, the arrangement must be open to *all* the holders of the shares of the other company in question: s. 103(4).

(*b*) Where the company is making an allotment of its shares in connection with a *merger* between itself and another company.

Both these operations are considered in more detail in Chapter 32.

22. Disclosure in prospectus where issue not fully subscribed. It is necessary also to deal with s. 84 which relates to allotment where an issue has not been fully subscribed.

Section 84(1) prohibits any allotment of shares in a public company, whether *for cash or otherwise*, unless *either*:

(*a*) the shares are fully subscribed; *or*
(*b*) the offer states that, even if the shares are not fully subscribed, those subscribed for will be allotted in any event.

Section 84(2) provides that if shares are prohibited from being allotted by subsection (1) and 40 days have elapsed after the first issue of the prospectus, all money received from applicants for shares must be repaid to them at once. By s. 84(3), if it is not repaid within 48 days after the issue of the prospectus, the directors become jointly and severally liable to repay it with interest at 5 per cent from the end of the 48th day, unless they can prove that the default in repayment was not due to their misconduct or negligence.

23. Effect of allotment which is irregular under s. 84. Section 85 deals with the effect of any allotment which is irregular under s. 84.

Section 85(1) provides that such an allotment is *voidable* by the applicant within one month after the date of the allotment even if the company is in liquidation.

Section 85(2) makes a director who knowingly contravenes s. 84 liable to compensate the company and the allottee for the resulting loss or damage, but s. 85(3) stipulates that the action to recover this compensation must be brought within *two years* – an unusual period of limitation, found also, however, in s. 92(2) in connection with contravention of the rules as to pre-emption rights (*see* 12).

24. The return of allotments. The final section on allotment to be considered is s. 88, dealing with the return of allotments. This important document must be delivered to the registrar within one month of the allotment whenever any limited company, public or private, allots shares. Capital duty of £1 per cent on the actual value of assets contributed must be paid at the same time. In the case of a public company, s. 711 then requires the registrar to publish his receipt of the return in the *Gazette*.

Section 88(2) states that the company must deliver:

(*a*) a return of allotments, stating:

    (*i*) the number and nominal amount of the shares allotted;

    (*ii*) the names, addresses and descriptions of the allottees;

    (*iii*) the amount paid and payable on each share; *and*

(*b*) where shares are allotted fully or partly paid up *otherwise than in cash:*

    (*i*) a written contract constituting the title of the allottee to the shares,

    (*ii*) the contract of sale or for services or other consideration for which the allotment was made, and

    (*iii*) a return stating the number and nominal amount of the shares so allotted, the extent to which they are paid up, and the consideration for which they were allotted.

Section 88(3) states that where there is no written contract available the company must deliver particulars of it, stamped with the same stamp duty as would have been payable if the contract had been in writing.

Section 88(2) must be studied and learnt very carefully. It is not difficult to understand, but it is not easy to learn. It will help if it is seen that *in every case* the company will have to deliver the return under (*a*) above, but will only have to deliver the contracts and return under (*b*) where the shares have been paid for *otherwise than in cash*, i.e. with property, goods or services.

Where the company makes a *capitalization issue* (**20:13**) and issues bonus shares paid up out of undistributed profits or reserves, it is nevertheless necessary to make not only a return of allotments (*a*), but also to file a contract between the company and the members constituting the title of the allottees (*b*). This is because bonus shares, though not paid for with property, goods or services, are not paid for in 'cash' within the meaning of the section, for this expression is confined to cases where the member provides the company with further capital. For the same reason, issues of bonus shares are not subject to capital duty.

If the company fails to comply with s. 88, there is a fine on every officer in default, but the *validity of the allotments is not affected*. Thus whether or not they are irregular in any other way, the fact that no return of allotments is made will not render them void.

25. Summary of statutory provisions on allotment. The statutory provisions on allotment are so numerous that it is sometimes helpful to have a summary for easy reference, such as that given below.

PUBLIC AND PRIVATE COMPANIES

SECTION		EFFECT OF CONTRAVENTION
s. 80	Company's authority required for allotment	Penalty on directors: s. 80(9) Allotment remains VALID: s. 80(10)

| ss. 89–96 | Pre-emption rights | Company and officers liable to pay compensation: s. 92 |
| s. 88 | Return of allotments | Penalty on officers in default: s. 88(5) Allotment remains VALID |

PUBLIC COMPANIES ONLY

SECTION		EFFECT OF CONTRAVENTION
s. 101	25% of nominal value to be paid before allotment	Penalty on company and officers in default: s. 114 Allottee liable to pay amount due: s. 101(4). Liability extended to all subsequent holders except purchasers for value without notice: s. 112(1)(3)
s. 102	Non-cash consideration to be transferred within 5 years of allotment	Same as for s. 101: s. 102(2) and s. 112(1)(3)(5) + Relief from liability: s. 113
s. 103	Non-cash consideration to be valued by independent person	Same as for s. 102: s. 103(6) and s. 112(1)(3) + Relief from liability: s. 113
s. 84	Disclosure in prospectus before allotment where issue not fully subscribed	Directors liable to pay compensation: s. 85(2)(3) Allotment VOIDABLE: s. 85(1)

Progress test 9

1. When are shares regarded as being allotted? (**1**)

2. How does a company deal with the legal difficulty which arises where an issue of shares is over-subscribed? (**4**)

3. What is the legal effect of a conditional application? (**6**)

4. What is the legal effect of an application subject to a condition subsequent or accompanied by a collateral agreement? (**7**)

5. How may directors be authorized to make an allotment of shares? For how long may the authority last? (**9**)

6. Give the rules relating to pre-emption rights. (**10–14**)

7. What is the minimum amount payable for shares before allotment? (**15**)

8. What special rules apply where allotment is made for non-cash consideration consisting of an undertaking to be performed in the future? (**16**)

9. Outline the rules governing the valuation of non-cash consideration. (**18–21**)

10. What special rules apply where an issue of shares in a public company is not fully subscribed? What is the effect of contravention of those rules? (**22–23**)

11. What rules govern the delivery and contents of the return of allotments? (**25**)

10

Payment for shares

1. Methods of payment for shares. It is essential to understand at the outset that shares must always be paid for. The company cannot give them to the allottee, for the law always seeks to ensure that the company's actual capital is at least equal to the nominal value of its issued capital.

The basic rule at common law was that as long as the company received some consideration for the shares, it was immaterial whether they were issued for money, i.e. *cash*, or for property, goods or services, i.e. *consideration other than cash*.

This rule was given statutory form by the Companies Act 1980 and is now stated in s. 99(1) Companies Act 1985, which provides that shares allotted by a company may be paid up in *money or money's worth* (including goodwill and know-how). There are, however, three limitations on it which are applicable only to *public* companies:

(*a*) Section 99(2) prohibits a public company from accepting payment for its shares, whether on account of the nominal value or of premium, by means of an *undertaking to do work or perform services* for the company.

The result of this prohibition is that shares in a public company must necessarily be paid up either in *cash* or in *non-cash assets*.

Section 738(2) states that a share shall be taken to have been paid up in *cash* if the consideration is:

(*i*) cash received by the company; *or*

(*ii*) a cheque received by the company in good faith which the directors have no reason for suspecting will not be paid; *or*

(*iii*) the release of a liability of the company for a liquidated sum; *or*

(*iv*) an undertaking to pay cash to the company at a future date.

Section 739(1) states that 'non-cash asset' means *any property or interest in property other than cash.*

Where a company contravenes s. 99(2) by accepting an undertaking for work or services in payment for its shares, the holder of those shares becomes liable to pay the amount of their nominal value, together with any premium, to the company, with interest at the appropriate rate.

Moreover, s. 112(1) and (3) applies here as it does to contravention of ss. 101–103 (*see* 9:**15–20**), with the result that where a person becomes liable through a contravention of s. 99 to pay an amount in respect of the shares, any subsequent holder also becomes liable, jointly and severally with him, to pay that amount unless *either*:

(*i*)   he is a purchaser for value without actual notice of the contravention at the time of the purchase; *or*

(*ii*)   he derived title to the shares from a person who acquired them after the contravention and was not himself so liable.

Section 113 again applies to any person liable under s. 99 (*see* 9:**17**).

(*b*)   Section 106 requires shares issued by a public company to a subscriber to the memorandum in pursuance of his undertaking in it, together with any premium, to be paid up in *cash*.

2. The meaning of payment otherwise than in cash.
If the allottee is simply buying the shares from the company and paying for them either on application (which is usual) or partly on application and partly when called upon later, no problems arise. The shares are either fully paid or partly paid according to their condition, and the only other relevant matters, namely premiums and discounts, are dealt with in this chapter.

If, however, he is providing the company with property, goods or services, there are two possible situations which should never be confused:

(*a*)   *Where there is no express agreement to pay for the shares otherwise than in cash:*

It sometimes happens that a shareholder provides the company with property, goods or services for which he is owed a sum of money, and that at the same time he has taken shares in the company for which he owes a sum of money.

There are *two separate transactions* here, one under which the company is receiving some benefit for which it has agreed to pay, and another under which the allottee is receiving shares for which he must pay, and concerning which no agreement to pay otherwise than in cash has been made. There are therefore *two debts*, one from the company to the allottee, and another from the allottee to the company.

Clearly, if the two debts are for exactly the same amount of money, it would be unnecessarily complicated for the company to pay the sum owed only to receive it back again. Even if the two debts are not for exactly the same amount, it is still easier for the party who owes the bigger debt to pay the balance due after deducting the amount he is owed than for each party to pay the full amount. Consequently, provided the two debts are presently payable, the law permits them to be set off against each other. But since this arrangement is only a substitute for two cash payments, the shares issued to the allottee are still paid for in *cash*.

Thus in *Spargo's Case* (1873), S bought shares from the company at the same time as he sold a mine to the company. The two debts were due on the two transactions at the same time, and one was set off against the other as described above. HELD: The shares were paid for in cash.

(*b*) *Where there is an express agreement to pay for shares otherwise than in cash:*
If in the first place the company agrees to allot shares to a person in return for property, goods or services, the shares are then said to be issued *otherwise than for cash*. There is *only one agreement* here, under which the shares are to be paid for with property, goods or services, and it will have to be registered under s. 88 (*see* 9:**24**).

Moreover, the limitations in respect of public companies mentioned in **1** must be borne in mind.

3. Inadequate consideration in private companies. It is no longer possible for consideration to be inadequate in a public company owing to the rules introduced by the Companies Act 1980. Shares in a public company must be paid for either in cash or non-cash assets under s. 99, and non-cash assets must be valued by an independent person under s. 103. Neither of these safeguards, however, applies to a private company which may therefore lawfully accept work or services, or non-cash assets without a valuation, in payment for its shares.

In any such arrangement there is always the possibility that the property, goods or services received by the company will be over-valued, so that they will not in fact be equal to the nominal value of the shares issued in exchange. The consideration is real, but inadequate. One might expect this to be unlawful, for it has the effect of an issue of shares at a discount, but this is not the case. The law here preserves the normal contractual rule that each man is free to make a bad bargain. Consideration must be real, but need not be adequate, and as a rule the court will not inquire into the true value of the consideration received by the company in return for the shares issued.

There are, however, three cases where it will do so:

(a) where there is *fraud*;

(b) where it appears *on the face of the agreement* that the consider-ation is, or may be, inadequate;

(c) where the consideration is in fact entirely *illusory*, i.e. unreal.

A good example of (b) occurred in *Hong Kong and China Gas Co.* v. *Glen* (1914), where the company agreed to allot *one-fifth of all future increases of capital* fully paid in return for the consideration it had received from the allottee. HELD: The agreement could not be allowed to stand, since in time the number of fully paid shares issued to the allottee might obviously become wholly dispropor-tionate to the consideration provided by him.

4. Issue of shares at a discount. So far we have seen two cases where shares may lawfully be issued at a discount, namely, under s. 97 by way of underwriting commission and, in a private company, where they are issued in exchange for over-valued consideration as described above.

Section 100(1) prohibits allotment at a discount in all other cases. Where shares are allotted in contravention of s. 100(1), the allottee remains liable to pay to the company an amount equal to the amount of the discount with interest at the appropriate rate:. s. 100(2). In such a case, as usual, any subsequent holder also becomes liable, jointly and severally with him, to pay that amount unless *either*:

(a) he is a purchaser for value without actual notice of the contravention at the time of the purchase; *or* (*b*) he derived title to the shares from a person who acquired them after the contravention and was not himself so liable: s. 112(1) and (3).

Lastly, it should be noted that s. 100 applies only to shares and not to debentures which, as was pointed out in 8:4, are not part of the share capital and may therefore be issued at a discount whenever required.

5. Issue of shares at a premium. In contrast to an issue at a discount, an issue of shares at a premium, i.e. at a price *above* the par or nominal value, may be made whenever desired. In practice it is usual to issue shares at a premium.

The only statutory requirement here concerns the premium, i.e. the amount in excess of the par value. This must be transferred, under s. 130(1), to the *share premium account*, whether the company is issuing the shares for cash, or otherwise than for cash, i.e. for property, goods or services which are worth more than the nominal amount of the shares issued in exchange.

In two cases, however, the Act relieves the company from this requirement, namely in mergers and in group reconstructions. These are dealt with in **7** and **8** below.

6. The nature and uses of the share premium account. Section 130(3) makes it quite clear that the share premium account is to be regarded as *share capital* as far as reduction of capital is concerned, even though it is not, of course, divided up into shares. However, s. 130(2) allows it to be used for *four specific purposes*:

(*a*) to pay up bonus shares to be issued fully paid to members;
(*b*) to write off the preliminary expenses;
(*c*) to write off commissions or discounts, or the expenses of any issue of shares or debentures;
(*d*) to provide the premium payable on the redemption of debentures.

The share premium account is often called a *statutory capital reserve*, since it is regarded as part of the company's capital and its use is strictly controlled by the Act. It must be disclosed in the balance sheet. The provisions of s. 130 are very important, and they will be discussed again later in Chapter 11.

7. Relief from s. 130 for mergers. Section 131 gives relief in the case of a merger from the requirement in s. 130 to form a share premium account whenever shares are issued at a premium. Before looking at the provisions of the section, however, it is helpful to note that it introduces two technical expressions not previously encountered in this book – 'equity shares' and 'non-equity shares'. These it defines in s. 131(7), stating that 'equity shares' means shares which form part of the company's equity share capital (*see* 13:**14**), while 'non-equity shares' means those which do not. This time one could almost have guessed as much!

Section 131(1) deals with the circumstances in which the section applies, prescribing two conditions:

(*a*) There must be an arrangement under which one company (the issuing company) is allotting *equity shares* to the shareholders of another company in exchange for the issue or transfer of *equity shares* in that other company to itself, or for the cancellation of *equity shares* in that other company not held by itself.

(*b*) As a result of the arrangement the issuing company must have obtained at least a 90 per cent equity holding in the other company, although it need not have acquired the entirety of that holding by means of the arrangement: s. 131(4). For instance, it might have had a small shareholding in the other company for many years and then decided to increase it.

Section 131(6) requires shares held by the issuing company's holding company, subsidiary or co-subsidiary in the other company to be regarded as held by the issuing company itself (*see* 13:**13–16**).

Section 131(2) then provides that if, in these circumstances, the equity shares in the issuing company are issued at a premium, s. 130 will not apply.

Finally, s. 131(3) extends the relief to where the arrangement provides *in addition* for the allotment of *any* shares in the issuing company in exchange for the issue, transfer or cancellation of *non-equity shares* in the other company.

8. Relief from s. 130 for group reconstructions. Section 132 gives relief in the case of a group reconstruction from the requirement in s. 130 to form a share premium account whenever shares are issued at a premium. Like s. 131, it includes two technical expressions which must be considered first – namely, 'the base value of the assets transferred' and 'the minimum premium value'.

'The base value of the assets transferred' is defined in s. 132(5) as:

(a) the cost of those assets to the company transferring them; or

(b) the amount at which those assets are stated in that company's accounting records immediately before the transfer;

whichever is the less.

'The minimum premium value' is defined in s. 132(3) as the amount, if any, by which the base value of the consideration for the shares allotted exceeds the nominal value of those shares.

Section 132(1) follows the same pattern as s. 131(1) and deals with the circumstances in which the section applies. There are, again, two conditions:

(a) The issuing company must be the wholly-owned subsidiary of another company (the holding company) (see 13:**13–16** and 16:**11**).

(b) The issuing company must be allotting shares to its holding company or to a wholly-owned co-subsidiary in consideration for the transfer to it of assets, other than cash, of any company which is a member of the group of companies comprising the holding company and all its wholly-owned subsidiaries.

Section 132(2) then provides that if, in these circumstances, the shares in the issuing company are allotted at a premium, the company is not required by s. 130 to transfer any amount in excess of the minimum premium value to the share premium account.

Progress test 10

1. What limitations exist on the allotment of shares for a consideration other than cash? (**1**)

2. Explain what is meant by payment for shares otherwise than in cash. (**2**)

3. In what cases may shares lawfully be issued at a discount? (**4**)

4. What is the legal effect of an unlawful issue of shares at a discount? (**4**)

5. What are the statutory requirements regarding the issue of shares at a premium? **(5)**

6. Outline the nature and uses of the share premium account. **(6)**

7. In what circumstances is a company given relief from the requirements of s. 130 Companies Act 1985? **(7, 8)**

11

Capital

1. The meaning of capital. The word 'capital' is as variable in meaning as the word 'company'. It means different things to different people, and in particular a lawyer will think of it in a different way from an accountant, and both of them will be perplexed by the economist. Since many students learn company law at the same time as accounting and economics, it is no wonder that they sometimes find definition impossible.

Most ordinary people – and lawyers, as far as accounting is concerned, are ordinary people – think of capital as *something the company has got*. It has got the money which it has raised by the issue of shares. It uses this money to buy the things which it needs, such as business premises and stock-in-trade, and these things are then called the *fixed* capital and the *circulating* capital respectively. Always the concept of capital is a *positive* one, based on the notion that what the company has obtained by issuing shares to members it must preserve at all costs.

There is nothing wrong with this idea and the lawyer survives happily until he looks at a company's balance sheet. Here he finds on the left-hand side clearly headed 'Liabilities' not only the share capital of the company, but also the debentures or 'loan capital' and, what is even worse, the trade creditors.

Slowly the truth begins to dawn upon him that the accountant thinks of capital in a *negative* way as *something the company owes*. The share capital is owed to the members, the loan capital is owed to the debenture-holders, and the trade debts are owed to the trade creditors. Almost certainly he will then wish that he knew some accounting principles, but when he asks an accountant for assistance he will probably be told that the idea of capital as a debt of the company flows directly from the law. Did not *Salomon* v. *Salomon &*

Co. show that a company is a separate legal person from the members? Why, then, should the money contributed by the members to the company not be regarded as a debt due back to them? What could be more logical? The lawyer will be compelled to agree, but his viewpoint will have been disturbed. The accountant sounds as though he knows what he is talking about, and the lawyer has suddenly seen the picture from a new angle.

NOTE: The only advice which can safely be given to students on this point is to tread warily and always try to find out in what sense the book or the lecturer is using the word 'capital'. Unless the term is defined at the beginning, any subsequent discussion will be both useless and dangerous.

In this chapter it is used in the sense adopted by most legal textbooks and means *share capital*, i.e. the money raised by the issue of shares. Money raised by the issue of *debentures* is simply money which the company has *borrowed* at a fixed rate of interest and *is not capital in this sense*, though the confusing expression 'loan capital' is often used in books on business management and economics to mean money raised in this way.

2. The use of the word. There are many expressions involving the use of the word 'capital'. The *issued capital* of the company, for instance, means as a rule the share capital which has been allotted to members, although 'issue' is also a variable word and is not always used in this sense. The *paid-up capital* means that amount of the issued capital which has been paid up by members, so that if the shares are not fully paid this will leave the *unpaid capital* which is the amount still unpaid on the issued capital and which can be called up at any time that it is required. The issued capital can of course never exceed the *nominal* or *authorized* capital, i.e. the figure given in the capital clause of the memorandum of association, and if it is desired to issue more shares than the number authorized by this clause, then the nominal capital must be increased to cover the required amount. In this chapter the method of doing this and of making other alterations to capital will be discussed.

Section 351(2) provides that if there is a reference to the company's share capital on its business stationery or order forms, that reference must be to the *paid-up* share capital.

3. Reserve capital. Lastly, there is the *reserve capital*. This must never be confused with a *capital reserve*, which is entirely different. *Reserve capital can only be created under s. 120*, and if one turns to s. 120 the expression is clearly explained. Note that the margin of the Act refers to the reserve *liability*, while the section itself states how this reserve capital or liability is created. It provides that a company may determine by special resolution that its uncalled capital (i.e. the amount of the issued capital which is still unpaid and which has not yet been called up by the directors) may not be called up except on liquidation.

Once the company has created reserve capital in this way, it cannot charge it as it can the uncalled capital. (It will be seen later that a charge on uncalled capital is one of the nine types of registrable charge mentioned in s. 396(1): **21:21**.) The reserve capital is not under the directors' control, and once the special resolution creating it has been passed, it cannot be revoked except under a scheme of arrangement with the consent of the court, for to do so would be a threat to the position of creditors who are relying on the existence of this fund of money. Reserve capital can, however, like all share capital, be reduced under s. 135 with the consent of the court.

Since it is possible to charge the uncalled capital, a difficult situation can arise if the company converts into reserve capital uncalled capital which has already been charged. In this case it would be injurious to the secured creditor with a charge on the uncalled capital if his charge could be destroyed by the simple expedient of converting the uncalled capital into reserve capital. The position here, therefore, is probably that the charge remains outstanding, although any further charges on what is now reserve capital are not permissible.

4. Provisions and reserves. As stated above, it is essential that the *reserve capital* should not be confused with a *capital reserve*. The meaning of the latter, however, becomes clear only if the term 'provision' is fully understood.

A provision is defined in para. 89 of the 4th Schedule to the Act (see **18:6**) as 'any amount retained as reasonably necessary for the purpose of providing for any liability or loss which is either likely to be incurred, or certain to be incurred but uncertain as to amount or as to the date on which it will arise'.

Thus if a company owes *a precise sum of money* to a creditor, this is a *liability*, for the company knows that it owes a debt and it knows the exact amount of it. If it sets aside a sum of money to meet a debt which is merely *likely* to be incurred, or *uncertain* in amount or date, this is a *provision*. If it sets aside a sum of money simply out of prudence and not because it has a known or possible debt in mind, then this is a *reserve*. If this reserve is regarded as *free for distribution* to the members, it is a *revenue reserve*, and if not, it is a *capital reserve*.

5. Types of capital reserve. It is clear that a revenue reserve is profit retained in the business, but which is distributable to the members when desired. It is also clear that a *capital* reserve is a fund which is not regarded as distributable in this way. But in fact there are two types of capital reserve:

(*a*) Those the use of which is strictly controlled by the Act, which impliedly makes them non-distributable by stating the only purposes for which they may be used.

These are:

    (*i*)   the share premium account: s. 130; and

    (*ii*) the capital redemption reserve: s. 170.

They are often termed the *statutory* capital reserves, since the Act controls both their creation and their use.

(*b*) Those the use of which is not controlled by the Act, and which are therefore often termed the *non-statutory* capital reserves. Their only characteristic is that they are *not regarded as free for distribution* to the members, but since they are not controlled by the Act in any way, they can in theory become regarded as free for distribution if desired and transferred to revenue reserve. This might be imprudent, but it would not be unlawful.

Non-statutory capital reserves can arise in several ways, e.g. where a fund is set aside out of profits to replace assets which are wearing out, such as heavy machinery. A well-managed company is one in which the directors plan for the future, and it would be imprudent not to provide for such demands on the company's resources.

NOTE: In Chapter 20 we shall see that, provided the rules on dividends are observed, there is no *legal* bar to distribution of such funds to the members, though in most cases good management requires their retention in the company's hands. Accountants as a body tend to regard all capital reserves as non-distributable, and view the legal position with gloomy mistrust, but this is due to the belief characteristic of the members of that profession that caution is the greatest of all virtues.

6. Reserve fund. Students may be required to distinguish capital reserves from reserve capital, or be asked for examples of capital reserves, or for the meaning of the capital redemption reserve which will be explained later in this chapter. But the simple expression 'reserve fund' is normally used to mean a sum of money which the company has invested in a readily realizable asset so that it can be made available quickly when needed. It has no technical legal significance.

7. Types of share capital. The shares in any company may be all exactly alike, i.e. they may all carry the same rights to attend and vote at company meetings and to dividends. But often they are of different types with varying rights: in this case the company is said to have different *classes* of shares, and the rights attached to the different classes are called *class rights*. The class rights normally relate to voting, dividends or the return of capital in liquidation, and they will be set out either in the memorandum or articles of association of the company or in the terms of issue of the shares concerned.

Section 28(1) and (2) provides that any company allotting shares with rights which are *not* stated in the memorandum, the articles, or a resolution required to be filed with the registrar under s. 380 (*see* **15:41**), and which are not uniform with shares previously allotted, must deliver to the registrar, within one month from the allotment, a statement containing particulars of those rights.

Similarly, under s. 128(3) and (4), where rights attached to shares are varied (*see* **13**), or a class of shares is given a name or other designation, *otherwise* than by an amendment of the memorandum or articles or a resolution required to be filed with the registrar under s. 380, a statement containing particulars of the variation, name or designation must be delivered to the registrar within one month.

These provisions ensure that in all cases, including that where the rights attached to shares are contained in or varied by an *ordinary* resolution, full details of the company's share capital reach the registrar who is then required, under s. 711, to publish his receipt of the statement in the *Gazette*.

There are the following types of share in existence:

(a) preference shares;
(b) ordinary shares;
(c) deferred shares.

8. Preference shares. The characteristic of the preference share is that it has a *preferred fixed dividend*, i.e. that the dividend payable on it is fixed at a certain figure, e.g. 7 per cent, and that this dividend must be paid *before* the ordinary shareholders receive anything.

It follows that preference shares are a safe, though far from stimulating, investment, and that when economic conditions are unstable they will be more in demand than when there is a period of prosperous growth or of inflation. On the other hand, nothing is more distressing than to own preference shares in a well-managed company which is making large profits. While the bulk of these profits will be distributed to the ordinary shareholders, whose shares will consequently rise on the market, the preference shareholder will continue to receive his modest fixed percentage. There are thus far more fluctuations in the market value of ordinary shares than of preference shares, providing more excitement to compensate for the greater risk.

Preference shares can be either:

(a) *cumulative*, i.e. if the company is unable to pay a dividend in any particular year, it must *accumulate* the arrears of dividend on the preference shares from year to year until they are all paid, before the ordinary shareholders can receive any of the profits; *or*

(b) *non-cumulative*, i.e. if the company is unable to pay a dividend in any particular year, the preference shareholder will never receive any dividend for that year.

NOTE: They are always *presumed to be cumulative* unless expressly described as non-cumulative.

Preference shares sometimes carry voting rights, but often carry different ones from those of the ordinary shares, or none at all.

Sometimes a company issues *participating* preference shares. These are preference shares which receive their fixed dividend, e.g. 6 per cent, in the normal way, but which then *participate further* in the distributed profits along with the ordinary shares after a certain fixed percentage has been paid on them as well. Note that a participating preference share will be part of the equity share capital unless it participates in profits only up to a further fixed percentage and there is also some restriction on its right to participate in surplus assets in a liquidation.

9. The rights attached to preference shares in a liquidation. In 1:**18** the order of distribution of assets in a liquidation was given. There it was seen that preference shares do not, contrary to popular belief, carry any priority to return of capital in a liquidation unless the memorandum or articles or the terms of issue confer it on them. Such a provision is, however, a common one and where it is made the preference shares *will not have any implied right to participate in the distribution of the surplus assets.* The right to receive the capital back in priority to the ordinary shareholders is said to be *exhaustive*, i.e. it implies that there is no right to receive anything more, and therefore if in such a case it is desired that the preference shares should also participate in the surplus assets, this right must be *expressly* given to them: *Scottish Insurance Corporation* v. *Wilsons and Clyde Coal Co.* (1949).

Difficulty sometimes arises over the payment of *arrears of dividend* on cumulative preference shares in a liquidation. Clearly, any dividend which has been declared must be paid, for it is a debt. But arrears of dividend, i.e. dividends which have *not* been declared, are not payable in a liquidation *unless the articles so provide*, for they do not constitute a debt. Moreover, the articles must provide for the payment of *arrears*. If they merely provide for payment of *arrears due*, the arrears of dividend will again not be payable unless they have been declared, for the word 'due' indicates that the sum is owing and therefore is a debt.

10. Ordinary shares. Ordinary shares normally carry the residue of distributed profits after the preference shares, if any, have received their fixed dividend. If the preference shareholders have priority as to return of capital in liquidation, the ordinary shares will then be entitled to all the surplus assets unless there are also deferred shares. Thus as a rule the ordinary shares are the *equity share capital* of the company.

(*a*) *Voting rights:* While preference shares often carry no voting rights, ordinary shares usually give the holder the right to vote; but this is not invariably the case. In some companies both voting and non-voting ordinary shares are issued, and this practice has been much criticized on several grounds. In principle, it is often thought to be wrong to divorce ownership from control so that those who may have invested the largest amount of money in the company may have no voice whatsoever in its management. Moreover, investors may not realize that their shares give them no voting rights until after they have bought them.

(b) *Control:* It is, however, always possible to keep control in the hands of a minority by the device of *weighted voting rights*, without issuing any non-voting shares, and it is sometimes desirable to be able to raise more capital without losing control.

11. Deferred shares. Deferred shares are not at all common. They usually give the holders the right to the residue of distributed profits after a certain fixed dividend has been paid on the ordinary shares. It follows that in such a case the deferred shares, not the ordinary shares, will constitute the equity share capital of the company (*see* 13:**14**).

Deferred shares may carry heavy voting rights as compared with the other shares in the company and may participate to a high degree in the surplus assets on the company's liquidation. For all these reasons they are normally issued to the promoters of the company, when they may be termed *founders' shares*, or to the directors, when they may be termed *management shares*.

12. No par value shares. So far all the types of share which we have considered have had a *par* or *nominal value*. This is because, as was explained in 2:**35**, shares with no par value cannot be issued in this country, though they exist in certain other countries, notably in the United States.

The rule that shares must have a par value is frequently criticized on two main grounds:

(a) The present form of balance sheet is linked to the figure of the nominal capital. This figure is almost certain to become entirely unrealistic in the course of time, for as the company's business expands and becomes more profitable, the market value of the shares will rise, bearing little or no relation to the original par value.

(b) Dividends are often declared in the form of a percentage of the nominal value. Thus a dividend of 25 per cent on shares with a par value of £1 but a market value of £5 gives the investor a yield of 5 per cent on his money, and although this is in fact a reasonable figure, it may not appear so to those who do not understand it.

13. Variation of rights. We have already seen in 7 that sometimes all the shares in a company are exactly alike, and sometimes they are divided up into different classes. We also saw that the rights attached to the shares are normally to be found in the memorandum, articles or terms of issue. These rights are described as 'class rights' only where there are different classes of shares in existence, in which case s. 128 ensures that the registrar receives particulars of them if they are not contained in a document already in his possession (*see* 7). It is now necessary to consider how these rights can be altered and for this purpose to study each of the two possible situations separately.

Where all the shares in a company are *exactly alike*, the rights – which will not, of course, be class rights – may be specified either in the articles or in the memorandum. If specified in the articles, they may be altered in the same way as any other clause in the articles, i.e. by special resolution. If specified in the memorandum, however, the clause will be covered by s. 17.

This section, as we saw in 2:**36**, covers with certain exceptions all the clauses in the memorandum other than the compulsory ones, and states that anything in the memorandum which could lawfully have been inserted in the articles instead can be altered by special resolution with the same provision for dissentients as is given by s. 5 for alterations of the objects clause.

Section 17, however, does not apply if the memorandum itself *stipulates a method* of altering the particular clause, in which case that method must be used. Nor does it apply if the memorandum *prohibits* alteration of the clause, in which case application must be made to the court under s. 425.

14. Variation of class rights. It must first be understood that s. 17 has no application here, for s. 17(2) expressly states that the section does not apply to a variation of class rights (*see* 2:**36**).

Such a variation is governed by s. 125 which lays down detailed rules. In an attempt to make these rules somewhat easier to learn, an initial distinction has been drawn between those which apply where no provision for variation is contained in either the memorandum or the articles, and those which apply where such a provision exists.

(*a*) *Where there is no provision for variation in either the memorandum or the articles*:

(*i*) Where the class rights are *specified in the memorandum*, any variation requires the consent of *all the members* of the company: s. 125(5).

(*ii*) Where the class rights are *specified elsewhere* (i.e. in the articles or terms of issue), any variation requires *either* the written consent of the *holders of three-quarters of the issued shares of that class, or* the sanction of an *extraordinary resolution* passed at a class meeting: s. 125(2).

In addition, any other existing requirements for variation must also be observed: s. 125(2), and s. 127, considered below, operate here to protect dissentients: s. 127(1).

(*b*) *Where there is provision for variation in either the memorandum or the articles:*

(*i*) Regardless of whether the class rights are specified in the memorandum or elsewhere, where the variation is connected with *either* the giving, variation, revocation or renewal of *the company's authority to the directors to allot shares* under s. 80, *or* a *reduction of capital* under s. 135, the rules for variation are *exactly the same as in* (*a*)(*ii*) *above*: s. 125(3).

(*ii*) Where the class rights are *specified in the memorandum* and the articles contain a provision for variation which was included at the time of the company's incorporation, a variation may be made only in accordance with that provision (unless it falls under (*i*) above): s. 125(4).

(*iii*) Where the class rights are *specified elsewhere* and the articles contain a provision for variation, whenever it was first included, a variation may be made only in accordance with that provision (unless it falls under (*i*) above): s. 125(4).

In *all three* of these cases s. 127 operates to protect dissentients. Thus the only time when s. 127 does *not* operate is in (*a*) (*i*) where no dissentients exist.

15. Protection of dissentients on variation of class rights. It will be clear from the wording of s. 127(1) that wherever there are class rights attached to shares in a company and *either the memorandum or the articles prescribe a method of variation* of those rights, the section operates to protect dissentients.

It also operates, under s. 127(1), in one case where a method of variation is *not* so prescribed – namely, where the class rights are specified elsewhere than in the memorandum (*see* **14** (*a*)(*ii*)).

Section 127(2) and (3) allows the holders of 15 per cent of the shares of the class in question, who did not consent to the variation, to apply to the court within 21 days to have it cancelled. The court may then, under s. 127(4), either cancel or confirm it.

Note that the required percentage of shareholdings by the applicants and the period for making the application are the same as under s. 5 regarding alterations of the objects clause and s. 17 regarding alterations of the non-compulsory clauses in the memorandum (i.e. 15 per cent and 21 days).

16. Further provisions on variation of class rights. Three further points are of importance when considering this topic:

(*a*) Section 125(7) states that any *alteration* of a provision in the articles prescribing a method of variation of class rights, or the *insertion* of such a provision into the articles, is itself to be treated as a variation of those rights.

This brings into operation all the safeguards described above.

(*b*) Section 125(6) states that class meetings connected with a variation of class rights are governed by the normal rules relating to general meetings found in the Act, but lays down two special rules:

(*i*) The *quorum* at such a meeting, except an adjourned meeting, is at least two persons holding, or representing by proxy, one-third of the issued shares of the class in question; the quorum at an adjourned meeting is one person holding shares of the class in question, or his proxy.

(*ii*) Any holder of shares of the class in question present in person or by proxy may *demand a poll*.

(*c*) The Schedule to the Companies (Tables A–F) Regulations 1985 (S.I. 1985, No. 805) contains no provision for variation of class rights but the articles of many existing companies include such a provision since Table A in the 1st Schedule to the Companies Act 1948 did so. Article 4 of that Table A stated that class rights might be varied with the written consent of the holders of three-quarters of the issued shares of that class, or the sanction of an extraordinary resolution passed at a class meeting.

Note that that article corresponded exactly with the requirements of s. 125(2): (*see* **14**(*a*)(*ii*)).

17. The meaning of variation. It is clear that if there are several classes of shares in a company, and the rights of one class are altered without the rights of the other class or classes being changed in any way, it is possible to change the *control* of the company. The voting rights attached to particular shares can be made quite ineffective by the giving of increased voting rights to another class, or by the issue of further shares of the same class.

In this context, however, the word 'variation' has a much more restricted meaning. It only covers *direct alterations*, i.e. if the rights attached to a particular class of shares are altered then that is a variation of rights, but the fact that the effect of the alteration is to remove control from another class of shareholders is immaterial, for this would merely be a *consequential* alteration. Of course the practical effect is to alter their rights, but this is not the meaning given by the law to the word 'variation'.

Section 125(8) provides, however, that in s. 125 and in any provision for variation of class rights contained in a company's memorandum or articles the word 'variation' includes *abrogation*. Similarly, s. 127(6) provides that 'variation' in s. 127 includes *abrogation*.

NOTE: A minority which can show that its interests are being *unfairly prejudiced* has, as will be seen later, a remedy under ss. 459–461. Furthermore, in *Clemens* v. *Clemens Bros Ltd* (1976), resolutions to increase the capital and issue the new shares in such a way as to deprive the plaintiff of her 'negative control' (i.e. diluting her voting power from 45 per cent to 24.6575 per cent) were set aside as having been passed by an inequitable use of the defendant's voting rights.

18. Alteration of capital. In Chapter 2 we considered the method of alteration of all the compulsory clauses in the memorandum except the capital clause. It must now be seen in what way this can be altered to suit the company's requirements.

Section 121(1)–(3) states that a company may alter the capital clause of the memorandum, i.e. its nominal capital, in the following ways:

(*a*) It may increase the nominal capital by creating new shares.

(*b*) It may consolidate its existing shares into larger shares, e.g. by consolidating five 5p shares into one 25p share.

(*c*) It may subdivide its existing shares into smaller shares, but it must keep the proportion paid and unpaid on each share the same. (Shares are sometimes subdivided to make them more marketable, for investors tend to prefer a large number of 'cheap' shares to a few 'expensive' ones, ignoring the fact that the yield on their investment will be the same whatever the nominal value of the shares.)

(*d*) It may convert fully paid up shares into stock, or vice versa.

(*e*) It may cancel shares which have not been taken up, and diminish the amount of the nominal capital by the number cancelled. (This is *not* a reduction of capital, for these shares have never been allotted to anyone. Section 121(5) makes this quite clear.)

In order to alter its capital clause in any of these ways, the company requires authority in its articles, but if the articles give no power to this effect it can be inserted. Since this involves altering the articles, a special resolution is required, and the same resolution may also be used to make the alteration of capital.

If, however, the articles already contain power to alter the capital an ordinary resolution will suffice to make the alteration, since s. 121 does not require a special one. The articles can, of course, prescribe a special resolution for this purpose, but Table A does not do so.

Section 123 states that notice of any increase in the capital must be given to the registrar within 15 days.

Section 122(1) states that notice of all alterations other than increases, including the redemption of redeemable shares under ss. 159–161 (*see* **24** below), must be given to the registrar within one month.

19. Stock. We have just seen that s. 121 allows the company to convert its fully paid up shares into stock, and it is therefore important to understand the nature of stock and any advantages which it may have.

Section 744, in defining a share, states that 'share includes stock'. The *relationship* of a shareholder to the company is in no way altered if his shares are converted into stock and he becomes a stockholder. Section 370(6) covers the case where the articles make no provision for the voting rights attached to the stock, stating that the member shall have one vote for each £10 of stock.

The provisions of s. 121, however, must be carefully observed. It only authorizes the conversion of shares into stock if the shares are fully paid. Moreover, it expressly states that shares may be *converted* into stock, and from this it follows that a *direct issue* of stock is not lawful. An issue of *partly paid* stock or of *bonus* stock is therefore *ultra vires* and void, and in theory the same result should ensue from a direct issue of *fully paid* stock. In *Re Home and Foreign Investment Co.* (1912), however, it was held that a direct issue of *fully paid* stock could be validated by *lapse of time*.

Once shares are converted into stock, the stockholder owns, say, £100 of stock where formerly he held 100 £1 shares. Thus though his *relationship* with the company remains the same, his *interest* in it is described in a different manner. It is no longer divided up into shares with a nominal value. This raises the question of its divisibility and brings us to consideration of its *advantages*:

(a) In legal theory *stock is divisible into any amount required*. Thus it is possible to transfer £4.32 worth of stock, while it is never possible to transfer a fraction of a share.

In practice, however, this advantage seldom exists, since the articles usually prescribe the minimum amount of stock transferable.

(b) *Since stock is not divided up into units, it cannot be numbered.* Shares, on the other hand, must have a number and this causes a certain amount of administrative work. But this advantage of stock is offset to a certain extent by s. 182(2), which, while requiring shares to be numbered, makes an exception for fully paid shares ranking *pari passu* for all purposes.

20. Serious loss of capital by public company. Section 142 applies whenever the net assets of a public company fall to *half or less* of its called-up share capital.

In such a case the section requires the directors, not later than 28 days from the day on which that fact first becomes known to a director, to convene an extraordinary general meeting for a date not less than 56 days from that day.

The purpose of the meeting is to consider whether any, and if so what, steps should be taken to deal with the situation. It is likely that this will lead, in many cases, to a reduction of capital, the procedure for which is described below.

21. Reduction of capital. A reduction of capital is, of course, an *alteration* of capital, but is an alteration of such importance and of such potential danger to creditors that it is strictly controlled by the Act in s. 135, the requirements of which are far more stringent than those of s. 121 for other types of alteration.

Section 135(1) and (2) states that with authority in its articles and the sanction of the court a company may by special resolution reduce its share capital in any way and make the necessary alteration to its memorandum. In particular, it may:

(*a*) extinguish or reduce the liability on unpaid share capital; *or*

(*b*) cancel paid up capital which has been lost or is unrepresented by available assets; *or*

(*c*) pay off any paid up share capital which is in excess of the company's wants.

NOTE:

(1) *The section naturally applies to stock as well as shares*, except that there can be no liability on stock to be extinguished or reduced since, as we have seen, it must always be fully paid. Reserve capital too, it will be remembered, can be reduced under this section, although (*b*) and (*c*) would be inapplicable to it since they can apply only to paid-up capital.

(2) *If the articles do not give the necessary authority*, it is not possible here, as it was under s. 121, to insert the authority and alter the capital in a single resolution. Here a special resolution must first be passed to alter the articles, and then a second special resolution to reduce the capital, though both can be passed at the same meeting.

(3) Where the ground of reduction is that the capital has been lost, the loss must be a permanent loss so far as is at the time foreseeable and not merely a temporary fall in the value of some capital asset: *Re Jupiter House Investments* (*Cambridge*) *Ltd* (1985). However, the court may confirm a reduction where the loss is not shown to be permanent if the company gives an undertaking to safeguard creditors' interests: *Re Grosvenor Press plc* (1985).

(4) *When capital is to be returned to the shareholders*, as under (*c*), it is not simply handed back to them in proportion to their holdings.

Their *class rights* will be considered, the court treating the reduction *as though it were a liquidation*. If, therefore, a certain class of shareholders would have priority to return of capital in liquidation, that class will also be the first to have the share capital returned to them in a reduction, and this is so even if they would prefer to remain members of the company: *Prudential Assurance Co. Ltd* v. *Chatterley-Whitfield Collieries Ltd* (1949).

22. Creditors' right to object to a reduction. Section 136(2) and (3) gives the creditors of the company a right to object to the reduction in any case where their interests are threatened, i.e. where the liability on unpaid share capital is extinguished or reduced, or where paid-up capital is returned to the shareholders. They can object in other cases if the court so directs.

The court settles the list of creditors entitled to object, as far as possible without requiring applications from creditors, and may publish notices fixing a day by which creditors not on the list must claim to be entered on it, or lose their right of objection: s. 136(4).

If a creditor on the list does not consent to the reduction, the court may dispense with his consent if the company secures payment of his debt by appropriating to it, where it admits the debt, the full amount, and where it does not admit it, the amount fixed by the court: s. 136(5).

Where a company owns leasehold properties, a list of landlords as creditors is not required if a sum sufficient to pay the rent is set aside or guaranteed. Ten years' rent will suffice for the court to dispense with the list, provided the leases are not onerous: *Re Lucania Temperance Billiard Halls (London)* (1966).

23. Confirmation and registration of reduction. Section 137(1) states that if the court is satisfied either that the creditors entitled to object have consented to the reduction, or that their debts have been paid or secured, it may confirm the reduction. Under s. 137(2) it may also direct that the words 'and reduced' be added to the company's name for a specified period, and that the company must publish the reasons for the reduction.

Section 138(1) states that when the court order confirming the reduction is produced to the registrar, and a copy of it together with a minute giving the details of the company's share capital are delivered to him, he must register the order and the minute.

The minute specifies:

(a) the amount of the share capital;
(b) the number of shares into which it is to be divided;
(c) the amount of each share;
(d) the amount paid up on each share.

Section 138(2) states that the reduction takes effect on registration, and s. 138(4) requires the registrar to give a certificate of the registration of the order and minute, and this certificate is conclusive evidence both that the requirements of the Act have been complied with, and that the share capital is now as set out in the minute. The registered minute, under s. 138(5), is deemed to be substituted for the corresponding part of the memorandum.

Section 139 contains special rules to apply where the court order confirming the reduction of the capital of a *public* company brings the nominal value of the company's allotted share capital *below the authorized minimum*. Section 139(2) then prohibits the registrar from registering the order under s. 138 unless the court directs otherwise or the company is first *re-registered as a private company*.

Under s. 139(3) the court, in these circumstances, may authorize the company to be re-registered as a private company under s. 53 (*see* 25:4) without its having passed the special resolution normally required for that operation. In these circumstances the court must then specify in its order the alterations to be made to the company's memorandum and articles connected with its re-registration.

24. Redeemable shares. In the normal way shares are not redeemable except on a reduction of capital effected with the consent of the court under s. 135, for if the company could give the members their money back at any time that it wished, the creditors could never rely on its having any money at all. For the same reason it is unlawful for a company to *convert* any of its share capital into redeemable shares and then redeem them.

Section 159, however, permits a company to issue shares which are redeemable at the option of either the company or the shareholder on compliance with the following conditions:

(a) There must be authority in the articles to make the issue: s. 159(1).

(*b*) There must be some non-redeemable issued shares in the company at the time: s. 159(2).

(*c*) The redeemable shares may be redeemed only if they are fully paid: s. 159(3).

(*d*) The terms of redemption must provide for payment on redemption: s. 159(3).

(*e*) The redeemable shares may be redeemed only out of distributable profits (*see* s. 181 and 20:**5-7**) or out of the proceeds of a fresh issue of shares made for the purpose: s. 160(1)(*a*). This does not apply to private companies (*see* **33**).

(*f*) Any premium payable on redemption must be paid out of distributable profits: s. 160(1)(*b*).

(*g*) Despite the rule in (*f*), where the redeemable shares were *issued at a premium*, any premium payable on redemption may be paid out of the proceeds of a fresh issue of shares made for the purpose of the redemption, up to an amount equal to:

(*i*) the aggregate premiums received by the company on the issue of the redeemable shares; *or*

(*ii*) the current amount of the company's share premium account, including any sum transferred to that account in respect of premiums on the new shares;
whichever is the less: s. 160(2).

The company's share premium account must in either case then be reduced by the amount of the payment made out of the proceeds of the new issue.

(*h*) The shares redeemed must be treated as cancelled on redemption and the company's issued share capital is to be diminished by the amount of their nominal value. The company's authorized share capital, however, is not affected by the redemption: s. 160(4).

(*i*) Where a company is about to redeem shares it may issue new shares up to the nominal amount of the shares to be redeemed as if the latter had never been issued: s. 160(5).

Accordingly provided the redemption takes place within a month after the issue of the new shares, there is no increase of capital for stamp duty purposes under s. 47 Finance Act 1973 unless the actual value of the new shares issued exceeds the value of the shares redeemed at the date of redemption. Duty is then payable only on the difference: s. 161(1) and (2).

(*j*) Where shares are redeemed out of profits a sum equal to the nominal amount of the shares redeemed must be transferred to the *capital redemption reserve*: s. 170(1).

(*k*) The capital redemption reserve, as explained in **5**, is a *statutory capital reserve* and s. 170(4) expressly states that it is to be treated as *share capital* for reduction purposes, although it may be used for paying up *bonus shares*.

Note how these rules maintain the capital of the company. If the redeemable shares are redeemed out of the proceeds of a fresh issue of shares, then the share capital is automatically replaced and no capital redemption reserve is required. If, however, they are redeemed out of distributable profits, then no shares are issued to replace them and a capital reserve must be formed in order to keep the total capital of the company constant. This capital reserve may be used for paying up bonus shares, but this merely converts it into share capital as opposed to a capital fund which is not divided into shares. The non-distributable funds are preserved throughout, for the total capital of the company does not alter (*see* 13:**22**).

Finally, s. 122(1) provides that notice of the redemption must be given to the registrar within one month. The registrar must then, under s. 711, publish his receipt of the notice in the *Gazette*.

25. Purchase by company of its own shares. It will be clear both from this chapter and from Chapter 13 that the preservation of a company's share capital is of fundamental importance. Not only the common law but also successive Companies Acts have developed this principle until it has now reached a highly sophisticated stage. It is all the more surprising, therefore, that the Companies Act 1985, in provisions derived from the Companies Act 1981, should appear to attack it by permitting companies to buy their own shares.

The attack is, however, more apparent than real, for when a company, in accordance with the Act, buys its own shares, all the safeguards which apply to the redemption of redeemable shares (*see* **24**) apply again. Private companies are permitted to buy their own shares out of capital, but only on certain conditions and with further safeguards. Moreover, even if the introduction of these rules is seen as a threat to the sanctity of share capital, there are a number of good reasons why it is justified. Thus a shareholder in a private company who wishes to sell his shares but cannot find a purchaser is now able to sell them to the company. An employee who has participated in an employees' share scheme can now sell his shares to the company if he ceases to be employed by it. A company which has issued redeemable shares can buy them back from the holder before the redemption date if the price is low, thus saving itself money – a practice which has always been possible in the case of debentures (*see* 21:**14**). There are many other ways in which the power of a company to buy its own shares may prove commercially useful without being dangerous.

The basic rule, which is of general application and therefore applies to every purchase by a company of its own shares, is found in s. 162. This permits a company to buy its own shares, including any redeemable shares (*see* **24**), if it is authorized to do so by its articles, *unless* as a result of the purchase there would no longer be any member of the company holding non-redeemable shares: s. 162(1) and (3).

Where a company buys its own shares under s. 162, the provisions of both ss. 159–161 and s. 170 apply in exactly the same way as in the case of the redemption of redeemable shares (*see* **24**): ss. 162(2) and 170. This ensures the replacement of the share capital purchased by the company with either a fresh issue of shares or a capital redemption reserve.

26. Off-market purchase by company of its own shares. Although the general rule is given by s. 162, later sections contain additional rules which apply to particular situations and accordingly vary with the circumstances of the purchase. The first of these is in ss. 163 and 164, governing off-market purchases.

Under s. 163(1) an off-market purchase by a company of its own shares occurs if *either*:

(*a*) the shares are purchased otherwise than on a recognized investment exchange; *or*

(*b*) they are purchased on a recognized investment exchange but are not subject to a marketing arrangement on it.

Such an arrangement exists if either the shares are listed under Part IV of the Financial Services Act 1986 or the company has been given facilities for them to be dealt in on that investment exchange without prior permission for individual transactions: s. 163(2).

Section 164(1) permits a company to make an off-market purchase of its own shares only in pursuance of *a contract approved in advance* in accordance with the section or under s. 165 (*see* **27**). The rules prescribed by s. 164 are as follows:

(*a*) Before the company enters into the contract of purchase, its terms must be authorized by special resolution: s. 164(2).

(*b*) The authority conferred by the special resolution may be varied, revoked or renewed by special resolution: s. 164(3).

(*c*) In a *public* company the authority conferred by the special resolution must specify its date of expiry which may not be later than 18 months after the date on which the resolution is passed: s. 164(4).

(*d*) No special resolution will be effective if any member who holds shares to which it relates exercises the voting rights attached to them and the resolution would not have been passed if he had not done so: s. 164(5).

(*e*) No special resolution will be effective unless a copy of the contract of purchase or, if it is not in writing, a written memorandum of its terms, is available for inspection by members both:

(*i*) at the registered office for at least 15 days ending with the date of the meeting at which the resolution is passed; and

(*ii*) at the meeting itself.

Any such memorandum must include the names of the members who hold the shares in question, while any copy of the contract must include them either in the contract itself or in an annexed memorandum: s. 164(6).

27. Contingent purchase contracts. A similar set of additional rules are stated in s. 165 and apply to contingent purchase contracts.

Under s. 165(1) a contingent purchase contract is one which does not amount to a contract by the company to purchase its own shares, but under which it may, on some condition, become entitled or bound to purchase them.

In this case too such a purchase may be made only *if the contract is approved in advance* and all the rules in s. 164 given in **26**(*a*)–(*e*) above apply again in exactly the same way: s. 165(2).

28. Market purchase by company of its own shares. The third and last set of additional rules is found in s. 166 and governs market purchases. Under s. 163(3) a market purchase is one made on a recognized investment exchange of shares which are either *listed* under Part IV of the Financial Services Act 1986 or in respect of which the company has been given *facilities for them to be dealt in* on that investment exchange without prior permission for individual transactions: s. 163(3).

Section 166 prescribes the following rules for a market purchase by a company of its own shares:

(*a*) The purchase must first be authorized by a resolution of the company: s. 166(1).

(*b*) The authority conferred by the resolution may be either conditional or unconditional and either general or limited to a particular class or type of share: s. 166(2).

(*c*) The authority must:

   (*i*)   specify the maximum number of shares which may be acquired;

   (*ii*) state the maximum and minimum price which may be paid for them; and

   (*iii*) specify its date of expiry which may not be later than 18 months after the date on which the resolution is passed: s. 166(3) and (4).

(*d*) The authority may be varied, revoked or renewed by resolution of the company: s. 166(4).

(*e*) Any resolution must be filed under s. 380: s. 166(7) (*see* 15:**41**).

This provision is necessary because the resolution is an *ordinary* one and there would not otherwise be any requirement to file it.

29. Assignment or release of company's right to purchase its own shares. Section 167(1) provides that a company's rights under any contract approved under s. 164 or s. 165 (*see* **26, 27**) or authorized under s. 166 (*see* **28**) cannot be *assigned*.

Further, s. 167(2) provides that any agreement by a company to *release* its rights under a contract approved under s. 164 or s. 165 is *void* unless the release is approved in advance in accordance with the following rules:

(*a*) Before the company enters into the release agreement its terms must be authorized by special resolution.

(*b*) All the rules in s. 164 given in **26**(*a*)–(*e*) above apply again in exactly the same way.

30. Payments by company other than purchase price. Section 168 applies where a company makes any payment in consideration of:

(*a*) *acquiring* a right under a contingent purchase contract;

(*b*) the *variation* of a contract for an off-market purchase or a contingent purchase contract; *or*

(*c*) the *release* of any of its obligations under a contract for an off-market purchase, a contingent purchase contract, or a contract for a market purchase.

In all three cases s. 168(1) requires the payment to be made out of the company's *distributable profits*.

If the company fails to comply with this rule any purchase of shares falling under (*a*) or (*b*) above will be unlawful and any release falling under (*c*) will be *void*: s. 168(2).

31. Disclosure of purchases and authorized contracts. Section 169(1) requires a company to file with the registrar, within 28 days from the date on which any shares purchased were delivered to the company, a *return* stating:

(*a*) the number and nominal value of the shares purchased; and

(*b*) the date on which they were delivered to the company.

In the case of a *public* company, s. 169(2) requires the return to state also:

(*a*) the total amount paid by the company for the shares; and

(*b*) the maximum and minimum prices paid for the shares of each class purchased.

Section 169(4) requires a company to keep for 10 years at its registered office:

(*a*) a copy of any contract approved under s. 164 or s. 165 or authorized under s. 166, if in writing, *or*

(*b*) if not in writing, a memorandum of its terms.

Under s. 169(5) every copy and memorandum must be open to inspection to any member of the company and, in the case of a public company, to the public. If inspection is refused, the court may order that it be allowed: s. 169(8).

32. Effect of company's failure to redeem or purchase its own

shares. Section 178(1) and (2) provides that where a company issues redeemable shares or agrees to purchase any of its own shares, it will not be liable in damages for failing to redeem or purchase them, as the case may be.

Any other rights which the shareholder may have are expressly preserved by the section, although his position is further weakened by s. 178(3) which prevents the court from granting an order for specific performance of the redemption or purchase terms if the company shows that it is unable to meet the cost of the redemption or purchase out of distributable profits.

33. Power of private company to redeem or purchase its own shares out of capital. The rules contained in the Act as to the issue of redeemable shares and purchase by a company of its own shares are considerably less stringent in the case of private companies. Section 171(1) permits a private company, with authority in its articles, to make a payment in respect of a redemption of its shares under s. 160 (*see* **24**) or a purchase of its shares under s. 162 (*see* **25**) *otherwise* than out of its distributable profits or the proceeds of a fresh issue, i.e. the payment may be made out of *capital*.

The amount payable out of capital is termed the *permissible capital payment*: s. 171(3). This is the amount which, together with any available profits and the proceeds of a fresh issue of shares made for the purpose of the redemption or purchase, is equal to the price of redemption or purchase, as the case may be: s. 171(3). Thus it appears that if there are no available profits and no fresh issue is made, the *whole* of the price of redemption or purchase can be paid out of capital.

If the permissible capital payment is *less* than the nominal amount of the shares redeemed or purchased, the amount of the difference must be *transferred* to the capital redemption reserve: s. 171(4). If it is *more*, the amount of the capital redemption reserve, share premium account or fully paid share capital (i.e. the capital in the legal sense: *see* **5**) and any amount representing unrealized profits arising on a revaluation of fixed assets (i.e. the revaluation reserve: *see* para. 34 of the 4th Schedule) may be *reduced* by the amount of the difference: s. 171(5).

34. Procedure required for private company for redemption or purchase out of capital. Under s. 173(1) a private company may not take advantage of the privilege afforded to it by s. 171 unless it complies with the requirements of ss. 173–175. These are as follows:

(*a*) The payment out of capital must be approved by special resolution: s. 173(2).

(*b*) The directors must make a statutory declaration specifying the amount of the permissible capital payment and stating that, after a full inquiry into the company's affairs and prospects, they have formed the opinion:

(*i*) as regards its initial situation immediately after the date of the proposed payment, that there will be no grounds on which it could then be found unable to pay its debts; *and*

(*ii*) as regards its prospects for the year following that date, that it will be able to carry on business as a going concern and pay its debts as they fall due throughout that year: s. 173(3).

(*c*) The statutory declaration must contain the prescribed information with respect to the nature of the company's business and have annexed to it an auditors' report addressed to the directors stating that:

(*i*) they have inquired into the company's state of affairs; *and*

(*ii*) the amount specified in the statutory declaration as the permissible capital payment is in their view properly determined; *and*

(*iii*) they are not aware of anything to indicate that the directors' opinion stated in the declaration is unreasonable: s. 173(5).

(*d*) The resolution must be passed on the date on which the directors make the statutory declaration, or within the following week: s. 174(1).

(*e*) The payment out of capital must be made not less than five nor more than seven weeks after the date of the resolution: s. 174(1).

(*f*) No special resolution will be effective if any member who holds shares to which it relates exercises the voting rights attached to them and the resolution would not have been passed if he had not done so: s. 174(2).

(*g*) No special resolution will be effective unless the statutory declaration and the auditors' report are available for inspection by members at the meeting at which the resolution is passed: s. 174(4).

(*h*) Within a week after the date of the resolution the company must publish a notice in the *Gazette* stating:

(*i*) that the company has approved a payment out of capital for the purposes of the redemption or purchase of its shares;

(*ii*) the amount of the permissible capital payment and the date of the resolution;

(*iii*) that the statutory declaration and the auditors' report are available for inspection at the registered office; *and*

(*iv*) that any creditor of the company may at any time within the five weeks after the date of the resolution apply to the court under s. 176 (*see* **35**) for an order prohibiting the payment: s. 175(1).

(*i*) Within a week after the date of the resolution the company must *either* publish a similar notice in an appropriate national newspaper *or* give notice in writing to that effect to each creditor: s. 175(2).

(*j*) Not later than the first notice date the company must deliver a copy of the statutory declaration and the auditors' report to the registrar: s. 175(5).

(*k*) The statutory declaration and auditors' report must be kept at the registered office from the first notice date until five weeks after the date of the resolution and must be open to the inspection of any member or creditor without charge: s. 175(6).

If inspection is refused, the court may order that it be allowed: s. 175(8).

35. Objections by members or creditors to redemption or purchase out of capital.

Where a private company passes a special resolution approving a payment out of capital for the redemption or purchase of its own shares, s. 176(1) permits any member who did not vote in favour of the resolution and any creditor of the company to apply to the court within five weeks of the date when it was passed for its cancellation.

Under s. 176(2) those entitled to make such an application may appoint one or more of their number to make it on their behalf. If an application is made, s. 176(3) requires the company to inform the registrar immediately and to deliver to him an office copy of the court order within 15 days from when it was made.

The court may confirm or cancel the resolution or adjourn the proceedings in order that an arrangement may be made for the purchase of the interests of dissentient members or the protection of dissentient creditors: s. 177(1) and (2).

The court order may provide for the purchase by the company of the shares of any members and for the resulting reduction of capital. It can also make any alteration to the memorandum or articles which are thereby rendered necessary and prohibit the company from making subsequent alterations to these documents. The company may then make such alterations only with the leave of the court: s. 177(3)–(5).

36. Liability of past members and directors in respect of redemption or purchase out of capital. Section 76(1) and (2) Insolvency Act 1986 provides that where a company is being wound up within a year from the date when it made a payment out of capital for the redemption or purchase of its own shares, and has not sufficient assets to pay its debts and the costs of winding up, the following persons are liable to contribute towards the deficiency:

(a) any person from whom the shares were redeemed or purchased; and

(b) any director who signed the statutory declaration, unless he can show that he had reasonable grounds for his opinion.

Under s. 76(3) of that Act a person falling under (a) above is liable to contribute to the company's assets up to the amount paid to him out of capital on his shares and the directors are jointly and severally liable with him.

Finally, under s. 124(3) Insolvency Act 1986 any person who is liable under s. 76 of that Act to contribute to the company's assets in a winding up may petition the court for a winding up order under s. 122(1) (f) or (g) of that Act, in addition to any other right to petition which he may have as a contributory of the company in the usual sense (see 30:1, 4).

Progress test 11

1. What do you understand by:

(a) the authorized capital?
(b) the issued capital?
(c) the unpaid capital?
(d) the reserve capital? (2, 3)

2. What is the difference between:

(*a*) a provision and a reserve?

(*b*) a capital reserve and a revenue reserve? (**4**)

3. What are the statutory capital reserves? Discuss their purpose. (**5, 24, 25**)

4. What is a class right? (**7**)

5. What is a preference share? Explain what is meant by the terms:

(*a*) cumulative and non-cumulative;

(*b*) participating and non-participating. (**8**)

6. How far are arrears of dividend on preference shares payable in the event of liquidation? (**9**)

7. What are:

(*a*) founders' shares? (**11**)

(*b*) management shares? (**11**)

(*c*) no par value shares? (**12**)

8. What criticisms are made of the rule that shares must have a par value? (**12**)

9. How may class rights be altered? (**14–16**)

10. How may a company alter its share capital? (**18, 21**)

11. What is stock? Discuss its advantages. (**19**)

12. What special rules apply where a public company incurs a serious loss of capital? (**20, 23**)

13. How may a company reduce its share capital? (**21**)

14. In what cases may a company's creditors object to a reduction of capital? (**22**)

15. Under what conditions may a company issue redeemable shares? (**24**)

16. Give a number of reasons why it may be beneficial for a company to buy its own shares. (**25**)

17. Under what conditions may a company purchase its own shares? (**25**)

18. What special rules apply to an off-market purchase by a company of its own shares? (**26**)

19. What special rules apply to a contingent purchase contract? (**27**)

20. What special rules apply to a market purchase by a company of its own shares? (**28**)

21. How far can a company either assign or release its right to buy its own shares? (**29**)

22. State the statutory provisions governing the disclosure of purchases by a company of its own shares. (**31**)

23. What is the effect of a company's failure to redeem or purchase its own shares when it is under an obligation to do so? (**32**)

24. What special rules apply to a *private* company which wishes to buy its own shares? (**33–36**)

12

Shares

1. The nature of a share. Section 182(1) provides that shares are personal property and that they are transferable in the manner laid down by the articles. Section 182(2), as was explained in 11:**19**, requires each share to be numbered, except where all the shares in a company, or all those of a particular class, are fully paid up and rank *pari passu* for all purposes. The remainder of the sections on shares deal with transfer, share certificates and share warrants, and will be discussed later in this chapter.

None of these provisions is very helpful in telling us what a share is. It follows from s. 182(1), of course, that a share is a chose in action, since personal property consists of chattels real (leaseholds) and chattels personal, and chattels personal in their turn consist of choses in possession (tangible things such as goods) and choses in action (intangible things such as debts, contractual rights and patents). Clearly a share is intangible, its ownership being evidenced by a document called a *share certificate*. But if we were to try to describe it in these terms, no-one would have much conception of what we were discussing.

Probably the best description of a share is not given in the Act at all, but in *Borland's Trustee* v. *Steel Brothers & Co. Ltd* (1901), by Farwell J.: 'A share is the interest of a shareholder in the company measured by a sum of money, for the purpose of liability in the first place, and of interest in the second'. This definition indicates the true position of the member: he is under a *liability* to the company, namely to pay for his shares on application, allotment, or when called upon to do so; but also he has an *interest* in the company which confers upon him certain rights, such as voting and dividend rights, and attendance at meetings. His interest is something he *owns*, so that he owns in reality a non-identified part of the company's undertaking. This is sometimes expressed by saying that the shareholders own the company, but of course no legal person can own another legal person. What the shareholders really own, collectively, is the entire undertaking of the company which, for convenience, is vested in the person of the company as soon as it is incorporated. It will readily be seen why it is sometimes said that the company is the *agent* of the shareholders.

2. Transfer of shares. A transfer of shares is simply a *voluntary assignment* and occurs, for example, where the shareholder sells his shares to another person or where he gives them away. In all cases of transfer s. 183(1) requires that a *proper instrument of transfer* must be delivered to the company. The word 'instrument' simply means a document, i.e. the transfer must be in writing. A deed is not necessary unless the articles require one, and Table A, Article 23, does not do so.

The effect of s. 183(1) is that an instrument of transfer is essential. An article, therefore, which attempts to provide for the *automatic* transfer of shares in the company to any particular person on the death of a member is illegal and void, for on death the legal ownership of the shares passes automatically to the personal representatives by transmission: *Re Greene* (1949). On the other hand an article which provides that on the death of a member his shares must be offered to certain other persons is valid, and will bind the personal representatives accordingly, for no avoidance of s. 183(1) is involved: *Jarvis Motors (Harrow) Ltd* v. *Carabott* (1964).

3. Form of transfer. At one time the instrument of transfer had to be executed both by the transferor and by the transferee and their signatures had to be witnessed. The Stock Transfer Act 1963, however, introduced a simplified 'stock transfer form' for fully paid shares. Such an instrument is signed by the transferor only, and need not be witnessed. The Act overrides any provision to the contrary in the company's articles.

Additional forms became permissible under the Stock Transfer (Addition of Forms) Order 1979 (S.I. 1979, No. 277), made under authority of the 1963 Act. These were introduced for the computerized 'Talisman' system of transfers on the stock exchange, and are the 'Talisman sold transfer', for use where shares are transferred to a 'stock exchange nominee', and the 'Talisman bought transfer', for use where shares are transferred from a 'stock exchange nominee'.

By s. 185(4) Companies Act 1985 'stock exchange nominee' means a person designated by statutory instrument as a nominee of the stock exchange, and by the Stock Exchange (Designation of Nominees) Order 1985 (S.I. 1985, No. 806) SEPON Ltd is designated as a nominee of the stock exchange.

Table A, Article 24, provides that the directors may refuse to register a transfer unless:

(a) it is lodged at the registered office or at such other place as the directors may appoint;

(b) it is accompanied by the share certificate;

(c) it is in respect of only one class of share; and

(d) it is in favour of not more than four transferees.

Section 183(4) states that on the application of the *transferor* of shares the company must enter the name of the transferee in the register of members in the same way as if the application for entry were made by the *transferee*.

4. Certification of transfers. Where a shareholder transfers only *some* of his shares in a company, it would be unsafe for him to part with the share certificate for his entire holding to the transferee. He therefore sends it to the company, which endorses the instrument of transfer with the words 'certificate lodged', returns it to the transferor, but retains the share certificate. This process is known as certification of the transfer.

The transferor then sends the certified instrument of transfer to the transferee, who applies to the company for registration. The company issues two new share certificates, one to the transferor to cover the shares which he continues to own, and one to the transferee to cover the shares he has acquired.

If the company is negligent and sends the transferor's original certificate for the entire holding back to him, it is not liable for any fraudulent act which he is able to do as a result, for that is *his* act and not that of the company.

5. The legal effect of certification. Section 184(1) states that the certification of a transfer amounts simply to a representation by the company that documents have been produced to it showing that the transferor has a *prima facie* title to the shares. The subsection carefully amplifies this by going on to say what certification is not: it is not a representation that the transferor has a title.

Thus, when the certification of a transfer is effected, the company is merely saying that it has seen a share certificate which appears to be in order, though it is *not* saying that it is in order. For the company to guarantee the title of the transferor would be to put altogether too heavy a burden on it.

NOTE: Naturally, if the company makes a *fraudulent* certification, i.e. with the intention to deceive, it will be liable for deceit. If, however, it makes a false certification *negligently*, there was at one time no liability at common law for negligent mis-statements. Section 184(2) covers this possibility by providing that a company should be under the same liability for a negligent certification as for a fraudulent one. Possibly today this provision is no longer necessary, for it is arguable that the company and the transferee are in a 'special relationship' within the principle laid down in *Hedley Byrne & Co. Ltd* v. *Heller & Partners Ltd* (1964), and that the common law would now cover the position.

6. Restrictions on transfer. Subject to the articles, shares may be freely transferred to any person provided the correct stamp duty is paid. Since 27 October 1986 the rate of stamp duty on share purchases has been one-half of one per cent. For administrative convenience, however, the articles sometimes provide for the suspension of the registration of transfers for a short time each year in order to enable dividend lists to be prepared. Table A, Article 26, contains such a provision, which must necessarily be within the period laid down by s. 358, i.e. not more than 30 days in the year. But not all companies take advantage of s. 358, and there are many which do not close their books at all.

(*a*) *Private companies:* Before the Companies Act 1980 a company could not satisfy the definition of a private company unless its articles contained a restriction of some kind on the transfer of its shares. Even now it is probable that private companies will normally find it desirable to continue to include restrictions on the transfer of shares in their articles.

(*b*) *Public companies:* Often there are restrictions on transfer in *public* companies, although in this case the stock exchange will not grant a listing for the shares if they are fully paid. Table A, Article 24, provides that the directors may refuse to register the transfer of *partly paid* shares to a person of whom they do not approve. Were it not for such a restriction, a member could transfer his shares to a 'man of straw' simply for the purpose of avoiding liability for the next call on them. Article 24 also provides that the directors may refuse to register a transfer of any share on which the company has a lien. Where a company exercises its power of sale of shares over which it has a lien (*see* **31**), it is subject to the same restrictions on transfer as would have applied to the shareholder himself under the company's articles: *Champagne Perrier-Jouet S.A.* v. *H. H. Finch Ltd* (1982).

7. The exercise of the company's power to refuse registration. The company's power to refuse registration of a transfer is, under Article 24 of Table A, exercised by the board of directors, but unless they actively exercise it the transferee must be registered. Thus there must be a *majority* of the board *opposing* the registration in order to constitute exercise of the power.

It follows that if the board are evenly divided with no casting vote, the transfer must be registered: *Re Hackney Pavilion Ltd* (1924). And if one of two directors intentionally fails to attend a board meeting so that the quorum of two will not be reached and accordingly transfers cannot be passed for registration, the transferee must, again, be registered: *Re Copal Varnish Co.* (1917). Moreover, the board's power to refuse registration of a transfer must be exercised within a reasonable time, or it will be lost: *Re Swaledale Cleaners Ltd* (1968).

So long as the directors act within the scope of the article, their decision cannot be challenged except on the grounds of bad faith. Since the onus of proving bad faith rests on the plaintiff, the directors' refusal to register the transfer can seldom be successfully attacked, for while a state of mind may be a fact, it is a fact which is exceedingly difficult to prove.

Thus in *Charles Forte Investments* v. *Amanda* (1964), the articles gave the directors power to refuse to register transfers 'in their absolute discretion and without assigning any reason'. They refused, giving no reason, to register a transfer by a former employee and minor shareholder who had quarrelled with one of the directors. He threatened to present a petition for winding up the company, whereupon the company applied for an injunction to prevent him from doing so. HELD: (*a*) the injunction should be granted, since the winding up would injure other members who were in no way responsible for the situation; (*b*) the directors were acting within the scope of the articles, unless bad faith could be proved, which it could not.

The articles may, of course, be more specific than they were in the *Forte* case; they may empower the directors to refuse to register transfers on certain specified grounds. The directors can then be interrogated as to the grounds for their refusal. But whether the article is widely phrased or narrowly expressed, they need show only that they were acting within its terms. They need give no reasons for their decision beyond this. If, on the other hand, they are foolish enough to give their reasons, then the court may consider whether those reasons were adequate. This is one of many legal situations in which the less that is said the less likelihood there is of liability.

Section 183(5) and Table A, Article 25, both provide that notice of a refusal to register a transfer must be sent to the transferee within two months from the date when the transfer was lodged with the company. If the transferee wishes to challenge the refusal, he should apply to the court for rectification of the register under s. 359.

8. Forged transfers. A forged document never has any legal effect. It can never move ownership from one person to another, however genuine it may appear. Thus a forged instrument of transfer leaves the ownership of the shares exactly where it always was: in the so-called transferor.

It follows that if the company registers a forged transfer, the true owner can apply to be replaced on the register. At the same time if the company has issued a new share certificate to a subsequent purchaser, it cannot, as will be seen later, deny his title to the shares, for the certificate estops it from doing so. It will therefore be under a liability to compensate him for his loss: *Re Bahia and San Francisco Railway* (1868).

In order to avoid this result, companies normally notify the transferor of the transfer so that he can object if he wishes, but such a notification does not enable the company to escape liability if in fact it registers a forged transfer and causes loss to a transferee. Nor is it always of much use to the company, for the transferor may be abroad at the time, or not trouble to reply.

The Forged Transfers Acts 1891–2, however, permit the company to form a fund out of which to pay compensation for forged transfers, and it is always possible for a company to insure against the risk.

If the company is compelled to pay compensation, it can claim an indemnity from the person who sent the forged transfer, even though that person was unaware of the forgery: *Sheffield Corporation* v. *Barclay* (1905). Moreover, that person, however innocent, cannot rely on a share certificate issued to him as an estoppel preventing the company from denying his title.

9. Share certificates. Section 185(1) states that a company must have the share certificate ready for delivery within two months after the allotment or the lodging of the transfer, unless the terms of issue of the shares otherwise provide. It imposes no requirements as regards the form of the certificate. In the case of listed companies, stock exchange rules require certificates to be ready for delivery within two weeks.

Table A, Article 6, however, requires the certificate to be under seal and to specify both the shares to which it relates and the amount paid up on them. Article 7 provides that if a share certificate is defaced, worn-out, lost or destroyed, it may be renewed on such terms as to evidence and indemnity, and payment of expenses reasonably incurred by the company in investigating evidence, as the directors may decide, but otherwise free of charge, and, in the case of defacement or wearing-out, on delivery up of the old certificate.

10. Legal effect of share certificates. Section 186 states that a share certificate under the common seal of the company specifying the shares held by the member is *prima facie evidence of his title to them*. It is important to understand the legal effect of this provision:

(*a*) *A share certificate is not a negotiable instrument*, for its transfer from one person to another does not move the ownership of the shares. To move the ownership, as we have seen, an instrument of transfer must be completed, lodged with the company, and approved by the directors, after which the transferee must be entered on the register. It is this final act of entry on the register which completes the shift of ownership. The physical whereabouts of the share *certificate* is legally immaterial even though it may be administratively inconvenient. If lost, damaged, or destroyed, it must be renewed. But whatever has happened to it and wherever it is, the legal title to the shares is in the registered holder.

(*b*) *Evidence of title*. All that the share certificate amounts to, then, is a statement by the company that *at the moment when it was issued* the person named on it was the legal owner of the shares specified in it, and that those shares were paid up to the extent stated. It does not constitute title but is merely evidence of title. It is, however, a statement of considerable importance for it is made with the knowledge that other persons may act upon it in the belief that it is true, and this fact brings into operation the doctrine of *estoppel*.

(c) *Estoppel* is not a principle of substantive law. It is a *rule of evidence which prevents a person from denying the legal implications of his conduct*. If he has behaved in a certain way, and if other persons have drawn certain natural and reasonable deductions from that behaviour as to his legal position, then he is not allowed to give evidence to show that his legal position is not in fact what it appeared to be. A company, therefore, is not allowed to deny the facts which it has stated to be true when it issued the share certificate.

This rule is expressed by saying that the share certificate acts as an estoppel against the company as regards:

(i) the title of the member: *Dixon* v. *Kennaway & Co.* (1900); and

(ii) the amount paid up on the shares: *Bloomenthal* v. *Ford* (1897).

The company, once it has issued the certificate, may not deny these facts, except, as stated above, against a person who sent in a forged transfer, or where the certificate itself is a forgery: *Ruben* v. *Great Fingall Consolidated* (1906).

11. The rights of a transferee. It will be apparent from the preceding pages of this chapter that there is of necessity a certain interval of time between the *contract* to sell a shareholding and the *registration* of the transferee. During this period the transferee clearly has certain rights, but his exact legal position is far from clear. It can be most easily considered if a transfer is divided into stages.

The first stage in a sale of shares is the *contract of sale*. If the vendor breaks this contract, the would-be purchaser has a right to damages for breach of contract, calculated on the normal basis, wherever damages would be an adequate remedy. However, if he is trying to buy shares in a private company, or if the shares in question are not readily available on the market, damages will be quite useless. In this case he may seek a decree of specific performance: *Duncuft* v. *Albrecht* (1841). He is then often said to have an *equitable interest* in the shares and indeed he has an interest which equity protects; nevertheless, it is an equitable interest of a qualified nature, for the only right which it confers on the purchaser is the 'right to enforce the contract in proceedings for specific performance': *Oughtred* v. *Inland Revenue Commissioners* (1960).

The second stage in a sale of shares – and the first stage of a gift – is the completion of an instrument of transfer by the transferor. This in itself confers no further rights on a purchaser, at least where the vendor is still unpaid: *Musselwhite* v. *Musselwhite & Son Ltd* (1962). A donee has no rights at all.

The third stage in a sale – and the second stage of a gift – is the delivery of an executed instrument of transfer accompanied by the relevant share certificate to the purchaser or donee, as the case may be. At this point the transferor has done all that he can do. The only remaining thing to be done in order to perfect the transferee's title is an act of the *company*, not of the transferor – namely, the entry of the transferee's name in the register of members. It has been held that the completion of this stage is the true moment of gift: *Re Rose* (1951). From this moment onwards the transferee has a full beneficial interest in the shares and the transferor holds them on trust for him until registration is effected. Thus the benefits attached to the shares, such as dividends, belong in equity to the transferee, while the exercise of the transferor's voting rights are controlled by the transferee.

The parties to the transaction can of course modify these rules as they wish. They can, for instance, agree that the shares are to be sold 'cum' (with) dividend or 'ex' (without) dividend, and the price paid for the shares will vary accordingly. The vendor can also agree to sell 'with registration guaranteed', the effect of which is to make the eventual registration of the purchaser a *condition* of the contract, failure of which gives the purchaser the right to recover his money. If registration is not expressly guaranteed in this way, the purchaser has no remedy against the vendor if the company, under the appropriate provisions in its articles, lawfully refuses to register the transfer. He will simply continue to own the *equitable interest* in the shares while the *legal title* remains in the vendor. The rules concerning equitable interests are more fully explained later (*see* 14:**8–14**).

The final stage of a transfer, whether by sale or gift, is the company's entry of the transferee in its register of members. This is the moment at which the *legal title* to the shares passes from the transferor to the transferee, and the transaction is now complete.

12. The register of interests in shares. The register of interests in shares was introduced into company law by the Companies Act 1967. Far more detailed rules became applicable under the Companies Act 1981 and these now form Part VI (ss. 198–220) Companies Act 1985.

Section 211(1) and (3) requires every *public* company to keep a register for the purposes of ss. 198–202 and, whenever it receives information under these sections, to inscribe it within three days in the register against the name of the person concerned, together with the date of the inscription. Under s. 211(2) the same rule applies where a company is notified that a person has ceased to be a party to an agreement to which s. 204 applies (*see* **20**).

In computing the three days, Saturdays, Sundays and bank holidays are to be disregarded: s. 220(2).

Section 211(4) prevents the company from becoming concerned in any question regarding a person's rights relating to shares. The section is imposing merely an administrative duty and the company must be protected from further involvement: cf. s. 360 (*see* 14:**12**) and s. 325 and para. 24 of the 13th Schedule (*see* 16:**17**).

Section 211(5) requires the register to be made up so that the entries against each name are in chronological order. Unless it is already in the form of an index, s. 211(6) requires the company to keep an index of the names inscribed in it which must indicate how the information with respect to each name may be readily found. Under s. 211(8) both the register and any index must be kept at the same place as the register of directors' interests (*see* 16:**13**) and, under ss. 211(8) and 219(1), be open for at least two hours a day during business hours to the inspection of any person without charge.

Section 219(2) authorizes any person to require a copy of the register, or any part of it, on payment of the prescribed fee not exceeding ten pence for every 100 words. The copy must be supplied within 10 days. If inspection is refused, or a copy not sent within the 10 days, the court may order that inspection be allowed or the copy sent: s. 219(4).

Finally, if a company ceases to be a public company and so is no longer governed by s. 211, it is required by s. 211(7) to keep the register and any index for six years.

13. Removal of entries from register of interests in shares. Section 218(1) prohibits a company from deleting any entry in its register of interests in shares unless it complies with the rules laid down in s. 217. If a company disregards this prohibition, the deleted entry must be restored to the register as soon as possible: s. 218(2).

Under s. 217(1) a company may remove an entry from its register only when more than six years have elapsed since the date of its inscription, and *either*:

(*a*) it recorded the fact that the person in question had *ceased* to have a notifiable interest in the company's relevant share capital under s. 198; *or*

(*b*) it has been superseded by a later entry inscribed under s. 211 against that person's name.

In the case of (*a*) above, the company may remove from the register not only the entry, but also the person's name.

Section 217(2) provides that where a person, in pursuance of a statutory obligation, gives a company the name and address of some other person as being interested in its shares, the company must within 15 days notify that other person that he has been so named and include:

(*a*) particulars of any entry made in the register as a result of the information given; and

(*b*) a statement informing him of his right to apply to have the entry removed in accordance with the section.

The right to apply for removal of the entry is given by s. 217(3). The application must be in writing and the company must remove the entry if it is satisfied that the information on which it was based was incorrect.

Section 217(4) deals with a person who appears in the register as a party to an agreement under s. 204 and who ceases to be such a party. He too may apply in writing for that fact to be recorded in the register and the company must comply.

If a company refuses an application under either of these subsections, s. 217(5) entitles the applicant to apply to the court for an order directing the company to remove the entry or record the information, as the case may be, and the court may make such an order if it thinks fit.

Lastly, where a person's name is removed from the register under s. 217(1), (3) or (5), any necessary alteration in the index must be made within 14 days: s. 217(6).

14. Notifiable interests. It is clear from **12** above that certain interests in shares must be notified to the company and entered in its register.

Section 208 deals with the question of which interests are caught by the Act and are therefore notifiable.

Section 208(2) shows that the scope of the provisions is intended to be very wide, for it provides that an interest *of any kind whatsoever* in shares is notifiable. Accordingly, while s. 209(1)(*a*) excludes a person who is a *bare trustee* of an interest in shares, since he has no enjoyment of it, a *beneficiary* under the trust has a notifiable interest: s. 208(3).

Further, under s. 208(4) and (5), a person will be taken to have a notifiable interest in shares if:

(*a*) he enters into a contract to buy them; *or*

(*b*) although not the registered holder, he is entitled to exercise or control the exercise of any right conferred by the holding; *or*

(*c*) he has a right to call for their delivery to himself or to his order, whether absolute or conditional; *or*

(*d*) he has a right to acquire, or is under an obligation to take, an interest in them, whether absolute or conditional.

Finally, s. 208(7) states that persons with a joint interest shall be taken each to have that interest, while s. 208(8) states that it is immaterial if the shares in which a person has an interest are unidentifiable.

15. Family and corporate interests. An interest may be notifiable not only when held by a particular person himself, but also when it is held by a member of his family or by a company which he controls.

Section 203(1) and (2) provides that a person must be taken to be interested in any shares:

(*a*) in which his spouse or infant child or step-child is interested; *or*

(*b*) if a company is interested in them and:

(*i*) that company or its directors are accustomed to act in accordance with his directions; *or*

(*ii*) he is entitled to exercise or control the exercise of one-third or more of the voting power at general meetings.

Section 203(3) goes even further along the same path, providing in effect that if Smith has one-third of the voting power in A Company and A Company has one-third of the voting power in B Company,

Smith is taken to be interested in shares held by B Company, as well as those held by A Company.

16. Meaning of 'relevant share capital' and 'notifiable percentage'. Although, as explained in **14** and **15**, the word 'interest' is given a wide meaning by the Act so that any interest held by a person, his immediate family, or a company which he controls, will as a rule be notifiable, the duty to notify does not extend to interests in any type of share nor of any size. Section 199(1) imposes a duty to notify the company only where the interest is in *relevant share capital*, while s. 199(2) requires it to be a minimum size, termed the *notifiable percentage*.

These expressions must therefore be considered. They are clarified by the Act as follows:

(*a*) Section 198(2) defines *relevant share capital* as the issued share capital carrying the *right to vote* in all circumstances at general meetings.

(*b*) Section 201(1) provides that the *notifiable percentage* is 5 per cent, although under s. 201(2) the Secretary of State is at any time empowered to prescribe another figure.

Where the relevant share capital is divided into different classes of shares, s. 198(2) makes it clear that 5 per cent of any *class* will be a notifiable percentage, since the percentage is based on the nominal value of each class taken separately.

17. Obligation to notify known interests in voting shares. Section 198 imposes on a person with a notifiable interest in a notifiable percentage of the relevant share capital of a public company an obligation to notify the company. Under ss. 198(1) and 202(1) and (2) where he:

(*a*) knowingly acquires or ceases to hold such an interest; *or*

(*b*) becomes aware that he has acquired or has ceased to hold such an interest;

he must notify the company in writing within five days, specifying the share capital concerned, and *either*:

(*a*) stating the number of shares in which he knows he had an interest immediately after the obligation to notify arose; *or*

(b) stating that he has ceased to hold an interest.

In computing the period of five days, Saturdays, Sundays and bank holidays are disregarded under s. 220(2) and the period runs, under s. 202(1), from the day after that on which the obligation to notify arose.

18. Time when obligation to notify arises. In order to see when the obligation to notify arises, it is first necessary to understand the meaning given to the term 'relevant time'. This is defined in s. 198(4) as the time of *the event or change of circumstances* mentioned in s. 198(1)(a), or the time when the person in question *acquires the knowledge* mentioned in s. 198(1)(b) (*see* **17**).

Under s. 199(4) and (5) the obligation to notify arises *either*:

(a) where such person has a notifiable interest immediately after the relevant time, but did not have one immediately before that time; *or*

(b) he had a notifiable interest immediately before the relevant time, but does not have one immediately after that time; *or*

(c) he has a notifiable interest both immediately before and immediately after the relevant time, but the percentage levels are not the same.

19. Particulars of registered holders. Further particulars which must be stated in any notification to the company under s. 198 are given in s. 202.

Section 202(3) requires the notification to include:

(a) the identity of each registered holder of any shares concerned; *and*

(b) the number of those shares held by each registered holder;

in so far as they are known to the person making the notification on the date when he makes it. He must also, under s. 202(4), notify the company within five days of any subsequent change in these particulars of which he becomes aware.

20. Notification of interests of persons acting together. Much criticism has long been levelled at persons who evade the disclosure rules by acquiring separately small quantities of shares, having previously agreed to combine their holdings at a suitable date. Such persons are often described as 'acting in concert' and the expression 'concert party' is used to indicate this type of agreement.

Sections 204–206 are directed at this kind of activity, the persons engaged in it being described as 'acting together'. Under s. 204(1) and (2) an agreement is caught by s. 204 if it is made between two or more persons and:

(a)   it includes provision for the acquisition by any of them of interests in shares in a particular public company, described as the *target company*;

(b)   it imposes obligations or restrictions on any of them concerning the *use, retention or disposal* of those interests; *and*

(c)   an interest in that company's shares is in fact acquired by any of them in pursuance of the agreement.

Section 204(6) provides that the section does not apply to any agreement which is not legally binding, unless it involves *mutuality* in the undertakings, expectations or understandings of the parties. Underwriting agreements are also excluded from its scope.

Where an agreement is subject to the section s. 205(4) applies, requiring any notification of his interest in shares in the target company made to that company under s. 198 by a person who is a party to the agreement to:

(a)   state that he is such a party;

(b)   include the names and, if known, the addresses of the other parties to the agreement; *and*

(c)   state whether or not any of the shares mentioned in the notification are covered by the agreement and, if so, their number.

Conversely, if a person is making a notification to the company under s. 198 that he has *ceased* to have an interest in its shares owing to the fact that he or some other person has ceased to be a party to an agreement governed by s. 204, the notification must include a statement to that effect and, where applicable, the name and address of that other person: s. 205(5).

21. Obligation of parties to a s. 204 agreement to notify each other. Where a person who is a party to an agreement caught by s. 204 knows:

(a)   that the target company is a public company;

(b) that the shares covered by the agreement are relevant share capital; *and*

(c) that the agreement is caught by s. 204;

he must within five days notify in writing every other party to it of any interest which he holds in the relevant share capital (*see* **16**) of the target company *independently of the agreement*: s. 206(1), (2) and (8).

Under s. 206(3) and (4) the notice must state:

(a) the number of shares in which he would be required to disclose his interest if it were notifiable under s. 198, apart from the agreement;

(b) particulars of the registered holders of those shares, if known to him; *and*

(c) particulars of the registered holders of any relevant share capital of the target company in which he has a notifiable interest apart from the agreement, and any change in them.

Further, s. 206(6) requires any party to a s. 204 agreement to notify in writing every other party of his current address and any change in it.

22. Power of company to require information concerning interests in its shares. Under s. 212(1), (2) and (4) a *public* company may serve notice in writing on any person whom it knows, or has reasonable cause to believe, to hold or to have held at any time during the *last three years* an interest in the company's relevant share capital. The notice requires him either to confirm that fact or to indicate whether or not it is the case and, if it is, to give the following information in writing within a reasonable time:

(a) particulars of his own past or present interest held at any time during the three-year period;

(b) particulars of any other interest which exists or existed at any time as his own during the three-year period, in so far as he knows them; *and*

(c) where his interest is a past interest, the identity of the person who held it immediately after him.

Under s. 212(3) the particulars required by (a) and (b) above include the identity of persons interested in the shares and whether they were parties to an agreement governed by s. 204 (*see* **20**), or to any agreement concerning the exercise of the rights conferred by the shareholding (e.g. a voting agreement).

23. Registration of interests disclosed under s. 212. Section 213(1) and (2) provides that where a company receives any information in response to its notice, it must inscribe against the name of the registered holder of the shares in question, in a *separate part* of its register of interests in shares (*see* **12**), the following matters:

(*a*) the fact that it served a notice and the date when it did so; *and*

(*b*) any information received in response which relates to the *present* interests in the shares in question held by any person.

Section 213(3) makes applicable by reference the provisions of s. 211 (*see* **12**) to this separate part of the register.

If a person on whom a notice is served fails to respond, the company may apply to the court under s. 216(1) for an order directing that the shares in question are to be subject to the restrictions imposed by Part XV (ss. 454–457) of the Act (*see* 22:**12**).

24. Exercise of company's powers under s. 212 on requisition. Section 214 (1) and (2) provides that members of a company who hold *one-tenth or more of the paid-up voting share capital* may requisition the company to exercise its powers under s. 212.

The requisition must be signed by the requisitionists and deposited at the company's registered office, and must:

(*a*) state that they are requiring the company to exercise its powers under s. 212;

(*b*) specify the manner in which they require the powers to be exercised; *and*

(*c*) give reasonable grounds for so requiring.

As soon as the requisition is deposited at the registered office, the company is under a duty to comply with it: s. 214(4). At the end of its inquiries it must prepare a report of the information received which must be available at the registered office within a reasonable time, not exceeding 15 days: s. 215(1) and (3). If the inquiries are not concluded within three months from the day after that on which the requisition was deposited, an interim report must be prepared for each period of three months which elapses. Interim reports too must be available at the registered office within a reasonable time, not exceeding 15 days: s. 215(2) and (3).

Within three days of making any report, final or interim, available at its registered office, the company must notify the requisitionists that it is there: s. 215(5). All reports must be kept at the registered office for the ensuing six years and be available for inspection during that time, under s. 215(7), in the same way as the register of interests in shares: s. 219(1).

25. Summary of statutory provisions on register of interests in shares. The Act contains such lengthy provisions on the register of interests in shares that a summary of the main points may perhaps be helpful:

(a) Only *public* companies are required to keep a register of interests in shares.

(b) 'Interest' is given a wide meaning in the expression 'notifiable interest'. Where there is a trust of shares, it includes an equitable interest but not the legal title of a bare trustee.

(c) The interests of a person's close family or of a company which he controls are regarded as his.

(d) An interest is not notifiable unless it comprises at least five per cent of the shares in question – the *notifiable percentage*.

(e) An interest is not notifiable unless the shares in question are *voting* shares – the *relevant share capital*.

(f) Persons who agree to act in concert and then proceed to do so must notify the company of their agreement.

(g) They must also notify each other of their interests in the target company, whether notifiable to the company or not, which are independent of the agreement.

(h) A company may require information from a person regarding his interest in shares, and that of any other person, during the last three years.

(i) The holders of one-tenth or more of the paid-up voting share capital may requisition the company to exercise these powers of inquiry.

26. Share warrants. Section 188(1) permits a company limited by shares to issue share warrants under its common seal provided:

(a) there is authority in the articles; and

(b) the shares are fully paid.

It also permits the company to provide for the payment of dividends on the shares included in the warrant by means of coupons.

Section 188(2) states that a share warrant entitles the bearer to the shares specified in it, and that the shares may be transferred by delivery of the warrant. It follows, therefore, that a share warrant, unlike a share certificate, *is a negotiable instrument*, and thus may be issued only by companies without restrictions on transfer in their articles.

Section 355(1) provides that on the issue of a share warrant the company must strike out of the register of members the name of the person who held the shares specified in the warrant, and enter in the register:

(a) the fact of the issue of the warrant;

(b) a statement of the shares included in the warrant, with distinguishing numbers, if any; and

(c) the date of the issue of the warrant.

Section 355(2) entitles the bearer of a share warrant to surrender it for cancellation and to have his name entered in the register in respect of the shares which were included in it.

Section 355(5) provides that the bearer of a share warrant may, if the articles so provide, be deemed to be a member of the company either to the full extent or for any purposes defined in the articles.

Section 291(2) states that a share warrant will not constitute the share qualification of a director, where one is imposed by the articles.

It will be seen in Chapter 15 that the annual return must give particulars of share warrants: s. 363(1) and the 15th Schedule. These are:

(a) the amount of shares for which warrants are outstanding;

(b) the amount of share warrants issued and surrendered since the date of the last return;

(c) the number of shares comprised in each share warrant.

Where a company has converted its shares into stock, stock warrants may be issued in exactly the same way. In practice neither share nor stock warrants are common.

27. Personation of a shareholder. The provision in the 1948 Act concerning personation of a shareholder or holder of a share warrant was repealed and superseded by the Theft Act 1968, ss. 15 and 20 of which are sufficiently widely drawn to embrace this offence.

28. Mortgage of shares. Shares, like any other form of property, may be mortgaged as security for a loan. The mortgage may be legal or equitable.

(*a*) *Legal mortgage:* Here the shares are *actually transferred* to the lender so that he becomes the registered holder with full membership rights. When the loan is repaid he transfers them back again to the borrower, with whom he has made an agreement to this effect.

Clearly this type of mortgage gives the lender complete security. He obtains the *legal* title to the shares, not merely an equitable interest in them. But it is cumbersome, liability for stamp duty will be incurred on each transfer, and if the shares are only partly paid the lender becomes personally liable for calls while his name is on the register.

(*b*) *Equitable mortgage:* Here the shares are not transferred to the lender, but the share certificate is merely deposited with him, sometimes accompanied by a *blank transfer*, i.e. an instrument of transfer signed by the borrower but with the name of the transferee left 'blank'.

In this case the lender's security is not complete, for he has merely an *equitable* interest in the shares unless he fills in the blank transfer when the borrower defaults and becomes the registered holder. He cannot inform the company that he has an equitable interest in the shares, for s. 360 states that the company may not take notice of trusts. The only way in which he can protect his interest, then, is by serving a stop notice on the company.

Equitable mortgages are more common, however, than legal mortgages, for they do not have the same disadvantages.

29. Calls. A call in the strict sense is a demand by the company for money due on the shares *excluding* the amounts payable on application, allotment or by instalments. Often the full amount of the share is payable on application, in which case the member is never liable to pay any more (with the exception of those rare cases when his liability can become unlimited). Sometimes a certain amount is payable on application and the balance on allotment or by instalments, i.e. at certain fixed dates. The date of a call, however, is not fixed until the call is made, and it will not be made until the company requires more capital.

Despite this distinction, Table A, Article 16, provides that for the purposes of Table A sums payable on allotment or at a fixed date, i.e. by instalments, shall be deemed to be calls, and all the provisions of the articles relating to calls apply to them as well.

The method of making calls depends entirely on the articles. Table A, Article 12, empowers the directors to make calls provided each member is given at least 14 days' notice of the time and place of payment. It also authorizes the directors to revoke or postpone a call if they wish.

Table A, Article 15, provides that if the member does not pay the call he must pay interest on the sum due from the date fixed for payment until he actually pays it, though the directors may waive the payment of interest. Under s. 14(2), as was explained in 3:**10**, a call is a specialty debt.

The directors' power to make calls must, like all their other powers, be exercised *bona fide* for the benefit of the company, and they may not abuse it. Thus they may not make calls on all the shareholders except themselves: *Alexander* v. *Automatic Telephone Co.* (1900), nor on one particular shareholder alone because he happens to annoy them: *Galloway* v. *Hallé Concerts Society* (1915).

Section 119, however, permits a company, with authority in its articles, to arrange on the issue of the shares for a difference between the shareholders in the amounts and times of payment of calls, and Table A, Article 17, gives the necessary authority. It is important to remember, however, that such an arrangement must be made *on issue*, and so is a term of the contract between the shareholder and the company, and that even when it exists the directors cannot avoid their duty to act in *good faith*.

Under the Finance Act 1973 capital duty of £1 per cent is payable on the amount of the calls received.

30. Payment of calls in advance. Section 119 also permits a company, with authority in its articles, to accept from a member the whole or part of the amount unpaid on his shares, even though it has not been called up. Table A, however, gives no such authority.

The advance payment, although in reality share capital, is treated as a *loan* to the company, for interest is a debt payable regardless of whether profits are available (*see* 20:**2**). Moreover, in liquidation (*see*

1:18) it must be repaid to the appropriate shareholders *after* the debts have been paid, but *before* the share capital is repaid to the shareholders generally. It cannot, however, be repaid to the shareholders while the company is a going concern, except under a reduction of capital complying with s. 135, so that in this respect it is treated as capital.

Where the articles authorize an advance payment they will also usually make it clear that the advance payment does *not* count as paid-up capital for dividend purposes. The reason for such a provision is, of course, that it would be inequitable if the advance payment carried a right to dividend as well as to interest. Once again, any power which the directors have to accept calls in advance must be exercised *bona fide*.

In *Sykes' Case* (1872), the directors, who knew that the company was insolvent, paid up the amount unpaid on their own shares in advance, and then at once applied it in payment of their own fees. HELD: They were still liable for the amount unpaid on their shares.

31. Lien. A lien, like a mortgage or pledge, is a form of security. It can arise at common law, such as the possessory lien of a repairer on the article repaired, or in equity, or under maritime law. The lien of a company on the shares of a member is an example of an equitable lien, giving the company an *equitable* interest in the shares of the member.

Apart from s. 150 (*see* below) the Act itself contains no reference to lien, but the articles of companies frequently give the company a lien on the shares of a member for money owed by him to the company. Table A, Article 8, gives the company a lien on all *partly paid* shares in respect of *money due on the shares*. This lien extends to the dividends as well.

If the member does not pay the sum which he owes to the company, the lien can be enforced by applying to the court for an order for the sale of the shares. Possibly, under the Law of Property Act 1925, this power of sale is exercisable without application to the court, but in any case the articles of the company usually give a power of sale in such circumstances. Table A, Article 9, accordingly gives the company *power to sell* any shares on which a lien exists provided:

(a) the sum in respect of which the lien exists is presently payable;

(b) written notice demanding payment has been given to the registered holder; and

(c) 14 days after the notice has expired.

Article 10 permits the directors to authorize a transfer of the shares to the purchaser, who can then be registered in respect of them. His title is not affected by any irregularity in the proceedings.

Article 11 states that the proceeds of the sale are to be applied in payment of the amount due to the company, the balance being paid to the original owner.

Since, as stated above, a lien gives the company an equitable interest, students should make sure that they fully grasp the rules relating to the priority of equitable interests explained in Chapter 14.

Section 150(1) greatly restricts the taking of a lien or other charge on its own shares by a *public* company. Such a lien or charge is *void* unless authorized by s. 150(2) which expressly permits a public company to take:

(a) a charge on its own *partly paid* shares for an amount payable in respect of them; and

(b) if it is a money-lending company, a charge on its own shares, *whether fully or partly paid*, as security in connection with a transaction entered into in the ordinary course of its business.

32. Forfeiture. When shares are forfeited the company *takes them away* from the member. This is obviously a serious step to take, for not only does it deprive the shareholder of his property but, unless the shares are re-issued, it involves a *reduction of capital* without the consent of the court and is the only example of this apart from surrender.

It is unlawful to forfeit shares unless the articles authorize it. Table A, Article 18, authorizes forfeiture for non-payment of calls and this includes, by Article 16, non-payment of sums payable at a fixed time, i.e. by instalments. Forfeiture of shares for any debt which does not arise from the shares is invalid. Consequently it has a much narrower scope than a lien.

Article 18 empowers the directors to serve a notice on the defaulting member requiring him to pay the company. It states that this notice must name a day at least 14 days ahead on or before which payment must be made, and must inform the member that unless he makes the required payment his shares will be liable to be forfeited. Article 19 empowers the directors to forfeit the shares concerned by resolution if the member does not comply with the notice.

Article 20 permits the directors to sell the forfeited shares or otherwise dispose of them as they wish. It also allows them to cancel the forfeiture up to the time when they have disposed of the shares. Where, for the purposes of its disposal, a forfeited share is to be transferred to any person, the directors may authorize some person to execute a transfer of the share to that person, who then becomes the registered holder and, by Article 22, is not bound to see to the application of the purchase-money; nor is his title affected by any irregularity in the proceedings. These provisions are similar to the provisions of Article 10 relating to sale of the shares on exercise of the company's lien.

As stated above, unless the shares are re-issued forfeiture results in a reduction of capital. Normally, therefore, the company re-issues them. It can re-issue at any price provided that the total of the *sum paid by the former holder* of the shares, together with the *amount paid on re-issue* and the *amount for which the purchaser is liable in the future* is not less than the par value for, if it were, this would be an issue at a discount. Usually it is *more* than the par value, and the excess is of course a *premium* and must go into the share premium account.

The shares are forfeited in the condition in which they then are. Thus if they are £1 shares 50p paid up, and the shareholder is unable to pay a call of 25p, the shares will be re-issued 50p paid up, and the new holder becomes liable for the whole amount unpaid on the shares, including the call of 25p which resulted in the forfeiture. In this case the price the purchaser pays for the re-issued shares is a *premium*.

Meanwhile the original holder is discharged from all liability on the shares, except that he will go on the 'B' list if the company goes into liquidation within a year. To preserve his liability, an express provision in the articles is required, and Table A, Article 21, has this effect. Such an article makes him liable as a *debtor* for, as stated above, he is liable as a *contributory* in a liquidation in any case. The debt, as we have seen, is under s. 14(2) a specialty debt, and accordingly he will be liable for 12 years: *Ladies' Dress Association* v. *Pulbrook* (1900).

33. Lien and forfeiture compared. Students are sometimes asked to compare the enforcement of the company's lien with forfeiture. The following points should then be borne in mind:

(a) A lien *never involves a reduction of capital*, for the shares are necessarily sold. Forfeiture *will involve a reduction of capital* unless the shares are re-issued.

(*b*) A lien is enforced by *sale*. Forfeiture is effected by *depriving the member of his shares*.

(*c*) Lien is a form of *security* for a debt. Forfeiture is a *penal proceeding*.

(*d*) In the case of lien, the liability of the former owner is only as a 'B' list *contributory* in a liquidation. After forfeiture an article similar to Table A, Article 21, can impose the liability of a *debtor* upon him.

(*e*) In the case of lien, the former owner *receives*, on the sale of the shares, the difference between *the amount received for them* and *the amount of his debt*. After forfeiture, he receives *nothing* and never recovers what he has already paid on the shares.

34. Surrender. The surrender of shares, like forfeiture, is lawful only where the articles authorize it, and Table A does not do so. Sometimes, however, a company's articles authorize the directors to accept a surrender of shares where it would be proper to do so.

Surrender is permissible only in two cases:

(*a*) as a short cut to forfeiture, to avoid the formalities;

(*b*) where shares are surrendered in exchange for new shares of the same nominal value (but with different rights).

Surrendered shares may be re-issued in the same way as forfeited shares, and if this is done no reduction of capital occurs in (*a*) above. In (*b*) there is of course no reduction because the capital is replaced.

35. Cancellation of shares after forfeiture or surrender. Section 146 gives two further rules applicable only to *public* companies:

(*a*) By s. 146(1)–(3) where shares are forfeited or surrendered, then unless the company has disposed of them (by re-issue) within the following three years, it must:

(*i*) cancel them and diminish the amount of its share capital accordingly; and

(*ii*) where the cancellation brings the nominal value of the allotted share capital below the authorized minimum, apply for *re-registration as a private company*.

Section 147(1) makes it clear that it is not necessary to comply with the rules in ss. 135 and 136 governing reduction of capital, although a board resolution altering the company's memorandum is required.

Under s. 147(2) the board resolution must be filed with the registrar within 15 days in accordance with s. 382 (*see* **15:41**).

(*b*) Section 146(4) prohibits the company from exercising any voting rights in respect of shares which have been forfeited or surrendered.

Progress test 12

1. What is a share? (**1**)

2. By what method must shares be transferred? Discuss the forms of transfer. (**2, 3**)

3. What do you understand by certification of transfers? What is the legal effect of certification? (**4, 5**)

4. How far can a company refuse to register a transfer of shares? (**6, 7**)

5. What is the legal effect of a forged transfer? What steps can a company take to minimize losses which it may sustain due to forged transfers? (**8**)

6. What are the requirements of the Act and Table A with regard to the completion and the form of the share certificate? (**9**)

7. What is the legal effect of a share certificate? (**10**)

8. What is the legal position with regard to shares during the period of time from the making of the contract of sale until the registration of the transfer? (**11**)

9. Give an account of the duty of a company to keep a register of interests in shares. (**12**)

10. Under what circumstances may a company remove an entry from its register of interests in shares? (**13**)

11. What do you understand by a 'notifiable interest'? (**14, 15**)

12. What do you understand by 'relevant share capital' and 'notifiable percentage'? (**16**)

13. Give the statutory provisions regarding a person's duty to notify a company of his interest in its shares. (**17–19**)

14. What do you understand by the expression 'acting in concert'? (**20**)

15. Give the statutory rules which apply to 'concert parties'. (**20–21**)

16. What powers has a company to require information concerning interests in its shares? (**22**)

17. What must a company do with information which it receives in response to its inquiries? (**23**)

18. Can a company be compelled to exercise its powers of inquiry and, if so, by whom? (**24**)

19. Give the statutory provisions with regard to share warrants. (**26**)

20. How far is the bearer of a share warrant a member of the company? (**26**)

21. In what ways may a mortgage of shares be effected? (**28**)

22. What is a call? What are the provisions of Table A regarding calls? (**29**)

23. Under what circumstances may a company accept payment of calls in advance from a member? How should the advance payment be treated? (**30**)

24. Give the provisions of Table A regarding the lien of a company on the shares of its members. (**31**)

25. What are the special rules relating to liens in public companies? (**31**)

26. Give the provisions of Table A regarding the forfeiture of shares. (**32**)

27. Compare and contrast the company's enforcement of its lien with its power of forfeiture. (**33**)

28. Under what circumstances is a surrender of shares lawful? (**34**)

29. What special rules apply in public companies when shares have been forfeited or surrendered? (**35**)

13
Membership

1. Methods of becoming a member. A person may become a member in the following ways:

(a) *Allotment:* Here the member takes the shares *directly from the company*. The statutory provisions on allotment have been fully discussed in Chapter 9.

(b) *Transfer:* Here the member acquires the shares *from an existing member* by sale, gift or some other transaction.

(c) *Transmission:* This is an involuntary transfer occurring on the *death* or *bankruptcy* of a member. Later it will be seen that the ownership in the shares then *automatically*, i.e. by operation of law, passes from the dead or bankrupt member to his personal representatives or trustee in bankruptcy, as the case may be, who may then be registered in respect of them. (The student who wrote that transfer was by act of parties, while transmission was by act of God, was somewhat overstating the divine responsibility.)

(d) *Subscribing the memorandum:* The subscribers must take their shares directly from the company, and not by transfer from another member.

Section 22(1) states that the subscribers to the memorandum shall be deemed to have agreed to become members, and must be entered in the register of members.

(e) *Estoppel:* If a person's name is improperly placed on the register of members, and he knows and assents to it, he will then be *estopped from denying* that he is a member.

Estoppel is simply a *rule of evidence* which prevents a person from denying the legal implications of his conduct. Thus a man may behave as though he is a partner in a firm, and be 'held out' by the other partners as being one of their number: neither he nor they will then be allowed to deny that he is a partner, for they will be estopped from doing so. The same rule applies to a person who behaves as though he is a member of a company by allowing his name to be placed on the register.

NOTE: Section 22(2) states that every other person who agrees to become a member and whose name is entered on the register of members shall be a member. This clearly covers allotment, transfer, transmission and estoppel.

2. The conditions of membership. It will be seen from the above that there are two conditions to membership:

(*a*) the *agreement* to become a member, either by subscribing the memorandum, or by allotment or transfer, or after transmission has occurred, or as a result of estoppel; *and*

(*b*) the *entry on the register of members* of the shareholder's name.

Thus as a general rule all members are shareholders, and all shareholders are members, so that the two words are synonymous. It has, however, been seen in Chapter 12 that there is an exception to this, namely, where share warrants have been issued. Also, in the case of death or bankruptcy, there will be a period of time when the person on the register no longer owns the shares, because he is either dead or bankrupt and transmission has occurred.

3. Joint holders. Where two or more persons own shares jointly, the *jus accrescendi* or right of survivorship applies. This means that on the death of any joint holder, the survivor or survivors simply *continue to own* the shares, which do not pass to the personal representatives of the deceased for distribution under the will or intestacy.

Joint holders may be entered on the company's register of members in any order which they desire, and the articles usually provide that the vote of the senior must be accepted to the exclusion of the votes of the others. Seniority is determined by the order in which the names stand in the register. Table A, Article 55, contains a provision to this effect.

Joint holders may require the company to split their holding equally among them. This will give them each a smaller holding but an equal number of votes. A similar result is obtained if their holding is split and their names in respect of each holding are placed in a different order. They will then all continue to own all the shares, but each will have the same voting rights as the others.

4. Methods of ceasing to be a member. There are a large number of ways in which a person may cease to be a member of a company, many of which are discussed in detail in other chapters:

(a) *Transfer:* Here the transferor ceases to be a member when the transferee is placed on the register.

(b) *Forfeiture:* The articles may provide that a member's shares may be forfeited for non-payment of calls.

(c) *Surrender:* This is a short-cut to forfeiture, in order to avoid the formalities.

(d) *Sale by the company under its lien.*

(e) *Transmission to personal representatives on death of member:* Later in this chapter we shall see that the dead member only ceases to be a member of the company when some other person is registered in his place.

(f) *Transmission to trustee in bankruptcy of member:* Here again the bankrupt member only ceases to be a member when some other person is registered in his place.

(g) *Disclaimer by trustee in bankruptcy of member.*

(h) *Liquidation:* On liquidation the company will be dissolved and members will have their capital returned to them as far as possible. Since the existence of the company comes to an end, membership also ceases.

(i) *Issue of share warrants:* Under s. 355 a member is struck off the register on the issue of a share warrant, but it should be noted that s. 355(5) provides that the bearer of a share warrant may be deemed to be a member to the extent to which the articles provide.

(j) *Redemption of redeemable shares under s. 159.*

(k) *Purchase by company of its own shares under s. 162.*

(l) *Repudiation by infant.*

(m) *Rescission for misrepresentation in the prospectus.*

(n) *Court order:* For example, ss. 5, 54 and 459–461.

(o) *Section 428:* Where a 'take-over bid' is made, the shares of the dissenting minority may under certain conditions be bought by the transferee company.

(p) *Sections 110 and 111 Insolvency Act 1986:* Where a liquidator is empowered to sell the company's property in return for shares in another company, those members who dissent from the arrangement can compel the liquidator either to abandon it or to buy their shares.

5. Legally abnormal persons. A *legally normal* person is any natural legal person of full age who is sane, sober and solvent.

Some legal persons are abnormal from their beginning, such as corporations which, as we have seen, are artificial legal persons. Others, whether by a disorder of their mind, body or finances, become abnormal in the course of their lives. Moreover, all normal persons are born: they are therefore minors, and legally abnormal for the first 18 years. They also die, creating a legal situation to which special rules apply.

It is now necessary to consider the rules which apply to legally abnormal persons as shareholders, i.e. to deal with minors, mentally disordered persons, personal representatives, trustees in bankruptcy and corporations. Drunkenness, though studied in the law of contract, does not affect shareholding unless of so persistent a nature that it leads to incapacity of mind, when the rules regarding lunacy will apply.

6. Minors. A minor may hold shares in a company, provided the company is willing to place his name on the register. Often the articles prohibit the transfer of shares to a minor, but even if they do not the company cannot be compelled to register him as a member.

(*a*) *A transfer to a minor is voidable.* If, therefore, the company has unknowingly registered a minor, it can still apply to the court to have the transfer set aside and the transferor put back on the register, but it must act promptly. If it acquiesces in the transfer, or delays too long before applying to have the register rectified, the minor shareholder will have to be recognized.

(*b*) *A minor shareholder may likewise repudiate his contract* either before attaining majority or within a reasonable time afterwards, and on doing so can avoid all future liability on partly paid shares. He cannot, however, recover money already paid on the shares unless there has been a total failure of consideration. If the shares have a market value, however small, the minor has received some consideration and therefore cannot recover his money: *Steinberg* v. *Scala Ltd* (1923).

(*c*) *A minor may subscribe the memorandum*, but can afterwards repudiate liability in the normal way.

(*d*) *A transfer of shares by a minor* is usually said to require an order from the court, though there is conflict of opinion on the point.

7. Mentally disordered persons. A person declared mentally disordered by the court may be a shareholder, but his voting rights will be exercised by his receiver or other person appointed by the court to deal with his affairs. Table A, Article 56, specifically authorizes this.

Such person may also be given authority to transfer the shares and to deal generally with the mentally disordered person's property.

8. Personal representatives. The expression 'personal representatives' covers both *executors*, who are appointed by the testator in his will, and *administrators*, who are appointed by the court when the testator fails to appoint an executor, or when the deceased has made no will.

It is essential to understand first that when a person dies, all his property vests at the moment of death in his personal representatives. This is known as *transmission*, or *transfer by operation of law*, or *involuntary assignment*, according to the context, but it can be expressed most simply by saying that because a deceased person cannot own anything, the ownership of all his property passes at the moment of death to those who legally represent him. These persons, under the Administration of Estates Act 1925, are his personal representatives.

This raises no difficulties where the deceased has appointed an executor, but if he has not, there will be a period of time which must obviously elapse before the court makes the necessary appointment of an administrator. Nevertheless, the ownership of the property vests in the administrator, once he is appointed, *from the moment of death*, and his title *relates back* to the date when the deceased died.

Personal representatives, therefore, have in all cases the *legal* ownership of the deceased's property. But they are *trustees*: they hold the property *on trust* for those entitled to it under the will or the rules of intestacy. The position which arises where a person is a trustee of shares will be fully discussed later, but meanwhile these basic principles should be kept in mind.

9. Provisions of the Act and Table A regarding personal representatives. There are two sections in the Act concerning personal representatives.

Section 187 states simply that the production to a company of any document which is by law sufficient evidence of probate of the will, or letters of administration of the estate, or confirmation as executor of a deceased person, must be accepted by the company as sufficient evidence of the grant, regardless of anything in the articles.

> NOTE: This section does not make the personal representatives members of the company. The deceased is still on the register. But it impliedly recognizes that the *ownership* in the shares has passed from the deceased to the personal representatives. Note here how membership is divorced from ownership, an exceptional position.

Section 183(3) proceeds further to implement this principle. It states that a transfer of the shares of the deceased made by a personal representative who is not a member of the company is as valid as if he were a member. Not only does he own the shares, but he may deal with them without his name being entered on the register of members.

Table A, Article 38, states that notice of meetings must be sent to the personal representative. But Article 31, while it gives him the right to dividends and other benefits attached to the shares, states that he shall not have any rights relating to meetings until his name is on the register of members. Thus while he receives the notice of a meeting, he will not be able to attend it or vote at it unless he has become registered as a member.

10. Registration of personal representatives as members. Unless the articles provide otherwise, personal representatives are entitled to be registered as members of the company if they wish, and may make their desire known to the directors by a *letter of request*. They may, however, prefer not to be registered but to transfer the shares to another person. Article 30 allows personal representatives to choose *either* to give notice to the company that they wish to be registered *or* to execute a transfer to another person, and provides that all the articles relating to transfer apply equally to the notice or to the transfer in this case.

If the shares are partly paid, personal representatives who are on the register of members are personally liable for calls, but they will have a right of indemnity against the deceased's estate for the amount paid.

If they have not become registered as members, then the calls will be made on the estate and payable out of it. Section 509 provides that if the personal representatives default in paying the calls, the company itself may take administration proceedings in order to obtain the money due to it.

11. Trustees in bankruptcy. When a member of a company becomes bankrupt, the legal position is very similar to that arising on death. The debtor's name will be on the register of members, but he will no longer own the shares, for when he was adjudged bankrupt the ownership passed by operation of law to his trustee in bankruptcy. Moreover, the title of the trustee in bankruptcy again *relates back* to a previous moment of time, namely the *commencement of the bankruptcy*, i.e. the date of the bankruptcy order made by the court.

NOTE

(1) *The trustee in bankruptcy*, though not on the register of members, becomes *entitled as owner of the shares* to deal with them, to control the debtor's vote, and to be registered as a member if he wishes. Article 38 provides that notice of meetings is to be sent to him, and Article 31 applies to him in the same way as to personal representatives.

(2) *If the shares are partly paid*, the company may prove in the bankruptcy both for calls in arrears and liability for future calls, but the trustee in bankruptcy may *disclaim* the shares under s. 315 Insolvency Act 1986 if they are onerous. If he disclaims, the company may prove for the damage resulting to it from the disclaimer, which will of course be the loss of the amount unpaid on the shares. The company may mitigate this damage by re-issuing the shares, as in the case of a forfeiture.

12. Corporations. A company may own shares in *another company*, and s. 375 then authorizes it to appoint a person to act as its representative at meetings.

It is also lawful for two companies to own shares *in each other*, though when this position is carefully considered it will be seen that if the share capital of *both* companies is regarded *as a whole*, then *that capital is always reduced by the amount of the cross-holdings*.

Thus if Mr and Mrs Smith form Company A with a share capital of 100 £1 shares, taking 40 shares each, and then Company B with a share capital of 100 £1 shares, again taking 40 shares each, and if Company A then buys the remaining 20 shares in Company B, while Company B buys the remaining 20 shares in Company A, the combined issued share capital will be 200 £1 shares, though the actual cash in both companies together will be £160.

Nevertheless, there is nothing unlawful about this situation, with one important exception: cross-holdings are lawful *provided the companies involved do not constitute a group*.

It is therefore essential to know what a group is, and how it arises.

13. The nature of a group. A group exists wherever two or more companies are in the relationship of *holding* and *subsidiary* to each other. The Act gives an important definition of a subsidiary company in s. 736.

Section 736(1) states that a company is a subsidiary of another where that other:

(*a*) is a member of it and controls the composition of the board of directors; *or*

(*b*) holds more than half its equity share capital.

This definition must be studied with the utmost care. Often students do not understand its implications.

NOTE

(1) *Observe that (a) and (b) are alternatives. Either* situation will result in a group. In order to satisfy the requirements of (*a*), the holding company *need own only one share*: the section states that it must be a member, and the ownership of a single share is enough to constitute membership. But membership alone does not suffice: the holding company must also control the composition of the board of directors. This means that, in the normal way, it has *voting control*, for the directors are appointed and removed by the company, and the company acts by a majority of votes. Usually in order to have voting control it is necessary to hold the majority of the voting shares, but sometimes *weighted voting* exists so that very few shares carry the majority of the votes, and the owner of those few shares has control without having a large shareholding.

For instance, in *Investment Trust Corporation* v. *Singapore Traction Co.* (1935), where there were 400,000 shares, a particular single share could outvote the other 399,999.

(2) *In order to satisfy the requirements of (b)*, on the other hand, the holding company need only hold more than half of the equity share capital, and *votes are irrelevant*. The shares held may carry votes, or they may not; it is immaterial. It is common for companies to issue non-voting shares to maintain control in present hands, so that sometimes part of the equity share capital may consist of such shares. But the group relationship here depends simply on whether or not *more than half* of the equity share capital is owned by another company and not, as in (a), on voting control.

14. Meaning of equity share capital. This is defined in s. 744 in language calculated to depress the most enthusiastic student. The meaning of the definition can be more simply expressed by saying that equity share capital consists of those shares which carry a right to unrestricted participation *either* in distributed profits (i.e. dividends) *or* in surplus assets on liquidation.

Thus preference shares, which carry the right to a fixed dividend and are often precluded by the articles from participation in surplus assets on winding up, are not normally equity share capital. Participating preference shares, however (where there is no ultimate limit on the dividend payable since they participate along with the ordinary shares once a certain level has been reached), will be part of the equity share capital even if there is a limit to participation in surplus assets on liquidation.

Ordinary shares are normally equity share capital unless there are deferred shares, which carry the residue of profits after a certain level has been reached on the dividend to the ordinary shareholders. The test is always the *absence of a limit to participation* with regard either to dividends or to surplus assets. If there is a limit on *both*, the shares are not part of the equity share capital.

15. Subsidiaries of subsidiaries. Section 736(1) further states that *the subsidiary of a subsidiary is also the subsidiary of the holding company*. In other words, where Company A is the holding company of Company B (e.g. by owning more than half its equity share capital), and Company B is the holding company of Company C (by owning more than half its equity share capital), then Company C is the subsidiary not only of Company B, but also of Company A. The result is that Company A has two subsidiaries, and Company C two holding companies, while the group relationship between them is *indirect*. It arises *only because* Company B is the subsidiary of Company A and the holding company of Company C.

16. Size of groups. From these statutory provisions it will be seen that a group can be quite small, e.g. two companies, one of which is the holding company of the other, or very large, e.g. one holding company with 20 subsidiaries, which in turn have subsidiaries of their own. The chain can be very long; in theory it is infinite. Where there are several subsidiaries, the term *co-subsidiary* is sometimes used to describe their relationship with one another. Often companies in a group are said to be similar to a family, and the holding company is referred to as the 'parent' company, but non-technical descriptions must be viewed with caution for it is the legal technicalities which are important here. No grandparent has ever yet become the parent of its grandchild, despite strenuous efforts.

17. Unlawful cross-holdings. It will now be clear that in all cases where two companies are in a *direct* group relationship the holding company is a member of the subsidiary. If the relationship arises under (*a*) (*see* **13**), then the holding company must own at least one share; if it arises under (*b*), then it must own more than half the equity share capital. If, therefore, the subsidiary company owns shares in the holding company, this will be a *cross-holding*, and it may here be affected by s. 23. In fact, s. 23 is intended to cover *all* group relationships, even where they are *indirect* as described in **15** so that there is no cross-holding.

Section 23(1) states that a subsidiary company cannot be a member of its holding company, and any allotment or transfer of shares in the holding company to its subsidiary is void.

The section was a new one in 1948, and therefore it was obvious that when the Act came into force there would be many groups in which the subsidiary owned shares in the holding company. This suddenly became unlawful. Consequently s. 23(2) carefully provides for these circumstances, stating that where a subsidiary company owned shares in the holding company *at the commencement of the Companies Act 1948*, it can continue to hold them, but cannot vote at meetings.

18. The exceptions to s. 23(1). Finally, there are two statutory exceptions to s. 23(1). Section 23(4) expressly permits a subsidiary company to own shares in the holding company where it does so in the capacity of:

(a) personal representative (e.g. if the subsidiary is a banking company acting as executor to a deceased owner of shares in its holding company); or

(b) trustee, provided the equitable interest in the shares is owned by persons outside the group (e.g. if the subsidiary is a banking company appointed the trustee of a family settlement created by a settlor owning shares in the holding company).

There is one case, however, where the equitable interest may be owned by a company within the group, namely, when it arises by way of security for a loan made by a money-lending company in the ordinary course of business (e.g. where the trustee wishes to raise a temporary loan, and mortgages the shares as security to a banking company within the group).

19. Disclosure in accounts of holding and subsidiary companies. The 5th Schedule to the Act (which relates to miscellaneous matters to be disclosed in notes to company accounts), by paras 1 and 14–16, requires a holding company to state with respect to each subsidiary:

(a) its name;

(b) if it is incorporated in Great Britain but in a different country from that in which the holding company is registered, the country in which it is registered, and if incorporated outside Great Britain, the country in which it is incorporated;

(c) the class or classes of shares and the proportion of nominal value of the allotted shares of each class held;

(d) the amount of its capital and reserves at the end of the last financial year; and

(e) its profit or loss for that financial year.

Conversely, para. 20 of the 5th Schedule requires a subsidiary company to disclose in a note to its accounts the name of the company regarded by the directors as being its ultimate holding company and, if known to them, the country in which it is incorporated.

20. Associated companies. The expression 'associated companies' is a commercial one with no precise technical legal significance. It is normally used to indicate a shareholding of 10–50 per cent by one company in another, so that the two companies are not usually in the group relationship described in **13** above. Such a holding is often acquired for business reasons and may well lead to the formation of a group at a later date by the companies concerned.

The only recognition given by the Companies Act to this type of relationship between companies is in regard to accounts. Section 231 and paras 7–9 of the 5th Schedule require any company which holds:

(a) more than *one-tenth in nominal value* of the allotted shares of any class of equity share capital;

(b) shares of an amount exceeding *one-tenth of the assets*; or

(c) more than *one-tenth in nominal value* of the allotted share capital

of another company which is *not its subsidiary* to disclose in a note to its accounts with respect to that company the information stated in **19** (a)–(c) above. Where the company holds more than *one-fifth in nominal value* of the allotted share capital of another company, s. 231 and paras 15 and 16 require it to disclose the information in **19**(d) and (e) as well.

21. Acquisition by company of its own shares. In **12** it was explained that a company may own shares in another company and that, with one exception, companies may own shares in each other.

A company may not, however, normally own shares *in itself*. This was formerly known as the rule in *Trevor* v. *Whitworth* (1887), where the articles authorized the company to buy its own shares, but were held illegal on the grounds that this would amount to a reduction of capital.

The rule is now given statutory form by s. 143(1) which, with one exception given below, prohibits any limited company from acquiring its own shares, whether by purchase, subscription or otherwise. In subsection (2) the Act imposes penalties on the company and every officer in default for contravention of the section and provides that any illegal acquisition of shares is *void*.

The single exception to the rule is found in s. 143(3). This expressly permits a company limited by shares to acquire any of its own *fully paid* shares *otherwise than for valuable consideration* (i.e. by way of gift). The exception is not new. A more limited version of it was formerly found in two well-known cases – *Kirby* v. *Wilkins* (1929) and *Re*

Castiglione's Will Trusts (1958) – but it is helpful to have it in a broader statutory form.

It is clear, of course, that if a company has issued 100 £1 shares at par, and then uses £25 of that share capital to buy 25 shares from an existing member, it will still have an issued capital of 100 shares, but will have only £75 in cash. The capital of the company is reduced by the amount which it has used to buy its own shares.

If, however, a company has been in existence for some time, and has accumulated revenue reserves, and then uses those reserves to buy its own shares from an existing member, this is not a reduction of *capital* in the strict sense of the word. Nevertheless, it would still be unlawful, both at common law and under s. 143, for it has reduced the amount of the company's *assets*, and on liquidation there would be less available to meet the claims of creditors. Thus the rule seems to be based not so much on an illegal reduction of capital, as on an illegal use of the company's assets generally, by returning money to a share-holder and so potentially depriving creditors of that amount.

22. Cases falling outside s. 143. Section 143(3) gives seven cases which fall outside the prohibition in s. 143(1), despite the fact that in five cases out of the seven the company purchases its own shares.

These seven cases are:

(*a*) where the company redeems or purchases its own shares in accordance with the relevant provisions of the Act (*see* 11:**24, 25**). Here, owing to the requirements of s. 170, no reduction of capital occurs;

(*b*) where the company acquires its own shares in a reduction of capital duly made;

(*c*) where the court makes an order for the purchase of shares in the company by the company under s. 5 (*see* 2:**27**);

(*d*) where the court makes an order for the purchase of shares in the company by the company under s. 54 (*see* 25:**5**);

(*e*) where the court makes an order for the purchase of shares in the company by the company under ss. 459–461 (*see* 23:**9**).

In these last three cases the court will also by order provide for the resulting reduction of the company's capital.

(*f*) where, under the company's articles, forfeiture of shares occurs (*see* 12:**32**);

(g) where the company accepts a surrender of shares in lieu of forfeiture (*see* 12:**34**).

23. Statutory extension of s. 143. Statutory rules which prohibited a company from giving financial assistance for the purchase of its own shares were formerly regarded as an extension of the common law rule in *Trevor* v. *Whitworth*. The rules are now in ss. 151–154 of the Act. Their effect is to broaden s. 143 in order to prevent attempted evasions of it.

Thus, if a company is approached by Smith and asked if it will *lend* him money in order to enable him to buy shares in that company, and it does so, then the company will have parted with some of its assets in return for a *debt* due to it from Smith. Probably Smith will repay it in due course, with interest, and the company may benefit from the arrangement. But possibly he will not. He might be adjudged bankrupt, or he might disappear. Then the loan will not be repaid and the company will have lost that amount of money.

Again, if Smith approaches the company saying that he wishes to buy shares in it, but has no cash available, and has therefore asked his bank manager for a loan which will be forthcoming provided the company acts as his *guarantor*, the same situation will result. Possibly Smith will repay the loan to the bank, and the company will never be liable on its guarantee, but possibly he will not, and the company may then have to pay to the bank the amount of the loan. There is a potential liability to the company here, a potential reduction of its assets.

Even if the company obliges Smith by providing *security* to his bank, e.g. by charging its assets in favour of the bank as security for the loan made to Smith, there is the same possibility that Smith will not repay the bank, which will then enforce its security. The company's assets will therefore be diminished by the value of that security.

Section 151 makes all these transactions illegal. Section 151(1) states the general rule that where a person *is either acquiring or proposing to acquire* any shares in a company, it is unlawful for the company or any of its subsidiaries to give *financial assistance*, directly or indirectly, for the purpose of that acquisition before or at the same time as the acquisition takes place. However, s. 153(1) provides that this general rule does not apply if:

(a) the acquisition is *either:*

(*i*) not the company's principal purpose in giving such assistance; *or*

(*ii*) merely an incidental part of some larger purpose of the company; *and*

(*b*) the assistance is given in good faith in the interests of the company.

Section 151(2) deals with slightly different circumstances, stating that where a person *has already acquired* any shares in a company and a liability has been incurred, either by him or some other person, for the purpose of that acquisition, it is not lawful for the company or any of its subsidiaries to give any *financial assistance*, directly or indirectly, for the purpose of reducing or discharging that liability. However, s. 153(2) provides that this does not prohibit a company from giving financial assistance if:

(*a*) the reduction or discharge of the liability is *either:*

(*i*) not the company's principal purpose in giving such assistance; *or*

(*ii*) merely an incidental part of some larger purpose of the company; and

(*b*) the assistance is given in good faith in the interests of the company.

Under s. 152(3) the expression 'incurring a liability' includes a case where a person *changes his financial position*, no matter by what means. The restoration of his financial position to what it was before the acquisition took place falls within the prohibition.

It would seem that ss. 151–153 have given express statutory form to the decision in *Belmont Finance Corporation* v. *Williams Furniture Ltd* (1980). In that case it was held that there was a contravention of the general rule against financial assistance (then stated in s. 54 Companies Act 1948) where a company buys something from a vendor without regard to its own commercial interests, the purpose of the transaction being to provide the vendor with funds to buy shares in the company, and it was irrelevant that the price paid was a fair one.

Clearly the expression 'financial assistance' is of major importance and it is helpful to have it defined by the Act in considerable detail. This definition is considered in **24** below.

24. The meaning of 'financial assistance'. Section 152(1) defines 'financial assistance' as that given:

(*a*) by way of gift;

(*b*) by way of guarantee, security, indemnity, release or waiver;

(*c*) by way of:

(*i*) a loan; *or*

(*ii*) any other agreement under which any obligation of the person giving the assistance is to be fulfilled at a time when an obligation of some other party to the agreement remains outstanding; *or*

(*iii*) the novation or assignment of any right arising under a loan or such other agreement; *or*

(*d*) in some other manner by a company the net assets of which are thereby reduced to a material extent, or which has no net assets.

'Net assets' here means the aggregate assets less the aggregate liabilities: s. 152(2).

The section is silent, as was its predecessor, concerning the identity of the recipient of the financial assistance. However, in *Armour Hick Northern Ltd* v. *Whitehouse* (1980), it was held that the prohibition against financial assistance is not confined to that given to a purchaser, but extends to financial assistance *to whomsoever it is given* for the purpose of a purchase of the company's shares. Doubtless this rule still applies.

25. Transactions given unqualified exemption from the s. 151 prohibitions. Although the provisions of s. 151 mentioned above are widely worded, s. 153(3) exempts a large number of operations which fall outside their ambit and are therefore lawful. These are as follows:

(*a*) a distribution of a company's assets lawfully made by way of dividend or in the course of winding up;

(*b*) the allotment of bonus shares;

(*c*) a reduction of capital confirmed by order of the court under s. 137 (*see* 11:**21–23**);

(*d*) a redemption or purchase of any shares made in accordance with ss. 159–181 on redeemable shares and purchase by a company of its own shares (*see* 11:**24–35**);

(*e*) anything done in pursuance of an order of the court under s.

425 (compromises and arrangements with creditors and members) (*see* 32:**1–4**);

(*f*) anything done under an arrangement made in pursuance of s. 110 Insolvency Act 1986 (acceptance of shares by liquidator in winding up as consideration for sale of property) (*see* 29:**21**).

26. Transactions given qualified exemption from the s. 151 prohibitions. Section 153(4) exempts three further operations from the prohibitions in s. 151. These are:

(*a*) The lending of money by the company in the *ordinary course of its business*, where it is a *money-lending company*.

In *Steen* v. *Law* (1964) it was held that this exception, which existed in identical terms under the earlier section, can apply only where the money lent is at the free disposition of the borrower so that he can do what he likes with it, and that it can never cover a loan made for the direct purpose of financing a purchase of the company's shares.

(*b*) The provision by a company under an employees' share scheme of money for the acquisition of fully paid shares in the company or its holding company.

(*c*) The making of loans by a company to persons other than directors who are employed in good faith by the company with a view to enabling those persons to acquire fully paid shares in the company or its holding company to be held by themselves as beneficial owners.

These three exceptions differ from those in **25** above in that where the company in question is a *public* company they are subject to qualification. Section 154(1) permits a public company to give financial assistance of any of these three kinds only if:

(*i*) its net assets are not thereby reduced; or

(*ii*) to the extent that they are thereby reduced, the assistance is provided out of distributable profits.

27. The effect of contravention of s. 151. Section 151(3), taken along with the 24th Schedule, imposes criminal liability for breach of the section. If a company contravenes its provisions, the company is liable:

(*a*) on conviction on indictment, to a fine;

(*b*) on summary conviction, to a fine not exceeding the statutory maximum;

and any officer who is in default is liable:

(*a*) on conviction on indictment, to imprisonment not exceeding two years or a fine, or both;

(*b*) on summary conviction, to imprisonment not exceeding six months or a fine not exceeding the statutory maximum, or both.

With regard to civil liability, it would seem that the effect of contravention of the section is still uncertain. If, for instance, a company contravenes s. 151 by providing unlawful security, it might be expected that the transaction would be void for illegality. At the present time, however, its effect remains doubtful.

In *Victor Battery Co. Ltd* v. *Curry's Ltd* (1946) *security* given in breach of the equivalent provision in the Companies Act 1929 was held to be valid, while in *Selangor United Rubber Estates Ltd* v. *Cradock* (1968) a *loan* contravening s. 54 Companies Act 1948 was held to be void. In *Heald* v. *O'Connor* (1971) Fisher J. reviewed these decisions and held that a debenture giving a charge on the company's assets in breach of the section was void. It is regrettable that later Companies Acts have not yet expressly dealt with the matter.

The effect on the directors of the company is nevertheless quite clear. In *Wallersteiner* v. *Moir* (1974) Lord Denning M.R., with his customary lucidity, said:

'Every director who is a party to a breach of s. 54 [*Companies Act 1948*] is guilty of a misfeasance and breach of trust; and is liable to recoup to the company any loss occasioned to it by the default.'

Doubtless this statement can be applied in the same way to a breach of s. 151 Companies Act 1985.

28. Relaxation of the rules in s. 151 for private companies. It is already clear from **26** above that the Act treats private companies more favourably than public companies in relation to the rules laid down by s. 151. In ss. 155–158, however, it goes much further in this direction.

Section 155 removes the prohibitions in s. 151 in their entirety for a private company wishing to give financial assistance for the purpose of the acquisition of shares either in itself or, where its holding company is also a private company, in the holding company, provided that it complies with the rules laid down by ss. 155–158. The rules prescribe both conditions to be fulfilled and a procedure to be followed. They are set out below:

(1) The company's net assets must not be thereby reduced or, to the extent that they are reduced, the financial assistance must be provided out of distributable profits: s. 155(2).

(2) Where the company is giving financial assistance for the purpose of the acquisition of shares in its holding company, it must not be a subsidiary of a public company which is itself a subsidiary of that holding company: s. 155(3).

The situation envisaged here is that of the 'chain' explained in **15** and **16** above. The section is ensuring that the group chain consists entirely of private companies.

(3) Unless the company is a *wholly-owned subsidiary* (*see* 16:**11**), the financial assistance to be given must be approved by a *special resolution*: s. 155(4).

The resolution must be passed on the date when the directors make the statutory declaration mentioned below, or within the following week: s. 157(1).

(4) Where the financial assistance to be given by the company is for the purpose of the acquisition of shares in its holding company, it must also be approved by a special resolution of that holding company and of any other holding company which is a subsidiary of that holding company, except in the case of a wholly-owned subsidiary: s. 155(5) (*see*, again, **15** and **16** above).

Section 157(1) applies to all special resolutions (*see* (3) above).

(5) Where any special resolution is passed by a company, an application for its cancellation may be made to the court by:

(*a*) the holders of not less than 10 per cent in nominal value of the company's issued share capital or any class of it; *or*

(*b*) if the company is not limited by shares, not less than 10 per cent of its members: s. 157(2).

Under s. 157(3) the application will be governed by the rules laid down in s. 54(3)–(10) (litigation to cancel resolution for re-registration of public company as private) (*see* 25:**5**).

(6) Under s. 157(4) no special resolution will be effective:

(*a*) unless the statutory declaration and auditors' report mentioned below are available for inspection by members at the meeting at which the resolution is passed;

(b) if it is cancelled by the court on an application under s. 157(2).

(7) The directors of the company giving the financial assistance and, where the shares to be acquired are shares in its holding company, the directors of that holding company and of any other holding company which is a subsidiary of that holding company, must make a *statutory declaration* before the assistance is given, stating:

(a) the prescribed particulars of the assistance to be given, the company's business and the identity of the recipient;

(b) that they have formed the opinion that immediately after the date when the assistance is to be given there will be no ground on which the company could be found unable to pay its debts; and *either*:

(i) if it is intended to commence the company's winding up within 12 months of that date, that the company will be able to pay its debts in full within 12 months of the commencement of the winding up; *or*

(ii) if there is no such intention, that the company will be able to pay its debts as they fall due during the year immediately after that date: ss. 155(6) and 156(1) and (2).

(8) The statutory declaration must have annexed to it a *report* by the company's auditors, addressed to the directors, stating that they have inquired into the state of affairs of the company and are not aware of anything to indicate that the directors' opinion is unreasonable: s. 156(4).

(9) The statutory declaration and auditors' report must be delivered to the registrar when the special resolution is filed under s. 380 (*see* 15:**41**) or, if no special resolution is required, within 15 days after the declaration is made: s. 156(5).

(10) The financial assistance proposed may not be given:

(a) until four weeks have elapsed since the passing of any special resolution required or, if more than one, the last of them, unless every member of the company who is entitled to vote at general meetings voted in favour of it;

(b) until any application for cancellation of such a resolution under s. 157(2) has been determined, unless the court orders otherwise;

(c) after eight weeks have elapsed since the date of the making of the statutory declaration or, if more than one, the earliest of them, unless the court, on any application for cancellation of the resolution, orders otherwise: s. 158.

It will be seen from the above list that the technicalities prescribed by ss. 155–158 are distressingly detailed. For anyone who is compelled to commit them to memory, it may be helpful to suggest a simple framework in which they may be arranged. This might appear in the following form:

(a) the 'net assets' rule;

(b) the 'chain' rule;

(c) special resolution;

(d) statutory declaration;

(e) auditors' report;

(f) time limits.

29. Acquisition of shares in company by the company's nominee. The prohibition imposed in s. 143 against a company's acquiring its own shares is fortified not only by the rules in ss. 151–158 as to financial assistance by a company for acquisition of its own shares, but also by ss. 144–149 concerning acquisition of shares in a company by the company's nominee. Fortunately the provisions of this section are less extensive.

Under ss. 144(1) and 145(2)(a), where a limited company has a beneficial (i.e. equitable) interest in:

(a) shares which are issued, not to the company itself, but to its nominee; *or*

(b) partly paid shares which are acquired by the company's nominee from a third person,

the shares in question must be treated as held by the nominee on his own account and the company must be regarded as having no beneficial interest in them.

If he is called on to pay an amount in respect of them, s. 144(2) provides that he must comply within 21 days. If he fails to do so, then:

(a) if the shares were issued to him as a subscriber to the memorandum, the *other subscribers; or* (*b*) if not, the *directors* of the company at the time when he acquired them,

are jointly and severally liable with him to pay the amount in question.

30. Special rules applicable only to public companies. Sections 146–149 impose stringent additional rules applying to *public companies only*. Section 146(1) gives four cases where these rules apply, the first of which has been considered in 12:**35** since it relates to forfeiture or surrender of shares.

The remaining three comprise cases where the company has a beneficial interest in its own shares and the shares in question were acquired:

(*a*) by the *company* otherwise than by any of the methods mentioned in s. 143(3)(*a*)–(*d*) (*see* **22**);

(*b*) by the *company's nominee* from a third person *without* financial assistance from the company; *or*

(*c*) by *any person with* financial assistance from the company.

In each of these three cases s. 146(2) and (3) provides that the shares in question, or the company's interest in them, must, within three years from their acquisition in the case of (*a*) and (*b*) and within one year in the case of (*c*), be either disposed of or cancelled by the company. If they are cancelled the company's share capital must be diminished accordingly and if in consequence it falls below the authorized minimum, the company must apply for re-registration as a private company.

By s. 147(1) and (2) the directors may take such steps as are necessary to enable the company to comply with s. 146(2) and (3) including the passing of a resolution to alter the company's memorandum. Any such resolution must be filed with the registrar within 15 days in accordance with s. 380 (*see* 15:**41**).

Thus in each of these cases the company's shareholding or interest will be purely temporary and the holder of the shares in question is meantime debarred by s. 146(4) from exercising any voting rights in respect of them.

Finally, s. 150 places strict limits on the cases where a public company may acquire an equitable interest in its own shares by way of security, e.g. a lien. This topic was discussed in 12:**31**.

Progress test 13

1. In what ways may a person become a member of a company? **(1)**

2. What is the legal position of joint holders of shares? **(3)**

3. In what ways may a person cease to be a member of a company? **(4)**

4. What is the legal position of a minor shareholder? **(6)**

5. Can a minor subscribe the memorandum? **(6)**

6. Give an account of the statutory provisions concerning the position of personal representatives of a deceased member. **(9)**

7. Give an account of the clauses of Table A concerning the position of personal representatives of a deceased member. **(9, 10)**

8. What is the legal position of a trustee in bankruptcy regarding the shares of a bankrupt member of a company? **(11)**

9. May a company own shares in another company? **(12)**

10. Explain what is meant by a cross-holding. How far are cross-holdings lawful? **(12)**

11. Define a subsidiary company. **(13)**

12. Define equity share capital. **(14)**

13. In what cases is it lawful for a subsidiary company to own shares in its holding company? **(17, 18)**

14. How far may a company lawfully acquire its own shares? **(21, 22)**

15. Give an account of the provisions in s. 151 which restrain a company from providing financial assistance to any person for the acquisition of shares in itself. **(23)**

16. What do you understand by the expression 'financial assistance' as employed in s. 151? **(24)**

17. What transactions are given exemption from the prohibitions in s. 151? **(25, 26)**

18. What is the effect of contravention of s. 151? **(27)**

19. In what way are the rules in s. 151 relaxed for private companies? **(28)**

20. What special rules apply to shares acquired by the company's nominee? **(29)**

21. What special rules apply in public companies where the company has a beneficial interest in its own shares? **(30)**

14
The register of members

1. The sections to be studied. In 2:**16** the register of members was listed as one of the statutory books, and in 2:**15** as one of the registers and documents which the company must keep at its registered office. It must now be considered in detail.

The sections of the Act which are concerned with it range from ss. 352–361, but the student should commit to memory only the main points. These are given below, where it will be seen that s. 357 has been entirely omitted, while s. 355 relating to share warrants has been considered in an earlier chapter (*see* 12:**26**). The sections have not been dealt with in their statutory order, since s. 360 is of major importance and requires more lengthy explanation.

The provisions of s. 362 on overseas branch registers are also given in this chapter.

2. The contents of the register of members. Section 352(1)–(3) requires every company to keep a register of its members and to enter in it:

(*a*) the names and addresses of members, the shares held by each member distinguishing each share by its number and class, if any, and the amount paid up;

(*b*) the date of entry in the register;

(*c*) the date of cessation of membership.

Stock is entered instead of shares where appropriate.

Section 361 states that the register is *prima facie* evidence of the matters inserted in it while s. 352(6) permits any entry relating to a *former* member of the company to be removed from the register after the expiration of 20 years from the date on which he ceased to be a member.

Finally, s. 352(7) imposes a limitation period of 20 years on any liability incurred by the company through the making or deletion of an entry in the register.

3. The place where the register of members must be kept.

Section 353(1) requires the register of members to be kept at the registered office unless it is made up at another office of the company, when it may be kept there, or by some other person, when it may be kept at his office. It may never be kept outside the company's domicile.

Section 353(2) and (3) states that notice must be given to the registrar of where the register is kept, and of any changes, unless it has always been kept at the registered office.

4. The index of members.

Section 354(1) requires every company with more than 50 members to keep an index, unless the register is already in the form of an index. It must alter the index within 14 days of altering the register.

Section 354(2) states that the index must indicate how the account of each member may be readily found in the register of members.

Section 354(3) requires the index to be kept at the same place as the register of members.

5. Inspection of the register of members and index.

Section 356(1) and (2) states that, except when closed under the provisions of the Act, the register of members and the index must be open to inspection by members free, and by other persons on payment of the appropriate charge, for at least two hours a day during business hours. The appropriate charge is 5p or such less sum as the company may prescribe: s. 356(4).

Section 356(3) and (4) authorizes any person to require a copy of the register, or of any part of it, on payment of a charge of 10p or such less sum as the company may prescribe for every 100 words. The copy must be supplied within 10 days.

Section 356(6) states that if inspection is refused, or a copy not sent within the 10 days, the court may order that inspection be allowed or that the copy should be sent.

Section 358, however, permits the company, on giving notice in a local newspaper, to close the register for not more than 30 days in each year.

6. Rectification of the register. Section 359(1) states that if:

(a) the name of a person is entered in or omitted from the register of members without sufficient cause; or

(b) default or delay occurs in entering a cessation of membership;

the aggrieved person, or any member, or the company may apply to the court for rectification.

Section 359(2) states that the court may either refuse the application, or may order rectification and payment by the company of damages for losses sustained by an aggrieved party.

Section 359(3) empowers the court also to decide questions of title (i.e. ownership of the shares) and any other necessary questions.

Section 359(4) requires the court to order that notice of any rectification shall be given to the registrar.

NOTE: This useful section deserves careful study, as much for its practical as for its academic importance. Note especially the three possible applicants, and the width of the powers given to the court. Often rectification proceedings provide the only remedy available to a person who thinks that he ought to be registered as a member, but who is rejected by the company.

7. Notice of trusts. Section 360 is a short section in simple language but with far-reaching consequences. It states merely that *no notice of any trust shall be entered on the register*, but many students find the concept of the trust difficult to understand and so do not entirely follow the meaning and purpose of the section.

An attempt, therefore, has been made to give a brief explanation of the trust before embarking on the effect of the section.

8. Legal ownership. In the normal way a person accepts the idea of *ownership* without question or analysis. If a student leaves a pen-knife behind after a class, and the lecturer asks to whom it belongs, he will reply: 'Me'. He seldom troubles to think of what he means because this one word, if true, gives him the right to pick it up and take it with him.

If, however, he is asked to think about it, he will readily agree that because he owns the knife he can carry it around with him, or keep it in his desk, or use it for its intended purpose of sharpening pencils, or its unintended purposes such as opening tins and bottles or slicing cucumber. He can sell it, or lend it to a friend, or hire it out to a friend at 10p per week, or pledge it to a pawnbroker. He can throw it in the dustbin or lose it without incurring liability to anyone. In fact, the only things which he may *not* do with it are *acts unlawful in themselves*, such as stabbing the lecturer or cutting the pages out of a library book.

Provided he is acting lawfully, then, the ownership of the knife gives him the right to do a very large number of things with it, and has therefore been described as 'a bundle of rights'. Intangible property, like shares, can be treated in the same way within the limits of its non-physical existence. Thus the owner of shares whose name, as we have seen, normally appears on the register of members, can deal with his shares in any lawful way, and can give them to a friend, sell them, mortgage them or dispose of them by will.

When we talk of ownership in this way, we are referring to a right, or a bundle of rights, recognized and protected by the *common law*. Common law ownership is often called *legal* ownership, to distinguish it from *equitable* ownership which arises under a *trust*.

A brief account of equitable ownership is given below.

9. The origin of equitable ownership.

(*a*) The royal courts of common law had superseded the local and feudal courts and were giving general protection to litigants by the end of the 13th century. Their growth since the Conquest in 1066 had by this time led to jurisdiction in all types of case. It was only because the common law had severe disadvantages that the Chancellor, in his court of 'equity' or *natural justice*, started to protect a petitioner who could claim merely a *moral* or *equitable* right to property, and his jurisdiction in this field did not become comprehensive until at least a century later. The first independent decree of the Chancellor in the Court of Chancery was given in 1474. Thus common law or legal ownership is historically earlier, and the idea of equitable ownership emerged afterwards to meet difficulties and defects.

(*b*) We cannot here consider all the disadvantages of the common law ownership of land, the most important type of property in mediaeval times. It is enough to know, for explanatory purposes, that a man could not devise his land by will at common law, and that all conveyances of land were required to be effected in public so that the ownership should never be in doubt. This latter rule was aimed mainly at preventing the evasion of the feudal incidents, i.e. the dues and other burdens which fell on the common law owner of land, whoever he might be. It is hardly surprising that the mediaeval landowner set out to improve his position in much the same way as the modern citizen wrestles with the Inland Revenue.

(*c*) Though the earliest examples of trusts of land appeared in the 13th century, it was not until the 14th century that it became a common practice for an owner of land to transfer it to a number of friends *on trust for himself*. By this device he had, *at common law*, no interest in the land at all, yet continued to enjoy it. As far as the common law courts were concerned, his friends owned it, and that was the end of the matter. They owned it as joint tenants, so that if any one of them died, the others merely continued as owners by the right of survivorship or *jus accrescendi*. As long as there were at least two of them, this avoided the worst of the feudal burdens, since these arose on the death of the landowner. If the original owner died, no dues became payable since at common law he was no longer connected with the land in any way. Moreover, he could dispose of the land by will by directing his friends to hold it on trust after his death for anyone he wished to name.

(*d*) Of course, at first a landowner who adopted this method of evading the disadvantages of common law ownership was taking the risk of his friends proving dishonest and taking advantage of their impregnable position at common law by depriving him of enjoyment. He had no remedy against them in that event, for at common law they were the owners and he was not. But from about the beginning of the 15th century the Chancellor, in the early court of equity, started to intervene to protect him.

(*e*) The Chancellor did this not by opposing the common law, but by ordering the defaulting friends to act equitably, and threatening them with imprisonment if they refused. In other words, he gave the petitioner a *remedy*, and where a court gives a remedy, the citizen has a *right*. The right here was merely in the Court of Chancery, but it was none the less effective against dishonest persons, and because it was recognized by the Chancellor in his equitable jurisdiction, it is called an *equitable right*, or, more usually, an *equitable interest*.

10. The enforceability of equitable interests. In the course of time the Chancellor protected the equitable interest of the petitioner not only against his defaulting friends, but against *any person to whom they should transfer the land* in breach of trust, with *one exception*: the petitioner *was never allowed to enforce his equitable interest against a person who took the land for valuable consideration and without notice of the equitable interest*.

From this development we can now see that there are *two essential rules* to remember:

(*a*) A legal or common law interest in property cannot be defeated by anyone.

At common law, with the exception of a sale in market overt, only the owner can deprive himself of ownership.

(*b*) An equitable interest in property can always be defeated by a *bona fide* purchaser for value of the legal interest in that property, though it cannot be defeated by anyone else.

Later these rules will be studied in relation to shares.

11. The nature of a trust. It will be seen from the above explanation that wherever there is an equitable interest in property, there is what is often called *duality of ownership*. By this expression we mean that one person is regarded as the owner of the property *at common law* (i.e. he is the *legal* owner), while another is regarded as the owner in *equity*.

Wherever this duality of ownership exists, there is a *trust*. The *legal* owner is the *trustee*, while the equitable owner is called the *beneficiary* or *cestui que trust*. There are many types of transactions which produce this duality of ownership, for the trust has developed enormously since mediaeval times, and is often said to be the most important feature of our law. An account of the occasions on which a trust arises is, however, outside the scope of this book and should be sought in manuals dealing with equity.

12. The purpose of s. 360. Let us now return to s. 360 which, as we have seen, states that *no notice of a trust shall be entered on the register of members*. It must be understood that the section does *not* say that there cannot be a trust of shares. It merely says that if there is a trust, it must not be entered on the register. We already know that the correct entry in the register is the name of the member, i.e. the person who *owns* the shares. This, of course, is the person who is the *legal* or *common law* owner, the *trustee* in the case of a trust. It is the *equitable* owner who must be kept off the register, whom the company must not recognize. Note that this is a purely *administrative* section. Its whole object is to simplify administration from the company's viewpoint.

There are in fact *two main reasons* for the section. First, it is possible for *several equitable interests* to arise in a single piece of property. Thus there can be several equitable interests in one holding of shares, while the legal ownership is in the member whose name is on the register. It is therefore possible for a dispute to arise among the owners of the equitable interests as to which of them has priority, i.e. the better claim to the shares.

If their names were to appear on the register, the company might be involved in this dispute, and therefore to prevent the company from being implicated in lengthy argument as to which owner of an equitable interest in the shares has priority, the section simply forbids the company from taking any notice of equitable interests at all. It is concerned solely with the *legal* owner, and if he happens to be a trustee and decides to commit a flagrant breach of trust, the company is not to blame unless it has actual knowledge not only of the trust, but also of the breach – a very unlikely circumstance.

NOTE: An extreme example of the protection afforded to the company can be seen in *Simpson* v. *Molsons' Bank* (1895), where the company registered a transfer of shares by executors (who are trustees) in breach of the terms of the will of the deceased. The Act incorporating the company provided that it should not be bound to see to the execution of any trust to which its shares were subject. The company had a copy of the will in its possession and its president was one of the defaulting executors and the testator's brother. The company and the executors employed the same law agent. It was held that though the company knew that the shares in question were held by the executors in that capacity, it had no knowledge of their breach of trust, and the knowledge of the executor and law agent could not be imputed to the company so as to affect it with liability.

Without a statutory provision of this kind a company might never dare to register a transfer of shares at all, for fear that it might be party to a breach of trust. It already has been seen that equivalent provisions exist with regard to the register of interests in shares (12:**12**), and later it will be seen that equivalent provisions also exist with regard to the register of directors' interests (16:**17**). While equitable interests must be shown on both these registers, the company is protected from involvement.

Secondly, it is a rule of equity that anyone who meddles with trust property becomes himself a trustee. If the company, therefore, were able to recognize trusts it might become concerned with trust property and so become a trustee, with all the attendant duties and liabilities. This is hardly the proper function of a trading company, and so the section prevents this result from occurring by entirely precluding the company from recognizing trusts.

13. Priority of equitable interests. Although s. 360 simplifies the position of the company, it is still sometimes necessary to know how the priority of equitable interests is regulated if there should be several in a single shareholding. There are *two basic rules* for this:

(*a*) If none of the owners of the equitable interests has succeeded in getting his name put on the company's register of members, then the person whose equitable interest is the earliest has priority.

This rule is often much more neatly expressed by the equitable maxim: *Where the equities are equal, the first in time prevails.* By 'equal' here is meant that the *moral* or equitable claims of the persons concerned are all equally good. Priority must obviously be regulated by something, so it is based on time.

Thus in *Peat* v. *Clayton* (1906), C assigned his property, including some shares, to P who never obtained the share certificates and never became the registered holder, so that he had merely an equitable interest in them. C subsequently sold the shares to a purchaser who, under the contract of sale, also obtained an equitable interest in the shares. Before either party became registered, P started proceedings claiming that he had the prior equity and therefore the right to have the shares registered in his name. HELD: He was entitled to registration. (He had in fact notified the company of his equitable interest, but the notice was of course quite ineffective because of the section, and his priority depended simply on the rule given above.)

(*b*) If any one of the owners of the equitable interests succeeds in getting his name put on the register of members, so that he becomes the *legal* owner of the shares, the equitable interests of other persons, even though created earlier, will be destroyed provided he acted *bona fide*.

This rule is expressed by the equitable maxim: *Where the equities are equal, the law prevails*. By 'law' here is meant the *common law*, and we have already seen (**10**) that an equitable interest has a single but important weakness: it can be destroyed by what Maitland describes as that 'extremely rare and extremely lucky person' – the *bona fide* purchaser for value of the legal interest in the property.

The good faith of the person who succeeds in getting registered is an essential factor.

> Thus in *Coleman* v. *London County and Westminster Bank* (1916), a debenture-holder transferred some debentures to a trustee on trust for his own sons, but the transfer was never registered so that the legal interest remained in the original holder. One of the sons sold his equitable interest to a purchaser. Many years later the registered holder deposited the debentures with the bank as security, thus giving the bank an equitable interest in them. When the bank discovered that a purchaser of an equitable interest in the debentures already existed, it applied for registration and succeeded in becoming registered as the legal owner. HELD: It could not obtain priority over the earlier equitable interest in this way, for it was not acting *bona fide*. It *knew* that the earlier interest existed.

These rules are easy to apply provided they are carefully learnt. It cannot be sufficiently stressed that the priority of equitable interests in shares or debentures is regulated by time, but that all equitable interests can be destroyed by a *bona fide* purchaser for value of the legal interest in the property.

14. The stop notice. The student may at this stage feel that the owner of an equitable interest is in a very difficult position. He may not tell the company that he has such an interest, because if he does the company is simply not concerned with the information. Section 360 says so. Consequently he must remain in a precarious state: he has an interest in shares of which the registered holder is the legal owner. How can he protect himself against the holder's dishonesty? If he discovers that the holder is defrauding him, he can of course start legal proceedings. But how can he find out *in time*, i.e. before a *bona fide* purchaser for value has become the registered holder and so defeated his equitable interest entirely?

The answer is that there is a simple process by which he can compel the company to inform him of a pending transfer of the shares. This is to serve on the company a *stop notice* (formerly known as a notice in lieu of distringas), under Order 50, Rules of the Supreme Court, 1965.

The effect of this notice is that the company becomes bound to inform the person serving it of any request to transfer the shares. Thus the owner of the equitable interest will be told of any impending threat to his position. He can then, if he likes, apply to the court within eight days for an injunction restraining the company from transferring the shares. If he does not do so, the company may register the transfer in the normal way.

NOTE: The company is not concerned with the equitable interest; its sole duty is to inform the owner of an impending transfer of the shares. It is entirely up to him to protect his equitable interest by application to the court, and if he does not wish to do this the company is under no obligation to protect it for him.

15. Legal position where company acquires equitable interest. One final problem can arise where *the company itself* acquires an equitable interest in the shares of a member, e.g. under its lien. It has already been seen that where the articles of a company give it a lien on the shares of a member for money due in respect of them, the lien is an equitable interest (*see* 12:**31**).

If in such a case there were already earlier equitable interests in the shares, and if a dispute broke out between their owners and the company so that all claimed to be entitled to the legal ownership of the shares, it might be thought that s. 360 gives the company an unfair advantage in that it prevents the company from having notice of the equitable interests of other persons.

This is not so. The rule applying here is that *the company's equitable interest ranks after any prior equitable interest of which it knows*, and *it cannot rely on s. 360 to say that it does not know*. It must always be borne in mind that the purpose of s. 360 is administrative convenience, and not to place the company in a better legal position than the holders of other equitable interests.

Thus in *Bradford Banking Co.* v. *Briggs* (1886), the articles gave the company a lien on the shares for the debts of a member. A member deposited his share certificate with the bank as security, thus giving the bank an equitable interest. The bank notified the company – a notice which in the normal way would be completely ineffective because of s. 360. The member then became indebted to the company, so that a second equitable interest in his shares was created under the company's lien. The question of the priority of the interests arose. HELD: The bank had priority, since s. 360 never operates to deprive the company of notice of an equitable interest *when the company itself is involved*. It gives no undeserved priority.

16. Overseas branch registers. Section 362(1) and (2) states that a company with a share capital whose objects comprise the transaction of business in any of the countries or territories specified in Part I of the 14th Schedule may cause to be kept in such a country or territory a branch register of members resident there, called an 'overseas branch register'.

Part II of the 14th Schedule, in para. 1, requires the company to give notice to the registrar of the office where any overseas branch register is kept, and of any changes in that office, and of the discontinuance of the register, within 14 days.

It also states in para. 2 that an overseas branch register is deemed part of the company's principal register, and must be kept in the same manner as the principal register.

By para. 4 the company is required to:

(*a*) send to its registered office a copy of every entry in its overseas branch register as soon as possible; and

(*b*) keep a duplicate of its overseas branch register at the place where its principal register is kept.

Progress test 14

1. What are the contents of the register of members? (**2**)

2. What are the statutory requirements as to the index of members? (**4**)

3. What rights of inspection of the register and index of members are given by the Act? Can the register of members ever be closed? (**5**)

4. Who may apply for rectification of the register of members, and under what circumstances? (**6**)

5. What are the powers of the court when application is made for rectification of the register? **(6)**

6. What are the provisions of s. 360? What is their purpose? **(12)**

7. What are the rules for determining the priority of equitable interests in shares? **(13)**

8. What is a stop notice? **(14)**

9. What is the legal position where a company acquires an equitable interest in its own shares? **(15)**

10. Give an account of the statutory provisions concerning overseas branch registers. **(16)**

15

Company meetings and the annual return

1. Types of company meeting. There are three types of meetings attended by shareholders:

(a) annual general meetings;
(b) extraordinary general meetings;
(c) class meetings.

2. Annual general meetings. Section 366(1) requires every company in each year (i.e. calendar year) to hold a general meeting as its annual general meeting, and to specify it as such in the notices calling it. There must not be more than 15 months between the meetings: s. 366(3).

If, however, the *first* annual general meeting is held *within 18 months of incorporation*, none need be held in the year of incorporation or the following year. Thus a company incorporated in September 1986 need not hold an annual general meeting in either 1986 or 1987, since it can hold its first annual general meeting early in 1988 without infringing the provisions of the Act.

3. Default in holding the annual general meeting. Section 367 states that if the company does not comply with s. 366, any member may apply to the Department of Trade and Industry, which may then itself call a general meeting and give such directions as it thinks fit, including a direction that *one member present in person or by proxy* shall be deemed to constitute a meeting.

Under s. 367(4) such a meeting is deemed to be an annual general meeting, but if it is not held in the year in which default occurred, it is not treated as the annual general meeting for the year in which it is actually held unless the company resolves that it be so treated.

4. The business transacted at an annual general meeting. The business usually transacted at an annual general meeting consists of:

(a) declaring a dividend;

(b) the consideration of the accounts, balance sheets, and directors' and auditors' reports;

(c) the election of directors; and

(d) the appointment and remuneration of the auditors.

Other business may also be transacted at the annual general meeting but it is in practice more usual to convene an extraordinary general meeting to deal with business other than that in (a) to (d) above.

5. The documents accompanying the notice of the annual general meeting. As stated in **4** above, the annual general meeting is normally the occasion on which the directors lay before the company the profit and loss account and balance sheet.

Sections 239 and 240 provide that a copy of the company's accounts (i.e. profit and loss account and balance sheet, the directors' report, the auditors' report and the company's group accounts if applicable) must, at least 21 days before the meeting, be sent to every member, every debenture-holder, and all other persons entitled to receive notice of general meetings.

If these documents are sent less than 21 days before the meeting, they are still deemed to have been duly sent if it is so agreed by all the members entitled to attend and vote.

By s. 241(3) the directors must deliver a copy of the accounts to the registrar and if any document comprised in the accounts is in a language other than English must annex to the document a certified translation of it into English.

6. The contents of the directors' report. The contents of the report which the directors must prepare for each financial year are to be found partly in s. 235 of the Act and partly in the 7th Schedule to the Act. The requirements were greatly increased by the Companies Acts of 1967, 1976 and 1981, but owing to the consolidation effected by the 1985 Act it is no longer necessary to look further than s. 235 and the 7th Schedule for a full view of the present requirements.

The order followed here is first to consider the matters provided for in s. 235 itself and then to consider separately the matters listed in Parts I–V of the 7th Schedule.

7. The requirements of s. 235. By s. 235(1) and (2) the directors' report must contain a fair review of the development of the business of the company and its subsidiaries during the financial year and of their position at the end of it and must state:

(a) the amount, if any, which the directors recommend should be paid as dividend;

(b) the amount, if any, which they propose to carry to reserves;

(c) the names of the persons who, at any time during the financial year, were directors of the company; and

(d) the principal activities of the company and its subsidiaries in the course of the year and any significant change in those activities in the year.

8. Matters of a general nature to be dealt with in directors' report. Part I of the 7th Schedule under its heading 'Matters of a General Nature' requires the following to be stated:

(a) *Asset values.* If significant changes in the fixed assets of the company or of any of its subsidiaries have occurred in the financial year, the report must contain particulars of the changes, and in the case of assets which consist of interests in land, any substantial difference which there may be between their market value and the amount at which they are included in the balance sheet must be indicated in the report.

(b) *Directors' interests.* Under ss. 324–328 a director has an obligation to notify his interests in the company and companies in the same group and a register must be kept by the company for recording such interests (*see* 16:**13–17**). The particulars entered in this register must be stated in the report (or, alternatively, given by way of notes to the accounts).

(c) *Political and charitable gifts.* Particulars of donations exceeding £200 for political or charitable purposes must be included in the report (*see* 2:**25**).

(d) *Miscellaneous.* The report must contain:

(*i*) particulars of any important events affecting the company or any of its subsidiaries which have occurred since the end of the financial year;

(*ii*) an indication of likely future developments in the business of the company and of its subsidiaries; and

(*iii*) an indication of the activities, if any, of the company and its subsidiaries in the field of research and development.

9. Disclosure by company acquiring its own shares. Part II of the 7th Schedule applies in the following cases:

(*a*) where shares in the company are:

(*i*) purchased by the company; *or*

(*ii*) acquired by the company by forfeiture or surrender; *or*

(*iii*) acquired by the company under s. 143(3) (company acquiring its own shares) (*see* 13:**21**);

(*b*) where shares in the company are acquired by some other person in circumstances to which para. (*c*) or (*d*) of s. 146(1) applies (acquisition by company's nominee, or by another with financial assistance from the company) (*see* 13:**30**);

(*c*) where the company acquires a lien or charge over its own shares which is permitted by s. 150(2) (exception to rule against company having a lien or charge on its own shares) (*see* 12:**31**).

In each of these cases the directors' report is required by Part II of the 7th Schedule to state, with respect to the financial year:

(*a*) the number and nominal value of the shares purchased, the amount paid for them by the company and the reasons for their purchase;

(*b*) the number and nominal value of the shares acquired by the company or the other person and of the shares charged during that year, together with:

(*i*) the maximum number and nominal value of such shares which were *held* by the company or that other person at any time during that year; and

(*ii*) the number and nominal value of such shares which were *disposed of* by the company or that other person or *cancelled* by the company during that year;

(*c*) in every case, the percentage of the called-up share capital which the shares in question represent;

(*d*) in any case where shares have been charged, the amount of the charge; and

(*e*) in any case where shares have been disposed of by the company or the other person for money or money's worth, the amount or value of the consideration.

10. Disclosure concerning employment of disabled persons.
Part III of the 7th Schedule applies only where the average number of persons employed by the company in each week during the financial year exceeded 250.

The report must in that case contain a statement describing the policy applied by the company:

(*a*) for giving full and fair consideration to applications for employment made by disabled persons;

(*b*) for continuing the employment of employees who have become disabled while employed by the company and for arranging appropriate training for them; and

(*c*) for the training, career development and promotion of disabled employees.

11. Health, safety and welfare at work of company's employees.
In the case of companies prescribed by regulations made by the Secretary of State, the report must by Part IV of the 7th Schedule contain prescribed information about the arrangements in force in the financial year for securing the health, safety and welfare at work of employees of the company and its subsidiaries, and for protecting other persons against risks to health or safety arising out of or in connection with the activities at work of those employees.

The regulations may make different provision with regard to companies of different classes.

12. Employee involvement.
Part V of the 7th Schedule applies only where the average number of persons employed by the company in each week during the financial year exceeded 250.

The report must in that case contain a statement describing the action taken during the financial year to introduce, maintain or develop arrangements aimed at:

(*a*) providing employees systematically with information on matters of concern to them as employees;

(*b*) consulting employees or their representatives on a regular basis so that the views of employees can be taken into account in making decisions which are likely to affect their interests;

(*c*) encouraging the involvement of employees in the company's performance through an employees' share scheme or by some other means; and

(*d*) achieving a common awareness on the part of all employees of the financial and economic factors affecting the performance of the company.

13. Extraordinary general meetings. All general meetings other than the annual general meeting are extraordinary general meetings. The directors may convene one whenever they wish.

Table A, Article 37, authorizes the directors to call general meetings, and provides that if there are not within the United Kingdom sufficient directors to call a general meeting, any director or any member of the company may call a general meeting.

14. Convening of extraordinary general meeting on requisition. Section 368(1) and (2) states that despite anything in the articles, the directors *must* convene an extraordinary general meeting on the requisition of members holding *not less than one-tenth of the paid up capital carrying the right to vote* or, if the company has no share capital, members representing not less than one-tenth of the total voting rights.

Section 368(3) requires the requisition to state the objects of the meeting, to be signed by the requisitionists, and deposited at the registered office.

Section 368(4) states that if the directors do not proceed to convene a meeting within 21 days from the deposit of the requisition, the requisitionists, or those representing more than half their total voting rights, may themselves convene a meeting. This meeting must not be held more than three months after the date of the deposit. Section 368(5) requires it to be convened in the same manner as meetings convened by the directors.

Section 368(6) states that any reasonable expenses incurred by the requisitionists must be repaid to them by the company, and that sum retained by the company out of the remuneration due to the defaulting directors.

Table A, Article 37, requires the directors to convene a meeting held on requisition for a date not later than eight weeks after receipt of the requisition. The purpose of this provision is to prevent the directors from fixing a date so far into the future that the value of the right to requisition a meeting will have, in effect, been lost.

15. The business transacted at an extraordinary general meeting. This can comprise anything which under the Act or the articles is required to be done by the company in general meeting. Usually the business will be something other than the usual business of annual general meetings (*see* **4**), e.g. it may be an alteration of the articles.

16. Provisions enabling members to call a meeting. Section 370(1) and (3) states that unless the articles otherwise provide, *two or more members holding not less than one-tenth of the issued share capital* (whether with voting rights or not), or if the company has no share capital, not less than 5 per cent of the members, may call a meeting.

17. Power of court to order a meeting. Section 371 provides that if for any reason it is impracticable to call or conduct a meeting, the court may, either of its own motion or on the application of any director or any member who would be entitled to vote, order a meeting to be called, held and conducted in such manner as the court thinks fit, and may give such directions as it thinks expedient, including a direction that *one member present in person or by proxy* shall be deemed to constitute a meeting.

18. Class meetings. Sometimes a meeting of a particular class of shareholders is held. At a class meeting the holders of the remainder of the company's shares have no right to be present.

The usual business of a class meeting is to consider a variation of class rights. This topic has been extensively treated in Chapter 11 but, in relation to meetings, 11:**16** is of special relevance here since it deals with the provisions of s. 125(7).

19. The requisites of a valid meeting. For a meeting to be valid the following conditions must be satisfied:

(*a*) It must be properly convened. This means:

convene a meeting specially to enable the resolution to be considered. It can be deferred until the next annual general meeting or extraordinary general meeting which is convened.

It should also be noted that if the resolution is considered at an extraordinary general meeting, 14 days' notice is adequate provided it is given at the same time and in the same manner as the notice of the meeting.

The following are the resolutions requiring special notice:

(a) a resolution to remove a director: s. 303(2) (**16:23**);

(b) a resolution to appoint another director in his place: s. 303(2);

(c) a resolution appointing a director over the age limit: s. 293(5) (**16:19**);

(d) a resolution to appoint as auditor a person other than a retiring auditor: s. 388(1) (**19:8**);

(e) a resolution to fill a casual vacancy in the office of auditor: s. 388(1);

(f) a resolution to reappoint as auditor a retiring auditor who was appointed by the directors to fill a casual vacancy: s. 388(1);

(g) a resolution to remove an auditor before the expiration of his term of office: s. 388(1).

Students should be careful to observe that *special notice* (s. 379) has no connection whatever with *special resolutions* (s. 378). The terminology is confusing, but once it is understood that these two things are quite unconnected, there is less likelihood of error.

25. The chairman. Section 370(1) and (5) states that unless the articles otherwise provide, *any member* elected by the members present at a meeting may be the chairman. Normally, however, the articles in fact provide otherwise, and Table A, Article 42, states that the *chairman of the board of directors* shall preside as chairman at every general meeting. It also states that if the chairman is not present within *15 minutes* of the time appointed for the commencement of the meeting, or is unwilling to act, the directors present must elect one of their number to be chairman.

Article 43 states that if no director is willing to act as chairman, or if no director is present within 15 minutes, the members present and entitled to vote must choose one of their number to be chairman.

At common law a chairman has no casting vote, but Table A, Article 50, gives him one in the case of an *equality of votes*, either on a show of hands or on a poll. If he is not also a shareholder in the company, this will be his only vote, and he is not bound to exercise it.

26. Duties of the chairman. The chairman's position is of great importance, and his many duties include the following:

(a) He must act at all times *bona fide* and in the interests of the company as a whole.

(b) He must ensure that the meeting is properly convened and constituted, i.e. that proper notice has been given, that the rules as to quorum are observed, and that his own appointment is in order.

(c) He must ensure that the provisions of the Act and the articles are observed, that the business is taken in the order set out in the agenda, and that the business is within the scope of the meeting.

(d) He must preserve order.

(e) He must take the sense of the meeting by putting the motions in their proper form, and declare the result of the voting.

(f) He must exercise his casting vote, if any, *bona fide* in the interests of the company. This probably involves voting *against* the motion.

(g) He must exercise correctly his powers of adjournment and of demanding a poll.

27. Quorum. A quorum is the minimum number of persons whose presence is necessary for the transaction of business. At *common law,* *one* person cannot constitute a meeting, even though he holds proxies for several other persons, and the minimum quorum is therefore two persons entitled to vote and present in person: *Sharp* v. *Dawes* (1876).

In the case of registered companies s. 370(1) and (4) adopts the common law rule and states that, unless the articles otherwise provide, the quorum shall be *two members personally present*. Table A, article 40 repeats this provision with recognition for proxies, stating that *two* persons, each being a member or a proxy for a member, shall be a quorum.

An interesting construction was put on an article which required *three members present in person* in the Scottish case of *Neil McLeod and Sons, Petitioners* (1967). There two shareholders attended the meeting, one of them in the dual capacity of individual and trustee. It was held that the required quorum was present. A different result might well have been reached in England where s. 360 applies (*see* 14:**12**).

Table A, Article 40, provides that no business shall be transacted at any meeting unless a quorum is present. This is in accordance with the common law, by which it is essential that the quorum remains present throughout the proceedings. If, however, the articles provide, as the Table A in the 1st Schedule to the 1948 Act provided, that no business shall be transacted unless a quorum is present *at the time when the meeting proceeds to business*, then the court may hold, as it did in *Re Hartley Baird Ltd* (1955), that a quorum need be present only when the meeting commences, it being immaterial that there is no longer a quorum present when a vote is taken.

Article 41 states that if within half an hour a quorum is not present, or if during a meeting a quorum ceases to be present, the meeting shall stand adjourned to the same day in the next week, at the same time and place, or to such time and place as the directors may determine.

28. Exceptions to the rule in *Sharp* v. *Dawes*. There are certain exceptional cases where, despite the rule in *Sharp* v. *Dawes, one* person may constitute a meeting. These are as follows:

 (*a*) under s. 367 (*see* **3** above);

 (*b*) under s. 371 (*see* **17** above);

 (*c*) where there is a committee of one (*see* **16:62**);

 (*d*) where there is a class meeting of shareholders, and all the shares of that class are held by one person: *East* v. *Bennett Bros. Ltd* (1911);

 (*e*) under Article 89, where the directors fix the quorum for board meetings at one.

29. Adjournments. Table A, Article 45, states that the chairman may, with the consent of any meeting at which a quorum is present, and shall if so directed by the meeting, adjourn the meeting.

Under such an article a chairman has no power to adjourn the meeting without its consent, unless there is disorder, and if he wrongly adjourns it, the meeting may appoint another chairman and continue the business.

At *common law* no notice is required of an adjourned meeting unless the original meeting is adjourned *sine die* (without a day being fixed for the holding of the adjourned meeting) or unless *fresh business* is to be discussed. Articles often vary this rule, and Table A, Article 45, provides that no business shall be transacted at an adjourned meeting other than business which might properly have been transacted at the original meeting. Moreover, when the meeting is adjourned for 14 days or more, Article 45 requires at least seven clear days' notice of the adjourned meeting to be given.

A properly convened meeting *cannot be postponed* by subsequent notice to that effect. It should be held and then immediately adjourned without transacting any business.

30. Resolutions passed at adjourned meetings. Section 381 provides that resolutions passed at adjourned meetings are to be treated as having been passed on the date on which they were in fact passed.

This provision is necessary because in law an adjourned meeting is merely a continuation of the original meeting, so that a resolution passed at an adjourned meeting would otherwise take effect as if passed at the *original* meeting.

31. Voting. The common law method of taking a vote is on a *show of hands*, and this is adopted by registered companies.

Table A, Article 46, states that a resolution shall be decided on a show of hands unless a poll is demanded by the proper persons, and Article 54 states that on a show of hands *every member present shall have one vote*. It follows that under Article 54 *proxies* cannot vote on a show of hands.

Section 372(2)(c) states that unless the articles otherwise provide, a proxy is not entitled to vote on a show of hands, but even where the articles confer this right, a member present who holds proxies for several other absent members still has only one vote.

Section 375 states that a representative appointed by a corporation to attend and vote at meetings of a company of which it is a member or creditor has the same powers as it would have if it were an individual. Thus he can vote on a show of hands, and is not a proxy.

Section 378(4) states that at a meeting at which an extraordinary or special resolution is to be passed, a declaration by the chairman that it is carried is, unless a poll is demanded, conclusive evidence of that fact without proof of the number of votes recorded for or against the resolution. Table A, Article 47, contains an even stronger provision to the same effect, stating that unless a poll is demanded, a declaration by the chairman that a resolution has been carried, or carried unanimously, or by a particular majority, or lost, or not carried by a particular majority and an entry in the minutes to that effect, is conclusive evidence of the fact without proof of the number of votes recorded for or against the resolution.

NOTE: Article 31(13:9), Article 55 (13:3), and Article 56 (13:7) are all relevant here, but have already been discussed. Article 57 states that a member may not vote unless all calls or other sums presently payable by him in respect of his shares have been paid. Lastly, Article 58 states that no objection may be raised to the qualification of any voter *except at the meeting* or adjourned meeting at which the vote objected to is given, and every vote not disallowed at such meeting is valid. Any objection made in due time must be referred to the chairman, whose decision is final.

32. Voting on a poll. Voting on a show of hands ceases to have any effect once a poll has been properly demanded; indeed, a poll can be demanded without going through the formality of a show of hands at all: *Holmes* v. *Keyes* (1959). The chairman must then allow a poll and decide when and where it is to be taken.

Table A, Article 51, provides that a poll demanded on the *election of a chairman* or on a *question of adjournment* must be taken forthwith. A poll demanded on *any other question* must be taken either forthwith or within the next 30 days at such time and place as the chairman directs, and meanwhile any other business may be proceeded with.

On a poll, members have the number of votes attached to their shares. Table A, Article 54, states that a member has one vote for each share, and s. 370(1) and (6) states that unless the articles otherwise provide, every member has one vote for each share or each £10 of stock. Article 59 states that on a poll votes may be given either *personally* or *by proxy*.

Section 374 states that on a poll, a member entitled to more than one vote need not use all his votes, nor cast all those used in the same way. This enables a nominee shareholder holding shares on trust for more than one beneficial owner to exercise the votes as the beneficial owners direct.

If the chairman decides that a poll should be taken at some future date, the question arises as to whether proxies lodged between the date of the meeting and the date of the poll can be accepted. A poll is an enlargement or *continuation* of the meeting at which it was demanded, and *not an adjournment* of it, so that in *Shaw* v. *Tati Concessions Ltd* (1913), where the articles allowed lodgement of proxies 48 hours before *a meeting or any adjournment thereof*, it was held that fresh proxies could *not* be lodged between the meeting and the poll.

Table A, Article 61, however, resolves this difficulty by providing that proxies must be lodged at least 48 hours before the time of the meeting or any adjournment of it, or, in the case of a poll taken more than 48 hours after it is demanded, at least 24 hours before the time appointed for the taking of the poll. In the case of a poll not taken forthwith but taken within 48 hours after it is demanded, the proxy must be delivered at the meeting at which the poll is demanded to the chairman or to the secretary or to any director. Thus, if the poll is not taken within the next 48 hours, fresh proxies can under this article be accepted between the date of the meeting and that of the poll.

33. The right to demand a poll. The right to demand a poll is a *common law* right which normally may be excluded by the regulations of any association. In the case of registered companies, however, s. 373(1)(*a*) gives members a *statutory right* to demand a poll on any question *except*:

(*a*) the election of the chairman; and

(*b*) the adjournment of the meeting.

This statutory right cannot be excluded by the articles.

Section 373(1)(*b*) states that an article which *makes ineffective* a demand for a poll by any of the following is *void*:

(*a*) by five or more members having the right to vote;

(*b*) by members having at least one-tenth of the total voting rights of members having the right to vote at the meeting;

(*c*) by members holding voting shares on which one-tenth of the sum paid up on all voting shares has been paid up.

Students often find this provision difficult, especially (*a*). Perhaps this can be more simply expressed by saying that *any five or more members have a right to demand a poll, no matter what the articles may say*. In fact, Table A, Article 46, gives *wider rights* than the section, for it states that a poll may be demanded by:

(*a*) the chairman; *or*

(*b*) at least two members having the right to vote; *or*

(c) members representing at least one-tenth of the total voting rights of all members having the right to vote at the meeting; *or*

(d) members holding voting shares on which one-tenth of the total sum paid up on all voting shares has been paid up.

It is important to understand that there is no conflict between s. 373(1)(b) and Article 46. The Act is merely ensuring that the articles do not insist on a poll being demanded by, e.g., 20 persons before the demand is valid. There is nothing to prevent the articles from stating that a poll may be validly demanded by *one* member, if this is thought desirable.

Section 373(2) states that an instrument appointing a proxy to vote is deemed also to confer authority to demand a poll, and Table A, Article 46, contains a provision to the same effect.

Finally, Article 48 states that a demand for a poll may, before the poll is taken, be withdrawn, but only with the consent of the chairman.

34. Proxies. The term 'proxy' covers not only the *person* who is appointed to act on behalf of a member at a meeting, but also the *instrument* by which the appointment is made. There is no right to appoint a proxy at *common law*, but s. 372 gives members a statutory right to do so.

Section 372(1) states that any member entitled to attend and vote is entitled to appoint another person (*whether a member or not*) as his proxy to attend and vote instead of him. In a *private* company a proxy also has the same right as the member to *speak*.

However, by s. 372(2), unless the articles otherwise provide:

(a) subsection (1) applies only to companies with share capital;

(b) a member of a *private* company may appoint only one proxy on each occasion;

(c) a proxy may vote only on a poll.

Section 372(3) has already been discussed (*see* **22**).

Section 372(5) states that any provision in the articles is *void* if it requires the instrument appointing the proxy to be received by the company more than 48 hours before a meeting or adjourned meeting. Table A, Article 61, specifies the maximum period permitted by the subsection, i.e. 48 hours.

A member who has appointed a proxy, however, may still attend the meeting and exercise his vote if he wishes, though this will revoke his proxy. Proxies may also be revoked by notice to the company at any time before they are acted upon, or by the death of the member. Accordingly Table A, Article 63, states that a vote of a proxy is valid despite the termination of the proxy's authority unless notice of the termination has been received by the company before the commencement of the meeting.

35. Specified proxies. Many companies send along with the notice of the meeting a form of proxy in favour of the directors. Members who cannot attend the meeting merely have to complete the form and send it back to the company. These proxy forms may be sent at the expense of the company, but some control is obviously necessary to prevent the directors sending them only to persons who will support their policy.

Section 372(6) accordingly provides that if invitations to appoint as proxy a person *specified in the invitations* are issued at the company's expense to *some only* of the members, every officer who knowingly and wilfully authorizes their issue is liable to a fine, unless he does so at the written request of the member, and the form would be available to every member on his written request. The fine must not exceed one-fifth of the statutory maximum: s. 730 and 24th Schedule.

36. Form of proxy. Table A, Article 60, states that the instrument appointing a proxy shall be in writing executed by or on behalf of the appointor. *A proxy need not be a member*: s. 372(1).

Two forms of proxy are in use:

(*a*) The *ordinary* form, as shown in Table A, Article 60, which simply authorizes the proxy to *vote on behalf of the member* (a *general* proxy).

(*b*) The *two-way* form, as shown in Table A, Article 61, which directs the proxy to *vote for or against the resolution*; here only if the member fails to give the proxy express directions how to vote may he exercise his discretion (a *special* proxy).

37. Minutes. In 2:16 we saw that s. 382(1) requires every company to keep minutes of the proceedings at both general and board meetings.

Section 382(2) provides that minutes, if signed by the chairman of the meeting or the next succeeding meeting, are evidence of the proceedings. They are normally only *prima facie* evidence, though Article 47 (*see* **31**) gives an exception to this.

Section 382(4) states that where minutes have been made in accordance with the section, the meeting is deemed duly held and convened, the proceedings duly had, and appointments of directors or liquidators valid, until the contrary is proved.

Section 383(1) and (2) requires the minute books of proceedings at general meetings to be kept at the registered office (*see* 2:**15**), and to be open to inspection for at least two hours a day during business hours to any member free. Section 383(3) entitles any member to a copy of the minutes within seven days on payment of a small charge, and s. 383(5) empowers the court to order inspection or the provision of copies if the company fails to comply with the section.

38. Resolutions. There are three types of resolutions: ordinary (passed by a simple majority) extraordinary (passed by a majority of 75 per cent) and special (passed by a majority of 75 per cent on 21 days' notice). In all cases, the majority is of those members present and voting, i.e. absentees and abstentions are not counted. It is important to understand that unless an Act or the articles expressly require a special or extraordinary resolution, an ordinary resolution will suffice.

It is therefore essential to know the occasions on which an Act requires a special or extraordinary resolution.

39. Purposes for which a special resolution is required. A special resolution is required:

(*a*) under s. 4, to alter the objects clause of the memorandum;

(*b*) under s. 9, to alter the articles;

(*c*) under s. 17, to alter any condition in the memorandum other than the compulsory clauses and class rights;

(*d*) under s. 28, to change the name of the company;

(*e*) under s. 43, to re-register a private company with a share capital as a public company;

(*f*) under ss. 43 and 48, to re-register an unlimited private company as a public company;

(*g*) under s. 51, to re-register an unlimited (private) company as limited;

(*h*) under s. 53, to re-register a public company as a private company;

(*i*)   under s. 95, to withdraw or modify the statutory pre-emption rights;

(*j*)   under s. 120, to create reserve capital;

(*k*)   under s. 135, to reduce capital, with the consent of the court;

(*l*)   under s. 155, to approve the giving of financial assistance by a private company for the acquisition of shares in itself;

(*m*)   under s. 173, to approve a payment out of capital by a private company for the redemption or purchase of its own shares;

(*n*)   under s. 307, to make the liability of the directors unlimited;

(*o*)   under s. 308, to approve the assignment of office by a director;

(*p*)   under s. 84 Insolvency Act 1986, to wind up voluntarily;

(*q*)   under s. 110 Insolvency Act 1986, to sanction the sale of the company's property by the liquidator in a members' voluntary winding up for shares in another company;

(*r*)   under s. 122 Insolvency Act 1986, to effect a winding up by the court.

40. Purposes for which an extraordinary resolution is required. An extraordinary resolution is required:

(*a*)   under s. 125, at a class meeting to sanction a variation of class rights in certain circumstances;

(*b*)   under s. 84 Insolvency Act 1986, to wind up the company voluntarily because it cannot continue its business owing to its liabilities;

(*c*)   under s. 165 and the 4th Schedule, Part I, Insolvency Act 1986, in a members' voluntary winding up, to sanction the exercise by the liquidator of the following powers:

(*i*)   to pay any class of creditors in full;

(*ii*)   to make a compromise or arrangement with creditors;

(*iii*)   to compromise all calls, debts and claims between the company and a contributory or other debtor.

41. The filing of resolutions. Section 380(1) and (4) requires a copy of the following resolutions or agreements to be sent to the registrar within 15 days:

(*a*)   *special* resolutions;

(*b*)   *extraordinary* resolutions;

(*c*)   resolutions or agreements which have been agreed to by *all the members,* but which would not otherwise have been effective unless they had been passed as special or extraordinary resolutions;

(*d*) resolutions or agreements which have been agreed to by *all the members of some class* of shareholders, but which would not otherwise have been effective unless passed by some *particular majority* or in some *particular manner,* and all resolutions or agreements which *bind all the members of a class* of shareholders though not agreed to by all of them;

(*e*) a resolution passed by the *directors* to comply with a direction under s. 31(2) (change of name on Secretary of State's direction) (*see* 2:**13**);

(*f*) a resolution passed under s. 80 (authority conferred on directors for certain allotments) (*see* 9:**9**);

(*g*) a resolution of the *directors* passed under s. 147(2) (alteration of memorandum on company ceasing to be a public company, following acquisition of its own shares) (*see* 12:**35** and 13:**30**);

(*h*) a resolution passed under s. 166 (authority conferred for market purchase of company's own shares) (*see* 11:**28**);

(*i*) a resolution for voluntary winding up passed under s. 84(1) (*a*) Insolvency Act 1986, when the period fixed by the articles for the company's duration expires.

Further, by s. 111(2) there must also be delivered to the registrar within 15 days:

(*j*) a resolution passed under s. 104 (transfer to public company of non-cash asset in initial period) (*see* 6:**5**).

Section 380(2) states that where articles have been registered, a copy of every resolution and agreement to which the section applies must be annexed to every future copy of the articles. If the alterations to the articles become too numerous, reprinting may be desirable, but the section does not require it. Note, however, the provisions of s. 18(2) (*see* 3:**9**).

Section 380(3) states that where articles have not been registered, a copy of every resolution and agreement to which the section applies must be sent to any member at his request, on payment of a small fee.

Finally, s. 711 requires the registrar to publish in the *Gazette* a copy of any resolution or agreement to which s. 380 applies and which:

(*a*) *states the rights attached to any shares in a public company,* other than shares which are in all respects uniform with those previously allotted;

(b) *varies rights* attached to any shares in a public company; *or*

(c) *assigns a name or other designation*, or a new name or designation, to any class of shares in a public company.

42. Circulation of members' resolutions. Section 376(1) and (2) states that on the requisition in writing of:

(a) *any number of members* representing *at least one-twentieth of the total voting rights* of all the members with a right to vote at the date of the requisition; *or*

(b) *at least 100 members* (whether entitled to vote or not) who have *paid up* on their shares *an average sum of at least £100 per member*,

the company must, at the requisitionists' expense unless the company otherwise resolves, give members entitled to receive notice of the next *annual* general meeting notice of any resolution which may properly be moved and is intended to be moved at that meeting.

It must also circulate to members entitled to notice of *any* general meeting any statement of not more than 1000 words concerning the subject-matter of any proposed resolution or the business to be dealt with at that meeting.

Section 376(5) requires the notice of the resolution to be given, and the statement to be circulated, in the same manner and, as far as is practicable, at the same time as the notice of the meeting, though under s. 377(3) it need not circulate any statement if, on the application of the company or any aggrieved person, the court is satisfied that these rights are being abused to secure *needless publicity for defamatory matter*.

Section 377(1) states that a company need not comply with s. 376 unless:

(a) a copy of the requisition signed by the requisitionists is deposited at the registered office:

(i) in the case of a requisition requiring notice of a resolution, at least *six weeks* before the meeting, and

(ii) in the case of any other requisition, at least *one week* before the meeting, *and*

(b) there is deposited or tendered with the requisition a sum reasonably sufficient to meet the company's expenses.

However, by s. 377(2), if after a copy of a requisition requiring notice of a resolution has been deposited at the registered office, an annual general meeting is called for a date six weeks or less afterwards, the copy is still deemed to have been properly deposited.

43. Power to dispense with general meeting. When any particular act of the company requires the assent of the shareholders in general meeting, it was at one time doubtful whether there could ever be any effective substitute for the holding of a meeting and the passing of a resolution in a formal manner.

The courts, however, became progressively more lenient in their view, and in *Re Duomatic* (1969), Buckley J. held that where *all* the shareholders with the right to attend and vote at a general meeting assent to some matter which a general meeting of the company could carry into effect, that assent is as binding as a resolution in general meeting.

Table A, Article 53, gives formal expression to this rule by stating that a resolution in writing signed by all the members entitled to attend and vote is as effectual as if passed at a general meeting.

44. The duty to make the annual return. Section 363(1) states that every company with a share capital must, at least once in every calendar year, make a return to the registrar in accordance with the 15th Schedule.

It need not, however, do so in the year of its incorporation, nor in the following year if the company is not required to hold an annual general meeting in that year (*see* **2**).

Section 365(1) states that the annual return must be completed within 42 days after the annual general meeting, and the company must at once send a copy signed by a director and the secretary to the registrar.

There is a registration fee of £20: Companies (Fees) Regulations 1980 (S.I. 1980, No. 1749).

45. The contents of the annual return. The 15th Schedule states that the contents of the annual return are:

(*a*) the address of the registered office;
(*b*) the address where the registers of members and debenture-holders are kept, if they are kept elsewhere;

(c) a summary distinguishing between shares issued for cash and shares issued as paid up otherwise than in cash, stating:

(i) the amount of share capital and the number of shares;

(ii) the number of shares taken up to the date of the return;

(iii) the amount called up, received and unpaid;

(iv) commission and discount in respect of shares or debentures;

(v) forfeitures;

(vi) details of share warrants;

(d) total amount of indebtedness in respect of registrable charges;

(e) a list containing:

(i) the names and addresses of those who are members on the 14th day after the annual general meeting, and of those who have ceased to be members since the date of the last return;

(ii) the number of shares held by each member, stating the shares transferred since the date of the last return;

(iii) an index of names where necessary;

(f) particulars of the directors and secretary.

This very important list of contents has been shortened and slightly re-arranged to facilitate learning, but it has been reduced to its minimum and every student should make sure that he is thoroughly familiar with it.

Section 363(4) also states that if the company has converted its shares into stock, the return should give the same particulars with regard to the stock as are required for shares. Moreover, s. 363(5) requires a complete list of members and their holdings only every third year. In the intervening years only changes need be given.

All statements in the return are admissible as evidence of the truth of their contents: *R.* v. *Halpin* (1975).

46. Destruction of old records. Section 715 authorizes the registrar to destroy any annual returns which he has kept for 10 years, but he must retain a copy (e.g. microfilm) of any document destroyed.

Progress test 15

1. What are the statutory provisions regarding the holding of the annual general meeting? (**2**)

2. Under what circumstances may the Department of Trade and Industry call a general meeting of a company? (**3**)

3. What type of business is usually transacted at an annual general meeting? (**4**)

4. What documents accompany the notice of the annual general meeting when it is sent out to the members? (**5**)

5. What are the contents of the directors' report? · (**6–12**)

6. Give the statutory provisions regarding requisitioned meetings. (**14**)

7. Under what circumstances may the court call a meeting? (**17**)

8. In what manner must notice of meetings be served? Under Table A, on whom must it be served? (**20, 21**)

9. What is the legal effect of:

(a) waiver of his right to notice by a member?

(b) the accidental failure to give notice to a member? (**20**)

10. What are the statutory requirements as to length of notice? Who may validly consent to shorter notice being given? (**23**)

11. What is special notice, and for which resolutions is it required? (**24**)

12. What do you understand by a quorum? Must a quorum be present throughout the meeting? What is the correct procedure if a quorum is never formed? (**27**)

13. Under what circumstances may one person constitute a meeting? (**28**)

14. What are the statutory provisions regarding the right to demand a poll? (**33**)

15. What are the provisions in Table A regarding the right to demand a poll? Can a demand for a poll be withdrawn? (**33**)

16. What do you understand by the term 'proxy'? What are the statutory provisions regarding proxies? (**34**)

17. What is:

(a) a specified proxy?

(b) a general proxy?

(c) a special proxy? (**35, 36**)

18. For what purposes is a special resolution required? (**39**)

19. For what purposes is an extraordinary resolution required? (**40**)

20. Which resolutions are required to be filed with the registrar? (**41**)

21. What rights are given by the Act regarding the circulation of members' resolutions? (**42**)

22. Is it ever possible to dispense with the holding of a meeting? (**43**)

23. What are the statutory provisions regarding the duty to make the annual return? (**44**)

24. Within what period must the annual return be completed, and who is required to sign the copy sent to the registrar? (**44**)

25. What are the contents of the annual return? (**45**)

16
Directors and secretary

1. Definition of a director. Section 741(1) defines a director as including 'any person occupying the position of director, by whatever name called'. This is a definition based purely on *function*: a person is a director if he does whatever a director normally does. But the Act gives little guidance on the function and duties of a director.

A director is an *officer* of the company, for s. 744, as we saw in 2:**10**, states that officer 'includes a director, manager or secretary'. He is also an *agent* of the company, though the Act does not say so. But he is *not an employee* and is therefore not entitled to preferential payment when the company goes into liquidation.

2. Shadow directors. Several provisions of the Act relating to directors are made applicable also to 'shadow directors', e.g. s. 309, which requires directors to have regard to the interests of the company's employees, and s. 319, which relates to a director's contract of employment for more than five years.

The term 'shadow director', by s. 741(2), means 'a person in accordance with whose directions or instructions the directors are accustomed to act'. However, a person is not deemed to be a shadow director merely because the directors act on advice given by him in a professional capacity.

3. The number of directors required. Section 282 states that every public company must have at least two directors, and every private company must have at least one.

The Act also contains a number of provisions designed to ensure that the offices of director and secretary do not fall into the same hands in companies with only one director.

Thus s. 283(1) states that every company must have a secretary, but

s. 283(2) then provides that a sole director may not be the secretary. Of course, if there are two or more directors, one of them may be the secretary and in practice often is.

Section 283(4), in language which students find a parody of legal expression, is designed to prevent evasion of s. 283(2) by using the device of the corporate person. Section 283(4)(*a*) provides that where two companies have the same person as sole director, neither company may be the secretary of the other. Section 283(4)(*b*) provides that where the same person is sole director of X company and secretary of Y company, X company may not be the sole director of Y company.

Finally, s. 284 provides that anything which must be done by the secretary and a director must be done by *two separate individuals*, and not by one person acting in both capacities.

NOTE: Students who are still mystified by s. 283(4) in spite of the attempted simplification above are advised to make a pictorial representation of the forbidden situation. They will then see the purpose of the section, having regard to s. 283(2).

4. Appointment of the first directors. Section 13(5) provides that the persons named in the statement required by s. 10 (*see* 4:**1**) as the directors of the company shall, on incorporation, be deemed to have been appointed the first directors. In practice, the articles often name the first directors, but s. 10(5) invalidates any such appointment unless the persons mentioned have also been named as directors in the statement.

5. Subsequent appointments. Table A, Article 73, states that at the first annual general meeting all the directors retire, and at every subsequent annual general meeting one-third or the number nearest one-third, retire. This is *retirement by rotation*.

Article 74 states that those to retire are those who have been longest in office, but if they all took office on the same day, those to retire must (unless they otherwise agree among themselves) be determined by lot.

Article 80 provides that retiring directors are eligible for re-election.

Article 75 provides that if the company, at the meeting at which a director retires by rotation, does not fill the vacancy the retiring director shall be *automatically re-elected*, unless:

(*a*) it is resolved not to fill the vacancy; *or*

(*b*) a resolution for his re-election is lost.

Article 76 provides that if it is desired to propose a person other than a director retiring by rotation or a person recommended by the directors for election as a director, then at least 14 and not more than 35 clear days before the meeting a written notice must be left at the registered office. It must be signed by a member entitled to attend and vote, and give notice of his intention to propose that person for election. It must be accompanied by that person's written consent to stand.

6. Appointment of directors to fill casual vacancies. Article 79 states that if a vacancy on the board occurs in between two annual general meetings, the remaining directors may appoint a person to fill it. It also authorizes the directors to appoint additional directors, so long as the maximum number permitted by the regulations is not exceeded.

In both cases the directors so appointed hold office only until the next annual general meeting. They are then eligible for re-election, but are not taken into account in determining those who are to retire by rotation at that meeting.

7. Voting on the appointment of directors. Section 292(1) provides that in a *public* company (*see* 25:6) directors must be elected *individually*, unless the meeting has first resolved *nem. con.* (*nemine contradicente* = with no vote cast *against* the resolution) to vote on them together.

The purpose of this section is to ensure that the will of the meeting is expressed on each director as an individual. If two or more directors could be elected by a single resolution, this would be impossible. Accordingly s. 292(2) invalidates any resolution which contravenes the section by attempting to apply to more than one director.

8. Permanent directors. Sometimes the articles appoint a person a permanent director, i.e. for life. In such a case it is not necessary to re-elect him, and the articles usually expressly exclude him from the operation of the clauses relating to retirement by rotation. He is normally given wide powers of management, and in practice he will probably be a major shareholder in the company.

It should not, however, be thought that he is truly 'permanent'. He is, like any other director, removable under s. 303, the provisions of which will be discussed later in this chapter. It follows that unless he has voting control, he can be removed at any time. We have already seen (*see* 3:**10**) that the articles never constitute a *contract* between the company and any person in a capacity other than that of *member*. But even if a permanent director has taken care to see that, quite apart from the appropriate clause in the articles, he has entered into a valid service contract with the company as, for example, its managing director, he can still be removed. He will in this case have a right of action for breach of contract, but no right to continue in office.

9. Assignment of office by directors. If the articles or any agreement empower a director to assign his office to another person, s. 308 states that the assignment will be void unless approved by a special resolution of the company.

10. Alternate directors. Alternate directors are entirely different from assignees of office, and are not affected by s. 308. The main distinction between them is that in the case of alternate directors there is only a *temporary* delegation of authority and function.

An alternate director cannot be appointed unless there is authority in the articles to that effect. Most articles nowadays contain the necessary authority.

Table A, Article 65, provides that any director may appoint any other director, or any other person approved by resolution of the directors, to be an alternate director. By Article 66 an alternate director is entitled to receive notices of all directors' meetings, to attend and vote at such meetings and generally to perform all the functions of his appointor, but he is not entitled to receive any remuneration from the company for his services as an alternate director. Article 67 provides that an alternate director ceases to be an alternate director if his appointor ceases to be a director. By Article 68 the procedure for appointment or removal of an alternate director is by notice to the company, signed by the director making or revoking the appointment, or any other procedure approved by the directors. Most important is Article 69 which provides that an alternate director is to be alone responsible for his own acts and defaults and is not to be deemed to be the agent of the director appointing him. (If the alternate director were the agent of his appointor, the appointing director would be responsible for all acts done by the alternate.)

Most of the statutory provisions apply to alternate directors in the same way as to ordinary directors. Thus ss. 285 (validity of acts of directors), 288–289 (register of directors and secretaries) and 291 (share qualification of directors) are applicable. So also are ss. 305 (directors' names on company correspondence, etc.), 314–316 (disclosure of payment for loss of office) and 317 (disclosure of interest in contracts). All these sections are considered later in this chapter. Section 282(1) however, requiring a minimum of two directors in a public company, is not satisfied by the company having one director with his alternate, for an alternate director is essentially a *substitute*.

11. The register of directors and secretaries. Section 288(1) requires every company to keep a register of its directors and secretaries at its registered office (*see* 2:**15, 16**).

Section 289(1) states that this register must contain the following particulars with respect to each director:

(*a*) his name and former name, if any;

(*b*) his address;

(*c*) his nationality;

(*d*) his business occupation, if any;

(*e*) particulars of any other directorships held by him or formerly held by him within the last five years, with two exceptions mentioned below;

(*f*) his date of birth, where the company is subject to s. 293 (age-limit).

Where the director is a corporation, the register must specify its corporate name and its registered or principal office.

NOTE

(1) *Particulars of other directorships.* The exceptions to (*e*) mentioned above are in s. 289(3) and (4) and relate to:

(*i*) directorships of *dormant* companies (*see* 19:**5**); and

(*ii*) directorships of a company grouped with the company keeping the register.

For the purposes of (*ii*), the Act gives a meaning of 'grouped with' which is difficult to understand unless specific companies are inserted as follows:

A company (A Ltd) is regarded as being grouped with another (B Ltd) if:

(*a*) B Ltd is a wholly-owned subsidiary of A Ltd; *or*

(*b*) A Ltd is a wholly-owned subsidiary of B Ltd; *or*

(*c*) A Ltd is a wholly-owned subsidiary of C Ltd *and* B Ltd is a wholly-owned subsidiary of C Ltd.

The underlying purpose of these complicated statutory provisions is to make it unnecessary, where there is such a closely-knit group, to include in the register of directors of any one company the directorships held by the directors in other companies within the same group.

(2) *Notification to registrar, publication and inspection of register.* Section 288(2) requires the company to notify the registrar of any change among its directors or in its secretary, or any change in the particulars contained in the register, within 14 days. Any notification of a person having become a director or secretary must contain a signed consent by that person to act in the relevant capacity.

Section 711 requires the registrar to publish in the *Gazette* the receipt by him of any notification of a change among its directors. If the change was not officially notified by the registrar at the material time and if the company cannot show that it was known at the time to the person concerned, then the company cannot rely on the change against that person: s. 42.

Finally, s. 288(3) requires the register to be kept open for at least two hours a day during business hours to members free, and to other persons on payment of 5p or such less sum as the company may prescribe.

12. Particulars of directors on documents. Section 305 prohibits a company from stating, in any form, the name of any of its directors (except in the text of the letter or as a signatory) on any business letter on which the company's name appears, unless it also states the Christian name or initials and surname of *every* director who is an individual, and the corporate name of *every* corporate director. The provisions extend to shadow directors.

13. Directors' interests in shares or debentures. Section 324(1), taken along with the 13th Schedule, para. 14, requires a director within five days to notify the company in writing of his interests in shares or debentures of the company or any other company within the group, giving particulars of the amount of shares or debentures of each class held by him.

Section 324(2), taken along with the 13th Schedule, para. 15, requires him within five days to notify the company in writing of any of the following events:

(a) an event as a result of which he becomes, or ceases to be, interested in such shares or debentures;

(b) the making by him of a contract to sell such shares or debentures;

(c) the assignment by him of any right granted to him by the company to subscribe for shares or debentures;

(d) the grant to him by any other company within the group of a right to subscribe for shares or debentures of that company, and his exercise or assignment of it.

In each case the amount and class of shares or debentures involved must be stated.

The 13th Schedule, para. 16, states that in computing the five days, Saturdays, Sundays and bank holidays must be disregarded.

Section 324(6) states that the section applies to shadow directors but that there is no duty under the section to disclose interests in shares in a company which is the wholly owned subsidiary of another company.

14. Extension of s. 324 to spouses and children. Section 328 extends the application of s. 324 by providing in s. 328(1)(a) that an interest of a director's spouse or infant child in shares or debentures must be treated as being the director's interest.

Section 328(2) states that a contract, assignment or right of subscription exercised or made by a director's spouse or infant child must be treated as having been exercised or made by the director, and a grant made to a director's spouse or infant child must be treated as having been made to the director.

Section 328(3) and (5) requires a director within five days to notify the company in writing of the occurrence of either of the following events:

    (*a*) the grant by the company to the director's spouse or infant child of a right to subscribe for shares or debentures of the company; and

    (*b*) the exercise of that right by the director's spouse or infant child.

15. Duty of company to notify stock exchange of directors' interests. Section 329(1) and (2) states that whenever a *listed* company is notified by a director under s. 324 or 328 of any matter relating to *listed* shares or debentures, it must, before the end of the following day, notify the investment exchange which may publish the information received.

16. The nature of an interest. Part I of the 13th Schedule explains what constitutes an interest within ss. 324 and 328.

The 13th Schedule, paras 2, 9 and 10, states that where shares or debentures are held on trust, any *beneficiary under that trust* (including discretionary trusts) shall be taken to have an interest within ss. 324 and 328, while a person who is a *bare trustee* of shares or debentures shall be treated as having none.

The same Schedule, in para. 3, states that a person is taken to have an interest in shares or debentures if:

    (*a*) he enters into a contract to buy them, whether for cash or other consideration; *or*

    (*b*) although not a registered holder, he is entitled (other than as a proxy or corporation representative) to exercise or control the exercise of any right conferred by the holding.

The Schedule, in para. 4, states that a person is taken to be interested in shares or debentures if a *company* is interested in them and:

    (*a*) that company or its directors are accustomed to act according to his instructions; *or*

    (*b*) he exercises or controls the exercise of *one-third or more* of the voting power at general meetings of that company.

The rule in (*b*) applies, under para. 5, even if a person exercises the control through another company. Thus if Smith controls one-third of the voting power in X Company and X Company controls one-third of the voting power in Y Company, Smith will be taken to control one-third of the voting power in Y Company.

The Schedule, in para. 6, states that a person is taken to have an interest in shares or debentures if (otherwise than through an interest under a trust):

(a) he has a right to call for delivery of them; or

(b) he has a right to acquire or an obligation to take an interest in them.

It is immaterial whether the right or obligation is conditional or absolute. However rights or obligations to *subscribe* for shares or debentures are expressly excluded.

Finally, para. 7 states that persons with a joint interest are deemed each to have that interest, while para. 8 states that it is immaterial if the shares or debentures in which a person has an interest are unidentifiable.

17. The register of directors' interests. Section 325, which is to be taken along with Part IV of the 13th Schedule, requires every company to keep a register for the purpose of recording the information furnished under ss. 324 and 328 (*see* **13** and **14**). Whenever it obtains such information, it must within three days inscribe it in the register against the name of the director concerned, together with the date of the inscription. In computing the three days, Saturdays, Sundays and bank holidays are to be disregarded.

Section 325(3) and (4), with the 13th Schedule, para. 3, requires every company:

(a) whenever it *grants to a director a right to subscribe* for shares or debentures of the company, within three days to inscribe in the register against his name:

(i) the date on which the right is granted;

(ii) the period during which it is exercisable;

(iii) the consideration for the grant or, if none, that fact;

(iv) the description of the shares or debentures involved; and

(v) the amount of shares or debentures involved;

(vi) the price to be paid for them.

(b) whenever *a right to subscribe* for shares or debentures of the company is *exercised* by a director, within three days to inscribe in the register against his name:

(i) the fact that the right was exercised;

(ii) the amount of shares or debentures involved;

(*iii*) if they were registered in his name, that fact, and if not, the name of the registered holder.

The 13th Schedule, para. 21, requires the register to be made up so that the entries against each name appear in chronological order.

The same Schedule, in para. 24, contains a provision similar to s. 211(4) (*see* 12:**12**), except that it applies to debentures as well as to shares.

The Schedule, para. 25, requires the register to be kept at the registered office or at the same place as the company's register of members (*see* 14:**3**), and to be open for at least two hours a day during business hours to the inspection of any member without charge, and of any other person on payment of 5p, or such less sum as the company may prescribe.

The Schedule, para. 26, authorizes any person to require a copy of the register, or of any part of it, on payment of 10p per 100 words, or such less sum as the company may prescribe. The copy must be supplied within 10 days.

Section 326(6) of the Act provides that if inspection is refused or a copy not sent within the 10 days, the court may order that inspection be allowed or that the copy be sent.

The 13th Schedule, para. 27, requires the company to notify the registrar of the place where the register is kept, unless it has at all times been kept at the registered office.

Finally, the Schedule, para. 29, requires the register to be produced at the company's annual general meeting, and to remain open and accessible during the meeting to any person attending it.

18. Qualification shares. There is a widespread misconception that a director is necessarily a member of the company. This is not so. The Act imposes no share qualification on the directors, so that unless the company's *articles* contain a requirement to that effect, a director need not be a shareholder unless he wishes. While the articles of many companies provide that the directors must hold a specified number of shares in the company, those of many other companies do not. Table A, for instance, does not require any share qualification for directors.

If the articles impose a share qualification on the directors, s. 291 applies. Section 291(1) requires them to obtain their share qualification within a maximum period of two months after appointment. The articles may fix a shorter period. Section 291(2) states that the holding of a *share warrant* will not suffice for this purpose. Section 291(3) states that if a director fails to obtain his share qualification within the specified time after his appointment, or at any time after appointment ceases to hold it, he vacates office.

NOTE: Care must be taken in computing the period of time when a poll is demanded on the election of a director and there is an interval between the taking of the poll and the declaration of the result. The period of time is calculated as running from the date when the result of the poll is *ascertained*, not from the earlier date when the votes were cast: *Holmes* v. *Keyes* (1958).

Where a share qualification is imposed by the articles, a joint holding will suffice unless the articles provide otherwise. The holding of stock instead of shares is also permissible. The shares or stock need not necessarily have been allotted to the director by the company; he may have acquired them by transfer from another member. Moreover, as long as his name appears on the register of members as the holder of the shares, it is immaterial that he is a mere trustee and does not own the *equitable* interest in them. This is so even where the articles provide, as they sometimes do, that he shall own them 'in his own right', though this curious expression has been held not to cover the case where a director held the shares as liquidator of another company.

19. The age limit for directors. Section 293 contains provisions regarding age limit, but s. 293(1) states that the section applies only to *public* companies or to private companies which are *subsidiaries of public companies*.

Section 293(2) provides that a person cannot be appointed a director of such a company if he has attained the age of 70. Section 293(3) further provides that an existing director of such a company must vacate office at the end of the next annual general meeting held after he attains the age of 70.

These stringent provisions, however, are rendered considerably less harsh by the remainder of the section. Section 293(7) states that the articles may alter or entirely remove the age limit, and s. 293(5) states that a director may be appointed at any age if the appointment is approved by the company in general meeting, so long as *special notice* of the resolution is given, stating his age. It also contains a similar provision regarding existing directors who attain the age of 70.

Section 294 requires any person who is appointed, or is proposed to be appointed, director of such a company to give notice of his age to the company when he has attained the age limit either under the Act or the company's articles.

20. Disqualification orders.

A disqualification order is an order made by a court forbidding a person, without leave of the court, from being:

(a) a director of a company; *or*

(b) a liquidator or administrator of a company; *or*

(c) a receiver or manager of a company's property; *or*

(d) in any way, directly or indirectly, concerned in the promotion, formation or management of a company.

The provisions of the Companies Act 1985 on this subject were strengthened by the Insolvency Act 1985, and these two sets of provisions were consolidated in the Company Directors Disqualification Act 1986. References in the rest of this paragraph are, therefore, unless the contrary is indicated, to that Act of 1986.

The Act deals with the grounds of disqualification under three headings:

(a) *Disqualification for general misconduct in connection with companies:*

By s. 2 the court may make a disqualification order where the person is convicted of an indictable offence in connection with the promotion, formation, management or liquidation of a company, or with the receivership or management of a company's property.

The maximum period of disqualification in this case is 15 years.

By s. 3 the court may make a disqualification order where it appears that the person has been persistently in default in delivering returns, accounts or other documents to the registrar. 'Persistent' default is conclusively proved if it is shown that in the five previous years he has been 'adjudged guilty' of three or more defaults. The phrase 'adjudged guilty' involves either a conviction for an offence or a default order under one of the following provisions:

(i) s. 244 Companies Act 1985 (order requiring delivery of company accounts);

(ii) s. 713 Companies Act 1985 (enforcement of company's duty to make returns);

(*iii*) s. 41 Insolvency Act 1986 (enforcement of receiver's or manager's duty to make returns); *or*

(*iv*) s. 170 Insolvency Act 1986 (corresponding provision for liquidator in winding up).

The maximum period of disqualification under s. 3 is five years.

By s. 4 the court may make a disqualification order if in the course of winding up it appears that the person:

(*i*) has been guilty of an offence for which he is *liable* (whether he has been convicted or not) under s. 458 Companies Act 1985 (fraudulent trading); *or*

(*ii*) has otherwise been guilty, while an officer (including a shadow director) or liquidator of the company or receiver or manager of its property, of any fraud in relation to the company or of any breach of his duty.

The maximum period of disqualification under this section is 15 years.

Section 5 relates to convictions for summary offences consisting of failure to deliver a return, account or other document to the registrar. The court convicting the person of the offence may, if it is at least his third offence within five years, make a disqualification order for a maximum period of five years.

(*b*) *Disqualification for unfitness:*

By s. 6 the court *must* make a disqualification order against a director (including a shadow director) if it is satisfied:

(*i*) that he is or has been a director of a company which has at any time become insolvent (whether while he was a director or subsequently); and

(*ii*) that his conduct as a director makes him unfit to be concerned in the management of a company.

A company becomes insolvent for the purposes of this section if:

(*i*) the company goes into liquidation at a time when its assets are insufficient for the payment of its debts and other liabilities and the expenses of the winding up; *or*

(*ii*) an administration order is made in relation to the company; *or*

(*iii*) an administrative receiver of the company is appointed.

The minimum period of disqualification is two years and the maximum period is 15 years.

Section 7 contains the following further provisions relating to a disqualification order under s. 6:

(*i*) An application for such an order may be made by the Secretary of State if it appears to him that such an order is expedient in the public interest. Alternatively, if the company is being wound up by the court in England and Wales, the application may be made by the official receiver on the Secretary of State's direction.

(*ii*) The application must be made within two years of the company's having become insolvent, unless the court grants leave for the application to be made later.

(*iii*) The office-holder responsible (i.e. the official receiver in the case of a winding up by the court in England and Wales, the liquidator in any other mode of winding up, the administrator if an administration order is in force, or the administrative receiver if such has been appointed) if it appears to him that the conditions for the making of a s. 6 order are satisfied must immediately report the matter to the Secretary of State.

(*iv*) The Secretary of State or the official receiver may require the liquidator, administrator or administrative receiver to furnish him with information concerning any person's conduct as a director and to produce books, papers and other records relevant to such conduct.

By s. 8 if it appears to the Secretary of State from a report made by inspectors under s. 437 Companies Act 1985 or from information or documents obtained under ss. 447 or 448 of that Act, that it is expedient in the public interest that a disqualification order should be made against a director or shadow director, he may apply to the court for an order, and the court may make an order if it is satisfied that the person's conduct in relation to the company makes him unfit to be concerned in the management of a company.

The maximum period of disqualification under this section is 15 years.

It should be noted that for both an order under s. 6 and an order under s. 8 the court must be satisfied that the person's conduct as a director or shadow director makes him unfit to be concerned in the management of a company. This is enlarged on by the 1st Schedule, which consists of a list of specific instances indicating unfitness, and by s. 9 the court must have particular regard to that list. The Schedule may be modified by statutory instrument.

(*c*) *Other cases of disqualification:*

Section 10 is linked to s. 213 Insolvency Act 1986, which provides that if in the course of winding up it appears that any business of the company has been carried on with intent to defraud creditors of the company or of any other person, or for any fraudulent purpose, the liquidator may apply to the court for a declaration that any persons who were knowingly parties to such fraudulent trading are to be liable to make such contributions to the company's assets as the court thinks proper. Section 10 Company Directors Disqualification Act 1986 enables the court also to make a disqualification order against the person concerned.

The maximum period of disqualification is 15 years.

By s. 11 it is an offence for a person who is an undischarged bankrupt to act as director of, or directly or indirectly to take part in or be concerned in the promotion, formation or management of, a company, except with the leave of the court.

Section 12 relates to the situation where a person fails to make any payment which he is required to make by an administration order under Part VI of the County Courts Act 1984, and the court, under s. 429 Insolvency Act 1986, revokes the administration order. Section 12 Company Directors Disqualification Act 1986 provides that such a person must not, except with the leave of the court, act as director or liquidator of, or directly or indirectly take part or be concerned in the promotion, formation or management of, a company.

Penalties are imposed by s. 13 for contravention of any of the above-mentioned provisions of the Act, and in addition, by s. 15, the person contravening becomes personally responsible for all the debts and other liabilities of the company incurred when he was involved in its management.

21. The register of disqualification orders. Section 18 Company Directors Disqualification Act 1986 requires officers of courts to furnish the Secretary of State with prescribed particulars of cases in which a disqualification order is made or, by action taken by the court, is varied or ceases to be in force, or in which leave is granted by the court for a person who is subject to an order to do anything which otherwise the order prohibits him from doing.

From the particulars so furnished the Secretary of State must maintain a register of orders, which is open to inspection on payment of a prescribed fee. The Secretary of State must delete an entry from the register when the order ceases to be in force.

22. Vacation of office. Apart from the sections mentioned above, and s. 303 which is discussed in the next paragraph, the articles usually contain a clause setting out the events which will cause a director to vacate office.

Thus Table A, Article 81, states that the office of director shall be vacated if:

(*a*) he ceases to be a director by any provision of the Acts or becomes prohibited by law from being a director; *or*

(*b*) he becomes bankrupt or makes any arrangement with his creditors generally; *or*

(*c*) he suffers from mental disorder; *or*

(*d*) he resigns office by notice to the company; *or*

(*e*) he is absent for more than six consecutive months, without permission of the directors, from meetings of directors *and* the directors resolve that his office be vacated.

23. Removal of directors. Section 303 gives the company its ultimate power of control over the directors. While they are in office there is very little which the company can do to influence the way in which the directors choose to manage the company's affairs. But if the company disapproves strongly enough of the method of management, it can resort to removing the board under this section. The only time this will be impossible is where the directors themselves have voting control.

The section does not, however, prevent the company from weighting the votes (*see* 13:**13**), i.e. attaching greater voting rights to certain shares for certain matters, e.g. to directors' shares on any resolution for their removal: *Bushell* v. *Faith* (1970).

Section 303(1) states that a company may by ordinary resolution remove a director before the expiration of his period of office and despite anything in the company's articles or in any agreement between the company and the director. There is one exception for certain directors of private companies (*see* 25:**6**).

The intention of the section is clear: the shareholders must have power to remove the board. But the director so removed is not without his remedy. Section 303(5) provides that the section does not deprive him of his right to sue for damages for breach of contract, if in fact he has one.

Section 303(2) requires *special notice* to be given of any resolution to *remove a director*, or to *appoint another director in his place*.

By s. 304, the company, on receiving notice of an intended

resolution to remove a director under s. 303, must immediately send a copy of the notice to the director and he is entitled to be heard on the resolution at the meeting. The director may also make written representations to the company (not exceeding a reasonable length) and request that they be notified to members. The company must then, unless the representations are received too late:

(*a*) in the notice of the resolution given to members state the fact that representations have been made; and

(*b*) send a copy of the representations to every member to whom notice of the meeting is sent.

If a copy is not sent out in this way because the representations were received too late or because of the company's default, then the director may require them to be read out at the meeting: s. 304(3).

It may perhaps occur that a director reacts sharply to the copy of the special notice of the resolution to remove him, and makes a statement in his own defence which is highly defamatory of some other person. Section 304(4) provides for this situation, stating that copies of the representations need not be sent out, nor need the representations be read out, if the company or any aggrieved person applies to the court and the court thinks that the director is abusing his rights *to secure needless publicity for defamatory matter*. Moreover, by s. 304(5), the court may order that the company's costs on such an application shall be paid by the director.

NOTE: These provisions in s. 304 concerning the written representations are *exactly the same as those in s. 388* relating to auditors. Once learnt, they apply to both directors and auditors alike.

Finally, it should be noted that difficulties may arise regarding the use of the provisions of s. 303. It appears from *Pedley* v. *Inland Waterways Association Ltd* (1977) that an *individual* member has no right to compel the inclusion of a resolution in the agenda of a company meeting unless the provisions of ss. 376 and 377 (*see* 15:42) have also been complied with. He can serve special notice under s. 379, but that is as far as he can go. If this decision represents the law, it would appear that the same problem would arise with the procedure for the removal of an auditor which, as stated above, is exactly the same.

24. Validity of directors' acts. Section 285 states that the acts of a director are valid despite any defect which may afterwards be discovered in his appointment or qualification. Table A, Article 92, repeats this provision.

The effect of this section must not be over-stated. It does *not* permit an improperly appointed or unqualified director to do whatever he likes. It simply means that provided the director's act is in other respects *a proper act*, the mere fact that he has not been properly appointed or is not qualified is immaterial and does not invalidate that act. This can be clearly seen in *Craven-Ellis* v. *Canons Ltd* (1936), the facts of which are given in 3:**14**, and where the act which the improperly qualified directors were trying to do, namely to appoint another improperly qualified director, was an *improper act* in itself and therefore not protected by what is now s. 285 of the 1985 Act.

The section is stating in a narrow form what is really a well-known and fundamental rule of *agency*, namely, that a principal is always bound by the act of his agent provided the agent is acting within the scope of his *actual or apparent authority*. This rule applies to companies and their agents in the same way as it applies to natural legal persons and their agents, and has been enunciated in the famous decision in *Royal British Bank* v. *Turquand* (1856).

25. The rule in Royal British Bank *v.* Turquand. By the time a decision of the courts has become familiar even to beginners of a subject, the facts which gave rise to it have usually become lost in the same way as basic assumptions tend to get overlooked. The facts should never be disregarded.

> In *Royal British Bank* v. *Turquand* (1856), the company's deed of settlement (corresponding to a modern memorandum and articles) empowered the directors to borrow such sums as were authorized by an ordinary resolution of a general meeting. The directors issued a bond to T, from whom they borrowed money. The bond was under the company's seal, but no resolution was passed by the company authorizing it. HELD: The company was bound.

It should be remembered that a third party has no means of knowing whether an *ordinary* resolution has been passed by the company. He can read the memorandum and study the *vires*, or inspect the register of charges, or discover whether a *special* or *extraordinary* resolution has been passed. He can read the articles and obtain particulars of the directors. But he cannot know, unless he has been told, whether an ordinary resolution such as was required in this case has been passed by a general meeting. The loan was clearly within the *vires* of the company. The company therefore had the necessary *capacity*. It was also clear from the articles that the directors had the necessary *authority*. A third party need go no further: he need not make sure that the rules of internal management have been observed. If a principal places secret restrictions on the apparent authority of his agent, they do not affect the third party; the third party need not take steps to ensure that there are no such restrictions, for this would make the carrying on of business a practical impossibility.

NOTE: There are two further points which should be borne in mind in connection with this case:

(1) If a document apparently issued by a company in a regular manner turns out to be a forgery, it can never bind the company. This is the basic principle applicable to all forgeries: they are totally ineffectual.

(2) If the authority of the company's agent is based on *estoppel*, i.e. on the *behaviour* of the company, which has 'held him out' as having authority, then the public documents are not regarded as 'holding out' for this purpose, whatever they say, *unless the third party has actually read them.*

This is because estoppel is always based on the effect which the behaviour of one person has on the mind of another, and if that other has not seen the behaviour he cannot have been affected by it.

Despite the tremendous amount of material which has been written concerning this formerly important case, it seems that the decision is entirely in accordance with the usual principles of the law of agency, and that it enunciated nothing new. It was deprived of much of its significance by s. 9(1) European Communities Act 1972 which destroyed the doctrine of constructive notice of a company's memorandum and articles both as regards the *vires* of the company and the *authority* of the directors. The provision is now in s. 35 Companies Act 1985 (*see* 2:**24**).

26. Remuneration of directors. We have already seen in **1** that directors are officers and agents, but not servants. They have not, as directors, any contract with the company and are not employed by it, though often they are employed by it in another capacity and are then termed 'service directors'.

As directors, they accordingly have no right to remuneration. The articles, however, normally make provision for them, and Table A, Article 82, states that the directors shall be entitled to such remuneration as the company may by ordinary resolution determine. Article 83 allows them travelling and hotel expenses for meetings and for other expenses properly incurred by them in connection with the discharge of their duties: these would not otherwise be allowed. The articles are not, of course, a contract, but they make it proper for the company to make such payments as are authorized by them.

Section 311(1) makes it unlawful for a company to pay a director his remuneration tax-free, and s. 311(2) states that if a provision for tax-free payment is made, it will take effect as if the *net* sum payable were a *gross* sum subject to tax.

As stated in **1**, a director is not entitled to preferential payment when the company goes into liquidation, for he is not an 'employee' within s. 386 and the 6th Schedule Insolvency Act 1986.

27. Apportionment of directors' remuneration. The Apportionment Act 1870, provides that all salaries are apportionable, but it is undecided whether this Act applies to directors. If it does not, and the articles provide for payment 'at the rate of' a certain sum per annum, or are expressed in such a way as to indicate that the annual sum is to be apportioned, then a director who holds office for less than a year is entitled to a proportion of that annual sum. If, however, the articles provide for payment of an annual sum on an annual basis, the remuneration is not apportionable. Table A, Article 82, provides that, unless the resolution provides otherwise, the remuneration shall *accrue from* day to day, making the position quite clear wherever Table A is applicable.

Probably, however, the Apportionment Act applies, so that the wording of the articles is immaterial.

28. Right of inspection of directors' service contracts. In the case of a 'service director' (*see* **26**) s. 318 gives the members of the company a right to inspect any director's contract of service. A shadow director (*see* **2**) must be treated as a director for the purposes of this section: s. 318(6).

Section 318(1) requires every company to keep at an appropriate place:

(a) in the case of a director whose contract of service is in writing, *a copy of the contract*;

(b) in the case of a director whose contract of service is not in writing, *a written memorandum* setting out its terms; and

(c) in the case of a director employed under a contract of service with a *subsidiary* of the company, *a copy of the contract* or, if it is not in writing, *a written memorandum* setting out its terms.

All the copies and memoranda must be kept at the same place: s. 318(2).

Section 318(3) states that the following places are appropriate:

(a) the registered office;

(b) the place where the register of members is kept, if elsewhere;

(c) the principal place of business.

Section 318(4) requires every company to give notice to the registrar of the place where the copies and memoranda are kept, and of any change in that place, except where they have always been kept at the registered office.

Section 318(7) requires every copy and memorandum to be open to the inspection of any member without charge for at least two hours a day during business hours.

Section 318(9) states that if inspection is refused, the court may by order compel an immediate inspection.

Finally, there are two provisions which apply in special circumstances. Section 318(11) states that the section does not apply where the unexpired term of the contract is *less than a year*, or when the contract can be terminated by the company within the next year without payment of compensation. Section 318(5) states that s. 318(1) does not apply if the director's contract requires him to work wholly or mainly *outside the United Kingdom*. Instead it requires the company to keep a *memorandum* which sets out:

(a) the *name* of the director;

(b) the provisions of the contract relating to its *duration*; and

(c) in the case of a contract of service with a *subsidiary* of the company, the *name and place of incorporation* of that subsidiary.

29. Directors' contracts of employment exceeding five years.
Section 319 requires long-term contracts of employment of directors
to be approved by the company in general meeting. It should be noted
that the meaning of 'contract of employment' is somewhat wider than
'contract of service' since, under s. 319(7)(*a*), it includes a *contract for
services*, e.g. a consultancy agreement. A shadow director is treated as
a director for the purposes of s. 319: s. 319(7).

Section 319(1) provides that the section applies to any term by
which a director's employment with the company of which he is a
director or, where he is the director of a holding company, his
employment within the group, is to continue for a period of *more than
five years* during which it:

(*a*) cannot be terminated by the company by notice; *or*

(*b*) can be so terminated only in specified circumstances.

Section 319(3) prohibits a company from incorporating such a term
in any agreement unless it is first approved by a resolution of the
company in general meeting and, in the case of a director of a holding
company, by a resolution of the holding company in general meeting
as well. The only exception to this rule is in the case of a wholly owned
subsidiary where no approval by its members is required: s. 319(4).

Under s. 319(5) the resolution may not be passed unless a *written
memorandum* setting out the proposed agreement incorporating the
term is available for inspection by members of the company both:

(*a*) at the registered office for not less than 15 days ending with the
date of the meeting; and

(*b*) at the meeting itself.

If a term is incorporated in an agreement in contravention of the
section, it is *void* and the agreement, the rest of which remains valid,
is deemed to contain a term entitling the company to terminate it at
any time by giving reasonable notice: s. 319(6).

30. Connected persons. The Act contains a number of provisions
which refer to a person being 'connected' with a director and to a
director being 'associated with' or 'controlling' a body corporate. The
meaning of these words is found in s. 346 and should be borne in mind
whenever the expression appears.

Section 346(2) states that, unless a person is himself a director of the
company, he is connected with a director if he is:

(*a*) that director's *spouse, child* or *step-child* (including illegitimate children but not any person over 18 years of age: s. 346(3));

(*b*) a *body corporate* with which the director is associated;

(*c*) a person acting in his capacity as the *trustee* of any trust under which the beneficiaries include the director or any person falling under (*a*) or (*b*) above; *or*

(*d*) a person acting in his capacity as *partner* of that director or of any person falling under (*a*), (*b*) or (*c*) above.

Under s. 346(4) a director is associated with a body corporate if he and the persons connected with him together are *either*:

(*a*) interested in at least one-fifth in nominal value of its equity share capital (*see* 13:**14**); *or*

(*b*) entitled to exercise or control the exercise of more than one-fifth of the voting power at any general meeting.

Under s. 346(8) references to voting power the exercise of which is controlled by a director include references to voting power the exercise of which is controlled by a *body corporate* controlled by that director (a neat example of 'veil-lifting' (*see* 1:**23**)).

Under s. 346(5) a director is deemed to control a body corporate if:

(*a*) he or a person connected with him is interested in any part of its equity share capital or is entitled to exercise or control the exercise of any part of the voting power at any general meeting; and

(*b*) he, the persons connected with him, and the other directors of the company together are interested in more than half the equity share capital or are entitled to exercise or control the exercise of more than half of that voting power.

31. Substantial property transactions involving directors. Section 320 is in principle very much the same as s. 319. It too requires the approval by the company in general meeting – this time where a director acquires substantial non-cash assets from the company, or vice versa (*see* 10:**1**).

Section 320(1) prohibits a company from making any arrangement by which a director of the company or of its holding company, or a person connected with such a director (*see* **30**), is to acquire *a non-cash asset of the requisite value* from the company, or vice versa, unless that arrangement is first approved by a resolution of the company in general meeting. If the director or connected person is a director of the holding company or a person connected with such a director, approval by a resolution in general meeting of the holding company is required as well.

Under s. 320(2) a non-cash asset is of the requisite value if its value exceeds £50,000 or 10 per cent of the amount of the company's net assets normally determined by reference to the last annual accounts, and is not less than £1000. These amounts can be increased at any time by order of the Secretary of State under s. 345(1).

As in s. 319, there is one exception to this rule, namely, that in the case of a wholly owned subsidiary no approval by its members is required: s. 321(1).

32. Effect of contravention of s. 320. Section 322 deals with the effect of contravention of s. 320. Any unlawful arrangement, and any transaction entered into in pursuance of it, is *voidable by the company* unless:

(*a*) *restitution* of the subject-matter is *impossible*; *or*

(*b*) the company has been *indemnified* (*see* below) for the loss suffered; *or*

(*c*) *rights* acquired by a *third party* bona fide, for value, and without notice of the contravention would be affected by the avoidance; *or*

(*d*) the arrangement is, within a reasonable time, *affirmed* by the company in general meeting and, where applicable, by a resolution of its holding company in general meeting as well.

Contravention of s. 320 not only has an effect on the arrangement or transaction in question but, under s. 322(3), it renders the director, any person connected with him and any other director of the company who authorized it liable:

(*a*) to *account to the company for any gain* which he made by it, directly or indirectly; and

(*b*) jointly and severally with any other person liable, to *indemnify the company* for any resulting loss.

Whether or not the unlawful arrangement or transaction has been avoided under s. 322 is immaterial: s. 322(4).

Where an unlawful arrangement is made by a company and a person connected with a director, that director will not be liable if he shows that he took all reasonable steps to secure the company's compliance with s. 320, while the connected person and the other directors who authorized it can escape liability if they can show that at the time it was made, they did not know of the contravention: s. 322(5) and (6).

33. Arrangements exempted from s. 320. Section 321(2) and (3) entirely exempts from the provisions of s. 320 three types of arrangements:

(*a*) any arrangement for the acquisition of a non-cash asset by a holding company from any of its wholly owned subsidiaries or vice versa, or by one wholly owned subsidiary from another wholly owned subsidiary of the same holding company;

(*b*) any arrangement entered into by a company which is being wound up (unless the winding up is a members' voluntary winding up); and

(*c*) any arrangement by which a member acquires an asset from a company and which is made with him in his character of member.

34. Legislation on loans to directors. Before embarking on the highly technical and sophisticated rules in ss. 330–346, which deal with loans to directors, including shadow directors, it is essential to understand the meaning given by the Act to three expressions:

(*a*) a relevant company;
(*b*) a quasi-loan;
(*c*) a credit transaction.

35. Meaning of 'relevant company'. Section 331 is the interpretation section for ss. 330–346. In subsection (6) it states that 'relevant company' means company which:

(*a*) is a public company; *or*
(*b*) is a subsidiary of a public company; *or*
(*c*) is a subsidiary of a company which has as another subsidiary a public company; *or*
(*d*) has a subsidiary which is a public company.

The gist of this definition is that a relevant company is *either*:

(*a*) a public company; *or*
(*b*) a private company which forms part of a group containing a public company.

36. Meaning of 'quasi-loan'. Section 331(3) defines a quasi-loan as a transaction under which one party ('the creditor') pays or agrees to pay a sum for another ('the borrower'), or reimburses or agrees to reimburse expenditure incurred by another party for another ('the borrower'):

(a) on terms that the borrower will reimburse the creditor; or

(b) in circumstances giving rise to a liability on the borrower to reimburse the creditor.

An example of a quasi-loan is where the company pays a debt which is owed by a director to a third party on terms that the director will repay the company over a period of time at his convenience.

37. Meaning of 'credit transaction'. Section 331(7) defines a credit transaction as a transaction under which one party ('the creditor'):

(a) sells any land or supplies any goods under a hire-purchase or conditional sale agreement;

(b) leases or hires any land or goods in return for periodical payments;

(c) otherwise disposes of land or supplies goods or services on the understanding that payment (however made) is to be deferred.

38. Loans to directors. Section 330(2) provides that, with certain exceptions, no company may:

(a) make a *loan* to any of its directors or to any director of its holding company;

(b) enter into any *guarantee* or provide any *security* in connection with a loan made by any other person to such a director.

This comprehensive prohibition applicable to all companies is followed by one which applies only to *relevant companies* (*see* **35**).

Section 330(3) and (4) provides that, again with certain exceptions, no *relevant company* may:

(a) make a *quasi-loan* to any of its directors or to any director of its holding company (*see* **36**);

(b) make a *loan or quasi-loan* to a person connected with such a director (*see* **30**);

(c) enter into a *guarantee* or provide any *security* in connection with a loan or quasi-loan made by any other person for such a director or connected person: s. 330(3);

(*d*) enter into a *credit transaction* as creditor for such a director or connected person (*see* 37);

(*e*) enter into any *guarantee* or provide any *security* in connection with a credit transaction made by any other person for such a director or connected person: s. 330(4).

39. Extension of prohibitions in s. 330 to indirect arrangements. Section 330(6) and (7) extends to indirect arrangements by which a company may try to evade the rules stated above.

Section 330(6) provides that no company may arrange for the assignment to it of rights, or the assumption by it of obligations, under a transaction which would have contravened subsections (2), (3) or (4) if it had been entered into by the company itself.

Section 330(7) provides that no company may take part in any arrangement by which another person:

(*a*) enters into a transaction which would have contravened subsections (2), (3), (4) or (6) if it had been entered into by the company itself; and

(*b*) obtains a benefit from the company or any company within the group.

40. General exceptions to s. 330. Sections 332–338 give a large number of exceptions to the rules laid down in s. 330. The exceptions in ss. 332–335 are exceptions to specific provisions within s. 330, whereas the exceptions in ss. 336–338 are general exceptions in the sense that they exclude *all* the provisions of s. 330 in particular situations. It is simplest to start with this latter category of exceptions.

There are four cases where s. 330 does not apply at all:

(*a*) A *loan* or *quasi-loan* by a company to its *holding company*, or a *guarantee* or *security* given by a company in connection with a loan or quasi-loan made by any other person to its holding company: s. 336(*a*).

(*b*) A company's entering into a *credit transaction* as creditor for its *holding company*, or giving a *guarantee* or *security* in connection with any credit transaction made by any other person for its holding company: s. 336(*b*).

(*c*) A company's doing anything to provide any of its directors with funds to meet *expenditure incurred for the purposes of the company* or to enable him *properly to perform his duties as an officer*, or anything to enable any of its directors to avoid incurring such expenditure, provided *either*:

(*i*) that thing is done with the *prior approval of the company in general meeting* at which all the details are disclosed; *or*

(*ii*) it is done on the condition that if the approval of the company is not so obtained at or before the next annual general meeting, the loan will be repaid or the liability discharged *within six months* from the end of that meeting: s. 337.

Even if one of these conditions is satisfied, the exception is subject to a financial limit in the case of any *relevant company*. Such a company may not enter into any transaction under (*c*) if the *aggregate of the relevant amounts* exceeds £10,000: s. 337(3).

(*d*) A loan or quasi-loan made by a *money-lending company* to any person, or a guarantee given by a money-lending company in connection with any other loan or quasi-loan, provided:

(*i*) the loan or quasi-loan is made, or the guarantee given, in the *ordinary course of its business*; and

(*ii*) the amount of the loan, quasi-loan or guarantee is not greater, and the terms not more favourable, than the company could reasonably be expected to offer to a person of the *same financial standing but unconnected with the company*: s. 338.

Even if these two conditions are satisfied, this exception is also subject to a financial limit in the case of *any relevant company which is not a recognized bank* (i.e. not recognized as a bank for the purposes of the Banking Act 1979: s. 331(5)). Such a company may not enter into any transaction under (*d*) if the *aggregate of the relevant amounts* exceeds £50,000: s. 338(4).

The second condition, however, is itself subject to an exception regarding a *dwelling-house*. Section 338(6) provides that (*d*)(*ii*) above does not prevent a company from making a loan to one of its directors or a director of its holding company:

(*i*) for the purpose of the *purchase of a dwelling-house*, together with any land to be occupied with it, for use as that director's *only or main residence*;

(*ii*) for the purpose of *improving* such a dwelling-house or land;

(*iii*) in substitution for any loan made by any other person for either of the above purposes;

if loans of that description are ordinarily made by the company to its employees on terms which are no less favourable, and if the *aggregate of the relevant amounts* does not exceed £50,000.

41. Exception to s. 330(2). Section 334 gives a special exception for small loans.

The section provides that s. 330(2)(*a*) (*see* **38**) does not prohibit a company from making a loan to any of its directors or to any director of its holding company, provided the *aggregate of the relevant amounts* does not exceed £2500.

42. Exceptions to s. 330(3). Sections 332 and 333 give exceptions to s. 330(3) (*see* **38**(*a*), (*b*) and (*c*) above).

The prohibitions in s. 330(3), which in any case apply only to *relevant companies*, do not prevent such a company from making a quasi-loan to any of its directors or to any director of its holding company if:

(*a*) the quasi-loan contains a term requiring the director to reimburse the creditor within two months; *and*

(*b*) the aggregate of the amount of that quasi-loan and the amount outstanding on any others does not exceed £1000: s. 332.

Section 333 gives an exception to s. 330(3)(*b*) and (*c*) (*see* **38** (*b*) and (*c*) above).

Where a *relevant company* is part of a group of companies, the prohibitions in s. 330(3)(*b*) and (*c*) do not prevent it from:

(*a*) making a loan or quasi-loan to another company in that group; *or*

(*b*) giving a guarantee or security in connection with a loan or quasi-loan made by any other person to another company in that group;

merely because a director of one company within the group is associated with another (*see* **30**(*b*)).

43. Exception to s. 330(4). Section 335 gives an exception to s. 330(4) (*see* **38** (*d*) and (*e*) above). These prohibitions in s. 330(4), which again apply only to relevant companies, do not prevent such a company from entering into any transaction for any person if:

(*a*) the *aggregate of the relevant amounts* does not exceed £5000; *or*

(b) (i) the company enters into the transaction in the *ordinary* course of its business; *and*

(ii) the value of the transaction is not greater, and its terms not more favourable, than the company could reasonably be expected to offer to a person of the *same financial standing, but unconnected with the company*.

44. Relevant amounts. When considering the rules on loans it should be borne in mind throughout that any of the amounts specified in the statutory provisions on this topic can be increased at any time by order of the Secretary of State under s. 345(1).

In several of the rules governing the exceptions, however, the expression 'aggregate of the relevant amounts' appears, namely in ss. 334 (*see* **41**), 335 (see **43**), 337(3) (*see* **40**) and 338(4) (*see* **40**). Its meaning is given in s. 339 but unfortunately, again, not without tears. Before 'relevant amounts' can be understood, it is necessary to understand the meaning of 'relevant arrangement' and 'relevant transaction'.

Section 339(3) provides that a *transaction* is relevant if it was made:

(a) for the director for whom the proposed transaction or arrangement is to be made, or for any person connected with him; *or*

(b) where the proposed transaction or arrangement is to be made for a person connected with a director, for that director or any person connected with him.

It concludes by stating that an *arrangement* is relevant if it relates to a relevant transaction.

Section 339(2) provides that the *relevant amounts* in relation to a proposed transaction or arrangement are:

(a) the value of the *proposed transaction or arrangement*;

(b) the value of any *existing relevant arrangement* falling under s. 330(6) or (7) (*see* **39**) but covered by one of the exceptions;

(c) the amount outstanding under *any other relevant transaction* covered by one of the exceptions.

The amounts to be included under (b) and (c) comprise not only those provided by the company, but also those provided by any of its subsidiaries or, where the proposed transaction or arrangement is to be made for a director of its holding company or a person connected with him, by that holding company or any of its subsidiaries (*see* 13:**16**).

45. Civil remedies for breach of s. 330. The provisions of s. 341 regarding the effect of contravention of s. 330 on the transaction or arrangement in question are, with one exception, *exactly the same* as those relating to substantial property transactions involving directors which are described in **31** above.

The single difference is that the provision regarding affirmation by the company (*see* (*d*) in **32**) does not appear in s. 341.

46. Criminal penalties for breach of s. 330. Section 342, which deals with the penalties for contravention of s. 330, applies only to *relevant companies*.

Under s. 342(1) a *director* of a relevant company who authorizes or permits the company to enter into a transaction or arrangement, knowing or having reasonable cause to believe that the company was thereby contravening s. 330, is guilty of an offence.

Under s. 342(2) and (5) a *relevant company* which enters into a transaction or arrangement for one of its directors or for a director of its holding company in contravention of s. 330 is also guilty of an offence, unless it shows that at the time the transaction was entered into it did not know the relevant circumstances.

Under s. 342(3) a person who *procures* a relevant company to enter into a transaction or arrangement, knowing or having reasonable cause to believe that the company was thereby contravening s. 330, is guilty of an offence.

Finally, s. 342(4), taken along with the 24th Schedule, states the penalties. A director, company or other person guilty of an offence under the section is liable:

(*a*) on conviction on indictment, to imprisonment not exceeding two years or a fine, or both;

(*b*) on summary conviction, to imprisonment not exceeding six months or a fine not exceeding the statutory maximum, or both.

47. Summary of statutory provisions on loans to directors. It can be seen from **34–46** above that the rules relating to loans by a company to its directors are not easy to master. It is probably best to acquire a thorough knowledge of **38** and then, given a transaction which appears to be prohibited by it, see which, if any, of the exceptions are applicable.

To assist the student in this exercise this approach is adopted below.

(1) First make sure that you have read and understood the definitions in s. 331(3) and (7) of the terms: 'quasi-loan' and 'credit transaction'.

(2) Then be quite clear on what is meant in s. 331(6) by: 'relevant company', i.e. a company which is *either*:

(*a*) a *public* company; *or*
(*b*) in the *same group* as a public company.

(3) Now make sure that the transaction in question *falls within one of the prohibitions in s. 330*.

Notice that while *all* companies are caught by the prohibitions on *loans* in s. 330(2), *only relevant companies* are caught by the prohibitions on *quasi-loans* and *credit transactions* in s. 330(3) and (4).

(4) Once you are sure that the transaction in question is caught by s. 330, see if it can be saved by any of the following exceptions:

LAWFUL LOANS TO DIRECTORS
ALL COMPANIES

Section 334	Section 336(*a*),(*b*)	Section 337
Loan to director of the company or of its holding company.	Loan, quasi-loan or credit transaction for *holding company*.	*Anything done* to provide a director with funds to meet expenditure incurred for the purposes of the company, or to enable him properly to perform his duties as an officer.
Limit: £2500	Guarantee or security for loan, quasi-loan or credit transaction by any other person for *holding company*.	
		Requirements: *Either:* prior approval of company in general meeting; *Or:* thing done on condition that, if not approved at or before the next AGM, loan must be repaid or liability discharged

within six months from end of AGM.

Limit: £10,000 in the case of a relevant company.

Section 333	Section 332	Section 335
Loan or quasi-loan to another company in same group.	*Quasi-loan* to director of the company or of its holding company.	*Credit transaction* for director or connected person.
Guarantee or security for loan or quasi-loan by any other person to another company in same group.	*Requirements:* Term for reimbursement within two months.	Guarantee or security for credit transaction made by any other person for director or connected person.
	Limit: £1000	*Requirements:* (1) In ordinary course of company's business; and (2) On usual commercial terms.
		Limit: £5000

MONEY-LENDING COMPANIES ONLY
(Section 338)

Loan or quasi-loan to any person.
Guarantee of any loan or quasi-loan.

Requirements:
(1) In ordinary course of company's business; and
(2) On usual commercial terms.

Limit: £50,000 in the case of a *relevant company other than a recognized bank.*

Dwelling-House:
Requirement (2) above (usual commercial terms) *does not apply* to loan to director of the company or of its holding company for *purchase* or *improvement of dwelling-house* provided two conditions are satisfied.

(a) Loans of that kind are normally made by the company to its *employees* on the same terms; and
(b) Loan does not exceed £50,000.

48. Disclosure in accounts of transactions involving directors. There are detailed provisions in ss. 232–234 and Part I of the 6th Schedule concerning disclosure, in *notes to the accounts*, of loans and other transactions favouring directors and officers.

Section 232(2) and (3) and the 6th Schedule, para. 2, require a note to the accounts of *any company other than a holding company* to contain *specified particulars (see* **49**) of:

(a) any transaction or arrangement *of a kind described in s. 330* entered into by the company for any of its directors, or a director of its holding company, or for any person connected with such a director;

(b) an agreement by the company to enter into any such transaction or arrangement; and

(c) any other transaction or arrangement with the company in which any of its directors, or a director of its holding company, had, directly or indirectly, a *material interest*.

Section 232(1) and (3) and the 6th Schedule, para. 1, require disclosure in a note to the *group accounts of a holding company* of specified particulars of the same transactions or arrangements, except that those entered into by any subsidiary of the company must also be included.

The 6th Schedule, para. 3, enlarges on (c) above, stating that:

(a) a transaction or arrangement between a company and any of its directors, or a director of its holding company, or a person connected with such a director, must be treated, if it would not otherwise be so, as one in which that director is interested; and

(b) an interest is not 'material' if it is not material in the opinion of the majority of the directors, other than that director, of the company which is preparing the accounts in question.

49. The specified particulars. The 6th Schedule, para. 9, gives details of the specified particulars which are to be disclosed under s. 232. It states that these consist of particulars of the *principal terms* of the transaction, arrangement or agreement including:

(a) a statement of the fact that it either was made or subsisted during the financial year in question;

(b) the name of the person for whom it was made and, where that person is connected with a director of the company or its holding company, the name of that director;

(*c*) the name of any director with a material interest and the nature of that interest;

(*d*) in the case of a loan, agreement for a loan, or arrangement within s. 330(6) or (7) relating to a loan (*see* **39**):

(*i*) the amount of the liability of the person to whom the loan was made or agreed to be made, in respect of principal and interest, at the beginning and at the end of the financial year in question;

(*ii*) the maximum amount of that liability during that financial year;

(*iii*) the amount of any interest which has fallen due but not been paid; and

(*iv*) the amount of any provision made in respect of any failure by the borrower to repay the loan or any interest on it;

(*e*) in the case of a guarantee, security, or arrangement within s. 330(6) relating to a guarantee or security (*see* **39**):

(*i*) the amount for which the company or its subsidiary was liable both at the beginning and at the end of the financial year in question;

(*ii*) the maximum amount for which the company or its subsidiary may become so liable; and

(*iii*) any amount paid or liability incurred by the company or its subsidiary in fulfilling the guarantee or discharging the security;

(*f*) in the case of any other transaction, arrangement or agreement, the value of the transaction or arrangement in question.

50. Types of transactions excluded from s. 232. Certain types of transactions are excluded from the disclosure requirements of s. 232. In the 6th Schedule, para. 5, these are stated to be:

(*a*) a transaction, arrangement or agreement between one company and another in which a director of the first company, or of its subsidiary or holding company, is interested only by virtue of his being a director of the latter;

(*b*) a contract of service between a company and any of its directors or a director of its holding company, or between a director of a company and any of its subsidiaries;

(*c*) a transaction, arrangement or agreement which was not entered into during the financial year in question and which did not subsist at any time during that year.

51. Exclusion of small transactions from s. 232. Even where a transaction does not fall within the types excluded by para. 5, paras 11 and 12 of the Schedule provide that no disclosure is required if:

(*a*) it is made by a company or its subsidiary for a person who at any time during the financial year in question was a director of the company or of its holding company, or connected with such a director; and

(*b*) *either:*

(*i*) it is a *credit transaction*, agreement to enter into a credit transaction, a guarantee or security given in connection with a credit transaction, or an arrangement within s. 300(6) or (7) (*see* **38**) relating to a credit transaction, and the *outstanding aggregate values* of each such transaction made for that person did not at any time during that year exceed £5000; *or*

(*ii*) it is a transaction or arrangement with the company or any of its subsidiaries in which a director of the company or of its holding company had a *material interest*, and the *outstanding aggregate values* of each such transaction made for that person did not at any time during that year exceed £1000 or, if more, did not exceed £5000 *or 1 per cent of the company's net assets*, whichever is the less.

The amounts specified in paras 11 and 12 can, like any amount specified in Part X of the Act, be increased at any time by order of the Secretary of State under s. 345(1) as applied by the 6th Schedule, para. 13.

52. Disclosure in accounts of transactions involving officers other than directors. Section 233 applies only to officers of the company other than directors. In subsections (1), (2) and (4), taken along with the 6th Schedule, para. 16, it provides that the group accounts of a holding company and the accounts of any other company must contain, by way of notes to those accounts, a *statement* relating to transactions, arrangements and agreements made by the company and, in the case of a holding company, its subsidiary, for persons who at any time during the financial year were *officers but not directors*.

The statement must give details of the aggregate amounts outstanding at the end of the financial year under transactions listed in para. 15, and the number of officers for whom such transactions were made.

The Schedule, in para. 15, lists the transactions in question as consisting of *loans, quasi-loans and credit transactions*, guarantees and securities relating to them, arrangements within s. 330(6) or (7) (*see* **39**) relating to them, and agreements to enter into any of these transactions or arrangements.

The Schedule, in para. 16, exempts transactions from such disclosure if the aggregate amount outstanding does not exceed £2500.

53. Duty of auditors regarding non-compliance with disclosure requirements. Section 237(5) provides that if a company fails to comply with the requirements of ss. 232 or 233 and the 6th Schedule regarding disclosure in the accounts, the auditors must include in their report a statement giving the required particulars, in so far as they are reasonably able to do so.

54. Compensation for loss of office. Section 312 states that it is not lawful for a company to pay a director compensation for loss of office or to make any payment to him in connection with his retirement, unless the amount of the proposed payment is disclosed to the members and approved by the company. If it is not so disclosed and approved the directors responsible for making it are liable to the company for misapplication of the company's funds: *Re Duomatic* (1969).

Section 313(1) contains an exactly similar provision regarding payments to directors when the undertaking or property of the company is being transferred, and s. 313(2) states that if such an illegal payment is in fact made, the director must hold the amount which he received in trust for the company.

Section 314 requires the amount of the payment to be stated in any notice given to shareholders of an offer for their shares wherever a transfer of all or any of the shares in the company results from:

(*a*) an offer to the general body of shareholders;

(*b*) an offer by some other company with a view to making the company its subsidiary;

(*c*) an offer by an individual with a view to his acquiring at least one-third of the voting power; *or*

(*d*) any other offer conditional on acceptance to a given extent; (i.e. the offer stands *provided* a specified fraction of the members accept it).

Offers for the shares of a company often result in its directors being virtually paid to go quietly, and the Act is merely making sure that the members know what is happening. Section 315 further provides that if the above rules are not complied with, the director must hold the amount which he has received in trust for any persons who have sold their shares as a result of the offer.

NOTE: The provisions of these three sections are also very important and must be studied carefully. It should be noted, however, that they apply only to payments *which the company is not legally obliged to make*. Payments made in fulfilment of the terms of a service contract are thus not subject to the requirement of approval by the company: *Taupo Totara Timber Co. Ltd* v. *Rowe* (1978).

Similarly, it is clear from s. 316(3) that a bona fide payment to a director by way of damages for breach of contract or pension for past services is also outside the scope of the sections.

55. Disclosure in accounts of payments to directors. Section 231(1), taken along with the 5th Schedule, Part V (i.e. paras 22–34), requires a note to the company's accounts to show:

(*a*) the aggregate amount of the directors' emoluments, distinguishing between those received by him *qua director* and those received *qua employee* if in fact he has a service contract with the company;

(*b*) the aggregate amount of directors' or past directors' pensions; and

(*c*) the aggregate amount of any compensation to directors or past directors for loss of office.

Section 231(4) requires a director to disclose to the company all the information necessary for the purposes of Part V of the 5th Schedule.

In Part V of the 5th Schedule, paras 24 and 25 require a note to the accounts to show also the *emoluments of the chairman*, and of the most highly paid director if he is paid *more than the chairman*. In addition, it must show the number of directors who had *no emoluments* and those who received £5000 or less. It must then proceed to show the number of directors receiving more than £5000 but not more than £10,000, the number receiving more than £10,000 but not more than £15,000, and so on up a scale of multiples of £5000. By para. 27, the Schedule requires a note to the accounts to show the number of directors who have *waived* their rights to emoluments, and the aggregate amount of the emoluments concerned.

The provisions in paras 24, 25 and 27 do not apply to any company which is neither a holding nor a subsidiary company if the amount shown in the note to its accounts under (*a*) above does not exceed £60,000: 5th Schedule, para. 23.

56. The legal position of directors.

We have already seen that directors are officers of the company and agents of it. All the normal rules of agency apply, e.g. a director may not make a *secret profit*.

Sometimes, however, the directors are in the position of agents of *the shareholders* as well. This can arise where the shareholders *expressly appoint* them to act as their agents: *Briess* v. *Woolley* (1954), or where by their own *behaviour* they render themselves agents for the shareholders: *Allen* v. *Hyatt* (1914). But this is not the normal legal position and arises only in exceptional circumstances.

Directors are also sometimes said to be *trustees* for the company, but this is not truly the case. A trustee is the *legal owner* of property which he holds on trust for a beneficiary; a director does not hold property on trust for the company, for the company itself is the legal owner. Moreover, the duties of a trustee are well defined by law, e.g. under a will or a settlement, but a director's duties are not capable of precise definition.

On the other hand a director, like a trustee, is in a *fiduciary relation* towards the company. He is, of course, in a fiduciary relation towards the company in any case where he is acting as the company's agent, for an agent is always in a fiduciary relation with his principal. But the fiduciary relation of the director towards the company covers not only his activities as its agent, i.e. the making of contracts on its behalf, but the entire field of operation. There is nothing he can do in his capacity of director which is *not* required to be done *in good faith*, for the *benefit of the company as a whole*. The care and control of its assets, the making of calls, the forfeiture of shares, the approval of transfers – all these things and any other things which are done by the directors as directors must be done in good faith. It is this that is meant when they are said to be trustees of their powers.

57. Directors' duties of good faith and care.

These can best be summed up by saying that a director is permitted to be very stupid so long as he is honest. In fact, if one were to draw any conclusions from the state of the law, one would imagine that the business world was full of honest, stupid men.

The courts have imposed two duties upon directors:

(a) the *fiduciary* duty; and

(b) the duty of *care*.

Statute law is almost silent concerning both, so that the source of all but one of the following rules is the decided cases.

(a) *The fiduciary duty:* We have already seen in **56** that directors must always act bona fide for the benefit of the company as a whole, but here there are a number of points which must be borne in mind:

(i) The directors owe their duty to the *company*, not to individual members.

Thus in *Percival* v. *Wright* (1902), the directors bought some shares in the company from a member who wished to sell them. The directors knew at the time that negotiations were in progress for the sale of all the shares in the company at a higher price than they were paying, but they did not disclose this fact to the member. HELD: The sale should not be set aside. The directors owed no duty to that individual member.

It should be borne in mind, however, that today the directors in question would have committed a criminal offence under the 'insider dealing' rules (*see* Chapter 24).

(ii) Their duty to the company as *directors* does not prevent them from voting as *members* at general meetings in any way that they wish: *North-West Transportation Co. Ltd* v. *Beatty* (1887).

They may not, however, use their voting control to ratify their own fraud: *Cook* v. *Deeks* (1916).

(iii) They must exercise their powers not only in good faith, but for a proper purpose: *Hogg* v. *Cramphorn Ltd* (1967).

Thus in *Howard Smith Ltd* v. *Ampol Petroleum Ltd* (1974), where the directors of R. W. Miller (Holdings) Ltd issued shares to Howard Smith with a view to diluting the majority voting power of two large existing shareholders, Ampol and Bulkships, and so facilitating a take-over bid from Howard Smith, the Privy Council dismissed Howard Smith's appeal from the decision of the Supreme Court of New South Wales setting aside the issue. The directors had used their fiduciary power 'solely for the purposes of shifting the power to decide to whom and at what price shares are to be sold', and this could not be 'related to any purpose for which the power over the share capital was conferred on them'.

However, the company in general meeting may choose to ratify an act done by directors for an improper purpose provided it is within the company's powers: *Bamford* v. *Bamford* (1970).

(*iv*) They must not place themselves in a position where their interests conflict with their duty without making full disclosure to the general meeting. If they fail to make full disclosure, any contract made in these circumstances may be *voidable* by the company in equity; and the director will be accountable to the company for any profits made out of the transaction: *Hely Hutchinson* v. *Brayhead Ltd* (1968).

The liability to account for the profit to the company 'arises from the mere fact of a profit having been made', and it is irrelevant that the profit could not have been obtained by the company: *Regal (Hastings) Ltd* v. *Gulliver* (1942). Thus in *Industrial Development Consultants Ltd* v. *Cooley* (1972) where Cooley obtained for himself the benefit of a contract which could not have been obtained by the company, but failed to make any disclosure to the company although he was a director at the time, he was held accountable for the profit.

(*v*) They must have regard in the performance of their functions to the interests of the company's *employees* in general, as well as those of the members.

This is the single statutory rule in the midst of well-developed case-law relating to fiduciary duties. It is found in s. 309(1) and the section makes it clear in subsection (2) that, like any other fiduciary duty, the duty of directors to consider the employees is owed to the *company* and thus enforceable by the company alone. The provision has been much criticised as being ineffective and indeed is illustrative, along with certain other sections of the Act, of the truth of the ancient proverb that barking dogs seldom bite.

(*b*) *The duty of care:* This was considered at length by Romer J. in *Re City Equitable Fire Insurance Co. Ltd* (1925) where the following propositions were stated:

(*i*) 'A director need not exhibit in the performance of his duties a greater degree of skill than may reasonably be expected from a person of his knowledge and experience....'

He may, however, have no knowledge of the company's business, and little experience, so that a reasonable standard of skill may be a very low one.

(*ii*) 'Directors are not liable for mere errors of judgment.' Brett L.J. had stated many years earlier in *Marzetti's Case* (1880): 'Mere imprudence is not negligence. Want of judgment is not'.

(*iii*) 'A director is not bound to give continuous attention to the affairs of his company. He is not bound to attend all (board) meetings, though he ought to attend whenever he is reasonably able to do so.'

(*iv*) 'In respect of all duties that may properly be left to some other official, a director is, in the absence of grounds for suspicion, justified in trusting that official to perform such duties honestly.'

It is clear that the standard of care required from a director is *subjective*, i.e. it is a variable standard depending on the skill and knowledge of the particular director in question. In law a director may safely be ignorant, inexperienced and lacking in judgment so long as he is honest and careful.

58. Disclosure by directors of interests in contracts. Section 317(1) requires a director who is in any way interested in a contract with the company to declare the nature of his interest at a *board meeting*. Unless the articles state otherwise, this duty to disclose to the board is in addition to, and not instead of, the duty to disclose to the general meeting imposed by the rules of equity considered in **57** and expressly preserved by s. 317(9).

Section 317(2) states that the declaration must be made at the board meeting at which the question of entering into the contract is first considered, or, if the director was not interested in it at that date, at the next board meeting held after he became interested. If he became interested in the contract only after it was made, he must declare his interest at the first board meeting held after he became so interested.

Section 317(3) states that if a director gives a *general notice* to the board that he is a member of a specified company or firm and is to be regarded as interested in any contract which is made with it, this is a sufficient declaration of interest. Such a notice, however, must either be given at a board meeting, or brought up and read at the next board meeting after it is given: s. 317(4).

If proper disclosure as required by the section is not made, the director is liable, under s. 317(7), taken along with the 24th Schedule, to a fine of an unspecified amount on conviction on indictment, and on summary conviction to a fine not exceeding the statutory maximum.

The articles often exclude the equitable duty to disclose an interest to the general meeting provided the director complies with s. 317. This is the effect of Article 85 of Table A, but see also Article 94, which restricts the interested director's right to vote, and Article 95, which provides that a director not entitled to vote cannot be counted in the quorum.

It should be noted that the meaning of the word 'contract' in s. 317 is extended by s. 317(5) to include any transaction or arrangement, whether constituting a contract or not. Moreover, under s. 317(6) a transaction or arrangement within s. 330 (*see* **38** and **39**) made by a company for any of its directors, or for a person connected with such director, must be treated, for the purposes of s. 317, as one in which that director is interested.

Lastly, s. 317(8) provides that s. 317 applies to a *shadow director* (*see* **2**) in the same way that it applies to a director, except that a shadow director must declare his interest, not at a board meeting, but by a *written notice* to the directors which is *either:*

(*a*) a *specific* notice given before the meeting at which, if he had been a director, the declaration would be required by s. 317(2) to be made; *or*

(*b*) a *general* notice which is sufficient under s. 317(3), disregarding the proviso in s. 317(4).

For the purpose of minutes, the declaration is treated as if it had formed part of the proceedings at the meeting in question.

59. Dealings in options by directors. Section 323(1) and (3) prohibits a director from purchasing any option, whether a 'call' option, a 'put' option or a 'double' option, with regard to shares or debentures of the company or any other company within the group if a stock exchange listing has been granted in respect of them. The prohibition applies to a shadow director as to a director: s. 323(4).

Section 323(5) nevertheless permits him to buy an option to *subscribe* for the shares or debentures of a company, or to buy debentures entitling the holder to subscribe for shares or convert the debentures into shares.

Section 327(1) extends the application of s. 323 to a director's spouse or infant child, though it is a defence for such a person to prove that he had no reason to believe that his spouse or parent, as the case may be, was a director of the company in question.

60. Liability for acts of co-directors and relief from liability.
A director is the agent of the *company* and not of the other members of the board. It follows that nothing done by the *board* can impose liability on a director who did not know of their action and did not participate in it, even if he attends the subsequent board meeting at which the minutes recording the wrongful action of the earlier meeting are confirmed. To incur liability he must either be a party to the wrongful act, or later acquiesce in it.

Where the directors have misappropriated the company's money, any director against whom an action is brought is entitled to *contribution* from as many of his co-directors as were parties to the misapplication.

Finally, in relation to a director's liability, note should be taken of the provisions of ss. 310 and 727. These sections apply not only to directors but to other officers and to auditors.

Section 310(1) and (2) states that any provision in the articles or in any contract exempting such persons from, or indemnifying them against, liability for negligence or breach of duty towards the company is *void*. Thus it is impossible for a director to limit or exclude liability for negligence by the terms of his contract.

If, however, the court thinks that, though liable, the director has acted honestly and reasonably and ought fairly to be excused, it may, under s. 727(1), relieve him from liability on such terms as it thinks fit. It has been decided that relief can be granted only in proceedings brought by or on behalf of a company against an officer or auditor for his negligence or breach of duty *in that capacity* and *in relation to the company*: *Customs and Excise Commissioners* v. *Hedon Alpha Ltd* (1981).

61. Powers of directors. The directors' powers are normally set out in the articles. Once these powers are vested in the directors, only they may exercise them. Thus the shareholders cannot control the way in which the directors choose to act, provided their actions are within the scope of the powers given to them. If the shareholders disapprove of the board's actions strongly enough, they can alter the articles to restrict the board's powers, or they can remove the directors under s. 303, but they cannot themselves try to perform the very functions which they have entrusted to the directors: *Salmon* v. *Quin & Axtens Ltd* (1909).

Table A, Article 70, states that the business of the company shall be managed by the directors, who may exercise all the powers of the company subject to the provisions of the Act, the memorandum and articles and any direction given by special resolution.

The effect of this article is to vest in the directors all the powers *except* those which the Act or the memorandum and articles or a special resolution specifically state must be exercised by the company in general meeting. It could not, therefore, be more widely expressed.

62. Delegation of directors' powers. The maxim *'delegatus non potest delegare'* applies to directors in the same way as to all agents. A person to whom a function has been delegated may not himself delegate it further without the consent of his principal.

Table A, Article 72, however, specifically permits delegation, stating that the directors may delegate any of their powers to committees consisting of such member or members of their body as they think fit. Thus a committee may consist of a single director under this article.

63. The managing director. The directors may not appoint a managing director unless the articles authorize them to do so. Table A, Article 72, empowers them to delegate to any managing director such of their powers as they consider desirable to be exercised by him. The delegation may be made subject to conditions and may be revoked or altered.

The managing director is normally a service director with a contract setting out his powers and duties and terms of employment. He has a dual capacity – that of director and that of employee.

If he has a service contract, the revocation of his appointment by the directors under Article 72, or an alteration of the articles, or his removal under s. 303 from the office of director, cannot deprive him of his right to damages for breach of contract, if indeed a breach has been committed. But it is for him to prove, as plaintiff, that his dismissal was contrary to the terms of his service agreement.

64. The secretary. A secretary, as we have already seen in **1**, is an officer of the company under s. 744, and s. 283 (*see* **3**) requires every company to have one.

Nevertheless, until recently, his important status was not recognized by the courts. In 1887 Lord Esher said: 'A secretary is a mere servant; his position is that he is to do what he is told, and no person can assume that he has any authority to represent anything at all': *Barnett, Hoares & Co.* v. *South London Tramways Co.* (1887). In 1902 Lord Macnaghten described his duties as 'of a limited and of a somewhat humble character': *George Whitechurch Ltd* v. *Cavanagh* (1902).

In *Panorama Developments (Guildford) Ltd* v. *Fidelis Furnishing Fabrics Ltd* (1971), however, the Court of Appeal were of the opinion that times had changed. The secretary was no longer a mere clerk, but the chief administrative officer of the company, and as regards *matters of administration* had ostensible authority to sign contracts on behalf of the company.

This change in the secretary's status is reflected in s. 286 which has its origin in the Companies Act 1980 and which deals with his qualifications. Section 286(1) provides that in a *public* company it is the directors' duty to take all reasonable steps to secure that the secretary is a person who appears to them to have the requisite *knowledge and experience* to discharge his functions *and*:

(*a*) held office as secretary, assistant secretary, or deputy secretary of the company when the 1980 Act came into operation; *or*

(*b*) for at least three out of the five years immediately preceding his appointment as secretary held office as secretary of a public company; *or*

(*c*) is a member of any of the bodies listed in subsection (2), (i.e. the Institutes of Chartered Accountants, the Association of Certified Accountants, the Institute of Chartered Secretaries and Administrators, the Chartered Institute of Management Accountants, and the Chartered Institute of Public Finance and Accountancy) *or*

(*d*) is a barrister, advocate or solicitor; *or*

(*e*) is a person who, by virtue of his having held some other position or being a member of some other body, appears to the directors to be capable of discharging those functions.

Progress test 16

1. Define a director. How far is he:

(a) an officer of the company?

(b) an agent of the company?

(c) a servant of the company? (**1**)

2. What do you understand by the expression 'shadow director'? (**2**)

3. How many directors are required by law in any company? Can a director also be the secretary of the company? (**3**)

4. Who appoints:

(a) the first directors of a company? (**4**)

(b) the subsequent directors? (**5**)

(c) persons to fill casual vacancies of directors? (**6**)

5. Under what circumstances, according to Table A, are retiring directors automatically re-elected? (**5**)

6. What is meant by retirement by rotation? (**5**)

7. Give the statutory provision regarding voting on the appointment of directors. (**7**)

8. Under what circumstances may a director assign his office? Compare the legal position of an assignee of office with that of an alternate director. (**9, 10**)

9. What details must be contained in the register of directors and secretaries as regards directors? (**11**)

10. Give the statutory provisions as to the contents and right of inspection of the register of directors' interests. (**13, 14, 17**)

11. Give the provisions of the Act regarding the share qualification of directors. (**18**)

12. It is said that a director must hold his qualification shares, if any, 'in his own right'. What does this expression mean? (**18**)

13. Give the statutory provisions regarding the age limit for directors. (**19**)

14. When may a disqualification order be made against a director? (**20**)

15. What is the purpose of the register of disqualification orders? (**20, 21**)

16. Give the provisions of Table A regarding vacation of office by directors. (**22**)

17. How may a director be removed from office? (**23**)

18. Outline the rule in *Royal British Bank* v. *Turquand*. (**24, 25**)

19. Give the provisions of Table A and of the Companies Act 1985 regarding the remuneration of directors and its apportionment. (**26, 27**)

20. Give the statutory provisions relating to the inspection of directors' service contracts. What special rules apply if a director's contract requires him to work outside the United Kingdom? (**28**)

21. What do you understand by the expression 'contract of employment' for the purposes of s. 319 Companies Act 1985 (directors' contracts of employment exceeding five years)? What special rules apply to long-term contracts of employment of directors? (**29**)

22. What do you understand by the expression 'person connected with a director'? (**30**)

23. What special rules apply to substantial property transactions between a company and any of its directors? (**31**)

24. What is the legal effect of contravention of the rules applying to substantial property transactions between a company and any of its directors? (**32**)

25. What do you understand, in the context of the legislation on loans to directors, by the expressions:

(*a*) 'relevant company'?

(*b*) 'quasi-loan'?

(*c*) 'credit transaction'? (**34–37**)

26. State the rules prohibiting a company from lending money, or assisting some other person to lend money, to any of its directors or persons connected with him. (**38, 39**)

27. Give the exceptions to the rules which prohibit a company from lending money, or assisting some other person to lend money, to any of its directors. (**40–43**)

28. What do you understand by the expressions:

(*a*) 'relevant transaction';

(*b*) 'relevant arrangement';

(*c*) 'relevant amount';

as they are used in the rules relating to loans to directors? (**44**)

29. What is the legal effect of contravention of the rules relating to loans to directors? Are there any criminal penalties? (**45, 46**)

30. State the rules relating to disclosure in the accounts of transactions between a company and any of its directors. What do you understand by the expression 'specified particulars' in relation to these rules? (**48, 49**)

31. State the transactions which are excluded from the rules of disclosure. (**50, 51**)

32. State the rules relating to disclosure in the accounts of transactions between a company and any of its officers other than a director. (**52**)

33. What is the duty of the company's auditors if the disclosure requirements are not complied with? (**53**)

34. Give the statutory provisions regarding payment to a director of compensation for loss of office. (**54**)

35. Give the statutory provisions regarding disclosure in the accounts of payments to directors. (**55**)

36. How far can it be said that a director:

   (*a*) is an agent of the *shareholders*?
   (*b*) is a trustee for the company? (**56**)

37. Outline the fiduciary duty of directors. How far do they owe such a duty to the employees of the company? (**57**)

38. Describe a director's duty of care. (**57**)

39. Give the statutory provisions regarding disclosure by directors of their interests in contracts. Comment on the meaning of the word 'contracts' in this context. (**58**)

40. How far is it lawful for a director to purchase an option relating to shares or debentures? (**59**)

41. How far is a director liable for an action by the board in which he had no part? (**60**)

42. How far has a director who is found liable for misappropriation of the company's money a right to contribution from the other directors? (**60**)

43. What is the extent of the powers of directors? Can they delegate such powers? (**61, 62**)

44. Give the provisions of Table A regarding the managing director and outline his legal position. (**63**)

45. What is the legal position of a company's secretary? What qualifications is he required to have? (**64**)

17
Board meetings

1. The holding of board meetings. Table A, Article 88, states that, subject to the provisions of the articles, the directors may regulate their proceedings as they think fit. Questions shall be decided *by a majority of votes*, and the chairman has a *casting vote*. A director may, and the secretary at the request of a director shall, at any time call a meeting. It is not necessary to give notice of a meeting to a director who is absent from the United Kingdom.

2. Notice of board meetings. Board meetings are often held regularly on the same day in each week or month, and in such cases notice is not required though it may be given in practice. If they are not held regularly in this way, then either *the period of notice prescribed by the articles* or, if none, *reasonable* notice must be given. Table A does not specify any particular period.

The notice need not be in writing, and oral notice will therefore suffice. If all the directors are assembled together and no-one objects, no notice at all is necessary and a meeting may be held then and there, but it is essential that they all consent to the holding of the meeting.

Thus in *Barron* v. *Potter* (1914), B and P, who were both directors of the company, disliked each other and refused to meet at board meetings. One day they met by chance at Paddington station, whereupon P insisted on holding a board meeting on the spot, claiming that he had proposed a motion and carried it with his chairman's casting vote. HELD: B had not consented to the holding of the meeting, and his mere physical presence without consent did not constitute a valid meeting.

3. The chairman of board meetings. Table A, Article 91, states that the directors may appoint one of their number to be the chairman of the board of directors and may at any time remove him from that office. If there is no director holding that office, or if the director holding it is unwilling to preside or is not present *within five minutes* after the time appointed for the meeting, the directors present may appoint one of their number to be chairman of the meeting.

This article may be compared with Article 42 (*see* 15:**25**) which contains a similar provision but requires less promptitude.

4. Quorum at board meetings. Table A, Article 89, states that the quorum necessary for the transaction of business may be fixed by the directors, and unless so fixed shall be two (*see* 15:**28**(*e*)).

If the articles *empower the directors* to fix the quorum, but fail to specify what the quorum shall be if they do not fix it, then the *number of directors who usually act* will form the quorum. If the articles make no provision concerning quorum at all, then the *majority* of the directors must be present to constitute a valid meeting.

The quorum at a board meeting must be a *disinterested quorum*. This means that directors who are disqualified from voting on a resolution because they have an interest in it (*see* 16:**58**) must not be counted in ascertaining whether a quorum is present, though they cannot be excluded from the meeting. Articles 85, 94 and 95 should be re-read at this point.

Table A, Article 90, permits the continuing directors to act in spite of any vacancies on the board so long as there are enough of them to form a quorum. Once, however, their number falls below that required for a quorum, *they may act only for two purposes*:

(*a*) to fill vacancies; and

(*b*) to call a general meeting of the company.

5. Power to dispense with board meeting. Table A, Article 93, states that a resolution in writing signed by all the directors entitled to receive notice of a board meeting shall be as valid as if it had been passed at a board meeting. The same applies to a meeting of a committee of directors.

Progress test 17

1. What are the provisions of Table A regarding the holding of board meetings? What period of notice is required? (**1, 2**)

2. What, under Table A, is the quorum for a board meeting? May a director who is disqualified from voting be counted in the quorum? (**4**)

The accounts

1. The statutory provisions on accounts. The statutory provisions on company accounts are contained in Part VII of the Act and in several of the Schedules to the Act, in particular:

(a) the 4th Schedule (form and contents of company accounts);

(b) the 5th Schedule (matters to be disclosed in notes to company accounts);

(c) the 6th Schedule (particulars in company accounts of loan and other transactions favouring directors and other officers – *see* 16:**48–52**);

(d) the 7th Schedule (matters to be dealt with in directors' report – *see* 15:**6–12**);

(e) the 8th Schedule (modified accounts of small and medium-sized companies).

The 9th, 10th and 11th Schedules deal with 'special category accounts'. These are defined in s. 257(1) as accounts of banking companies, shipping companies and insurance companies. The provisions are too specialized to be included in this book, and these three Schedules will, therefore, not be mentioned further.

It should be noted at the outset that by ss. 251 and 256 the Secretary of State has power to alter many of the accounting requirements in the Act and in the Schedules by regulations made by statutory instrument.

2. Keeping accounting records. The accounting records which every company must, by s. 221(1) and (2), cause to be kept must be sufficient to show and explain the company's transactions and be such as to disclose with reasonable accuracy the company's financial position and enable the directors to ensure that the company's annual accounts comply with the Act.

By s. 221(3) and (4) the accounting records must in particular contain:

(*a*) entries from day to day of receipts and payments;

(*b*) a record of assets and liabilities; and

(*c*) if the company's business involves dealing in goods, statements as to stock and stocktakings.

The accounting records must, by s. 222(1), be kept at the registered office or such other place as the directors think fit, and must at all times be open to inspection by the company's officers. If accounting records are kept at a place outside Great Britain, accounts and returns must be sent to, and kept at, a place in Great Britain and be likewise open to inspection by officers: s.222(2).

Accounting records must be preserved in the case of a private company for three years and in the case of a public company for six years: s. 222(4).

3. Penalties for non-compliance with ss. 221 and 222. If a company fails to comply with any provision of s. 221 or with s. 222(1) or (2), every officer who is in default is guilty of an offence unless he can show that he acted honestly and that in the circumstances in which the company's business was carried on the default was excusable: s. 223(1).

As regards s. 224(4), an officer is guilty of an offence if he fails to take all reasonable steps for securing compliance by the company with that subsection or has intentionally caused any default by the company under it: s. 223(2).

The penalties are:

(*a*) for conviction on indictment, two years' imprisonment or a fine, or both;

(*b*) for summary conviction, six months' imprisonment or a fine of the statutory maximum, or both: s. 223(3) and the 24th Schedule.

4. The accounting reference period. Section 224(2) and (3) of the Act permits any company to give notice to the registrar within six months from incorporation specifying a date on which, in each calendar year, the accounting reference period of the company is to end.

If the company gives such a notice, then the specified date becomes, under s. 224(2), the company's *accounting reference date*. If no such notice is given, the accounting reference date is 31 March: s. 224(3).

Section 225(1) permits a company to alter its *current and all subsequent* accounting reference periods by giving notice to the registrar at any time in the course of a period specifying a new accounting reference date. Section 225(2) and (3) permits a holding or subsidiary company (*see* 13:**13–16**) to alter its *previous and all subsequent* reference periods by giving notice to the registrar at any time after the end of a period specifying a new accounting reference date which *coincides* with the accounting reference date of its subsidiary or holding company, as the case may be.

5. Directors' duty to prepare annual accounts. Section 227(1) requires the directors of every company in respect of each accounting reference period to prepare a profit and loss account for the financial year, and s. 227(3) requires them to prepare a balance sheet as at the last day of the financial year.

The financial year, by s. 227(2), begins with the day after the date to which the last preceding profit and loss account was made up and ends with the date on which the accounting reference period ends or on another date determined by the directors provided it falls not more than seven days before nor more than seven days after the end of the accounting reference period.

By s. 227(4), in the case of a holding company the directors must secure that the financial year of each of its subsidiaries coincides with the company's own financial year, except where in the directors' opinion there are good reasons against that.

6. Form and content of individual accounts. A company's accounts prepared under s. 227 must comply with the 4th Schedule as regards the form and content of the balance sheet and profit and loss account and any additional information to be provided by way of notes to the accounts: s. 228(1).

The overriding principle of the accounts is stated in s. 228(2) as being that the balance sheet must give a true and fair view of the state of affairs of the company as at the end of the financial year and the profit and loss account must give a true and fair view of the profit or loss of the company for the financial year. This overrides the requirements of the 4th Schedule and all other requirements of the Act as to the matters to be included in the accounts or in notes to the accounts: s. 228(3).

If the balance sheet or profit and loss account drawn up in accordance with the specific requirements would not provide sufficient information to comply with the overriding principle, any necessary additional information must be provided in the balance sheet or profit and loss account or in a note to the accounts: s. 228(4).

Further, if, owing to special circumstances in the case of any company, compliance with requirements in relation to the balance sheet or profit and loss account would prevent compliance with the overriding principle (even with the additional information provided under s. 228(4)), the directors must depart from the requirements so far as necessary in order to comply with the overriding principle, and must give particulars of the departure, the reasons for it and its effect, in a note to the accounts: s. 228(5) and (6).

7. Group accounts. By s. 229(1), if at the end of its financial year a company has subsidiaries, the directors must, as well as preparing individual accounts for that year, also prepare group accounts, i.e. accounts or statements which deal with the state of affairs and profit or loss of the company and the subsidiaries. This does not apply if the company is, at the end of the financial year, the wholly-owned subsidiary of another British company: s. 229(2).

By s. 229(3), group accounts need not deal with a subsidiary if the company's directors are of opinion that:

(*a*) it is impracticable, or would be of no real value to the company's members, in view of the insignificant amount involved; *or*

(*b*) it would involve expense or delay out of proportion to the value to members; *or*

(*c*) the result would be misleading, or harmful to the business of the company or any of its subsidiaries; *or*

(*d*) the business of the holding company and that of the subsidiary are so different that they cannot reasonably be treated as a single undertaking.

If the directors are of that opinion about each of the company's subsidiaries, group accounts are not required at all.

However, as regards (*c*) and (*d*) above, the approval of the Secretary of State is required for not dealing with a subsidiary in group accounts if the ground is that the result would be harmful or if the ground is difference between the business of the holding company and that of the subsidiary: s. 229(4).

A holding company's group accounts must be consolidated accounts, i.e. a consolidated balance sheet dealing with the state of affairs of the company and its subsidiaries, and a consolidated profit and loss account dealing with the profit or loss of the company and its subsidiaries, except that if the directors are of opinion that the information would be better presented or would be more readily appreciated by the company's members if the group accounts were prepared in other than consolidated form, that other form may be adopted: s. 229(5) and (6).

Group accounts may be wholly or partly incorporated in the holding company's individual balance sheet and profit and loss account: s. 229(7).

Section 230(1) provides that a holding company's group accounts must comply with the requirements of the 4th Schedule with respect to the form and content of those accounts and any additional information to be provided as notes to those accounts.

The overriding principle as to true and fair view applies to group accounts as it does to individual accounts: s. 230(2)–(6) (*see* **6**).

By s. 230(7), if the financial year of a subsidiary does not coincide with that of the holding company, the group accounts must deal with the subsidiary's state of affairs at the end of its immediately previous financial year, but the holding company's directors may apply to the Secretary of State for a direction to the contrary.

8. The laying of accounts before the general meeting. Section 241(1) requires the directors, in respect of each financial year of the company, to lay before the company in general meeting a copy of the company's accounts for that year.

The 'company's accounts' for a financial year are, by s. 239, to be taken as consisting of the following documents:

(*a*) the company's profit and loss account and balance sheet;

(*b*) the directors' report (*see* 15:**6–12**);

(*c*) the auditors' report (*see* 19:**15**); and

(*d*) where the company has subsidiaries and s. 229 applies, the company's group accounts.

By s. 238(1) the balance sheet and every copy of it which is laid before the company in general meeting or delivered to the registrar (*see* **9**), must be signed on behalf of the board of directors by two of the directors or, if there is only one director, by that one, and every copy issued, circulated or published must include a copy of the signatures or signature. Failure to comply with these provisions makes the company and every officer of it who is in default liable to a fine: s. 238(2).

A company's profit and loss account and any group accounts of a holding company (in so far as such group accounts are not incorporated in the holding company's individual accounts) must be annexed to the balance sheet and be approved by the board of directors before the balance sheet is signed on their behalf: s. 238(3) and (4).

Section 240(1) provides that a copy of the company's accounts must, not less than 21 days before the meeting at which they are to be laid, be sent to every member (including those not entitled to receive notice of general meetings) and every debenture-holder. If copies of the accounts are sent less than 21 days before the meeting, they are deemed to have been duly sent if it is so agreed by all the members entitled to attend and vote at the meeting: s. 240(4). If default is made in complying with s. 240(1), the company and every officer of it who is in default is liable to a fine: s. 240(5).

9. Delivery of the accounts to the registrar. Section 241(3) provides that in respect of each financial year the directors must deliver to the registrar a copy of the accounts for the year. Unlimited companies, provided they are neither the subsidiaries of limited companies nor the holding companies of limited companies, are exempt from this provision: s. 241(4).

10. Period allowed for laying and delivering accounts. Section 242(2) provides that the period allowed for laying and delivering accounts (*see* **8, 9**) is:

(*a*) for a private company, 10 months after the end of the accounting reference period; and

(*b*) for a public company, seven months after the end of that period.

By s. 242(3) a company which has interests abroad may, by giving notice to the registrar, extend these periods for a further three months, and by s. 242(6) the Secretary of State may extend the period for a specified company if for any special reason he thinks fit to do so.

11. Penalties and default orders. Section 243(1) provides that if for a financial year the requirements for laying and delivering accounts are not complied with before the end of the permitted period, every director is guilty of an offence and liable to a fine and, for continued contravention, to a daily default fine. It is, however, a defence for him to prove that he took all reasonable steps for securing compliance: s. 243(2).

For failure to deliver accounts as required by s. 241(3) provision has been made that the company be liable to a scale of penalties varying according to the length of time elapsing before compliance: s. 243(3) and (4).

Section 244(1) further provides that where there is failure to deliver the accounts a notice may be served on the directors requiring them to make good the default within 14 days, and that if they still fail to comply, any member or creditor of the company or the registrar of companies may apply to the court for an order directing the directors to make good the default within a time specified in the order. The court's order may provide that all costs of the application are to be borne by the directors: s. 244(2).

Section 245 makes it an offence for directors to lay before the company or deliver to the registrar accounts which do not comply with the requirements of the Act, but it is a defence for a director to prove that he took all reasonable steps for securing compliance with the requirements in question.

12. Right to obtain copies of accounts. Section 246(1) provides that any member of a company, whether or not entitled to have copies of the accounts sent to him, and any debenture-holder is entitled to be furnished, on demand and without charge, with a copy of its last accounts.

Failure to comply with such a demand within seven days makes the company and every officer of it who is in default liable to a fine and, for continued contravention, to a daily default fine, unless it is proved that the person has already made a demand for, and been supplied with, a copy: s. 246(2).

13. Modified accounts. In **9** it was explained that under s. 241(3) there is a general duty on the directors of all limited companies to deliver annually to the registrar a copy of the company's accounts. However, s. 247(1) entitles directors in certain cases to deliver modified accounts in accordance with the 8th Schedule. To enjoy this privilege the company must qualify as small or medium-sized.

It is important to note that under s. 247(2) certain types of companies can never be entitled to deliver modified accounts, whatever their size. These types of companies are:

(*a*) public companies;

(*b*) 'special category companies', i.e., by s. 257(1), banking, shipping and insurance companies; and

(*c*) companies which are not dormant companies and which form part of 'an ineligible group', i.e., by s. 247(3), a group which includes a public company or a special category company.

Thus, the privilege of delivering modified accounts is necessarily confined to *private* companies which are not in a group containing a public company. Further, the privilege applies only in relation to the delivery of accounts to the registrar and has no application to the duty to lay accounts before the general meeting (*see* **8**).

14. The qualifying conditions as to size. Section 248(1) provides that a company qualifies as small in a financial year if, for that year, two or more of the following conditions are satisfied:

(*a*) The amount of its turnover for the year is not more than £1.4 million.

(*b*) Its balance sheet total is not more than £700,000.

(*c*) The average number of its employees in the year does not exceed 50.

By s. 248(2) a company qualifies as medium-sized in a financial year if for that year two or more of the following conditions are satisfied:

(*a*) The amount of its turnover for the year is not more than £5.75 million.

(*b*) Its balance sheet total is not more than £2.8 million.

(*c*) The average number of its employees in the year does not exceed 250.

15. Modified individual accounts. Section 249 and Part I of the 8th Schedule deal with the cases in which a company's directors may deliver individual accounts modified as for a small or a medium-sized company.

By s. 249(2) in respect of the company's first financial year the directors may deliver modified accounts if in that year the company qualifies as small or medium-sized. As regards later financial years, however, regard must be had to the preceding year as well as to the year in question: the directors are entitled to deliver modified accounts only if the company has qualified in two consecutive years as a small or medium-sized company, but once the status of small or medium-sized has been obtained, it continues to be enjoyed by the company until for two consecutive years the company is no longer qualified as small or medium-sized. The effect is that the directors may deliver modified accounts provided one of the following is satisfied:

(*a*) The financial year is the company's first financial year and the company qualifies as small or medium-sized in that year.

(*b*) The financial year is the company's second financial year and the company qualifies as small or medium-sized both in that year and in its first year.

(*c*) The financial year is any later year than the first or second and the company *either* in the year in question *or* in the immediately preceding year (but not necessarily in both) qualifies as small or medium-sized.

By Part I of the 8th Schedule the permitted modifications for a small company include the following:

(*a*) Instead of the full balance sheet there may be delivered an abbreviated version showing only certain specified items.

(*b*) No copy of the profit and loss account or the directors' report need be delivered.

(*c*) The information required by the 4th Schedule to be given in notes to the accounts need not, with certain exceptions, be given.

(*d*) The information required by Parts V and VI of the 5th Schedule (as to the remuneration of the chairman, of directors and of employees paid at higher rates) need not be given.

The permitted modifications for a medium-sized company are that a modified profit and loss account may be delivered instead of a full profit and loss account, and in the notes to the accounts no particulars of turnover need be given.

The 8th Schedule further provides that the company's balance sheet must contain a statement by the directors, immediately above their signatures, that the company is entitled to the benefit of ss. 247–249 as a small or medium-sized company, and the accounts delivered must be accompanied by a special report of the auditors stating that in their opinion the directors are entitled to deliver modified accounts and that these accounts have been properly prepared in accordance with the 8th Schedule.

16. Modified group accounts. Modified group accounts are governed by s. 250 and Parts II and III of the 8th Schedule.

Section 250(2) provides that the directors of a holding company are not entitled to deliver accounts modified as for a small or medium-sized company unless the group is small or medium-sized. The figures to be taken into account in deciding whether the group is small or medium-sized are the group account figures, i.e.:

(*a*) in consolidated accounts the figures for turnover, balance sheet total and numbers employed which are shown in those accounts; and

(*b*) in group accounts not prepared as consolidated accounts the corresponding figures given in the group accounts, with the same adjustment as would have been made if the accounts had been prepared in consolidated form.

If a subsidiary has been omitted from the group accounts on one of the grounds specified in s. 229(3) (*see* 7) (other than the first ground of impracticability, etc.), the relevant figures from the omitted subsidiaries must be added: s. 250(3).

17. Modification of ss. 247–250 and 8th Schedule. Section 251 enables the Secretary of State to modify the provisions in ss. 247–250 and the 8th Schedule by regulations made by statutory instrument.

18. Unaudited accounts of dormant companies. Section 252(1) provides that in certain circumstances a dormant company may pass a special resolution making itself exempt from the obligation to appoint auditors. Then, by s. 253(2), a report by the company's auditors need not be included with the accounts laid before the company in general meeting and delivered to the registrar.

By s. 252(5) a company is 'dormant' during any period in which no transaction occurs which is for the company a significant accounting transaction, i.e. a transaction which is required to be entered in the company's accounting records under s. 221 (*see* 2), and a company ceases to be dormant on the occurrence of any such transaction.

Only a company whose directors are entitled to deliver, under s. 249, accounts modified as for a small company can qualify for this exemption: s. 252(2). It is not available to a public company or to a 'special category' company (*see* 13): s. 252(4).

19. Publication of accounts. Although English company law has for many years required companies to file accounts with the registrar, it has never required publication in newspapers or journals. The Act does, however, include certain safeguards applicable where a company chooses to publish accounts.

A distinction is made between publication of full company accounts and publication of abridged accounts.

Section 254 applies to publication of full individual or group accounts, i.e. the accounts required by s. 241 to be laid before the company in general meeting and delivered to the registrar, including the directors' report unless dispensed with under the 8th Schedule (see 15).

Section 254(2) provides that if a company publishes individual accounts (modified or other), it must publish with them the relevant auditors' report. By s. 254(3), if a company required by s. 229 to prepare group accounts publishes individual accounts, it must also publish with them its group accounts, and by s. 254(4), if a company publishes group accounts otherwise than along with its individual accounts, it must publish with them the relevant auditors' report.

Section 255 applies to publication of abridged accounts. Section 255(3) provides that if a company chooses to publish abridged accounts, it must publish with them a statement indicating:

(*a*) that the accounts are not full accounts;

(*b*) whether full individual or full group accounts have been delivered to the registrar;

(*c*) whether the company's auditors have made a report on the accounts for the financial year with which the abridged accounts purport to deal; and (*d*) whether the auditors' report was unqualified, i.e. was to the effect that the company's accounts had been properly prepared.

By s. 255(4) a company must not publish the auditors' report along with abridged accounts.

Contravention of any of the provisions of ss. 254 and 255 makes the companies and any officers who are in default liable to fines: ss. 254(6) and 255(5).

20. Destruction of old records. Section 715 authorizes the registrar to destroy any company accounts which he has kept for 10 years. He must, however, retain a copy (e.g. microfilm) of any document which he destroys.

Progress test 18

1. What are the essential contents of a company's accounting records? (**2**)

2. What is the overriding general principle governing a company's accounts? (**6**)

3. When are group accounts required, and what form do they take? (**7**)

4. What documents comprise the 'accounts' which the directors must lay before the company in general meeting? (**8**)

5. What period is allowed for laying and delivering accounts? (**10**)

6. What companies can never be entitled to deliver modified accounts? (**13**)

7. What are the qualifying conditions entitling a company to the accounting exemptions (*a*) as a medium-sized company and (*b*) as a small company? (**14**)

8. What modifications are permitted by Part I of the 8th Schedule in the accounts of (*a*) a small company and (*b*) a medium-sized company? (**15**)

9. What do you understand by a 'special auditors' report'? (**15**)

10. When can a holding company which is required to prepare group accounts claim the benefit of modified accounts? (**16**)

11. What rules apply to a company which publishes its accounts in the press? (**19**)

12. For how long does the registrar of companies require to keep company accounts which have been delivered to him? (**20**)

19
Auditors

1. Appointment of the first auditors. Section 384(2) states that the *first* auditors may be appointed by the *directors* at any time before the first general meeting at which accounts are laid. The auditors so appointed hold office until the end of that meeting.

Section 384(3) states that if the directors do not exercise their power of appointment, the company in general meeting may appoint the first auditors.

2. Appointment of auditors to fill casual vacancies. Section 384(4) provides that the *directors,* or the *company in general meeting,* may appoint auditors to fill casual vacancies, but that the surviving auditors may continue to act during any vacancy.

3. Subsequent appointment of auditors. Section 384(1) requires every company to appoint one or more auditors at each general meeting at which accounts are laid in accordance with s. 241. Such auditors hold office from the end of that meeting until the end of the next general meeting at which the requirements of s. 241 are complied with.

4. Power of Secretary of State to appoint an auditor. Section 384(5) states that if no auditors are appointed or reappointed at a general meeting at which accounts are laid as required by s. 241, the Secretary of State may appoint a person to fill the vacancy. The company must give the Secretary of State notice within one week of the fact that his power has become exercisable.

5. Dormant companies. Section 252 provides that in certain circumstances a 'dormant' company may pass a special resolution exempting itself from the obligation to appoint auditors (*see* 18:18).

If a company ceases to be dormant it also ceases to be exempt from the obligation to appoint auditors. The directors may then appoint an auditor at any time before the next general meeting at which accounts are laid before members and if they do so those auditors hold office until the end of that meeting. If the directors do not exercise their power of appointment, the company in general meeting may do so: s. 252(7).

6. Remuneration of auditors. Section 385(2) states that if the directors appoint an auditor they may fix his remuneration, and if the Secretary of State makes an appointment, he may fix the remuneration. Apart from this, however, the company must fix it, or else determine the way in which it will be fixed: s. 385(1). 'Remuneration' here includes sums paid by the company for the auditors' expenses: s. 385(3).

7. Removal of auditors. Section 386(1) states that a company may by ordinary resolution remove an auditor before the expiration of his term of office and despite any agreement between it and him.

Notice of the fact that such a resolution has been passed must be given to the registrar within 14 days: s. 386(2).

8. Resolutions relating to appointment and removal of auditors. Section 388(1) states that *special notice* (*see* 15:24) must be given of a resolution at a general meeting:

    (*a*) to appoint as auditor a person other than a retiring auditor;

    (*b*) to fill a casual vacancy in the office of auditor;

    (*c*) to reappoint as auditor a retiring auditor who was appointed by the directors to fill a casual vacancy;

    (*d*) to remove an auditor before the expiration of his term of office.

9. The auditor's right to make written representations. Section 388(2) states that when the company receives this notice, it must at once send a copy of it:

    (*a*) to the person proposed to be appointed or removed, as the case may be;

(*b*) to the retiring auditor where it is proposed to appoint another person as auditor;

(*c*) to the auditor who resigned where a casual vacancy was caused by his resignation.

Section 388(3) states that where notice is given of a resolution to appoint as auditor a person *other than the retiring auditor*, or to *remove* an auditor before the expiration of his term of office, and the retiring auditor or the auditor proposed to be removed makes *written representations* to the company and asks that these should be notified to the members, the company must, unless it receives them too late:

(*a*) state the fact that they were made in any notice of the resolution to the members; and

(*b*) send a copy of them to every member to whom notice of the meeting is sent.

If a copy is not sent out in this way because the representations were received too late or because of the company's default, then the auditor may demand that his statement shall be read out at the meeting: s. 388(4).

It may perhaps occur that an auditor reacts sharply to the copy of the special notice of the resolution to appoint someone in his place or to remove him, and makes a statement in his own defence which is highly defamatory of some other person. Section 388(5) provides for this situation, stating that copies of the representations need not be sent out, nor need the representations be read out, if the company or any aggrieved person applies to the court and the court is satisfied that the auditor is abusing his rights *to secure needless publicity for defamatory matter*. Moreover, the court may order that the company's costs on such an application shall be paid by the auditor.

NOTE: These provisions concerning the written representations are *exactly the same as those in s. 304* relating to directors. Once learnt, they apply to both directors and auditors alike.

10. Rights of auditors in respect of meetings. Section 387(1) provides that a company's auditors are entitled to attend any general meetings of the company and to receive all notices of, and other communications relating to, any general meeting which a member is entitled to receive and to speak at any general meeting which they attend on any part of the business which concerns them as auditors.

Section 387(2) entitles an auditor who has been removed:

(*a*) to attend the general meeting at which his term of office would have expired;

(*b*) to attend any general meeting at which it is proposed to fill the vacancy caused by his removal;

(*c*) to receive all notices and communications relating to such meetings which a member is entitled to receive;

(*d*) to speak at such meetings on any part of the business which concerns him as former auditor.

11. Qualifications of auditors. Section 389(1) and (3) states that an auditor must be *either*:

(*a*) a member of a body of accountants established in the United Kingdom and recognized by the Department of Trade and Industry (i.e. the Institute of Chartered Accountants or the Chartered Association of Certified Accountants); *or*

(*b*) authorized by the Department as having similar qualifications obtained elsewhere.

Section 389(5) spitefully enables the Secretary of State to refuse an authorization under (*b*) above to a person who has qualifications obtained outside the United Kingdom if the country in which they were obtained does not confer corresponding privileges on persons qualified in the United Kingdom.

12. Disqualifications of auditors. Under s. 389(6) and (7) even a qualified accountant cannot act as auditor to a company if he is:

(*a*) an officer or servant of the company; *or*

(*b*) a partner or employee of an officer or servant of the company; *or*

(*c*) an officer or servant, or partner or employee of an officer or servant, of any company within the same group (i.e. if he is disqualified under (*a*) or (*b*) for *any* company within a group, he is disqualified for *all* companies within that group).

Section 389(6) also states that a body corporate cannot act as auditor. It does not prohibit a shareholder in the company from acting as its auditor, but the rules of his professional association are likely to do so.

Finally, s. 389(9) prohibits any person from acting as the auditor of a company if he knows that he is disqualified for appointment. If he knowingly becomes disqualified during his term of office he must at once vacate his office and give written notice to the company of his reason for doing so. In *Secretary of State for Trade and Industry* v. *Hart* (1982), however, it was held that a person who acts as an auditor when he is disqualified is not guilty of an offence under this subsection unless he knows not only the facts but also the statutory provisions which disqualify him, since the subsection expressly requires 'some form of *mens rea*' (*per* Woolf J.).

13. Resignation of auditors. Section 390(1) provides that an auditor may resign by giving written notice to the company at the registered office. Section 390(2), however, states that this notice is not effective unless it contains *either*:

(*a*) a statement that there are no circumstances connected with his resignation which he considers should be brought to the notice of the company's members or creditors; *or*

(*b*) a statement of such circumstances.

Once an effective notice has been given, s. 390(3) requires the company within 14 days to send a copy of it:

(*a*) to the registrar; and

(*b*) if it contained a statement of the connected circumstances, to every member and debenture-holder of the company.

Under s. 390(4) and (5) the company or any aggrieved person may, within 14 days of the company's receipt of a notice containing a statement of the connected circumstances, apply to the court which, if it is satisfied that the auditor is using the notice *to secure needless publicity for defamatory matter*, may order that copies need not be sent out. Moreover, it may also order that the company's costs on such an application shall be paid by the auditor.

Finally, s. 390(6) requires the company, within 14 days of the court's decision, to send to the registrar and to every member and debenture-holder:

(*a*) a statement of the effect of the court order, if any;

(*b*) if none, a copy of the notice containing the statement of the connected circumstances.

14. Resigning auditor's rights. Section 391(1) and (2) confers two rights on the resigning auditor where his notice of resignation contains a statement of the connected circumstances (*see* **13**):

(*a*) He may deposit with the notice a signed requisition calling on the directors of the company to convene an extraordinary general meeting to receive and consider his explanation of those circumstances.

The directors must then, under s. 391(4), within 21 days proceed to convene a meeting for a day not more than 28 days after the date on which the notice of the meeting is given.

(*b*) If he requests the company to circulate to the members before the general meeting at which his term of office expires, or at which it is proposed to fill the vacancy caused by his resignation, or which is convened on his requisition, a written statement of the connected circumstances, the company must, unless it receives it too late:

(*i*) state the fact that it was made in any notice of the meeting given to the members, and

(*ii*) send a copy of it to every member to whom notice of the meeting is sent.

Section 391(5), once again, states that if a copy is not sent out in this way because the statement was received too late or because of the company's default, the auditor may demand that his statement be read out at the meeting.

As before, s. 391(6) provides that copies of the statement need not be sent out, nor need the statement be read out, if the company or any aggrieved person applies to the court and the court is satisfied that the auditor is abusing his rights to *secure needless publicity for defamatory matter*. Moreover, the court may also order that the company's costs on such an application shall be paid by the auditor.

Finally, s. 391(7) entitles a resigning auditor to attend any meeting mentioned in (*b*) above, and to receive all notices and communications relating to such a meeting which a member is entitled to receive. He may also speak at such a meeting on any part of the business which concerns him as former auditor.

15. Auditors' report. Section 236(1) states that the auditors must make a report to the members on the accounts examined by them.

Section 241(2) states that this report must be read before the company in general meeting, and be open to inspection by any member.

Section 236(2) requires the report to state whether in the auditors' opinion the company's balance sheet, profit and loss account and group accounts, if any, have been properly prepared and a true and fair view given:

(a) in the case of the balance sheet, of the state of the company's affairs as at the end of its financial year;

(b) in the case of the profit and loss account, of the company's profit or loss for its financial year;

(c) in the case of group accounts, of the state of affairs and profit or loss of the company and its subsidiaries.

Section 237(1) requires the auditors, in preparing their report, to carry out such investigations as will enable them to form an opinion as to the following matters:

(a) whether proper accounting records have been kept by the company, and adequate returns have been received from branches not visited by them;

(b) whether the balance sheet and profit and loss account agree with the accounting records and returns.

If they think that this is not the case, they must state that fact in their report: s. 237(2).

Section 237(3) states that the auditors have a right of access to books, accounts and vouchers of the company. This presumably includes the minutes of board meetings. They may require from the officers of the company any information and explanations which they think necessary and if they fail to obtain these they must, under s. 237(4), state that fact in their report.

Finally, s. 237(6) requires the auditors, when preparing their report, to consider whether the information given in the directors' report is *consistent* with the accounts. If they think that it is not, they must state that fact in their report.

16. Auditors' powers relating to subsidiaries. Section 392(1) provides that where a company has a subsidiary (*see* 13:**13–15**) incorporated in Great Britain, that subsidiary and its auditors must give the auditors of the holding company such information and explanation as they may reasonably require for the purposes of their duties.

Where a company has a subsidiary incorporated elsewhere, it is the duty of the holding company, if required by its auditors, to take all reasonable steps to obtain such information and explanation from the subsidiary.

17. False statements to auditors. Section 393 makes it a criminal offence for any officer of a company knowingly or recklessly to make, either orally or in writing, to the company's auditors any statement conveying any information or explanation which the auditors require or to which they are entitled and which is misleading, false or deceptive in a material particular.

18. Legal position of auditors. An auditor is not an officer of the company within s. 744, which defines an officer as including a director, manager or secretary. He is, however, an officer for the purposes of certain sections, e.g. ss. 206–211 Insolvency Act 1986, which impose criminal liability on officers of companies in liquidation, and s. 212 Insolvency Act 1986, dealing with misfeasance by officers of companies which comes to light in liquidation.

He is, on the other hand, a servant of the company, and for certain purposes he is also an agent, e.g. s. 434, dealing with an investigation of the company's affairs by the Department of Trade and Industry. He is not, however, an agent of the company for the purposes of acknowledging a debt on its behalf within the Limitation Act 1980 when he signs his report on the balance sheet.

19. Auditors' liability for negligence. An auditor is naturally liable to the *company* for loss occasioned by breach of his duty of care, i.e. negligence, for he is in a contractual relationship with it.

Thus in *Re Thomas Gerrard and Son Ltd* (1968), a director of a company falsified the company's accounts by fraudulent entries, *inter alia*, regarding stock. The auditors were suspicious and asked him for an explanation, but made no further investigation. As a result their estimate of the company's profits was wrong and the company declared dividends which it would not otherwise have done, paying tax which would not otherwise have been payable. The company went into liquidation and the liquidator took misfeasance proceedings against the auditors under s. 333 Companies Act 1948 (now s. 212 Insolvency Act 1986). HELD: The damages recoverable by the liquidator included the dividends, the costs of recovering the tax, and any tax not recoverable.

Further, as a result of the decision in *Hedley Byrne & Co. Ltd* v. *Heller & Partners Ltd* (1964), it was established that a person may be liable for a negligent mis-statement even where there is no contractual relationship between him and the party to whom he makes it, provided there is some 'special relationship' between them, and provided he does not expressly disclaim responsibility. The House of Lords did not define the expression 'special relationship', but thought that it arose wherever one person relies on the skill or knowledge of another who is using it responsibly, though gratuitously, to assist him. This would seem to cover an auditor who, for example, makes a negligent mis-statement to a potential investor.

The scope of the auditor's duty of care has been still further widened by the decision of Woolf J. in *JEB Fasteners Ltd* v. *Marks, Bloom & Co.* (1981). There the plaintiffs, who had taken over the company, brought an action for damages against the auditors alleging that they had been negligent in preparing the company's accounts in that they had over-valued the stock. HELD: An auditor owes a duty of care to any person whom he ought to have foreseen as relying on the accounts for the purpose of deciding whether or not to take over the company. In the present case, however, the defendants were not liable since the plaintiffs, although they had seen and considered the accounts, would have acted no differently even if they had known the true position. This decision was subsequently upheld in the Court of Appeal.

20. Duties of auditors.

(a) *An auditor must act honestly*, and with *reasonable skill, care and caution*.

(b) *He must show the true financial position as shown by the books*. If proper accounting records have not been kept, or they do not, in his opinion, show a true and fair view of the company's affairs, he must state that fact in his report and even refuse to certify the accounts and resign.

(*c*) *He must know his duties* under the articles and the Companies Acts, and in particular his report must comply with s. 236.

(*d*) *He must verify the existence of the company's securities* and see that they are in safe custody. Thus he should actually see the securities unless they have been deposited with a third party with whom securities would normally be deposited in the ordinary course of business, e.g. a bank.

(*e*) He must check the *cash in hand* and *the bank balance*.

(*f*) *He is not concerned with policy or management.* He must simply state the effect of what has been done, and the remedy for bad management will lie with the shareholders, who can remove the directors or at least raise the matter at a meeting.

(*g*) *He is not under a duty to take stock*, unless there are suspicious circumstances, but he should make sure that the amount of stock stated to exist is a reasonably probable figure. In practice, an auditor often thinks it prudent to exceed his legal duty with regard to stock-taking.

(*h*) *A watchdog but not a bloodhound.* Although the famous words of Lopes L.J. in *Re Kingston Cotton Mill Co. Ltd (No. 2)* (1896), that an auditor 'is a watchdog but not a bloodhound' are invariably remembered by students and are often the only remark which they can make when asked for the duties of an auditor, constant repetition of even such a delightful phrase tends to depress the examiner. Lopes L.J. also said that 'an auditor is not bound to be a detective', which is another way of expressing the same idea and at least makes a change.

21. Relief from liability. Section 310 applies not only to officers of the company but also to auditors. Section 310(1) and (2) states that any provision in the articles or in any contract exempting them from, or indemnifying them against, liability for negligence or breach of duty towards the company is *void*. Thus it is impossible for an auditor to limit or exclude liability for negligence by the terms of his contract.

If, however, the court thinks that, though liable, the auditor has acted honestly and reasonably and ought fairly to be excused, it may, under s. 727, relieve him from liability on such terms as it thinks fit. This compassionate section, like s. 310, applies also to defaulting officers, and not only to auditors, but relief can be granted only in proceedings brought by or on behalf of a company against an officer or auditor for his negligence or breach of duty *in that capacity* and *in relation to the company*: *Customs and Excise Commissioners* v. *Hedon Alpha Ltd* (1981).

22. Share valuations by auditors. The valuation of shares is not an easy matter. It is not just a question of valuing the entire undertaking of the company and then dividing the figure reached by the number of shares issued, i.e. estimating what is called the 'break-up' value. A share in a going concern will be affected by many factors: the dividend yield, the number of times the dividend was covered, the marketability of the shares, the existence of reserves, the possibility of expansion and the making of 'rights' issues, and the hope of a takeover bid.

Auditors, therefore, are often required to make such valuations under the articles of a private company where there are no dealings in the shares and some price must be attached to them. When they perform this function they must of course act honestly, but they *need not give reasons for their valuation*. Indeed, the less said the better, for if they give reasons the court can inquire into the accuracy of the valuation and set it aside: *Burgess* v. *Purchase & Sons (Farms) Ltd* (1983). Their position here is similar to that of directors who refuse to register a transfer of shares under an article conferring on them an unrestricted discretion.

In valuing shares an auditor is not normally acting in a judicial or arbitral capacity and is therefore not entitled to the immunity from liability for negligence possessed by a judge or arbitrator. He is exercising a professional function, not settling a dispute, and will therefore be liable to the person who employs him for any loss caused to that person by his negligence: *Arenson* v. *Casson Beckman Rutley and Co.* (1977).

He will, of course, also be liable for fraud or collusion if he acts dishonestly.

Progress test 19

1. Who appoints:

(a) the first auditors of a company? (**1**)

(b) auditors to fill casual vacancies? (**2**)

(*c*) auditors at the general meeting before which the accounts are laid? (**3**)

2. Under what circumstances may the Secretary of State appoint an auditor? (**4**)

3. How is the remuneration of auditors fixed? (**6**)

4. How may an auditor be removed before the expiration of his term of office and what are his rights in respect of meetings? (**7, 10**)

5. What resolutions regarding auditors require special notice? (**8**)

6. Describe the statutory requirements and possible consequences when special notice is given of a resolution to appoint an auditor other than the retiring auditor, or to remove an auditor before the expiration of his term of office. (**9**)

7. Give the statutory provisions relating to:

(*a*) the qualifications of an auditor; (**11**)

(*b*) the disqualifications of an auditor. (**12**)

8. Give the statutory provisions relating to the resignation of auditors and the resigning auditor's rights. (**13, 14**)

9. What matters must be dealt with in the auditors' report? (**15**)

10. Give an account of the auditors' powers relating to subsidiary companies. (**16**)

11. How far is an auditor:

(*a*) an officer of the company?

(*b*) a servant of the company?

(*c*) an agent of the company? (**18**)

12. Discuss the duties of an auditor. (**15, 16, 20**)

13. Can an auditor exclude liability for negligence by the terms of his contract? (**21**)

20
Dividends

1. The nature of a dividend. A company pays *dividends* to its members, *interest* to its debenture-holders. It is important to distinguish between these two types of payment.

A dividend is a *proportion of the distributed profits* of the company. It may be a *fixed* annual percentage, as in the case of preference shares, or it may be *variable* according to the prosperity of the company, as in the case of ordinary shares, but since it is payable only out of the distributed profits, it follows that if no profits are made, or if none are distributed, no dividend will be declared.

The shareholder cannot insist on the company declaring a dividend, for this is a matter which is at the discretion of the directors. It is the directors who control the management and financial policy of the company, and it is they who recommend the amount of dividend to be paid. If, therefore, the members do not approve of the directors' policy, their proper remedy is to make appropriate changes to the board.

The articles normally contain provisions on payment of dividends but the only statutory provision is contained in s. 119(*c*). This states that a company, with authority in its articles, may pay dividends in proportion to the amount paid up on the shares where a larger amount is paid up on some shares than on others. Table A, Article 104, gives this authority.

2. The nature of interest. The payment of interest is in no way dependent on the existence of profits. Interest is a *debt*. It is payable whether profits are available or not, and may therefore lawfully be paid either out of capital or out of revenue.

In accounting, debenture-holders' interest and the dividends of preference shareholders are often collectively referred to as *prior charges*. This term simply indicates that both these types of payment must be made before the ordinary shareholders receive anything. It is a mistake to think that they are in any way similar in law; even though the debenture-holder is a creditor of the company to the extent of the sum which he has lent and the interest on it, while the shareholder, as we have seen in Chapter 11, is regarded in accounting as a creditor to the extent of the capital which he has invested, the *funds out of which they may be paid are different*. The debenture-holder may lawfully be paid his interest out of *any of the company's funds*, including capital. The shareholder, whether he holds preference or ordinary shares, may lawfully be paid dividends *only if profits are available*. Furthermore, while interest on a loan will accrue at the agreed rate per annum and will automatically become a debt, a dividend is not a debt until it is declared, and there is no obligation to declare it.

Thus there are two fundamental distinctions between interest and dividends:

(*a*) *They are payable out of different funds*, interest being payable out of any of the company's moneys, while dividends are payable only out of profits.

(*b*) *Interest is a debt, while a dividend is not a debt until it is declared*. Even then, under s. 74(2)(*f*) Insolvency Act 1986, in a liquidation it is not payable until *after* the company's debenture-holders and trade creditors have been paid, for it is a debt payable to a member in his capacity of member (*see* 1:**18**).

3. Meaning of distribution, profits and losses. There was formerly little difference between funds which were legally distributable and the concept of 'profits'. All 'profits' were normally distributable so long as the articles did not contain restrictive provisions and the fixed assets as a whole were maintaining their value. Thus the mere description of funds as 'profits' indicated that the company had almost complete freedom to use them as it desired.

These lenient rules for distribution were often criticized as a potential danger to creditors for they went far beyond the limits of prudence. It was, for instance, permissible to make a distribution on the strength of an unrealized accretion to a fixed asset: *Dimbula Valley (Ceylon) Tea Co. Ltd* v. *Laurie* (1961). There are now, however, provisions in the Act (derived from the Companies Act 1980) which, while leaving the concept of 'profits' unchanged, lay down stringent rules regarding dividends which considerably restrict the funds out of which they may lawfully be paid. In other words, not all 'profits' are now legally distributable.

Before considering these rules it is essential to grasp the meaning given by the Act to the words 'distribution', 'profits' and 'losses'.

Section 263(2) states that 'distribution' means every description of distribution of a company's assets to its members, whether in cash or otherwise, *except* those made by way of:

(*a*) an issue of fully or partly paid bonus shares;

(*b*) the redemption or purchase of any of the company's own shares out of capital (including the proceeds of any fresh issue of shares) or out of unrealized profits in accordance with the provisions of the Act concerning redeemable shares and purchase by the company of its own shares;

(*c*) the reduction of share capital by extinguishing or reducing the liability of members in respect of unpaid share capital or by paying off paid up share capital; and

(*d*) a distribution of assets to members on winding up.

Section 280(3) explains that the word 'profits' in the Act refers to *both revenue and capital profits*, while the word 'losses' refers to *both revenue and capital losses*.

4. Restriction on distribution of assets by public companies. Not only are there now more stringent rules regarding dividends in general but there is also an additional restriction on distributions of assets applicable only to public companies. By s. 264(1) a public company may make a distribution only:

(*a*) if the amount of its net assets at the time is not less than *the aggregate of its called-up share capital and its undistributable reserves*; and

(*b*) if, and to the extent that, the distribution does not reduce the amount of the net assets to less than that aggregate.

The undistributable reserves, for the purpose of this provision, are listed in s. 264(3). They are:

(*a*) the share premium account;

(*b*) the capital redemption reserve;

(*c*) the amount by which the company's accumulated *unrealized* profits exceed its accumulated *unrealized* losses; and

(*d*) any other reserve which the company is prohibited from distributing by any other enactment or by its memorandum or articles.

An example of (*d*) is found in s. 148(4) which provides that where a public company or its nominee acquires shares or an interest in shares in the company, and those shares or that interest appear in the balance sheet as an asset, then an amount equal to their value must be transferred out of distributable profits to a *reserve fund* which is not available for distribution.

5. Profits available for distribution. With the provisions of ss. 263 and 264 in mind, the general rules for the payment of dividends can be considered. (The special rules applying to investment companies and contained in s. 265 have been omitted here.)

The basic rule is found in s. 263(1) which prohibits any company, public or private, from making a distribution except out of *profits available for the purpose*. In s. 263(3) these are stated to be a company's *accumulated realized profits less its accumulated realized losses*.

This strict rule is fortified by s. 263(4) which prohibits a company from applying an *unrealized* profit in paying up debentures or amounts unpaid on issued shares. It also destroys, with a single statutory blow, all the former leniency of English rules on dividends.

6. Revaluation of fixed assets and provisions. Section 275(2) appears to throw a bone to the corporate dog by providing that if an unrealized profit is made on the revaluation of a fixed asset, and the sum allowed for depreciation after revaluation exceeds the sum which would have been allowed had no such profit been made, an amount equal to the amount of the extra depreciation is to be treated as *realized profit*. Without such a rule directors might be discouraged from effecting revaluations of the company's assets, since depreciation is normally charged against distributable profits.

Revaluation clearly raises difficulties where the cost of an asset is unknown. Accordingly s. 275(3) thoughtfully provides that where there is no record of the original cost, or one cannot be obtained without unreasonable expense or delay, the cost of an asset must be taken to be the value ascribed to it in the earliest available record made after the company acquired it.

Finally, s. 275(1) states that a *provision* (*see* 11:4) must be treated as a *realized loss*, except where it is in respect of a diminution in value of a fixed asset appearing on a revaluation of all the fixed assets of the company, or all of them other than goodwill. Under s. 275(4) any consideration by the directors of the value of a fixed asset must be *treated* as a revaluation for the purposes of this exception. If, however, this results in assets being treated as re-valued when this is not in fact the case, the exception applies *only* if the directors are satisfied that their value is not less than the amount at which they are stated in the accounts.

7. Development costs and distributions in kind. Two further sections, derived from the Companies Act 1981, deal with development costs and distributions in kind.

Firstly, s. 269 states that where *development costs* are shown as an asset in the accounts (which is not the usual procedure) the amount shown in respect of them must be treated, for the purposes of s. 263, as a *realized loss*.

Secondly, s. 276 states that where a company makes a distribution of any *non-cash asset*, any part of the amount at which that asset is stated in the accounts representing unrealized profit must be treated as *realized profit*.

8. Legality of distribution. Section 270 provides that the question whether a company may make a distribution without contravening s. 263 or s. 264, as well as the amount of the distribution, must be determined by reference to the *relevant accounts*, i.e. normally the last annual accounts. The distribution will be unlawful unless the requirements of s. 271 concerning those accounts are complied with.

Section 271(2)–(4) gives these requirements:

(*a*) The accounts must have been properly prepared.

(*b*) The auditors must have made a report in respect of them under s. 236.

(*c*) If, because of something referred to in it, their report is *not unqualified*, they must have stated in writing whether, in their opinion, that thing is *material* for the purpose of determining whether the distribution is unlawful.

(*d*) A copy of any such statement must have been laid before the company in general meeting.

By s. 271(3) an 'unqualified report' is a report without qualification to the effect that in the auditors' opinion the accounts have been properly prepared. It has been held that, since the requirement for an auditors' written statement under (*c*) above is designed for the protection of creditors, it is not a procedural matter which can be waived with the unanimous agreement of all members voting at meetings: *Precision Dippings Ltd* v. *Precision Dippings Ltd* (1985).

9. Restrictions in memorandum or articles. Section 281 makes it clear that all the above rules apply without prejudice to any further restrictions on distributions which may appear in the company's memorandum or articles. Thus the articles may stipulate that dividends may be paid only out of 'trading profits' or 'the profits of the business', in which case realized profits on fixed assets (capital profits) could not be used for this purpose. They may be even more restrictive, stating that dividends may be paid only out of 'the profits of the business for the year', in which case revenue reserves could not be used.

It is accordingly important always to look carefully at a company's articles on this point. Table A, however, does not contain any further restrictions.

10. The declaration of dividends. Under the articles of most companies, it is the company which *declares* the dividend, but the directors who recommend its *amount*. The articles usually provide that the dividend shall not exceed the amount recommended by the directors and Table A, Article 102, does this, so that while the shareholders can reduce the amount of the dividend, they cannot increase it.

Unless the company takes advantage of s. 119(*c*) and inserts a clause similar to Table A, Article 104, in its articles, dividends are declared either as a percentage based on the nominal value of the shares, or, with increasing frequency, as a specific sum per share. The amount paid up on the shares is irrelevant.

NOTE

(1) *Debt:* Once declared by the company, the dividend becomes a debt due to the members. It has been held that it is not a specialty

debt and the period of limitation is thus the normal one of six years: *Re Compania de Electricidad de la Provincia de Buenos Aires Ltd* (1978). Unclaimed dividends, however, may give rise to practical problems. It was held in *Jones* v. *Bellgrove Properties Ltd* (1949), that a statement of a debt in the balance sheet of a company signed by the company's officers constituted a written acknowledgment of that debt and prevented it from becoming statute-barred under the Limitation Act 1939. The point was further clarified in *Re Gee & Co. (Woolwich) Ltd* (1975), where it was held that a balance sheet duly signed by the directors was an effective acknowledgment of the state of indebtedness as at the date of the balance sheet, so that the cause of action was deemed to have accrued at that date. However, in *Re Compania de Electricidad de la Provincia de Buenos Aires Ltd* (1978) mentioned above, Slade J. further held that a written acknowledgment is not effectively made to a creditor within the Limitation Act unless it actually reaches him.

(2) *Interim dividends:* Sometimes the articles authorize the directors to pay *interim* dividends to the members, i.e. dividends which are paid in between two annual general meetings, usually six months after the final dividend. Table A, Article 103, gives the directors this power. Some companies apply the main part of their distributable profits towards the final dividend, so that the interim dividend is comparatively small. Others aim at making half-yearly dividend payments of approximately the same size.

Where a *public* company proposes to pay an interim dividend which would be unlawful if paid on the basis of the last annual accounts, *interim accounts* will be necessary to show that it is justified: ss. 270(4) and (5) and 272. These too must be properly prepared and a copy of them delivered to the registrar of companies, but they do not have to be audited: s. 272(2)–(4).

(3) *Method of payment of dividends:* Table A, Article 106, states that dividends may be paid by cheque sent through the post to the registered address of the holder, or to such person as the holder may direct. Many shareholders require the company to send their dividends to their bank, which then informs them of the amount. Article 107 provides that dividends shall not bear interest, and Article 108 provides that any dividend which has remained unclaimed for 12 years shall, if the directors so resolve, be forfeited and cease to remain owing by the company.

(4) *Payment in cash:* Since a shareholder has a right to receive his

dividend in *cash* unless there is a provision in the articles authorizing payment in some other way, Table A, Article 105, empowers the company, on the recommendation of the directors, to direct that the dividend be satisfied wholly or partly by the distribution of assets.

11. Consequences of unlawful distribution. We have already seen that dividends may be paid only out of profits available for distribution. If, however, other funds of the company are wrongly used for dividend purposes, s. 277(1) makes all shareholders who, when they received the improper dividend, knew or had reasonable ground for believing that it was paid out of undistributable funds, liable to repay it to the company.

Presumably where the shareholders are entirely innocent of the illegality, the directors will be liable to replace the funds improperly used, as was the case before there was any statutory provision on the matter.

12. The creation of reserves. As was stated earlier, the directors cannot be compelled to recommend a dividend. They may think it prudent to put all the profits for that year to reserve, and articles usually give them power to do this.

13. Capitalization issues. Section 280(2) states that the expression 'capitalization' in relation to the profits of a company means:

(*a*) applying profits in wholly or partly paying up unissued shares to be allotted to members as fully or partly paid *bonus shares; or*

(*b*) transferring profits to the capital redemption reserve.

The first of these operations, described in (*a*) above, is normally and correctly termed a *capitalization issue*. It is often called a *bonus issue* which is equally correct, but wrongly gives the impression that the shares are 'free' when in fact they have been paid for out of funds which could instead have been distributed to shareholders by way of dividend. Another term for the same operation is *scrip issue* – an expression commonly used by brokers.

In the case of a capitalization issue the new shares are allotted to members in proportion to their existing holdings fully, or occasionally partly, paid up. The members thus receive shares on which all or some of the money payable has been already paid out of profits retained by the company and on which there is no, or only a partial, further liability. Since this issue of shares is an addition to capital, the shareholder will not pay income tax on it.

NOTE

(1) *Effect of bonus issue:* Such an issue increases the company's capital, and often entails increasing the nominal capital under s. 121. A company may wish to bring its issued capital more into line with the true worth of its undertaking, and the bonus issue frequently achieves this. On the other hand, the increase in the issued capital causes an immediate fall in the market value of the shares of the company, since the cake is now divided up into a larger number of slices each of which must necessarily be smaller than before. The fall in the market price gives investors a good opportunity to buy the company's shares at a low price, for often it is accentuated by shareholders selling their bonus shares as soon as they receive them.

(2) *Authority in articles and funds available for a bonus issue:* In order to make a bonus issue, a company must have authority in its articles. Table A, Article 110, gives it, allowing a company to use for this purpose any amount standing to the credit of any of its reserve accounts or its profit and loss account which is *available for distribution.* Such funds may also be used under this article to pay up any partly paid shares *already held* by members, which would not, of course, result in any increase in the issued share capital although the shares so treated would have a bonus element.

In addition, Article 110 permits a company to apply its share premium account and its capital redemption reserve to pay up unissued shares to be allotted to members credited as fully paid shares. In either of these cases there is no true capitalization issue, for these funds are already, in law, capital and not profits (*see* 11:5).

Finally, Article 110 authorizes a company to use any profits *not available for distribution* to pay up unissued shares to be allotted to members credited as fully paid shares, e.g. an unrealized profit on a fixed asset.

14. Rights issues. A capitalization issue must not be confused with a rights issue. Here the company wishes to raise more share capital, and having effected any necessary increase in its nominal capital proceeds to issue new shares. These it first offers to its existing members, on favourable terms, in proportion to their existing holdings. The members may then subscribe for the shares and so increase their holdings, or sell their 'rights' on the market. If a large number of 'rights' are sold, this again may be a good opportunity for an investor to buy shares in the company while they are easily available and the price temporarily depressed.

In reality there is no bonus element in a rights issue, but the members of the company are often pleased to subscribe for more shares at a figure below the market price, and this advantage is often loosely referred to as the bonus element. Payment for the new shares, however, is made entirely by shareholders subscribing fresh capital and not, as in the case of a bonus issue, by the company applying its profits or reserves for that purpose.

It should be noted that where the statutory pre-emption rights apply, an issue of shares will necessarily be a rights issue (*see* 9:**10**).

Progress test 20

1. Distinguish between dividends and interest. (**1, 2**)

2. Explain what is meant by the words 'distribution', 'profits' and 'losses'. (**3**)

3. What special restrictions exist regarding the distribution of assets by public companies? (**4**)

4. What do you understand by 'profits available for distribution'? (**5–7**)

5. On what basis is the legality of a proposed dividend determined? Are there any special rules for interim dividends? (**8–10**)

6. How are dividends (*a*) declared, and (*b*) paid? (**10**)

7. What are the consequences of the payment of dividends out of undistributable funds? (**11**)

8. What do you understand by (*a*) a capitalization issue, and (*b*) a rights issue? (**13, 14**)

21
Debentures

1. The nature of a debenture. The statutory definition of a debenture in s. 744 is very wide. The Act here states that debenture includes debenture stock, bonds, and any other securities of a company whether constituting a charge on the assets or not.

The definition is juristically confused, for a debenture is strictly speaking a *document*, while debenture stock is not. The word 'securities' also sometimes misleads students here. It is used to mean the *undertaking to repay* the money borrowed, and the definition goes on to state that this undertaking may or may not be accompanied by a charge on the company's assets. Thus a mortgage of the company's property to a single individual as security is a debenture within the definition.

Usually, however, a debenture is *one of a series* issued to a number of lenders. It is often accompanied by a charge on the assets which may be either fixed or floating (*see* **7**). But sometimes no charge is given, and then the debenture is described as 'naked' or 'unsecured'. Moreover, the term 'mortgage debenture' is restricted by the Stock Exchange to debentures with *fixed* charges, although its legal meaning would appear to cover charges of both types.

Shares and debentures are commonly mentioned, even in the Act, as though they were similar, but their legal nature is entirely different. *A share is a chose in action, evidenced by a document* called a share certificate. *A debenture is a document which is evidence of a chose in action*, i.e. the debt. *Debenture stock*, however, is similar to *stock*, for it is evidenced by a document called a *debenture stock certificate*, while stockholders receive a *stock certificate*. Moreover, a debenture can be transferred only *as a whole*, i.e. if it is evidence of a debt from the company of £500, then the *whole debt* must be transferred. Debenture stock, on the other hand, is *divisible* into any amounts required, in the same way as stock.

Sometimes the debenture-holders are given a right, by the terms of the debenture, to convert their debentures into shares at some future date. Such debentures are called *convertible*, and if the holders exercise their right of conversion they cease to be lenders to the company and become members instead. The convertible debentures cannot, however, be issued at a discount entitling the holder to exchange them immediately for shares of the same par value, as this would be an indirect method of issuing shares at a discount and therefore unlawful under s. 100.

2. Power of company to borrow. The power of a company to borrow money is implied in the case of all trading companies. Non-trading companies, however, must be expressly authorized to borrow by their memorandum.

A power to borrow money, whether express or implied, includes the power to charge the assets of the company by way of security to the lender (*see* 6 and 7). The company can charge any type of property which it happens to own. It can also charge its uncalled capital, though not its reserve capital (*see* 11:3).

Borrowing powers are not exercisable until the company can *commence business*. Public companies, therefore, must first obtain their trading certificate by complying with the requirements of s. 117 which are set out in 5:2. Moreover, the memorandum may restrict the amount of money which the company may borrow.

The power of the company to borrow is exercised by the directors, who cannot of course borrow more than the sum authorized. Sometimes, however, the power of the *company* to borrow is *unrestricted*, but the authority of the *directors* acting as its agents is *limited* to a certain figure. For instance, the articles may prohibit (as Table A in the 1st Schedule to the Companies Act 1948 did) the directors from borrowing a sum which exceeds the nominal amount of the issued share capital unless they have first obtained the sanction of a general meeting of the company. There is, however, no restriction in Table A in the Companies (Tables A–F) Regulations 1985.

Formerly it was very important to distinguish between borrowing which was *ultra vires the company*, and borrowing which was *intra vires the company* but *outside the scope of the directors' authority*. However, s. 9(1) European Communities Act 1972, implementing the

First EEC Directive of 1968, substantially modified the position. The provisions are now in s. 35 Companies Act 1985, but in order to understand the effect of s. 35 it is necessary to consider also how the law stood before the 1972 Act.

3. *Ultra vires* borrowing before the European Communities Act 1972. Any act which was *ultra vires* the company was void. Here the behaviour of the directors, as the company's agents, could have no effect whatsoever on the validity of the loan, for no agent can ever have more capacity than his principal. If, therefore, the borrowing was *ultra vires* so that the company had no capacity to undertake it, the lender could have no right of action against the company in respect of it, nor could he enforce any security granted to him. This was so even where the company's memorandum empowered it to borrow if the loan, to the lender's knowledge, was to be used for an *ultra vires* purpose: *Introductions Ltd* v. *National Provincial Bank Ltd* (1969) (*see* 2:**19**).

The lender might, however, have the following remedies against the company:

(*a*) If he could *identify* the money lent, or any property which the company had bought with it, he could at common law recover the money or the property, as the case might be, since he was still regarded as its owner.

(*b*) If he could *not identify* the money lent, he might in equity be able to obtain a 'tracing order' giving him an equitable charge on a mixed mass of assets: *Sinclair* v. *Brougham* (1914) (*see* 2:**21**).

(*c*) If the company had used the borrowed money to pay off any of its *intra vires* debts, the lender ranked as a creditor up to the amount so used. He did not here obtain the security or the priority, if any, of the *intra vires* creditors, but he was able to enforce any security granted *to him*.

This remedy appeared to be based on the fact that the company still owed the same amount of money; it merely owed it to a different person. Its liabilities remained constant, but there was a change of creditor.

Finally, although the lender had no right of action on the contract of loan against the *company*, he might be able to sue the *directors* for *breach of warranty of authority*. If their lack of authority was obvious from the memorandum and articles, it must be remembered that these are public documents the contents of which the lender was *deemed to know*. He might therefore be met by the argument that he knew the directors had no authority, and so could not have been misled by their warranty. On the other hand, if the directors deliberately misrepresented their authority the lender ought in principle to have had a right of action. An analogy could perhaps have been drawn between this situation and that in *Curtis* v. *Chemical Cleaning and Dyeing Co*. (1951), where the document by its terms denied the plaintiff a remedy, but the plaintiff nevertheless sued successfully because the terms of the document had been misrepresented to her.

4. *Intra vires* borrowing outside the agent's authority before the European Communities Act 1972. This type of borrowing was often described as being '*ultra vires* the directors', but this was confusing. Strictly speaking, the terms '*intra vires*' and '*ultra vires*' should be reserved for describing the *company's capacity*, and should not be used to describe the *agent's authority*.

The legal position here, however, was quite simple. The company had the *power* to borrow, but it had restricted the authority of the agent to a certain sum which had been exceeded. There was no lack of *capacity*. It followed that the company might, if it wished, ratify the agent's act, in which case the loan bound both the lender and the company as if it had been made with the company's authority in the first place.

On the other hand, the company might refuse to ratify the agent's act. Here the normal principles of agency applied. A third party who deals with an agent knowing that the agent is exceeding his authority has no right of action against the principal. Bearing in mind that the memorandum and articles are public documents *the contents of which the third party was deemed to know*, he had no right of action against the company if the agent's lack of authority was obvious from reading them. A third party, however, is not affected by *secret* restrictions of the agent's authority, so that if the lack of authority was not clear from the public documents and the lender did not know of it from some other source, the company was bound (*see* 16:**24, 25**).

5. The provisions of s. 35 Companies Act 1985. Section 35(1) provides that in favour of a person dealing with a company in good faith, any transaction decided on by the directors is deemed to be one which it is within the capacity of the company to enter into, and the power of the directors to bind the company is deemed to be free of any limitation under the memorandum or articles. Further, by s. 35(2), a party to such a transaction is not bound to inquire as to the capacity of the company to enter into it or as to any limitation in the memorandum or articles on the power of the directors, and is presumed to have acted in good faith unless the contrary is proved.

Students are advised at this point to re-read 2:**20–24**.

6. Types of security. Before further consideration of debentures it is appropriate to look at the nature of security in general and in particular at security given by companies.

When a person owes money to another, either because he has borrowed it or for any other reason, the sum owed is a *debt*. This debt can be either *unsecured* or *secured*.

When the debt is unsecured, the creditor has only one remedy: to sue for the amount owed, i.e. a right of action. He is not, therefore, at all safe if the debtor goes bankrupt or disappears. He has no security. Ordinary trade debts are usually unsecured, as is money borrowed from a friend when a person unexpectedly finds that he has not enough money in his pocket for his fare home.

A wise creditor, therefore, will demand security, i.e. a right over the debtor's *property* which is *in addition* to his right of action. A bank overdraft, for instance, is often secured by a deposit of the title deeds of the borrower's house (a mortgage), or of his share certificates (*see* 12:**28**). An unpaid seller of goods who is still in possession of them has a lien on those goods for the price, under the Sale of Goods Act 1979. An unpaid repairer of goods, e.g. a cobbler, has a lien at common law on the goods he has repaired, i.e. he can retain them until he is paid the amount owed to him. A bank may ask a customer who wishes to borrow money whether he can find another person of means to guarantee his overdraft, i.e. someone who is willing to undertake to repay the bank if the borrower does not do so. And a pawnbroker or pledgee has possession of the goods pledged to him. Thus a mortgage, a charge, a lien, a guarantee and a pledge are all *types of security*, i.e. methods by which a creditor's position is made safer.

7. Security given by companies. A company, like any other person, can give its creditors security. Often it mortgages or charges its property to its *debenture-holders*, i.e. the persons who have lent money to it. These persons will then not only be able to sue the company for the amount of money which they have lent to it, but they will be able also to enforce their security, i.e. claim that the property charged belongs to them. The charges given by a company fall into two categories:

(*a*) *Fixed or specific charges:*

These are charges on definite or specific property of a permanent nature, e.g. land or heavy machinery, and may be either legal or equitable (*see* 14:**8–10**).

(*b*) *Floating charges:*

These are charges which do not initially attach to the property charged and are thus necessarily equitable. They are useful when the assets to be charged are of the kind turned over in the course of trade, e.g. stock, for the company may continue to deal in the usual way with the property charged without the consent of the creditor. A floating charge will attach to the particular property then in the company's possession if:

    (*i*) the company goes into liquidation; *or*

    (*ii*) the company ceases to carry on business; *or*

    (*iii*) the debenture-holders take steps to enforce their security, e.g. by appointing a receiver (*see* **15**).

It is then said to become fixed or to crystallize.

NOTE: Section 407(1) requires *all* charges given by a company to its creditors to be shown in the company's register of charges kept at the company's registered office. Each entry in that register must contain:

    (1) a short description of the property charged;

    (2) the amount of the charge; and

    (3) the names of the persons entitled to the charge (s. 407(2)).

8. Trust deeds. When a *series of debentures* is issued to numerous debenture-holders, a trust deed is normally drawn up. Under the terms of the deed the company undertakes to pay the debenture-holders their principal and interest, and normally charges its property to the trustees (usually a trust corporation) as security. If the charge is to be a *legal fixed* charge such a deed is essential, for a legal estate in land cannot be owned by more than four persons, and therefore could not be granted to a large number of debenture-holders.

The deed usually empowers the trustees to appoint a receiver to protect the property charged if the company defaults in payment of the principal or interest, and may contain other provisions concerning meetings of the debenture-holders, supervision of the assets charged, and the keeping of a register of debenture-holders.

A similar deed can be drawn up for debenture stock.

9. Advantages of a trust deed. A trust deed has two main advantages:

(*a*) As stated above, it makes it possible for the company to give the debenture-holders (through the trustees) a *legal fixed charge* over property of a permanent nature such as land.

(*b*) The rights of the debenture-holders and the company's covenants for payment of principal and interest and for the care and insurance of the property charged to them can be enforced by the trustees against the company.

It would be much more difficult for a large and fluctuating body of individual debenture-holders to do this.

The Act does not impose any specific statutory duties on the trustees, but s. 192 renders *void* any provision in the trust deed exempting them from, or indemnifying them against, liability for breach of trust.

10. Forms of debenture. A debenture may be either:

(*a*) a registered debenture; *or*
(*b*) a bearer debenture.

It is usually, though not necessarily, under the company's seal.

11. Registered debentures. These are subject to many of the same rules as shares. A register of debenture-holders is kept in the same way as a register of members, and must under s. 190 normally be kept at the registered office of the company (*see* 2:**15**). Section 191(7), imposes a limitation period of 20 years on any liability incurred by the company through the making or deletion of any entry in the register, as in the case of the register of members (*see* 14:**2**). Section 183(1) applies to debentures as well as to shares, requiring a *proper instrument of transfer* to be delivered to the company before a transfer can be registered. Section 185(1) applies to debentures and debenture stock certificates in the same way as it applies to share certificates (*see* 12:**9**) and so also does s. 183(5) concerning notice of the company's refusal to register a transfer (*see* 12:**7**).

The debenture itself consists of two parts:

(*a*) the covenants by the company to pay the principal and interest; and

(*b*) the endorsed conditions, i.e. the terms of the loan.

The endorsed conditions vary, but they normally contain a provision that the debenture is one of a series all ranking *pari passu*. This is necessary because without such a clause the debentures would rank *in the order of issue* regarding the assets charged by the company, and if a large issue of debentures is made it is obviously essential that the debenture-holders should all have the same rights as regards security.

Another usual endorsed condition is a provision keeping the trusts off the register. This is required because s. 360 (*see* 14:**7**) applies only to the register of members and not to the register of debenture-holders.

12. Bearer debentures. Bearer debentures are similar to share warrants in that they too are negotiable instruments, transferable by delivery. The interest on them is paid by means of attached coupons, as are dividends on share warrants (*see* 12:**26**).

13. Perpetual debentures. As a general rule when a mortgage is made by an individual, *equity will not permit it to be irredeemable*. The purpose of the transaction has been to borrow money: anything, therefore, which prevents the borrower from repaying the loan and recovering his security will be void in equity. This will be the position right up to the moment when the mortgagee has obtained an order for the sale or foreclosure of the mortgaged property, even if the legal or contractual right to redeem has long since expired. Equity expresses this rule in the maxim: 'Once a mortgage, always a mortgage'.

Thus the mortgagor normally has a *legal or contractual* right to repay the loan and redeem his property on the date specified in the contract of loan. Once this date has passed, he has an *equitable* right to redeem his property on payment of the loan and accrued interest. From the moment the mortgage is created, he has an *equitable interest* in the mortgaged property which remains in him so long as the mortgage endures, and which is called the *equity of redemption*. Equity will hold invalid any provision which 'clogs' the equity of redemption, i.e. fetters the rights of the mortgagor, and his most important right is his equitable right to redeem.

This rule, however, is subject to an exception in the case of companies. Section 193 expressly states that a condition in a *debenture* is *not invalid* on the grounds that it is *irredeemable* or *redeemable only* on the occurrence of an event, however remote, or on the expiration of a period of time, however long. It follows that debentures can be made *perpetual*, i.e. the loan is repayable only on winding up, or after a long period of time.

14. The company's power to re-issue redeemed debentures. Although in the last paragraph we saw that debentures may be perpetual or irredeemable, they are, unlike shares, normally redeemable at a certain specified future date. The company may then lawfully effect an economy by redeeming them, i.e. buying them back from any willing seller, *before* the specified redemption date has arrived.

When debentures are redeemed they are, at common law, extinguished and the company would therefore be unable to re-issue them were it not for the provisions of s. 194. This section permits the company to re-issue them, or to issue others in their place, *with the priority of the original series* provided:

(*a*) there is no provision to the contrary, express or implied, in the articles or in any contract made by the company; and

(*b*) the company has not shown an intention to cancel them, e.g. by passing a resolution to that effect.

15. The remedies of debenture-holders. The remedies of a debenture-holder vary according to whether he is secured or unsecured. He will naturally have wider protection in the former case.

An *unsecured* debenture-holder is in exactly the same position as an ordinary trade creditor. The fact that his debt arises from a loan to the company rather than the supply of goods to it or the performance of services for it is quite immaterial. He is owed money and he has no security. Like any other unsecured creditor, therefore, he has *only three remedies*:

(*a*) He can *sue* for his principal and interest, obtain judgment, and, if the judgment debt is not paid, levy execution against the company's property.

(*b*) He can apply to the court for the court to make an administration order under ss. 8 and 9 Insolvency Act 1986 on the ground that the company is or is likely to become unable to pay its debts.

(*c*) He can, if he wishes, *petition under s. 124 Insolvency Act 1986 for a winding up* of the company by the court on the ground specified in s. 122(1)(*f*) of that Act, namely, that the company is unable to pay its debts.

A *secured* debenture-holder has *each of the above remedies*, but in addition he also has the following courses open to him:

(*d*) He can *exercise any of the powers* which are given to him by the *debenture or the trust deed*, as the case may be, without applying to the court. Usually these include a power to appoint a receiver, and a power to sell the company's property.

(*e*) He can *apply to the court* for the appointment of a *receiver* or for an order for the *sale or foreclosure* of the property.

When the company defaults in payment of principal or interest, any debenture-holder may sue, but he normally brings the action on behalf of himself and the other debenture-holders of the same class. This is known as a *debenture-holders' action*, and if several individuals start to sue separately, the court can consolidate their actions into one.

16. Receivers. A receiver may be appointed:

(*a*) by the court; *or*

(*b*) under the terms of the debenture or the trust deed.

Section 30 Insolvency Act 1986 disqualifies a corporation from appointment as a receiver, and s. 31 of that Act disqualifies an undischarged bankrupt unless he is acting under a court order. Moreover, a receiver is caught by the provisions of the Company Directors Disqualification Act 1986, so that a disqualification order may be made against him by the court (*see* 16:20). If the company is in compulsory liquidation when the debenture-holders apply to the court to appoint a receiver, s. 32 Insolvency Act 1986 states that the official receiver may be appointed.

Once the appointment is made, every invoice, order for goods or business letter on which the company's name appears is required by s. 39 Insolvency Act 1986 to contain a statement that a receiver has been appointed.

Further, s. 405(1) Companies Act 1985 states that if any person obtains an order for the appointment of a receiver, or appoints a receiver under the terms of a document, he must notify the registrar within seven days from the order or the appointment, and the registrar must enter the fact in the register of charges. Notice of the fact that the receiver has ceased to act must likewise be given to the registrar under s. 405(2), and the registrar must make the appropriate entry in the register of charges.

17. A receiver appointed by the court. When a receiver is appointed by the court, he is not the agent either of the debenture-holders or of the company, but is an *officer of the court*. He must therefore act according to the court's directions. The court may appoint a receiver:

(*a*) if the principal or interest is in arrears, *or*

(*b*) if the security is in jeopardy, *i.e.* where the company or its other creditors are about to take steps which will put the assets charged beyond the reach of the debenture-holders.

A receiver appointed by the court is personally liable on contracts, but has a right of indemnity out of the company's assets. His remuneration is fixed by the court.

18. A receiver appointed under a power in the debenture or trust deed. When a receiver is appointed under the terms of the debenture or trust deed, he would naturally be the agent of the *debenture-holders*, if it were not for the terms of the debenture itself and of the Insolvency Act 1986. In fact, however, the debenture or trust deed normally provides that he shall be the agent of the *company* and s. 44(1) Insolvency Act 1986 provides that an 'administrative' receiver (i.e., by s. 29(2) of that Act, a receiver of the whole (or substantially the whole) of a company's property) is deemed to be the company's agent unless and until the company goes into liquidation, while ss. 37(1) and 44(1) of the same Act make any receiver personally liable on any contract entered into by him but entitled to an indemnity out of the company's assets.

Section 35 Insolvency Act 1986 entitles the receiver to apply to the court for directions whenever he wishes so that as a result his legal position is equivalent to that of a receiver appointed by the court. His remuneration is fixed by agreement except that the court may fix it if the company goes into liquidation and the liquidator applies to the court for that purpose under s. 36 of the 1986 Act.

The powers conferred on an administrative receiver by the debentures under which he was appointed are, by s. 42(1) Insolvency Act 1986, deemed to include the 23 powers listed in the 1st Schedule to that Act except in so far as these are inconsistent with any of the provisions of the debentures. By s. 42(3) a person dealing with an administrative receiver in good faith and for value is not concerned to inquire whether the receiver is acting within his powers.

Section 43 Insolvency Act 1986 enables an administrative receiver to apply to court for authority to dispose of property which is subject to a security. He must satisfy the court that a disposal of the property would be likely to promote a more advantageous realization of the company's assets than would otherwise be effected. The secured creditor who is thus deprived of his security is entitled to the net proceeds of the disposal together with any amount necessary to bring that amount up to the net amount which would have been realized if the property had been sold in the open market by a willing seller.

19. Provisions as to information when receiver is appointed.
The Insolvency Act 1986 requires certain information, prescribed in greater detail by regulations made under that Act, to be given by a receiver appointed under a power in the debenture or trust deed. The requirements are more elaborate in the case of administrative receivers than in the case of other receivers.

By s. 38(1) Insolvency Act 1986 a receiver other than an administrative receiver must deliver to the registrar an account of his receipts and payments. The time allowed for delivery of such accounts is one month (or such longer period as the registrar may allow) after the expiration of 12 months from the date of the receiver's appointment and of every later period of six months and also within one month after he ceases to act as receiver: s. 38(2). The accounts take the form of an abstract showing receipts and payments during the relevant period of 12 or six months as the case may be, except that in the case where the receiver ceases to act the period may be less in duration, but there must also be shown the aggregate amount of receipts and payments during all the preceding periods since the receiver's appointment: s. 38(3).

A receiver who makes default in complying with s. 38 is liable to a fine and, for continued contravention, to a daily default fine: s. 38(5).

The more stringent provisions applicable to administrative receivers are to be found in ss. 46–49 Insolvency Act 1986.

By s. 46 where an administrative receiver is appointed he must:

(a) immediately send to the company and publish in the prescribed manner a notice of his appointment; and

(b) within 28 days after his appointment, unless the court otherwise directs, send such a notice to all the creditors of the company, so far as he is aware of their addresses.

By s. 47 an administrative receiver must immediately after his appointment require some or all of the company's officers and employees (including persons who have been its officers or employees within the preceding year) to submit to him a statement in a prescribed form showing:

(a) particulars of the company's assets, debts and liabilities;

(b) the names and addresses of its creditors;

(c) the securities held by each of them;

(d) the dates when each of the securities was given; and

(e) any other information which is prescribed.

The statement must be submitted to the administrative receiver within 21 days, except that the administrative receiver, or, failing him, the court, may extend the period or may release a person altogether from the obligation to submit the statement.

Section 48 deals with an administrative receiver's report. By s. 48(1) within three months (or such longer period as the court may allow) after his appointment the administrative receiver must send to the registrar, to any trustees for secured creditors and (so far as he is aware of their addresses) to all secured creditors a report as to:

(a) the events leading up to his appointment, so far as he is aware of them;

(b) the disposal or proposed disposal by him of any property of the company and the carrying on or proposed carrying on by him of any business of the company;

(c) the amounts of principal and interest payable to the debenture-holders by whom or on whose behalf he was appointed and the amounts payable to preferential creditors (*see* **20**); and

(d) the amount, if any, likely to be available for the payment of other creditors.

By s. 48(2) the administrative receiver must also, within three months (or such longer period as the court may allow) after his appointment, *either*:

(*a*) send a copy of the report (so far as he is aware of their addresses) to all unsecured creditors; *or*

(*b*) publish in the prescribed manner a notice stating an address to which unsecured creditors should write for copies of the report to be sent to them free of charge.

In either case (unless the court directs otherwise) he must lay a copy of the report before a meeting of unsecured creditors summoned for the purpose on not less than 14 days' notice.

By s. 48(4) where the company goes into liquidation the receiver must send a copy of his report to the liquidator within seven days of the liquidator's nomination or appointment.

By s. 48(5) the administrative receiver's report must include a summary of the statement of affairs submitted to him under s. 47 and a summary of any comments made by him upon that statement.

The report need not include any information the disclosure of which would seriously prejudice the carrying out by the administrative receiver of his functions: s. 48(6).

If the administrative receiver fails without reasonable excuse to comply with ss. 46–48, he is liable to a fine and, for continued contravention, to a daily default fine: ss. 46(4), 47(6) and 48(8).

Section 49 provides that where a meeting of creditors is summoned under s. 48, the meeting may, if it thinks fit, establish a committee ('the creditors' committee'), and that that committee may require the administrative receiver to attend before it and furnish it with information relating to the carrying out by him of his functions.

20. Priority of preferential debts. Where any receiver is appointed on behalf of the holders of debentures secured by a floating charge and the company is *not in liquidation*, s. 40 Insolvency Act 1986 requires him to pay all preferential debts of the company (money due to the Inland Revenue for income tax deducted at source, VAT, car tax, betting and gaming duties, social security and pension scheme contributions, remuneration, etc. of employees, as listed in the 6th Schedule to the 1986 Act) out of the assets in his hands before meeting any claim for principal or interest in respect of the debentures.

(Note that if the company *is in liquidation*, the priority of the preferential debts is preserved by s. 175 Insolvency Act 1986 (*see* 1:**18**).)

21. Charges which must be registered with the registrar.

Quite apart from the company's own register of the charges which it has created over its property (*see* **7**), s. 401 Companies Act 1985 requires the registrar to keep another register of charges for each company. There are nine types of charge which are registrable in this register, and these are listed in s. 396(1). They are here re-arranged for memorization:

(*a*) a charge to secure debentures;

(*b*) a floating charge;

(*c*) a charge on uncalled share capital;

(*d*) a charge on calls made but not paid;

(*e*) a charge on land;

(*f*) a charge on a ship or aircraft;

(*g*) a charge on book debts;

(*h*) a charge on goodwill, patents, trademarks or copyrights;

(*i*) a charge created by an instrument which, if executed by an individual, would require registration as a bill of sale.

NOTE

(1) This list will be most easily memorized if learnt in four couples and one odd item at the end. Most of these charges require some explanation, so that they can be connected with each other.

(2) The first two are placed together because debentures, though they may be secured by a fixed charge, are very often secured by a floating charge and so the one reminds the student of the other. The third couple are placed together because ships and land have certain obvious similarities. The fourth couple are all choses in action (intangible personal property). But students are often puzzled by the second couple and the ninth charge at the end.

(3) The second couple are charges on capital. Let us assume that a company has a share capital of 100 £1 shares issued at par, of which A holds 50 and B holds 50. This means that both A and B can ultimately be compelled to pay £50 each to the company. Usually they will have done this when they applied for the shares, and if so they will then have no further liability towards the company. But sometimes they will have paid only part of this sum, so that their shares are partly paid and therefore partly unpaid.

Let us assume now that they have each paid up 50p per share. We then say that the company has an issued share capital of £100, but a paid-up capital of £50. It therefore has unpaid capital of £50, and at some point, when more money is required, the directors will call up, i.e. demand, this unpaid capital. Until they do so, this unpaid capital is also the uncalled capital of the company.

Since the uncalled capital has not been received, or even demanded, by the company, it is still a fund which can be charged in favour of a creditor, in the same way as a book debt. Thus, when it is finally received by the company, the creditor has a right to such part of it as will pay off the debt owed to him. This is the charge on *uncalled share capital*. Furthermore, at some point, as we have seen, the directors may call up this money, and even after they have done so it may still be charged by the company before it is actually received. This is the charge on *calls made but not paid*.

(4) The ninth charge is not as complicated as it sounds. When an individual, i.e. a human person, mortgages his goods as security to a creditor, he does so by a document, i.e. an instrument, called a mortgage or conditional bill of sale. When goods are mortgaged in this way, the debtor remains in possession of them, though he no longer owns them. His position is exactly the reverse of a pledgor, who loses possession but retains ownership. This might be very misleading to other persons, since the mortgagor will look much richer than he is, and therefore the Bills of Sale Act 1882 requires such instruments to be registered in a public registry so that they are available for inspection by any interested person.

This Act, however, does not apply to companies, and therefore s. 396(1) has to include in its list of registrable charges a *charge created by an instrument which, if executed by an individual, would be registrable as a bill of sale*, thus making the same provision for mortgages of goods by companies as does the Bills of Sale Act for those created by human persons.

(5) A book debt is a debt arising in the course of a business which would in the ordinary course of such a business be entered in well-kept books, whether it is in fact so entered or not, and includes a *future* book debt: *Independent Automatic Sales Ltd* v. *Knowles and Foster* (1962). It has been held, however, not to include a policy issued to a company by the Export Credits Guarantee Department of the Department of Trade and Industry guaranteeing payments to

cover losses sustained by the company in export transactions: *Paul and Frank Ltd* v. *Discount Bank (Overseas) Ltd* (1967).

(6) In a contract for the sale of land by a company *an unpaid vendor's lien* is not registrable under s. 396(1) because such a lien arises by operation of law, and is not 'created' by the company within s. 395(1): *London and Cheshire Insurance Co. Ltd* v. *Laplagrene Property Co. Ltd* (1971). On the other hand, the deposit of title deeds to land by a company in order to secure a debt creates an equitable charge on the land which is registrable under s. 396(1), for it arises by presumption of law into the contract made by the parties and therefore, although implied and not express, is 'created' by the company within s. 395(1): *Re Wallis and Simmonds (Builders) Ltd* (1974).

(7) Difficulties have arisen where a supplier of goods has, under the contract, retained an interest in those goods by way of security until he has been paid in full for them. Thus where a seller supplied goods to a company under a contract containing a 'reservation of title' clause providing that the title to the goods should not pass until full payment was made, the right to trace the proceeds of sale of the goods if the company re-sold them was held not to be a charge on a book debt within what is now s. 396(1), since those proceeds already belonged in equity to the supplier: *Aluminium Industrie Vaassen BV* v. *Romalpa Aluminium Ltd* (1976).

On the other hand, in *Re Bond Worth Ltd* (1980) where the supplier retained merely *equitable* ownership under the contract and the *legal* title to the goods passed to the company, Slade J. held that the reservation of equitable ownership amounted to the creation of a floating charge by the company over its property which was registrable within what is now s. 396(1).

Further, in *Borden (UK) Ltd* v. *Scottish Timber Products Ltd* (1981), where there was a reservation of the *legal* title to resin supplied by the seller for use in the manufacture of chipboard, the Court of Appeal held that since the resin had been amalgamated with other ingredients into a new product by an irreversible process, 'the resin and the title and the security disappeared without trace' (*per* Templeman L.J.), so that no charge was created. Had the wording of the contract been held to confer a charge on the chipboard, however, it is clear that such a charge would have been registrable as falling within (*i*) in the list given at the beginning of this section.

22. Particulars to be entered in the registrar's register of charges. When any of these nine charges is registered, the particulars which must be entered by the registrar in his register are, by s. 401(1)(*b*):

(*a*) the date of creation of the charge;
(*b*) the amount secured by the charge;
(*c*) short particulars of the property charged; and
(*d*) the persons entitled to the charge.

NOTE: These particulars are the same as those which must be entered in the company's register of charges, except for the addition of the date of creation.

If the charge is one to which the *holders of a series of debentures* are entitled, then the particulars which must be given, according to s. 401(1)(*a*), are those set out in s. 397(1). These are:

(*a*) the total amount secured by the whole series;
(*b*) the dates of the resolution authorizing the issue of the series and the deed, if any, creating the security;
(*c*) a general description of the property charged; and
(*d*) the names of the trustees, if any, for the debenture-holders.

The deed containing the charge, if any, or if none, one of the debentures of the series, must also be delivered to the registrar.

Section 401(2) provides that the registrar's certificate of registration of a charge is conclusive evidence that the statutory requirements as to registration have been complied with. It is thus conclusive evidence both of the date of creation of the charge and of the amount for which it was given: *Re C. L. Nye Ltd* (1971).

23. The effect of non-registration of a registrable charge. Section 395(1) as amended by the 6th Schedule to the Insolvency Act 1985 provides that if any registrable charge is not registered within 21 days from its creation by the company, it is *void* against the liquidator or the administrator and any creditor of the company. The charge is not made void against the *company*, however, so that the company itself cannot claim that the charge is void for non-registration: *Independent Automatic Sales Ltd* v. *Knowles and Foster* (1962).

Moreover, the debt in respect of which it was given remains *valid*, although the creditor has not got the security of the charge and is totally unsecured: *Re C. L. Nye Ltd* (1971). His debt becomes immediately payable under s. 395(2), and he can thus sue for it at once.

Section 399(1) states that it is the duty of the company to register the charge, but if it does not do so, then any person interested (normally the creditor) may do so. There is now no fee payable for registration.

Where a company borrows money in order to purchase land on the condition that once it has acquired the land it will grant the lender a first legal charge on it to secure the loan, and the charge, though duly granted, is void for non-registration under s. 395(1), the lender is a mere unsecured creditor. He cannot claim that he is entitled by way of subrogation to the unpaid vendor's lien which the vendor of the land would have had if he had not been paid with the lender's money and which would not, of course, have been registrable (*see* **21**, note (6)): *Burston Finance Ltd* v. *Speirway Ltd* (1974).

24. The memorandum of satisfaction. After a charge has been created and registered, the debt may be paid by the company, or the creditor may release some of the property charged to him, or the property may no longer form part of the company's assets.

In such a case the company should notify the registrar, who enters on the register of charges a *memorandum of satisfaction* recording this fact: s. 403(1).

25. Rectification of the register of charges. If a charge is not registered within the proper time, or if there is an omission or mis-statement in the register or in a memorandum of satisfaction, s. 404 empowers the court to extend the time for registration or rectify the omission or mis-statement. The section does not, however, give the court jurisdiction to delete a whole registration; it can merely rectify an omission by adding what is required, or a mis-statement by correcting it: *Re C. L. Nye Ltd* (1971). If the company has already gone into liquidation, no extension of time will be granted: *Re Resinoid and Mica Products Ltd* (1982).

The persons who may apply to the court for such an order are the company or any interested person, and the court must be satisfied that the failure to register the charge or the error or omission in doing so was accidental or due to inadvertence or some other sufficient cause, or not prejudicial to the creditors or shareholders, or that on other grounds it is just and equitable to grant relief.

Progress test 21

1. Distinguish debentures and shares. What is meant by a convertible debenture? **(1)**

2. What was the position prior to the European Communities Act 1972 of a person who had lent money to the company where the borrowing was *ultra vires* the company? **(2, 3)**

3. What was the position prior to the European Communities Act 1972 of a person who had lent money to the company where the borrowing was *intra vires* the company but outside the scope of the directors' authority? **(4)**

4. How did the European Communities Act 1972 affect (*a*) *ultra vires* borrowings by the company, and (*b*) *intra vires* borrowings which are outside the scope of the directors' authority? **(5 and 2:24)**

5. Outline the nature and advantages of a floating charge. **(7)**

6. Explain what is meant by 'crystallization' of a floating charge. **(7)**

7. What particulars must be entered in the *company's* register of charges? **(7)**

8. What is a trust deed in relation to debentures? What are its advantages? **(8, 9)**

9. What is meant by:

(*a*) a registered debenture? **(11)**

(*b*) a bearer debenture? **(12)**

(*c*) a perpetual debenture? **(13)**

10. Under what circumstances may a company re-issue redeemed debentures? **(14)**

11. Give an account of the remedies of debenture-holders. **(15)**

12. What is the legal position of a receiver appointed by the court? When may the court appoint a receiver? **(16, 17)**

13. What is meant by an 'administrative receiver' and what is his legal position? **(18)**

14. What are the statutory provisions relating to the account of receipts and payments which a receiver (other than an administrative receiver) appointed under a power in a debenture or trust deed must deliver to the registrar? **(19)**

15. What are the contents of an administrative receiver's report and to whom is the report sent? **(19)**

16. What provision governs the payment of preferential debts

when a receiver is appointed on behalf of the holders of debentures secured by a floating charge? (**20**)

17. What charges must be registered with the registrar? (**21**)

18. What particulars must be entered in the *registrar's* register of charges? (**22**)

19. What particulars must be entered in the registrar's register of charges where the charge is one to which the holders of a series of debentures are entitled? (**22**)

20. What is the legal effect of failure to register a registrable charge? (**23**)

21. Who is entitled to register a registrable charge? (**23**)

22. What is a memorandum of satisfaction? (**24**)

23. If a registrable charge is not registered within the prescribed period, is there any remedy? (**25**)

22

Investigations and inspection of documents

1. Part XIV Companies Act 1985. There are three types of investigation which can be carried out by the Department of Trade and Industry under Part XIV (i.e. ss. 431–453) Companies Act 1985. These are:

(a) an investigation of the company's *affairs*;

(b) an investigation of the company's *ownership*;

(c) an investigation of *share dealings*.

The provisions relating to an investigation of type (a) apply not only to companies registered under the 1985 Act, but also to companies incorporated outside Great Britain which carry on business in Great Britain, though the provisions may be adapted or modified by regulations in the case of such companies: s. 453.

Despite the wide powers conferred on the Department, s. 452 provides safeguards for privileged information in relation to all three types of investigation. Thus, by s. 452(1), no disclosure is required:

(i) by any person of any information which he would in an action be entitled to refuse to disclose on grounds of legal professional privilege except, if he is a lawyer, the name and address of his client;

(ii) by a company's bankers of any information about the affairs of any of their customers other than the company.

Part XIV of the Act and this chapter also deal with the Department's power to make:

(d) an inspection of the company's *documents*.

This power also extends to companies incorporated outside Great Britain which carry on business in Great Britain: s. 447(1).

Investigation of affairs

2. Power of Department to investigate affairs of company. Section 431(1) and (2) states that the Department *may* appoint inspectors to investigate and report on a company's affairs:

(a) in the case where it has a share capital, on the application of:
  (i) at least 200 members; *or*
  (ii) members holding at least one-tenth of the shares issued;
(b) in the case where it has no share capital, on the application of at least one-fifth of the members; and
(c) in any case, on the application of the company.

Section 431(3) states that the application must be supported by such evidence as the Department may require, showing good reason for the investigation. The Department may also require security for costs not exceeding £5000 from the applicants: s. 431(4).

Section 432(2) provides that the Department *may* appoint inspectors to investigate the company's affairs if it appears:

(a) that its affairs are being or have been conducted:
  (i) with intent to defraud creditors; *or*
  (ii) for a fraudulent or unlawful purpose; *or*
  (iii) in a manner unfairly prejudicial to any of its members; *or*
(b) that any actual or proposed act or omission of the company is or would be unfairly prejudicial to any of its members; *or*
(c) that the company was formed for a fraudulent or unlawful purpose; *or*
(d) that the persons concerned with formation or management have been guilty of fraud, misfeasance or other misconduct towards the company or its members; *or*
(e) that its members have not been given all the information about its affairs which they might reasonably expect.

Section 432(3) provides that the power of the Department under s. 432(2) is exercisable even if the company is in voluntary liquidation, and by s. 432(4) the word 'member' in (a) and (b) above includes a person who is not a member but to whom shares have been transferred or transmitted by operation of law (e.g. a personal representative).

3. Duty of Department to investigate affairs of company.
Section 432(1) states that the Department *must* appoint inspectors to investigate and report on a company's affairs if the court declares that its affairs require it.

4. Investigation into affairs of related companies.
Section 433(1) states that if an inspector appointed under either s. 431 or s. 432 thinks it necessary, he may also investigate and report on the affairs of any other company which is or has been within the same group.

Note that this section provides an example of 'lifting the veil of incorporation', for in order to discover whether or not a group exists, it is essential to establish the identity of the *members*.

5. Powers of the inspector.
Section 434(1) requires all officers and agents of the company and of any other company within the group to produce to the inspectors all books and documents in their custody or power relating to the company, or to a company within the group, to attend before them and to give them all the assistance that they can. An auditor is an agent for this purpose: s. 434(4). Section 434(2) extends this provision to any other person who, in the inspectors' opinion, has or may have information about the company's affairs.

Under s. 435 if an inspector has reasonable grounds for believing that a director or past director of the company or any other company within the group has or had, either in Great Britain or elsewhere, a bank account into which there has been paid:

(*a*) any emoluments of his office which have not been disclosed in the accounts as required by Part V of the 5th Schedule (*see* 16:55); *or*

(*b*) any money resulting from or used in the financing of any transaction, arrangement or agreement, particulars of which have not been disclosed in a note to the accounts as required by s. 232 and Part I of the 6th Schedule (*see* 16:48); *or*

(*c*) any money in any way connected with any act or omission amounting to misconduct on the part of that director, whether fraudulent or not, towards the company or any company within the group, or its members;

the inspector may require him to produce all documents in his possession or under his control relating to that bank account.

Section 434(3) empowers the inspector to examine on oath all the persons mentioned in s. 434(1) and (2). Moreover, if they refuse to comply with ss. 434 and 435 he may, under s. 436(2), certify their refusal to the court. They then become punishable as if guilty of contempt of court: s. 436(3).

6. The inspectors' report. Section 437(1) states that the inspectors may, and, if directed to do so by the Department, must make interim reports to the Department, and at the end of the investigation must make a final report. Reports must be either written or printed, as the Department directs.

Section 437(2) requires the Secretary of State, where the inspectors were appointed under s. 432(1) in pursuance of a court order, to furnish a copy of their report to the court. Under s. 437(3) in any case he may, if he thinks fit:

(*a*) forward a copy of the report to the company's registered office;
(*b*) provide a copy on request and payment of the prescribed fee to:

    (*i*) any member of the company or any other company which is the subject of the report;

    (*ii*) any person whose conduct is mentioned in the report;

    (*iii*) the auditors of the company or any other company which is the subject of the report;

    (*iv*) the applicants for the investigation;

    (*v*) any other person whose financial interests appear to the Secretary of State to be affected by the matters dealt with in the report, whether as a creditor of such company or other company, or otherwise; and

(*c*) cause the report to be printed and published.

Section 441(1) states that a copy of an inspectors' report certified by the Secretary of State to be a true copy is admissible in any legal proceedings as evidence of the inspectors' opinion concerning anything in it.

7. Powers of the Department arising from investigation. Section 440 states that if it appears to the Department from any inspector's report or from any information or document obtained under s. 447 or 448 (*see* **14**) that it is expedient in the public interest that the company should be wound up, it may, unless the company is already being wound up by the court, *present a petition for it to be so wound up* if the court thinks it just and equitable.

Section 460(1) states that if it appears to the Secretary of State from any inspectors' report or from any information or document obtained under s. 447 or 448 that there is any ground for a petition by a member under s. 459(1), he may, as well as or instead of presenting a winding-up petition, present a petition for an *order under s. 459 (see* 23:**6–10**).

Finally, s. 438(1) empowers the Department itself to bring *civil proceedings* in the name of any company wherever it appears in the public interest to do so.

Investigation of ownership

8. Power of Department to investigate ownership of company. Section 442(1) states that where there appears to be good reason to do so, the Department *may* appoint inspectors to investigate and report on the membership of any company in order to determine the true persons financially interested in its success or failure, or able to control or materially influence its policy.

9. Duty of Department to investigate ownership of company. Section 442(3) states that where members qualifying within s. 431(2)(*a*) and (*b*) as to numbers or shareholdings (*see* **2**) apply to the Department for the appointment of an inspector to make an investigation of ownership, it *must* appoint an inspector unless the application is vexatious.

Students should note carefully, when they have learnt the figures relating to the applicants under s. 431, that while s. 431 gives the Department a *power* to appoint an inspector, s. 442(3) imposes a *duty* to do so. This is an important practical and academic distinction which, if not accurately made, leads to confused answers to examination questions.

10. Powers of inspector in an investigation of ownership. Section 442(4) empowers the inspector to investigate arrangements which, though not legally binding, are observed in practice.

Under s. 443, the provisions of ss. 433(1) (investigation into affairs of related company), 434 (production of documents and evidence to inspectors), 436 (obstruction of inspectors treated as contempt of court) and 437 (inspectors' reports) also apply to an investigation of ownership. In an investigation of ownership, however, if the Secretary of State thinks that there is good reason for not divulging any part of a report, he may disclose the report under s. 437 with that part omitted.

11. Power of Department to require information. Section 444 applies where it appears to the Department that the ownership should be investigated, but that it is unnecessary to appoint an inspector. It empowers the Department to require any person whom they have reasonable cause to believe to have or to be able to obtain any information as to the present or past interests in the shares or debentures of the company to give such information to the Secretary of State.

12. Power of Department to impose restrictions on shares or debentures. Where the Department makes an investigation under either s. 442 or 444 and it finds difficulty in obtaining information, s. 445 and Part XV (i.e. ss. 454–457) empower it to impose restrictions on the shares or debentures as follows:

(a) Any transfer of shares or debentures or, if unissued, any transfer of the right to be issued with them, shall be void.

(b) Voting rights shall not be exercisable.

(c) No further rights issues may be made (see 20:**14**).

(d) No payment, either of capital or otherwise, shall be made of any sums due from the company on the shares or debentures, except in a liquidation: ss. 445(2) and 454(1).

Section 454(2) provides that where shares or debentures are subject to the restrictions in (a) above, any *agreement* to transfer them or, if they are unissued, the right to be issued with them, is *void*, unless it is made in pursuance of a court order for sale. Section 454(3) gives the same rule for agreements to transfer rights falling under (c) or (d) above.

Section 456(1) and (2) authorizes any person who is aggrieved by the restrictions imposed to apply to the court for an order directing that the shares or debentures shall cease to be subject to them. Section

456(3) permits an order of the court or of the Secretary of State lifting the restrictions to be made only if:

(a) the court or the Secretary of State, as the case may be, is satisfied that the relevant facts about the shares or debentures have been disclosed to the company and that no unfair advantage had accrued to any person as a result of the earlier failure to make that disclosure; or

(b) the shares or debentures are to be sold and the court or Secretary of State approves the sale.

Despite this rule, however, under s. 456(4), the court may always, on the application of either the Secretary of State or the company, order the shares or debentures to be sold and at the same time lift the restrictions on them. The proceeds of the sale, less the costs, must be paid into court for the benefit of those entitled to them: s. 457(1).

Investigation of share dealings

13. Power of Department to investigate share dealings. Section 446 authorizes the Department, if circumstances suggest that contravention of ss. 323 (directors dealing in share options) (see 16:59), 324 (duty of directors to disclose shareholdings) (see 16:13), or 328 (extension of s. 324 to spouses and children) (see 16:14) has occurred regarding a company's shares or debentures, to appoint an inspector to investigate in order to establish whether this is the case, and to report the result of his investigation to the Department.

Section 446(3) states that for the purposes of such an investigation, ss. 434–436 (see 5) apply.

Inspection of company's documents

14. Inspection of company's books and papers. Section 447(2)–(4) empowers the Department, if it thinks there is good reason to do so, to require the production of any specified books or papers from the company or from any person who appears to be in possession of them, without prejudice to that person's lien on them, if any.

Section 447(5) states that the power conferred by the section includes power:

(a) if the books or papers are produced:

(i) to take copies of or extracts from them; and

(ii) to require the person producing them, or any employee, or past or present officer of the company in question, to explain them;

(b) if they are not produced, to require the person required to produce them to state, to the best of his knowledge and belief, where they are.

Section 451 states that if such person gives an explanation or makes a statement which he *knows to be false in a material particular*, or gives a false explanation or makes a false statement *recklessly*, he is guilty of an offence.

Section 448 authorizes a justice of the peace, if satisfied by the Department that there are reasonable grounds for suspecting that there are on any premises books or papers which have been required but not produced, to issue a warrant authorizing any constable to enter (using such force as is reasonably necessary) and search the premises, and to take possession of the books or papers, or take any steps necessary for preserving them and preventing interference with them.

15. Security of information. Section 449(1) states that no information or document obtained under s. 447 or 448 shall be published or disclosed without the company's previous consent in writing, except to a competent authority, unless publication or disclosure is required:

(a) for the purpose of any criminal proceedings arising out of the Act or other specified Acts or for an offence involving misconduct in management or misapplication of property;

(b) for the purpose of the examination of a person by an inspector appointed under s. 431, 432, 442 or 446;

(c) for the purpose of enabling the Secretary of State to exercise any of his functions under the Act or other specified Acts;

(d) for the purpose of proceedings under s. 448.

Under s. 449(3), each of the following is a competent authority for the purposes of the section:

(a) the Department of Trade and Industry;

(b) an officer of the Department of Trade and Industry;

(c) an inspector appointed under Part XIV of the Act by the Department of Trade and Industry;

(d) the Treasury;

(e) an officer of the Treasury;

(f) the Director of Public Prosecutions; and

(g) any constable.

16. Destruction of documents. Section 450(1) makes it an offence for an officer of a company to destroy, mutilate or falsify a document relating to the company's property or affairs, or to make a false entry in it, unless he proves that he did not intend to conceal the state of affairs or defeat the law.

Section 450(2) makes it an offence for him fraudulently to part with, alter or make an omission in any such document.

Progress test 22

1. When may the Department of Trade and Industry investigate the affairs of a company, and when must it do so? (**2, 3**)

2. What are the powers and duties of an inspector appointed by the Department of Trade and Industry to investigate the affairs of a company? (**5, 6**)

3. What steps can be taken by the Department of Trade and Industry after an investigation of affairs has been carried out? (**7**)

4. When may the Department of Trade and Industry investigate the ownership of a company, and when must it do so? (**8, 9**)

5. What steps may be taken by the Department of Trade and Industry during an investigation of ownership if it finds difficulty in obtaining information? (**12**)

6. In what circumstances can the Department of Trade and Industry investigate share dealings? (**13 and 16:13, 14, 59**)

7. What power has the Department of Trade and Industry to inspect the company's books and documents?   (**14**)

8. What provisions exist for ensuring the security of the information so obtained?   (**15**)

23
Majority rule and minority protection

1. The rule in Foss v. Harbottle. Next after *Salomon* v. *Salomon & Co. Ltd.* (1897) the most fundamental case in company law is *Foss* v. *Harbottle* (1843). This case is usually considered in textbooks in connection with meetings. Strictly speaking, however, it relates, like Salomon's case, to the theory of the corporate personality. The facts were as follows:

> The minority shareholders brought an action against the directors to compel them to make good losses incurred by the company owing to the directors' fraud. HELD: The action failed, for the proper plaintiff for wrongs done to the company is the company itself, and the company can act only through its majority shareholders.

This decision is the logical result of the principle that a company is a separate legal person from the members who compose it. Once it is admitted that the company is a legal person, it follows that if a wrong is done to it, the company is the proper person to bring an action. This is a simple rule of *procedure* which applies to all wrongs: only the injured party may sue. If, for instance, A intentionally pushes B down the stairs because he does not like him, and B breaks his leg in consequence, it is no use if C, who has seen the whole incident, brings an action against A. C has not been hurt: he is not the injured party; he is the wrong plaintiff. The right plaintiff is B, or, sometimes, persons who are injured by having been deprived of B's services. But if a person has not been injured, he cannot sue.

Of course, as applied to companies, the rule appears a little more complicated. After all, the directors who have been fraudulent have injured the *company*. The company is composed of *members*. Losses to the company affect *all the members*, not simply the majority or the minority or any particular member. Why, then, should an individual member not sue, since he has been injured?

The answer is that injury is not enough. The plaintiff must show that the injury has been caused by a *breach of duty* to him. In the course of existence a person suffers many injuries for which no action can be brought, for no duty to him has been broken; and individual shareholders, or even the minority shareholders as a body, who try to show that the directors owe a duty to *them personally* in their management of the company's assets will assuredly fail. The directors owe no duty to the individual members, but only to *the company as a whole*. A company is a person, and if it suffers injury through breach of a duty owed to it, then the only possible plaintiff is the company itself acting, as it must always act, through its majority.

NOTE: *Foss* v. *Harbottle* concerned a wrong done to the company by the *directors*, but it is immaterial by whom it was done. In *Leon* v. *York-o-Matic Ltd*. (1966), it was stated that for wrongs done by a *liquidator*, such as selling the company's assets at an undervalue, the proper plaintiff would have been the *company*, and not a creditor or a director.

2. Advantages of the rule in Foss v. Harbottle. There are two main advantages of the rule in *Foss* v. *Harbottle*, of a purely practical nature:

(*a*) Clearly, if every individual member were permitted to sue anyone who had injured the company through a breach of duty, there could be as many actions as there are shareholders. Legal proceedings would never cease, and there would be enormous wastage of time and money.

(*b*) If an individual member could sue a person who had caused loss to the company, and the company then ratified that person's act at a general meeting, the legal proceedings would be quite useless, for a court will naturally hold that the will of the majority prevails.

3. Apparent exceptions to the rule in Foss v. Harbottle. There are a number of occasions on which *an individual member may bring an action*, and these are as follows:

(a) Where the act done is *ultra vires* the company or *illegal*.

(b) Where the act can validly be done only by a special or extraordinary resolution, but in fact has been done by a simple majority.

(c) Where the majority are committing a fraud on the minority.

In *Prudential Assurance Co. Ltd.* v. *Newman Industries Ltd (No. 2)* (1981) Vinelott J. held that dicta in *Foss* v. *Harbottle* indicated that an action might be brought not only where the wrongdoers were a majority with voting control, but also where they 'were able ... by manipulation of their position in the company to ensure that the action is not brought by the company', i.e. where they had merely *de facto control* and the interests of justice would be defeated if an action were not allowed. He further stated that the 'fraud' lies in the controllers' 'use of their voting power, not in the character of the act or transaction giving rise to the cause of action' – a useful and penetrating distinction.

The Court of Appeal, however, while observing that it could not properly decide the scope of the exception to *Foss* v. *Harbottle* in this case because Vinelott J. had already permitted the action to proceed, disapproved his view that there is an exception to the rule in *Foss* v. *Harbottle* whenever the justice of the case so requires. The court was 'not convinced that this is a practical test'.

More recently, in *Estmanco (Kilner House) Ltd.* v. *GLC* (1982) the Vice-Chancellor, Sir Robert Megarry, held that 'no right of a shareholder to vote in his own selfish interests or to ignore the interests of the company entitles him with impunity to injure his voteless fellow shareholders by depriving the company of a cause of action and stultifying the purpose for which the company was formed'. Accordingly, he allowed a voteless shareholder to bring a derivative action (*see* **4**) since in his judgment 'the exception usually known as "fraud on the minority" is wide enough to cover the present case'.

(d) Where a minority shareholder has no other remedy and the directors are using their powers, either fraudulently or negligently, in a manner which benefits themselves at the expense of the company: *Daniels* v. *Daniels* (1978).

(e) Where the *personal* rights of the *individual member* have been infringed: *Edwards* v. *Halliwell* (1950).

(f) Where a company meeting cannot be called in time to be of practical effect: *Hodgson* v. *National and Local Government Officers Association* (1972).

These six occasions are often said to be exceptions to the rule in *Foss* v. *Harbottle* – exceptions which, to quote the incisive Lord Lloyd of Kilgerran, 'have taken the matter into the realms of near incomprehensibility'. If, however, they are considered carefully it appears that five of them are unconnected with it and based not so much on legal logic as on common sense. In the first four, the wrongful act is done not so much *to* the company as *by* it. If the majority act *ultra vires* or illegally, or alter the objects clause by ordinary resolution, or oppress the minority, it is the *company* who is doing these things. One cannot say that the majority constitutes the company for one purpose and not for another. And if the company is doing these things, who is to stop it except the minority? Thus the law permits the minority to sue and, since the decision of the Court of Appeal in *Wallersteiner* v. *Moir* (*No. 2*) (1975), to be indemnified by the company against all costs reasonably incurred in the proceedings.

The fifth occasion is of an entirely different nature. Here the wrong has been done to the individual member *as such*. His dividend has been withheld, or his vote disallowed. The company's duty to him has been broken, and he is injured thereby. Naturally in such a case he is not merely the proper plaintiff, but the only possible one, for he has contractual rights against the company, and injury has been caused to him by their breach. Thus here we have not so much an exception to *Foss* v. *Harbottle* as an example of the very principle which *Foss* v. *Harbottle* enunciates.

Only in the sixth occasion, therefore, do we have a genuine and entirely proper exception.

4. Derivative and representative actions distinguished. On all the occasions mentioned above in **3** with the exception of (*e*), where the individual member is bringing his own action, the minority shareholders are bringing *the company's* action, since it is the company which has been injured. Because their right of action is *derived* from the company, the proceedings are known as a *derivative action* and the damages payable, if any, will be paid to the *company*.

It may well be, however, that in addition to the company's cause of action each of a number of shareholders has a separate claim in tort for injury caused to him. Because the injury to each of them will have been caused by the same illegal conduct, it is sufficient if one of them brings a *representative* action on behalf of himself and all other members who have been similarly injured. This avoids the necessity of repeatedly proving the illegal conduct before the court.

In a representative action the successful plaintiff will normally obtain only *declaratory* relief, i.e. the court will hold that the illegal conduct has been satisfactorily proved. The plaintiff can then go on to claim damages on the basis of the declaration and the other injured members can do likewise.

In *Prudential Assurance Co. Ltd.* v. *Newman Industries Ltd.* (*No. 2*) (1981) Vinelott J. held that the two claims are not mutually exclusive. Thus a derivative claim can be joined with a representative claim in the same proceedings. In a previous hearing, however, the judge had held that in order to succeed in a representative action three conditions must be satisfied:

(*a*) A court order for relief must not confer a right of action on a member who would not otherwise have been able to assert it in separate proceedings, or bar a defence otherwise available to the defendant in such proceedings.

(*b*) There must be an 'interest' shared by all the members of the injured class – a common ingredient in the cause of action of each of them.

(*c*) The court must be satisfied that it is for the benefit of the injured class that the plaintiff be allowed to sue in a representative capacity.

Further, the Court of Appeal made it clear that no shareholder is ever entitled to 'double recovery', i.e. he cannot recover damages merely because the company in which he is interested has suffered damage. He can bring a personal action only where he has suffered personal loss which is not 'merely a reflection of the loss suffered by the company', e.g. the expenses of attending a meeting.

5. Statutory protection of the minority. Throughout this book many statutory provisions for the protection of specified minorities of shareholders are included in the context of the statutory subject-matter to which they relate, e.g. the right of a 15 per cent minority to object to an alteration of the company's objects is dealt with in 2:**27**, the right of a 15 per cent minority to object to variation of class rights is dealt with in 11:**15** and the right of holders of one-tenth of issued shares to have an inspector appointed by the Department of Trade and Industry to investigate ownership of the company's shares is dealt with in 22:**9**.

It remains to consider in this chapter a group of provisions which stand on their own and now comprise Part XVII (ss. 459–461) of the Act under the heading 'Protection of Company Members against Unfair Prejudice'.

6. Former legislation. The first statutory provision in this area was s. 210 Companies Act 1948 which authorized any shareholder who complained that the company's affairs were being conducted in an *oppressive* manner to petition the court for an order to deal with the position.

Although this provision received a considerable amount of academic attention, it was in practice of very little value. It had two major weaknesses. First, it had no application to isolated acts – the petitioner had to show that there had been an oppressive *course of conduct*. Secondly, the petitioner was required to convince the court that the facts of which he complained would *justify the making of a winding-up order* by the court on the ground that it was *just and equitable* to wind the company up (*see* 30:**1** and **3**). Often he could not establish this and accordingly orders under the section were a rarity.

7. Present legislation. The Companies Act 1980 repealed and replaced s. 210 and removed both of the weaknesses mentioned above. It is the provisions derived from the 1980 Act which are now applicable under ss. 459–461 Companies Act 1985.

8. The petition. Section 459(1) provides that any member may petition the court for an order on the ground that the company's affairs are being or have been conducted in a manner which is *unfairly prejudicial* to the interests of some part of the members, including himself, or that any actual or proposed act or omission of the company is or would be so prejudicial.

This provision clearly enlarged the scope of the remedy in several respects. The remedy now covers the past conduct of affairs as well as the present. It covers not only an isolated act but also an isolated omission or failure to act; and it extends to a proposed or contemplated act or omission.

Further, under s. 461(1) the court may make such order as it thinks fit if it is satisfied that the petition is *well founded*. No mention is made of a winding-up order being justified.

By s. 459(2) the remedy is available to a person who is not a member but to whom shares have been transferred (i.e. an unregistered transferee) or transmitted by operation of law (i.e. a personal representative or trustee in bankruptcy).

Finally, s. 460 provides that in certain circumstances, mentioned in 22:7, the Secretary of State may petition under the section.

9. The court order. As stated in **8** above, the court may make such order as it thinks fit to give relief to the petitioner in respect of the matters complained of: s. 461(1).

Section 461(2), however, provides that, without prejudice to the generality of subsection (1), a court order may:

(*a*) regulate the conduct of the company's affairs in the future;

(*b*) require the company to refrain from doing an act complained of by the petitioner or to do an act which he has complained it has omitted to do;

(*c*) authorize civil proceedings to be brought in the name and on behalf of the company by such person as the court directs;

(*d*) provide for the purchase of the shares of any members of the company by other members or by the company itself, and in the latter case for the resulting reduction of capital (*see* 13:**22**).

It should be noted that (*c*) authorizes a *derivative action* – the first time that such a course has been given a statutory basis in English law (*see* **4**). Nothing is said, however, about the costs of such an action. Presumably the plaintiff would be entitled to be indemnified by the company against all costs reasonably incurred in the proceedings: *Wallersteiner* v. *Moir* (1975) (*see* **3**).

Lastly, it is clear from s. 461(4) that the court may alter the company's memorandum or articles if it so desires, while under s. 461(3) it can prohibit the company from altering these documents without the court's consent (*see* 3:**9**(*e*)).

10. Judicial decisions. Most of the cases which have been decided under the provisions since their amendment in the 1980 Act have arisen in small quasi-partnership companies and been concerned with attempts to exclude a shareholder from participation in the company's affairs.

The cases fall into three main groups:

(a) those on the interpretation of the term 'unfair prejudice';

(b) those in which the remedy was sought as an alternative to a winding-up order on 'just and equitable' grounds;

(c) those involving valuation of shares.

An instance of (a) is *Re Bovey Venture Holdings Ltd.* (1981). A company was owned in equal shares by husband and wife, with two nominee shareholders each holding one share. On the breakdown of the marriage the wife was excluded from the management. The company incurred a large VAT bill. The wife applied for an order under what is now s. 461(2)(d) for the purchase of either her own or her husband's shares on the ground of unfair prejudice. HELD: A shareholder could bring himself within the provision if he could show that the value of his shares had been seriously diminished or at least seriously jeopardized by a course of conduct by those in *de facto* control of the company. The test is objective: there is no need to show bad faith on the part of the controller and the question is whether a reasonable bystander would regard the conduct as unfairly prejudicial. In this case the exclusion from management and loss of profit by payment of the unpaid VAT diminished the value of the wife's shares and was unfairly prejudicial.

Re a Company No. 002612 of 1984 is an instance of a *proposed* act being held unfairly prejudicial. The petitioner wished to prevent a proposed rights issue from being placed before an extraordinary general meeting. HELD: Although the proposal was on the face of it fair, the petitioner was unfairly prejudiced because, owing to his financial position, he would be unable to take up his allocation in the issue. The judge issued orders restraining two members from voting in favour of the proposal.

An instance of (b) is *Re R A Noble & Son (Clothing) Ltd.* (1983). A small private company was incorporated by two persons, as shareholders and directors, to expand the business started by one of them and to be continued by him. Disputes as to the number of shares held by each and as to other financial matters arose and the second shareholder, wishing to sever his connections, petitioned alternatively for relief on the ground of unfair prejudice or a winding-up order on just and equitable grounds. HELD: As the second shareholder had for the previous five years taken no real interest in the company and the first shareholder had done little to involve him, the company's affairs were not being conducted in an unfairly prejudicial manner. Mutual trust had, however, been destroyed and a winding-up order on just and equitable grounds was justified.

An instance of (c) is *Re London School of Electronics* (1985). In a two-shareholder company which ran degree courses the majority appropriated potential students to its own courses. The minority shareholder set up a rival organization and took some students with him. He then petitioned the court on the grounds of unfair prejudice. HELD: Although *prima facie* an interest in a going concern ought to be valued at the date of the order, there were in some circumstances overriding considerations of fairness which required some other date to be chosen such as the date before the conduct complained of took place. In this case the valuation had to be on the basis that the students who had gone with the petitioner had remained with the company.

Progress test 23

1. Outline the rule in *Foss* v. *Harbottle*, explaining its practical advantages and its so-called exceptions. **(1–3)**

2. Distinguish between derivative and representative actions. **(4)**

3. In what circumstances may a shareholder petition the court for an order under Part XVII (ss. 459–461) of the Companies Act 1985? **(5, 8)**

4. State what persons other than those on the register of members may petition the court under these provisions. **(8)**

5. What remedies may be granted by a court order on such a petition. **(9)**

6. With what matters have most of such petitions so far been concerned? **(10)**

24
Insider dealing

1. Meaning of expression 'insider dealing'. The expression
'insider trading' or 'insider dealing' is used to mean the dealing in the
securities of a company for the purpose of private gain by a person
who has inside information about them which would affect their price
if it were generally known.

The topic was not covered by the Companies Act 1948 at all. The
earliest English legislation on it was contained in the Companies Act
1967 which made it a criminal offence in certain circumstances for a
director to deal in options (*see* 16:**59**).

After that Act was passed repeated attempts were made to draft
comprehensive provisions on the topic which would trap the culpable
without at the same time punishing the blameless. The result of these
efforts finally took statutory form in provisions of the Companies Act
1980.

In the 1985 consolidation these provisions became, without any
amendment, the Company Securities (Insider Dealing) Act 1985.
That consolidating Act has now been amended by Part VII (i.e. ss.
173–178) of the Financial Services Act 1986. The principal amendments relate to the widening of s. 2 of the 1985 Act ('Abuse of
information obtained in official capacity') by the substitution of
'public servant' for 'Crown servant' and to the introduction of an
investigation procedure for which the 1985 Act made no provision.

*In this chapter references to sections are to sections of the Company
Securities (Insider Dealing) Act 1985 unless the contrary is indicated.*

The Act creates three main types of offence:

(*a*) *dealing* in securities;
(*b*) *counselling or procuring* another person to deal in securities;

(c) *communicating information* knowing that the recipient will use it for the purpose of dealing in securities.

2. Definition of 'insider'. In order to understand the intricacies of the insider dealing legislation it is necessary first to grasp the meaning given by the Act to the language normally associated with this type of activity. The word of primary importance is clearly the word 'insider', a term which is used in the title of the Act, in the heading to Part I of the Act and in a marginal note to s. 1 but is not found in the actual provisions themselves.

Instead of the term 'insider' the Act employs the phrase 'individual connected with a company'. This would appear to indicate that a *company*, being a corporation, cannot be affected by the Act at all in this respect. Only 'individuals', i.e. people, can be insiders.

Section 9 provides that an individual is connected with a company, i.e. he is an insider, if:

(a) he is a director of that company or a related company; *or*

(b) he occupies a position:

(i) as an officer (other than director) or employee of that company or a related company; *or*

(ii) involving a professional or business relationship between himself (or his employer or a company of which he is a director) and that company or a related company which may reasonably be expected to give him access to unpublished price sensitive information relating to the securities of either company, and which it would be reasonable to expect a person in his position not to disclose except for the proper performance of his functions.

Even this initial definition is somewhat indigestible and requires some study. First, there is the expression 'related company'. In order to understand the nature of a related company we must turn to s. 11 which defines it as 'any body corporate which is that company's subsidiary or holding company, or a subsidiary of that company's holding company'. Rather than to memorize this cumbersome definition, it is simpler merely to regard a related company as one *within the same group*.

Secondly, while the persons who would fall under (a) and (b) (i) are obvious, those who would be caught by (b) (ii) are almost infinitely various. The words used would clearly cover persons in the professions commonly associated with corporate activities – i.e. solicitors and accountants – but would also cover financial advisers, management consultants, printers of securities or indeed almost anyone who managed by any lawful method to *obtain* unpublished price sensitive information, since it is difficult to see how one can lawfully obtain something to which one cannot reasonably be expected to have access.

Accordingly a shareholder in his capacity of shareholder is not an insider since he has no access to information of this kind.

3. Definition of 'unpublished price sensitive information'. Section 10 defines unpublished price sensitive information in relation to a company's securities as information which:

(a) relates to *specific matters* relating or of concern (directly or indirectly) to the company, i.e. is not of a general nature; and

(b) is *not generally known* to those persons who are accustomed or would be likely to deal in those securities but which would be likely materially to affect their price if it were.

4. Offences created by s. 1. Section 1(1) prohibits any individual who is knowingly connected with a company, or has been so connected at any time within the last six months, from dealing on a recognised stock exchange in that company's securities if he has information which:

(a) he holds by virtue of being connected with the company;

(b) it would be reasonable to expect him not to disclose except for the proper performance of his functions; and

(c) he knows is unpublished price sensitive information.

Under s. 1(2) this same individual is also prohibited from dealing in the securities of *any other company* if he has information which:

(a) he holds by virtue of being connected with the first company;

(b) it would be reasonable to expect him not to disclose except for the proper performance of his functions;

(c) he knows is unpublished price sensitive information in relation to the securities of that other company; and

(d) relates to any transaction (actual or contemplated) involving both companies, or one of them and the securities of the other, or to the fact that any such transaction is no longer contemplated.

It can be seen that under both these subsections a *present or recent insider* is prohibited from dealing. Under s. 1(3) and (4), however, any individual who is given a 'tip' by the insider, commonly known as a 'tippee', is also prohibited from dealing. Section 1(3) and (4) provides that where an individual:

(*a*) has information which he knowingly obtained (directly or indirectly) from a present or recent insider who he knows or has reasonable cause to believe held it by virtue of his connection with a particular company, and

(*b*) knows or has reasonable cause to believe that it would be reasonable to expect the insider not to disclose the information except for the proper performance of his functions,

he is prohibited from dealing on a recognised stock exchange:

(*a*) in securities of that company if he knows that the information is unpublished price sensitive information in relation to them, and

(*b*) in securities of any other company if he knows that the information is unpublished price sensitive information in relation to them, and it relates to any transaction (actual or contemplated) involving both companies, or one of them and the securities of the other, or to the fact that any such transaction is no longer contemplated.

Since s. 1 covers the 'tippee' it is not surprising that it also covers the 'tippor', i.e. the individual who gives a 'tip' to another person. Section 1(8) prohibits any individual who is forbidden by the section from dealing on a recognised stock exchange in any securities owing to the fact that he has certain information from *communicating* that information to any other person if he knows or has reasonable cause to believe that that person or some other person will use it for the purpose of dealing, or counselling or procuring any other person to deal, on a recognised stock exchange in those securities.

Two more subsections in s. 1 cover the position where a takeover bid is being considered. Section 1(5) prohibits any individual who is contemplating or has contemplated making a takeover offer for a company in a particular capacity from dealing on a recognised stock exchange in securities of that company in another capacity if he knows that information that the offer is, or is no longer, contemplated is unpublished price sensitive information in relation to them.

Section 1(6) prohibits that individual's 'tippee' from dealing in them if he knowingly obtained (directly or indirectly) the information in question and knows that it is unpublished price sensitive information in relation to them.

Lastly, s. 1(7) prohibits any individual who is forbidden *by any provision in the section* from dealing on a recognised stock exchange in any securities from *counselling or procuring* any other person to deal in them, knowing or having reasonable cause to believe that he would do so.

It should be noted that the expression 'recognised stock exchange' wherever it occurs in the Act includes an investment exchange, i.e. an organisation maintaining a system whereby an offer to deal in securities made by a subscriber to the organisation is communicated, without his identity being revealed, to other subscribers, and any acceptance of that offer is recorded and confirmed: ss. 13(2) and 16(1) (the latter amended by s. 212(2) and the 16th Schedule, para. 28, Financial Services Act 1986).

It should also be noted that all these prohibited activities require positive action of some kind to constitute an offence. Thus it can never be an offence to *refrain* from dealing, however profitable that may sometimes be.

5. Offences created by ss. 2, 4 and 5. It is clear that s. 1 covers insider dealing in great detail. Moreover, it is supplemented by s. 2, as amended by s. 173 Financial Services Act 1986, which contains similar provisions applicable to present and former *public servants* who hold unpublished price sensitive information concerning a company's securities by virtue of their position, and to individuals who knowingly obtain it from them (directly or indirectly).

The term 'public servant' was substituted for 'Crown servant' by s. 173(1) Financial Services Act 1986. The persons covered by this wider term are defined in s. 173(2) of that Act, and s. 173(5) and (6) enables the Secretary of State by statutory instrument to widen the definition even more if he considers that persons connected with any body appearing to him to exercise public functions may have access to unpublished price sensitive information.

Further, s. 4 extends the provisions of both s. 1 and s. 2 to *off-market deals*, i.e. deals in the advertised securities of a company otherwise than on a recognised stock exchange.

Lastly, s. 5 prohibits an individual who is subject to any prohibition under s. 1 or s. 2 from:

(a) *counselling or procuring* any other person to deal in the securities in question in the knowledge or with reasonable cause to believe that he would deal in them *outside Great Britain; or*

(b) *communicating* the information in question to any other person in the knowledge or with reasonable cause to believe that that person or some other person will use it for the purpose of dealing, or counselling or procuring any other person to deal, in the securities in question *outside Great Britain.*

It appears that the insider is not *himself* prohibited by this provision from dealing abroad otherwise than on a recognised stock exchange.

6. Summary of offences. The offences which can be committed under the head of insider dealing are so numerous that a summary may perhaps be helpful even though brevity necessarily imports a degree of inaccuracy where the rules are of such a technical nature.

The offences fall into the following categories:

(a) dealing by the insider in the securities of his own company;

(b) dealing by the insider in the securities of another company;

(c) communicating information by the insider, i.e. insider acting as 'tippor';

(d) dealing by insider's 'tippee';

(e) dealing by person contemplating a take-over bid;

(f) dealing by 'tippee' of person contemplating take-over bid;

(g) counselling or procuring another person to deal;

(h) public servants;

(i) off-market deals;

(j) foreign deals.

7. Exceptions to the prohibitions in ss. 1, 2, 4 and 5. Sections 3 and 7 contain provisions which expressly exempt certain transactions from the prohibitions imposed by ss. 1, 2, 4 and 5.

Section 3(1), as amended by s. 174(1) Financial Services Act 1986, states that an individual is not prohibited by reason of his having any information from:

(a) doing any particular thing *otherwise than with a view to making a profit or avoiding a loss* by the use of that information (e.g. realising securities because he is in immediate need of money);

(*b*) entering into a transaction in the course of the exercise in good faith of his functions as *liquidator, receiver* or *trustee in bankruptcy*;

(*c*) doing any particular thing in good faith in the course of his business as a *jobber* if the information:

(*i*) was obtained by him in the course of that business; and

(*ii*) was of a description which it would be reasonable to expect him to obtain in the ordinary course of that business; *or*

(*d*) doing any particular thing in the course of his business as a *market maker* if the information:

(*i*) was obtained by him in the course of that business; and

(*ii*) was of a description which it would be reasonable to expect him to obtain in the ordinary course of that business.

The term 'jobber' means any person dealing in securities on a recognised stock exchange and is recognised by the Stock Exchange as carrying on the business of a jobber, and the term 'market maker' means any person who holds himself out at all normal times in compliance with the rules of a recognised stock exchange as willing to buy and sell securities at prices specified by him and who is recognised as doing so by that recognised stock exchange.

Section 7 states that a trustee or personal representative who would otherwise be subject to the prohibitions in ss. 1, 2, 4 and 5 is *presumed* to have acted within the terms of s. 3(1)(*a*) above provided he acted on the advice of a person who:

(*a*) appeared to him to be an appropriate person from whom to seek such advice; and

(*b*) did not appear to him to be prohibited by ss. 1, 2, 4 or 5 from dealing in the securities in question.

This subsection would protect, for instance, a trustee who seeks the advice of an investment consultant.

Finally, s. 6, as substituted by s. 175 Financial Services Act 1986, gives exemption to individuals who do anything for the purpose of stabilising the price of securities if it is done according to conduct of business rules made under s. 48 Financial Services Act 1986.

8. Penalties. The penalties for committing any of the statutory offences are found in s. 8. Section 8(1) states that an individual who contravenes the provisions of ss. 1, 2, 4 or 5 is liable:

(*a*) on conviction on indictment to imprisonment for a term not exceeding two years (expected soon to be increased to seven years) or a fine, or both; and

(b) on summary conviction to imprisonment for a term not exceeding six months or a fine not exceeding the statutory maximum, or both.

The sting is taken out of this subsection, however, by s. 8(2) which states that proceedings for an offence cannot be instituted except by the Secretary of State or by or with the consent of the Director of Public Prosecutions. It is unlikely, therefore, that such proceedings will be a frequent occurrence.

9. Legal effect of unlawful transaction. Section 8(3) makes it clear that the illegality of a transaction prohibited by ss. 1, 2, 4 or 5 has no effect on its validity. It provides that no transaction shall be void or voidable merely because it contravenes any of these sections.

Another important feature of the statutory provisions is that they give no remedy to anyone who has suffered loss as a result of an offence having been committed. The courts, however, have not always been averse to the awarding of damages for loss suffered as the result of the commission of a statutory offence.

10. Investigations into insider dealing. Provisions for investigations into insider dealing were introduced by the Financial Services Act 1986 to enable the offences relating to insider dealing to be more effectively detected.

Section 177(1) of that Act provides that if it appears to the Secretary of State that there are circumstances suggesting a contravention of ss. 1, 2, 4 or 5 of the 1985 Act, he may appoint an inspector to investigate and report to him.

By s. 177(3) the inspector has power to require any person whom he considers may be able to give information concerning the subject of his investigation:

(a) to produce documents;

(b) to attend before him; and

(c) in any other way to give him all reasonable assistance in connection with the investigation.

By s. 177(5) the inspector may make interim reports if he thinks fit, and must make such reports if so directed by the Secretary of State.

At the end of the investigation he must make a final report to the Secretary of State.

Section 177(6) provides that a statement made by a person in compliance with a requirement imposed by s. 177 may be used in evidence against him, but by s. 177(7) it is permissible to refuse disclosure of information or production of documents on the grounds of legal professional privilege, and by s. 177(8) bankers have a more limited exemption.

Section 178 deals with penalties which may be imposed on a person who refuses to comply with a request made under s. 177(3) above or refuses to answer a question on a relevant matter.

By s. 178(1) the inspector may certify the refusal to the court and, by s. 178(2)–(4), if the court is satisfied that the alleged offender had no reasonable excuse for his refusal, it may:

(*a*) punish him as if he had been guilty of contempt of the court; or

(*b*) direct that the Secretary of State may cancel his authority to carry on investment business or may restrict his authority to do so to a specified extent.

Progress test 24

1. What do you understand by the expression 'insider dealing'? (**1**)

2. Define an 'insider'. (**2**)

3. Define 'unpublished price sensitive information'. (**3**)

4. What are the offences relating to insider dealing under the Company Securities (Insider Dealing) Act 1985 (as amended)? (**4–6**)

5. Give the exceptions to the criminal liability imposed by the Company Securities (Insider Dealing) Act 1985 (as amended) with respect to insider dealing. (**7**)

6. What penalties are imposed by the Company Securities (Insider Dealing) Act 1985 (as amended) for insider dealing? Who may bring proceedings against an individual alleged to have committed an offence of this kind? (**8**)

7. What is the legal effect of a transaction prohibited by the Company Securities (Insider Dealing) Act 1985 (as amended) by

reason of the fact that it constitutes an insider dealing offence? What remedy does the Act give to a person who has suffered loss as a result of the commission of an offence by an insider?   **(9)**

8. Outline the statutory provisions relating to investigations by the Secretary of State into insider dealing.   **(10)**

25
Private companies

1. Definition of a private company. The Companies Act 1985 in s. 1(3) defines a private company simply as a company which is not a public company (*see* 2:**2**).

Two restrictions on offers of shares in a private company were noted in 7:**1**: ss. 143(3) and 170 Financial Services Act 1986.

Apart from these two provisions, there are no further restrictions on a private company as such but the Act deals extensively with the procedure whereby a private company converts into a public company, and vice versa.

2. Capital requirements for conversion to public company. Section 45 imposes strict initial rules regarding the share capital of any private company seeking conversion. Before it can be re-registered as a public company, it must satisfy two of the same conditions required of a company registered as a public company on its original incorporation when such a company applies for a trading certificate, namely:

(*a*) the nominal value of its allotted share capital must be not less than the authorized minimum (*see* 2:**35**); and

(*b*) not less than one quarter of the nominal value of each allotted share, together with the whole of any premium on it, must have been paid up (*see* 5:**2** and 9:**15**).

There are, however, two further conditions to be satisfied under s. 45 owing to the fact that ss. 99(2) and 102(1) do not apply to private companies (*see* 10:**1** and 9:**16**). Thus safeguards are required when conversion is sought:

(*c*) where any share in the company, or any premium on it, has been paid up by *an undertaking to do work or perform services* for the company, that undertaking must have been performed; and

(*d*) where shares have been allotted as paid up as to their nominal value or any premium on them *otherwise than in cash*, and the consideration for the allotment includes an undertaking to the company which *does not fall within* (*c*) *above*, then *either*:

    (*i*) that undertaking must have been performed; *or*

    (*ii*) there must be a contract between the company and some person under which that undertaking is to be performed *within five years*.

Under s. 45(5) and (7), where (*b*) above has not been complied with as regards shares allotted under a share scheme for employees, those shares may be disregarded for the purpose of compliance with (*b*)–(*d*), but must then be treated for the purpose of (*a*) as though they were not part of the allotted share capital.

In addition to the four requirements of s. 45, s. 44(1) and (2) imposes two more conditions which apply where, between the date of the balance sheet and the passing of the special resolution for re-registration, shares are allotted as paid up as to their nominal value or any premium on them *otherwise than in cash*. In these circumstances the company may not apply for re-registration as a public company unless:

(*a*) the consideration has been valued in accordance with s. 108; and

(*b*) a report has been made on its value during the six months immediately preceding the allotment (*see* 9:**18** and **19**).

3. Procedure for re-registration of private company as public company. Section 43 governs the procedure to be followed for the re-registration of a private company with a share capital as a public company.

The first step is for the company to pass a special resolution for re-registration which:

(*a*) alters its memorandum so that it states that the company is to be a public company; and

(*b*) makes all other necessary alterations in both its memorandum and articles.

Next, an application for re-registration, signed by a director or secretary, must be delivered to the registrar along with the following documents:

(*a*) a printed copy of the *altered memorandum and articles*;

(*b*) a copy of a written *statement by the company's auditors* that in their opinion the relevant balance sheet shows that the amount of the company's net assets at the date of the balance sheet was not less than the aggregate of its called-up capital and undistributable reserves;

(*c*) a copy of the *relevant balance sheet*, i.e. one prepared as at a date not more than seven months before the company's application, together with a copy of an *unqualified report by the auditors*;

(*d*) a copy of any *report* prepared under s. 44(2) (*see* 2 *above*); and

(*e*) a *statutory declaration* by a director or secretary:

(*i*) that the special resolution for re-registration has been passed and the conditions specified in ss. 44 and 45 have been satisfied (*see* 2 *above*); and

(*ii*) that between the date of the balance sheet and the application for re-registration there has been no change in the company's financial position resulting in the amount of its net assets falling below the aggregate of its called-up capital and undistributable reserves.

Under s. 47(2) the registrar may accept this declaration as sufficient evidence that the special resolution has been passed and the conditions satisfied. Under s. 47(1) he then retains the application and other documents and issues the company with a certificate of incorporation stating that it is a public company. Section 47(4) states that on the issue of the certificate the company becomes a public company and the alteration in its memorandum and articles take effect, while under s. 47(5) the certificate is conclusive evidence that all the requirements of the Act regarding re-registration have been complied with, and that the company is a public company. Under the Companies (Fees) Regulations 1980 (S. I. 1980, No. 1749) there is a re-registration fee of £50.

It should be noted that under s. 48 the same procedure, with slight and obvious modifications, is required for the re-registration of an *unlimited* (and therefore necessarily private) company as a public company. Furthermore, s. 77 Insolvency Act 1986 protects the interests of creditors where an unlimited company re-registers as a limited company and then goes into liquidation within the next three years (*see* 28:4).

Finally, s. 104, which brings into play the rules in s. 109 relating to the valuation of non-cash assets when acquired by the company from a subscriber to the memorandum, applies under s. 104(3) where a private company re-registers as a public company and non-cash assets equal to one-tenth or more of the nominal value of its issued share capital are acquired by the company from persons who were members at the date of re-registration within two years from that date (*see* 6:5–7 and 9:18–20).

4. Procedure for re-registration of public company as private company. Section 53 prescribes the procedure for the converse operation, namely, the re-registration of a public company as a private company. Although this is a far less common occurence, it is sometimes seen where one company has taken over another and the holding company wishes to alter the status of its subsidiary (*see* 13:13).

The first step, once again, is the passing of a special resolution for re-registration by the company which:

(*a*) alters its memorandum so that it no longer states that the company is a public company; and

(*b*) makes all other necessary alterations in both its memorandum and articles.

Next, an application for re-registration, signed by a director or secretary, must be delivered to the registrar together with a printed copy of the altered memorandum and articles. Furthermore, either the period for making an application to the court under s. 54 to cancel the resolution must have expired without such an application having been made or, if such an application has been made, it must have been withdrawn or a court order made confirming the resolution and a copy of that order delivered to the registrar.

Under s. 55(1) the registrar then retains the application and other documents and issues the company with an appropriate certificate of incorporation. On the issue of the certificate the company, under s. 55(2) becomes a private company and the alterations in its memorandum and articles take effect, while under s. 55(3) the certificate is conclusive evidence that all the requirements of s. 53 regarding re-registration have been complied with, and that the company is a private company. Under the Companies (Fees) Regulations 1980 (S.I. 1980, No. 1749) there is a re-registration fee of £5.

5. Provision for dissentient members. It can be seen from **4**

above that an application can be made to the court to cancel a resolution passed by a public company for re-registration as a private company. Section 54 governs such an application, dealing with the applicants, the period of time allowed and the powers of the court.

Section 54(2) states that such an application may be made:

(a) by the holders of not less than 5 per cent in nominal value of the company's issued share capital or any class thereof;

(b) if the company is not limited by shares, by not less than 5 per cent of its members; *or*

(c) by not less than 50 of the company's members.

No person who has voted in favour of the resolution can apply.

Section 54(3) requires the application to be made within 28 days of the passing of the resolution. The court, under s. 5(5), must then make an order either cancelling or confirming the resolution on such terms as it thinks fit, and may adjourn the proceedings in order that an arrangement may be made for the purchase of the interests of the dissentient members.

Section 54(6) states that the court order may provide for the purchase by the company of the shares of any members and for the resulting reduction of capital (*see* 13:**22**). It can also make any alterations to the memorandum or articles which are thereby rendered necessary and, under s. 54(8), prohibit the company from making subsequent alterations to these documents. The company may then make such alterations only with the leave of the court (*see* 3:**9**(*d*)).

Finally, the registrar must be kept informed. As soon as an application to the court is made, s. 54(4) requires the company to notify him. Then, when the court order is made, the company must deliver to him within 15 days an office copy of it: s. 54(7).

6. Differences between public and private company. Private companies have a number of advantages which can sometimes be *dis*advantageous according to whose interests are being considered. Thus a 96-year-old director may cling to office with obvious enjoyment even though there is a point at which efficiency outweighs experience. It can at least be said, however, that a private company differs from a public company in the following ways:

(1) The statutory minimum of directors is one: s. 282.

(2) Two or more directors can be appointed by a single resolution of a general meeting: s. 292.

(3) A director holding office for life on 18 July 1945 (now almost extinct) cannot be removed by ordinary resolution under s. 303: s. 14 Companies Consolidation (Consequential Provisions) Act 1985.

(4) There is no statutory age-limit on the directors unless the company is a subsidiary of a public company: s. 293.

(5) There is no requirement that the secretary shall have qualifications: s. 286.

(6) A private company can convert from a limited company to an unlimited company: s. 49.

(7) A private company limited by guarantee is, on complying with certain conditions, exempt from the provisions of the Act regarding the use of the word 'limited' as part of its name: s. 30.

(8) A proxy may speak at general meetings: s. 372.

(9) The directors are not required to convene an extraordinary general meeting where the company's net assets fall to half or less of its called-up capital: s. 142.

(10) No minimum authorized capital is required on registration: s. 11.

(11) A private company can commence business immediately on registration and requires no trading certificates: s. 117.

(12) A private company must not apply for its shares to be listed on the Stock Exchange: s. 143(3) Financial Services Act 1986.

(13) A private company must not offer its shares by advertisement unless exempted by the Secretary of State for Trade and Industry: s. 170 Financial Service Act 1986.

(14) Shares issued by a private company to a subscriber to the memorandum are not required to be paid up in cash: s. 106.

(15) Where a subscriber to the memorandum of a private company sells non-cash assets to the company, there is no requirement that those assets shall be valued by an expert: s. 104.

(16) It is unnecessary for 25 per cent of the nominal value of the shares in a private company to be paid up on allotment: s. 101.

(17) A private company is not prohibited from accepting payment for its shares in the form of an undertaking to do work or perform services from the company: s. 99.

(18) Non-cash consideration to be furnished to a private company in respect of an allotment of shares need not be so furnished within five years: s. 102.

(19) Non-cash consideration furnished to a private company in respect of an allotment of shares need not be valued by an expert: s. 103.

(20) The statutory pre-emption rights can be totally excluded by the memorandum or articles of a private company: s. 91.

(21) A private company may declare a dividend even though the amount of its net assets is less than the aggregate of its called-up share capital and its undistributable reserves: s. 264.

(22) A private company is not required to file interim accounts to support a proposed interim dividend: s. 272.

(23) The strict rules applicable to shares in which the company itself has a beneficial interest do not apply to private companies: s. 146.

(24) A private company is not subject to the statutory restrictions on the taking of a lien or charge on its own shares: s. 150.

(25) A private company which is not in the same group as a public company is not prohibited from making quasi-loans to its directors or entering into credit transactions with them: ss. 330 and 331.

(26) A private company which is not in the same group as a public company is not prohibited from making loans to persons connected with a director: ss. 330 and 331.

(27) The rules relating to the giving of financial assistance by a company for the purpose of the acquisition of its own shares are less stringent for a private company: ss. 151–158.

(28) Only a private company may be entitled to deliver modified accounts to the registrar: s. 247.

(29) A private company is subject to one less rule than a public company in the case of an off-market purchase by the company of its own shares: s. 164.

(30) A private company is subject to fewer rules regarding the disclosure of purchases of its own shares: s. 169.

(31) Only a private company is permitted to purchase its own shares out of capital: s. 171.

(32) A private company is not required to keep a register of interests in shares under s. 211.

It should be noted that the Companies Acts 1980 and 1981 very greatly accentuated the difference between a public and a private company. Accordingly it now is considerably more advantageous to

register as a private company than was the case before those Acts were
passed.

Progress test 25

1. Define a private company. (**1**)
2. With what conditions must a private company comply as
regards share capital when it seeks conversion to a public
company? (**2**)
3. How does a private company convert into a public
company? (**3**)
4. By what procedure does a public company convert into a private
company? (**4**)
5. In what ways does a private company differ from a public
company? (**6**)

26
Dissolution and insolvency

1. Methods of dissolution. A company is like a contract in that, having been created by a legal process, it can only be destroyed by a legal process. It will not evaporate or disappear. A contract is created by agreement supported by consideration, and destroyed by one of the methods of discharge familiar to students of commercial law. A company is created by registration, and destroyed by one of the methods of dissolution which we are about to consider. They are as follows:

(a) A company which has been registered with *illegal* objects can be dissolved by the taking of proceedings by the Attorney-General for *cancellation of the registration.*

Thus in *Attorney-General* v. *Lindi St. Claire (Personal Services) Ltd.* (1980), Miss St. Claire, who was engaged in the business of prostitution, was advised to register a limited company for the purposes of her business. The registrar rejected the names of Prostitutes Ltd., Hookers Ltd., and Lindi St. Claire French Lessons Ltd., but finally accepted the name of Lindi St. Claire (Personal Services) Ltd. and the company was duly registered. The Attorney-General successfully applied to have the registration cancelled on the ground that the purpose of the company was unlawful.

(b) A company which is transferring its undertaking to another company under a scheme for reconstruction or amalgamation may, according to s. 427(3)(d), be *dissolved without winding up*, if the court so orders (*see* 32:**1-5**).

(c) A company which is *defunct* may be *struck off the register* by the registrar, under s. 652, and will then be *dissolved* (*see* 31:**26-27**).

This is now a very common method of dissolution, as it is both cheap and easy.

(*d*) A company may be *wound up*, i.e. *liquidated*.

It is unnecessary to say more about (*a*), and there is very little to be learnt about (*b*) and (*c*), both of which will be discussed later. Liquidation, however, is a lengthy topic and it must be studied in more detail (*see* Chapters 28–31).

2. The Insolvency Act 1986. The provisions of the Companies Act 1985 relating to winding up were amended by the Insolvency Act 1985. The amended provisions together with the unamended provisions were then consolidated in the Insolvency Act 1986. Therefore *in the remainder of this chapter and in Chapters 28–31* which are devoted to winding up *references to sections are to be taken as references to sections of the Insolvency Act 1986 unless the contrary is indicated*

It should be kept clearly in mind throughout this and the succeeding chapters that, while most companies which go into liquidation are insolvent, i.e. cannot pay their debts in full, insolvency is not an essential ingredient of liquidation. Indeed, it will be seen that in one type of liquidation – a members' voluntary winding up – it is essential that the company *is able* to pay its debts in full. Fortunately, *all* the winding-up provisions, including those relating to companies which are not insolvent, have been consolidated in the Insolvency Act 1986. One should not be misled by the short title 'Insolvency Act 1986' into thinking otherwise.

A further preliminary point which must be mentioned is that the Insolvency Act 1986 also includes Parts which deal with the bankruptcy of individuals. These Parts can for present purposes be omitted. However, there are certain provisions in the Act which relate both to insolvent companies and to insolvent individuals, e.g. the categories of preferential debts and the qualification of being an insolvency practitioner. Such matters, so far as they affect companies, are treated within Chapter 31, which deals with provisions of general application in winding up.

3. Methods of winding up and sections to be studied. There are two methods of winding up, according to s. 73(1):

(*a*) *voluntary* winding up, which may, by s. 90, be either:

    (*i*) a *members'* voluntary winding up; or

    (*ii*) a *creditors'* voluntary winding up; and

(*b*) winding up *by the court*, i.e. *compulsory* liquidation.

The main problem in studying liquidation is not its difficulty, but its length. Students find it an unmanageable topic, and do not know where to start. Here an attempt has been made to simplify it so that they will not feel too aware of the size of the subject, and it is hoped that they will then be able to read the many detailed books on it without losing their way.

The provisions to be studied comprise *principally Part IV* of the Insolvency Act 1986 and range from s. 73 to s. 219. This need cause no alarm, for there are many sections which can be omitted, and there are many to which a very short reference is enough. It is helpful if they are grouped so that the student knows where he is:

Sections 73–83	These are general sections applying to both methods of winding up and concerning *contributories*.
Sections 84–116	These sections deal with *voluntary* winding up, but are subdivided:
ss. 84–90	General sections.
ss. 91–96	*Members'* voluntary winding up.
ss. 97–106	*Creditors'* voluntary winding up.
ss. 107–116	Sections applying to both kinds of voluntary winding up.
Sections 117–162	These sections deal with winding up *by the court*.
Sections 163–219	These again are general sections applying to both methods of winding up.

In addition there are provisions in *Part VI* of the Act which must be looked at. Part VI covers miscellaneous provisions applying to *companies* which are *insolvent or in liquidation*, e.g. the liquidator's administration in getting in the company's property, his right to apply to court for inquiry to be made into the company's dealings, and what challenge can be made of transactions at an unvervalue, preferences, extortionate credit transactions and floating charges.

It should be noted that these provisions apply not only to a liquidator but also to the administrator, if an administration order is made under Part II of the Act (*see* Chapter 27).

Finally, as has been stated above, there are a few other provisions which are common to *company and individual insolvency*: of these, preferential debts are dealt with in Part XII of the Act and the qualifications of insolvency practitioners in Part XIII.

4. Company insolvency rules. Despite the numerous sections to be studied, there is also a substantial volume of subordinate legislation, since many of the detailed provisions relating to winding up are contained not in the Act itself but in company insolvency rules.

Section 411 provides for the making of such rules by the Lord Chancellor with the concurrence of the Secretary of State for Trade and Industry, and the 8th Schedule indicates the provisions which are capable of being included in the rules.

These provisions include provisions relating to:

(a)   *court procedure* when a court is involved in the winding up;

(b)   the form, contents and publication of *notices* and the persons to whom they are to be given;

(c)   the way in which a *provisional liquidator* is to carry out his functions;

(d)   the way in which the various *meetings* are to be summoned and conducted;

(e)   the establishment and proceedings of the various *committees* of creditors and liquidation committees for which the Act provides;

(f)   the *proving of debts*;

(g)   the *distribution* of the company's property, including unclaimed funds and dividends;

(h)   financial matters including the *liquidator's remuneration, investment* of receipts, winding-up *expenses*;

(i)   *records* required to be kept *by officers of courts* and the inspection of these records by contributories and creditors;

(j)   proceedings at *public examinations*;

(k)   the *liquidator's books*, accounts and other records and their inspection and disposal;

(l)   the *auditing* of the liquidator's accounts; and

(m)   making non-compliance with any of the rules a *criminal offence*.

The matters for which provisions may be made under the 8th Schedule include matters arising under voluntary arrangements (*see* **6–8**) or where there is an administration order (*see* Chapter 27).

The content of the rules is beyond the scope of this book, but the existence of the rules and the general nature of the matters for which they may provide must be constantly borne in mind in the study of the provisions of the Act itself as given in the remaining chapters of this book.

5. Alternatives to winding up. The winding-up procedure has been recognised as being in some situations an over-drastic means of dealing with a state of insolvency. The Insolvency Act 1985 introduced two new alternatives to liquidation, namely:

(a) company voluntary arrangements; and

(b) administration orders.

The provisions relating to (a) now comprise Part I of the Insolvency Act 1986 and are outlined in **6–8** below. The provisions relating to (b) now comprise Part II of that Act and are the subject-matter of Chapter 27.

6. Company voluntary arrangements. Sections 1–7 relate to a new procedure introduced by the Insolvency Act 1985 with a view to enabling a company which is nearly or actually insolvent to resolve its financial difficulties to the satisfaction of its creditors without the formality and expense necessarily involved in other procedures available under the Acts.

Safeguards are, however, necessary to prevent abuse of an informal procedure, and the principal safeguard in this case is the requirement that the person who acts in connection with the voluntary arrangement and sees to its implementation must be qualified as an 'insolvency practitioner'.

7. The proposal. Section 1(1) provides that the directors of a company may make a proposal to the company and to its creditors for a *composition in satisfaction of its debts* or a *scheme of arrangement of its affairs*. The term 'voluntary arrangement' is used to cover both of these.

By s. 1(2) the proposal is that some person (at this stage referred to as 'the nominee') should act in relation to the voluntary arrangement either as trustee or otherwise for the purpose of supervising its implementation, and the nominee must be a person who is qualified to act as an insolvency practitioner in relation to the company (*see* 31:**15**).

The proposal may be made even if an administration order (*see* Chapter 27) is in force and even if the company is being wound up, but in those circumstances it is not the directors who make the proposal but the administrator or the liquidator as the case may be: s. 1(3).

Section 2(1) and (2) provides that where the nominee is not the administrator or liquidator, he must, within 28 days after he has been given notice of the proposal (or longer if the court allows), submit a report to the court, stating:

(a) whether, in his opinion, meetings of the company and of its creditors should be summoned to consider the proposal; and

(b) the date, time and place at which he proposes that any such meetings should be held.

For the purposes of enabling the nominee to prepare his report, the person intending to make the proposal must, by s. 2(3), submit to the nominee:

(a) a document setting out the terms of the proposed voluntary arrangement; and

(b) a statement of the company's affairs containing prescribed information including particulars of its creditors, of its debts and other liabilities and of its assets.

If the nominee fails to submit the required report, the person intending to make the proposal may apply to the court for the nominee to be replaced by another qualified insolvency practitioner: s. 2(4).

By s. 3(1) the nominee, if he is not the administrator or liquidator and has reported to the court under s. 2(2) that meetings of the company and its creditors should be summoned, must proceed to do so unless the court directs otherwise.

Section 3(2) provides that where the nominee is the liquidator or administrator he must summon meetings of the company and of its creditors to consider the proposal for such a time, date and place as he thinks fit. There is no need for a report to be made to court in this situation.

8. Consideration and implementation of proposal. Section 4 provides that the meetings summoned under s. 3 must decide whether to approve the proposed voluntary arrangement, with or without modifications, e.g. they may make a change of nominee. However, a modification must not be so radical as to take the arrangement outside the definition of 'voluntary arrangement' in s. 1(1), and the rights of secured and preferential creditors cannot be altered by the proposal (or by any modification of it) without the concurrence of the creditor concerned. At the end of either meeting the chairman reports the result of it to the court and to prescribed persons.

By s. 5(1) and (2) where each of the meetings summoned under s. 3 approves the proposed voluntary arrangement either with the same modifications or without modifications, then the arrangement takes effect as if made by the company at the creditors' meeting and binds every person who had notice of, and was entitled to vote at, that meeting (whether or not he was present or represented) as if he were a party to the arrangement.

By s. 5(3) if an administration order is in force or the company is being wound up, the court may do one or both of the following:

(a) by order, discharge the administration order or stay the winding-up proceedings;

(b) give directions as to the conduct of the administration or winding up to facilitate the implementation of the voluntary arrangement.

An order under (a) must not be made until 28 days from the date of the chairman's reports or, where an application is made to court under s. 6, a final decision has been reached by the court.

Section 6(1) allows the decisions taken at the meetings to be challenged by an application to the court on one or both of the following grounds:

(a) that the arrangement unfairly prejudices the interests of a creditor, member or contributory of the company;

(b) that there has been some material irregularity at or in relation to either of the meetings.

By s. 6(2) the persons who may make such an application are:

(a) a person entitled to vote at either of the meetings;

(b) the nominee; and

(c) if an administration order is in force or the company is being wound up, the administrator or liquidator.

The application must be made within 28 days of the chairman's reports to the court under s. 4: s. 6(3).

If the court is satisfied as to either of the grounds mentioned above, it may, by s. 6(4), do one or both of the following:

(a) revoke or suspend the approval given by the meetings;

(b) give a direction to any person for the summoning of further meetings.

Section 7(1) and (2) provides that once a voluntary arrangement has taken effect, the nominee becomes known as the 'supervisor' of the arrangement.

The remainder of s. 7 concerns the role which the court may play in relation to the implementation of the proposal:

(a) By s. 7(3), if any of the company's creditors or any other person is dissatisfied by any act, omission or decision of the supervisor, he may apply to the court, and on such an application the court may:

    (*i*)   confirm, reverse or modify any act or decision of the supervisor;

    (*ii*) give him directions; or

    (*iii*) make such other order as it thinks fit.

  (*b*) By s. 7(4) the supervisor may apply to the court for directions as to any particular matter arising under the arrangement, and he is included among the persons who may apply to the court for an administration order or for winding up.

  (*c*) By s. 7(5) and (6) the court may make an order appointing a qualified insolvency practitioner in substitution for the existing supervisor to fill a vacancy or to be an additional supervisor. These powers are to be exercised only where it is difficult for an appointment to be made without the court's assistance.

Progress test 26

  1. In what ways may a registered company be dissolved? (**1**)

  2. Give a general description of the nature and contents of the Insolvency Act 1986. (**2, 3**)

  3. In what ways may a registered company be wound up? (**3**)

  4. List the matters which may be provided for in company insolvency rules. (**4**)

  5. Define the term 'voluntary arrangement' for the purposes of Part I of the Insolvency Act 1986. (**7**)

  6. What are the requirements regarding the holding of meetings of the company and of its creditors for the purposes of a voluntary arrangement under Part I of the Insolvency Act 1986? (**7, 8**)

  7. How may the decisions of the meetings be challenged? (**8**)

  8. Who is the 'supervisor' in a voluntary arrangement? (**8**)

  9. What are the powers of the court in relation to the implementation of a voluntary arrangement? (**8**)

27
Administration orders

1. The object of administration orders. The Insolvency Act 1985 introduced administration orders as a new procedure for dealing with the affairs of a company which was likely to be or which actually was insolvent. The aim is to rescue and rehabilitate the company so that it will survive as a going concern, or, if that proves impossible, to ensure a more advantageous realisation of its assets than would result from a winding up.

The statutory provisions on administration orders now comprise Part II (i.e. ss. 8–27) of the Insolvency Act 1986.

2. Definition of 'administration order'. By s. 8(2) an administration order is an order of the court directing that, during the period for which the order is in force, the affairs, business and property of the company shall be managed by a person ('the administrator') appointed for the purpose by the court.

3. Circumstances in which an administration order may be made. Section 8(1) and (3) provides that the court may make an administration order in relation to a company if the court:

(*a*) is satisfied that the company is or is likely to become unable to pay its debts; and

(*b*) considers that the making of an order would be likely to achieve one or more of the following purposes:

(*i*) the survival of the company, and the whole or any part of its undertaking, as a going concern;

(*ii*) the approval of a voluntary arrangement under Part I of the Act (*see* 26:**6–8**);

(*iii*) the sanctioning under s. 425 Companies Act 1985 of a compromise or arrangement between the company and its creditors or members (*see* 32:**1–5**); and

(*iv*) a more advantageous realisation of the company's assets than would be obtained on a winding up.

By s. 8(4) an administration order must not be made in relation to a company after it has gone into liquidation.

4. Application for and making the order. Section 9(1) provides that an application for an administrative order is by petition presented to the court by the company or its directors or by a creditor or creditors or by all or any of those parties.

By s. 9(2) notice of the petition must immediately be given to any person who has appointed, or is entitled to appoint, an administrative receiver and to other prescribed persons.

Where there is an administrative receiver of the company and the person by whom he was appointed has not consented to the making of an administration order, the court must dismiss the petition unless the security which led to the appointment of the receiver is open to challenge under the provisions dealing with transactions at an undervalue and preferences (*see* 31:**20, 21**) or avoidance of floating charges (*see* 31:**23**): s. 9(3).

Section 10(1) provides that during the period between the presentation of the petition and the making of the order (or the dismissal of the petition as the case may be):

(*a*) no resolution may be passed or order made for winding up the company;

(*b*) no steps may be taken to enforce any security over the company's property or to repossess goods in the company's possession under a hire-purchase agreement except with the leave of the court; and

(*c*) no other proceedings and no execution or other legal process may be begun or continued against the company or its property except with the leave of the court.

That provision, however, does not prevent a petition for winding up from being *presented*, or an administrative receiver from being appointed or a receiver (whenever appointed) from carrying out any of his functions: s. 10(2).

5. Effect of order. Section 11(1) and (2) provides that the making of an administration order has the following consequences:

(a) Any petition for the winding up of the company must be dismissed.

(b) Any administrative receiver of the company must vacate office.

(c) Any receiver of part of the company's property must vacate office on being required to do so by the administrator.

By s. 11(3) during the period for which an administration order is in force:

(a) no resolution may be passed or order made for the winding up of the company;

(b) no administrative receiver of the company may be appointed;

(c) no other steps may be taken to enforce any security over the company's property or to repossess goods in the company's possession under a hire-purchase agreement except with the consent of the administrator or the leave of the court; and

(d) no other proceedings and no execution or other legal process may be begun or continued against the company or its property except with the consent of the administrator or the leave of the court.

Further s. 12 provides that while the administration order is in force every document issued by the company or by the administrator on which the company's name appears must also contain the administrator's name and state that the affairs, business and property of the company are being managed by him. Failure to comply with this provision makes the company and any officer or the administrator who without reasonable excuse authorizes or permits the default liable to a fine.

6. Appointment of administrator. Section 13 provides that the administrator is appointed by the administration order or, if a vacancy occurs by death, resignation or otherwise, by the court on an application being made to it:

(a) by any continuing administrator; or

(b) where there is none, by the creditors' committee (*see* **10**); or

(c) where there is neither a continuing administrator nor a creditors' committee, by the company or the directors or any creditor.

7. Powers of administrator. Section 14(1) confers on the administrator the general power to do all such things as may be necessary for the management of the affairs, business and property of the company, and provides that that general power covers all the 23 specific powers listed in the 1st Schedule. The 23 listed powers are the same as the powers which, by s. 42, are conferred on the administrative receiver (unless they are inconsistent with the provisions of the debentures under which the administrative receiver was appointed) (*see* 21:**18**).

By s. 14(2) and (3) the administrator also has power:

(*a*) to remove any director and appoint a director;

(*b*) to call any meeting of members or creditors; and

(*c*) to apply to the court for directions with regard to any particular matter arising in carrying out his functions.

Any power conferred on the company or its officers by the Companies Act 1985 or the Insolvency Act 1986 or by the memorandum or articles cannot be exercised without the administrator's consent if its exercise would interfere with the exercise by the administrator of his powers: s. 14(4).

By s. 14(5) the administrator in exercising his powers is deemed to act as the company's agent, and s. 14(6) provides that a person dealing with him in good faith and for value is not concerned to inquire whether he is acting within his powers.

Section 15 makes special provision to enable the administrator to dispose of secured property as if it were not subject to the security.

If the security is a floating charge, the holder of it must be treated as having the same priority over company property representing the property disposed of as he would have had over the secured property itself.

In the case of a security other than a floating charge, the administrator must apply to court and satisfy the court that the disposal would be likely to promote one of the purposes specified in the administration order (*see* **3**). The net proceeds of the disposal and any sum necessary to make that amount up to the amount which would have been obtained if the property had been sold in the open market by a willing seller must be applied towards discharging the sum secured. An office copy of the court's order must be sent by the administrator to the registrar of companies within 14 days.

8. Duties of administrator. The Act imposes the following duties on the administrator:

(*a*) By s. 17(1) he must, on his appointment, *take into his custody* all the property to which the company is entitled.

(*b*) He must then, by s. 17(2), *manage* the affairs, business and property of the company in accordance with any directions given by the court up to the time when his proposals have been approved by a meeting of creditors (*see* 9). After that time he must act in accordance with the approved proposals.

(*c*) By s. 21(1) he must *immediately* after the administration order has been made send to the *company and publish in the prescribed manner a notice of the order*, and, *within 28 days* after the making of the order (unless the court otherwise directs), send the *same notice to all creditors* whose addresses he knows.

(*d*) By s. 21(2) he must also, *within 14 days* after the making of the order, send an office copy of the order to the *registrar of companies and other prescribed persons*.

(*e*) By s. 22(1) and (2) he must *immediately* after the order has been made require a *statement of the company's affairs* to be made out and submitted to him.

It must be in the prescribed form, verified by affidavit, and show:

(*i*) particulars of assets, debts and liabilities;

(*ii*) names and addresses of creditors;

(*iii*) securities held by them, and the dates when these were given; and

(*iv*) any further information which may be prescribed.

Section 22(3) provides that the persons who may be required to submit the statement are:

(*i*) past or present officers of the company;

(*ii*) persons who have taken part in its formation within one year before the date of the administration order;

(*iii*) persons who are, or have been within that year, in the company's 'employment' (widely defined as including employment under a contract for services) and who are capable of giving the required information;

(*iv*) persons who are, or have been within that year, officers or in the employment of another company which is or has been within that year, an officer of the company concerned.

By s. 22(4) the statement must be submitted *within 21 days* from the administrator's notice requiring it.

(*f*) By s. 23(1) the administrator must, *within three months* (or longer if the court allows) after the making of the order:

(*i*) send to the registrar of companies and to all creditors whose addresses he knows a *statement of his proposals* for achieving the purposes specified in the order; and

(*ii*) lay a copy of the statement before a meeting of creditors summoned for the purpose on not less than 14 days' notice.

(*g*) By s. 23(2) he must also, *within the same three months* (or longer if the court allows) *either*:

(*i*) send a copy of the statement to all members whose addresses he knows; *or*

(*ii*) publish in the prescribed manner a notice stating an address to which members should write for copies of the statement to be sent to them free of charge.

(*h*) After the creditors' meeting at which his proposals are considered, he must, by s. 24(4), *report the result* of the meeting to the court, and give notice of the result to the registrar of companies and to prescribed persons.

(*i*) When the administration order is discharged, he must, by ss. 18(4), 24(6) and 27(6), *within 14 days* after the order effecting the discharge, send an office copy of that order to the registrar of companies.

(*j*) If, after proposals have been approved, he proposes to make substantial revisions of them, he must, by s. 25, follow the same procedure as in (*f*), (*g*) and (*h*) above except that the result of the meeting need not in this case be reported to the court.

9. Consideration of proposals. Section 24(1) provides that the meeting of creditors summoned under s. 23(1) must decide whether to approve the administrator's proposals. By s. 24(2) the meeting may approve the proposals *with modifications*, but only if the administrator consents to each modification.

If the meeting declines to approve the administrator's proposals, the court may by order discharge the administration order or adjourn the hearing or make an interim or any other order that it thinks fit: s. 24(5).

10. Creditors' committee. Section 26(1) provides that where the creditors' meeting has approved the administrator's proposals (with or without modifications), the meeting may, if it thinks fit, establish a committee ('the creditors' committee') which, by s. 26(2), may, on giving not less than seven days' notice, require the administrator to attend before it and furnish it with such information relating to the carrying out of his functions as it may reasonably require.

11. Protection of creditors and members. Section 27 is designed to protect the interests of creditors and members where an administration order is in force.

By s. 27(1) a creditor or member may apply to the court by petition for an order on the ground that:

(a) the company's affairs, business and property are being managed by the administrator in a manner which is *unfairly prejudicial* to the interests of its creditors or members generally, or of some of them (including at least himself); or

(b) any actual or proposed act or omission of the administrator is or would be of that nature.

By s. 27(2) the court may make such order as it thinks fit for giving relief or it may adjourn the hearing or make an interim or any other order that it thinks fit. In particular, by s. 27(4), the order may:

(a) regulate the future management by the administrator of the company's affairs, business and property;

(b) require the administrator to refrain from doing or continuing an act complained of or to do an act which he has omitted to do;

(c) require the summoning of a meeting of creditors to consider such matter as the court may direct;

(d) discharge the administration order.

On the other hand, an order under s. 27 must not prevent either:

(a) the implementation of a voluntary arrangement under Part I of the Act (*see* 26:**6–8**) or any compromise or arrangement under s. 425 Companies Act 1985 (*see* 32:**1–5**); or

(b) the implementation of proposals or revised proposals if the application for the order has not been made within 28 days after the approval of the proposals or revised proposals as the case may be.

12. Discharge or variation of order. Section 18(1) provides that the administrator may at any time apply to the court for the administration order to be discharged or to be varied so as to specify an additional purpose.

By s. 18(2) the administrator *must* make such an application if:

(a) it appears to him that the purposes specified in the order either have been achieved or are incapable of being achieved; or

(b) he is required to do so by a meeting of the company's creditors.

On hearing the application, the court may order the administration order to be discharged or varied, or may adjourn the hearing or make any interim or other order that it thinks fit: s. 18(3).

13. Vacation of office. Section 19(1) provides that the administrator may at any time be removed from office by order of the court, and may, in prescribed circumstances, resign his office by giving notice to the court.

By s. 19(2) he *must* vacate office if:

(a) he ceases to be qualified to act as an insolvency practitioner in relation to the company; or

(b) the administration order is discharged.

Where a person ceases to be administrator, his remuneration, any expenses properly incurred and debts and liabilities arising out of contracts entered into or contracts of employment adopted by him in carrying out his functions are paid out of any property in his custody in priority to any floating charge over that property: s. 19(3)–(5).

14. Release of administrator. Section 20(1) provides that a person who has ceased to be the administrator has his release from the following times:

(a) if he has died, the time at which notice is given to the court;

(b) in any other case, the time decided on by the court.

The effect of the release is to discharge him from all liability for acts or omissions in his conduct as administrator, but this does not prevent the exercise against him of the summary remedy under s. 212 (misapplication of property or breach of duty to the company).

15. Other provisions applicable to administration orders. The account given above is confined to the provisions of Part II of the

Act. There are, however, provisions elsewhere in the Act which apply to administration orders. In particular, in Part VI of the Act ('Miscellaneous Provisions Applying to Companies which are Insolvent or in Liquidation'), s. 230(1) provides that the administrator must be a person who is qualified to act as an insolvency practitioner in relation to the company (*see* 31:**15**), and several later sections in that Part provide that the administrator is an 'office-holder' for the purposes of the section in question. These sections deal with supplies of the public utilities such as gas, electricity and water (s. 233), getting in the company's property (s. 234), the duty to co-operate with the office-holder (s. 235), application to court for inquiry (ss. 236–237), and the challenge of prior transactions which were at an undervalue (s. 238) or preferences (s. 239), or extortionate credit transactions (s. 244), or invalid floating charges (s. 245), or unenforceable liens (s. 246). These will be dealt with in Chapter 31 since they are provisions of general application in winding up as well as where an administration order has been made (*see* 31:**16–24**).

Progress test 27

1. Define 'administration order' for the purposes of the Insolvency Act 1986. (**2**)

2. Of what must the court be satisfied before it makes an administration order? (**3**)

3. Who may apply to the court for an administration order and by what procedure? (**4**)

4. What are the immediate and continuing effects of the making of an administration order? (**5**)

5. Who may apply to the court for the filling of a vacancy in the office of administrator? (**6**)

6. What powers does the administrator have to dispose of company property over which a creditor holds security? (**7**)

7. Who are the persons whom the administrator may require to submit a statement of the company's affairs to him? (**8**)

8. What procedure must the administrator follow in relation to his statement of proposals before the holding of the creditors' meeting at which the proposals are considered? (**8**)

9. What consequences follow if the creditors' meeting declines to approve the administrator's proposals? **(9)**

10. What type of order may the court make if it is satisfied, on a creditor's or member's application, that an act of the administrator is unfairly prejudicial to the interests of the creditor or member? **(11)**

11. In what circumstances is the administrator bound to apply to the court for the administration order to be discharged or varied? **(12)**

12. When is the administrator bound to vacate office? **(13)**

13. What is the effect of the release of the administrator? **(14)**

14. What statutory provisions other than those in Part II of the Insolvency Act 1986 apply to the administrator? **(15)**

28

Contributories

1. Definition of a contributory. Section 79(1) defines a contributory as *every person liable to contribute to the assets of a company in the event of its being wound up.*

Section 81(1) states that if a contributory dies, his personal representatives become liable to contribute to the assets and so become contributories. Moreover, s. 81(3) states that if they default in paying any money due, the company may take administration proceedings in order to compel payment out of the estate (*see* 13:**10**).

Section 82(2) states that if a contributory becomes bankrupt, his trustee in bankruptcy represents him and becomes a contributory, and s. 82(4) states that the estimated value of his liability to future calls, as well as calls already made, may be proved against the bankrupt's estate.

2. Liability of a contributory. Section 80 states that the liability of a contributory creates a *specialty debt* accruing due from him at the time when his liability commenced (i.e. when he acquired the shares), but *payable when calls are made.*

Section 74 is a lengthy section, giving the details of the liability of the contributories. It does not refer to the terms 'A list' and 'B list' so that these require some explanation. The term 'A list' denotes the list of all those persons whose names were on the company's register of members at the commencement of the liquidation. The term 'B list' denotes the list of all those persons who were members *within the year preceding the commencement of the liquidation*, but who had transferred their shares before liquidation commenced. The two lists together form the contributories, i.e. persons who are liable to contribute to the assets in accordance with s. 74.

Section 74(1) provides first in a general statement that every present and past member is liable to contribute to the assets of the company on liquidation an amount sufficient to pay its debts. It then proceeds, in s. 74(2), to qualify this statement in the following way:

(a) A *past* member (B list) is not liable to contribute if he ceased to be a member a year or more before the commencement of the winding up, i.e. he is liable *only* if he ceased to be a member *within a year* preceding the winding up.

(b) A *past* member is not liable in respect of any debt contracted after he ceased to be a member.

(c) A *past* member is not liable unless the *existing* members (A list) are unable to satisfy the contributions required from them.

(d) In a company limited by shares, no contribution is required from *any member*, past or present, exceeding the amount, if any, *unpaid on the shares* in respect of which he is liable (limited liability).

(e) In a company limited by guarantee, no amount is required from any member exceeding the amount of the guarantee. Section 74(3), however, adds that if such a company also has a share capital, then the member will be liable not only up to the amount of the guarantee, but also up to the amount unpaid on the shares, so that he has a double, if limited, liability.

(f) A sum due to a member *in his character of member*, by way of dividends, profits or otherwise, shall not be deemed a debt of the company payable to that member in the case of competition between himself and any other creditor not a member, though it may be taken into account in adjusting the rights of the contributories among themselves.

This curiously worded little paragraph is, of course, a reference to the order of distribution of assets. Students are often puzzled by it, asking what is the position if a trade creditor is also a member. Does the fact that he is a member deprive him of his priority, since the Act says 'creditor not a member'? Probably the correct view to take is that the Act means 'creditor regarding a debt which has *not arisen* in respect of his shares'.

3. Contribution and distribution. The rules given above, apart from (f), relate to *contribution*. They do not affect *distribution* by the liquidator of the assets on which he can lay his hands. This can have some odd practical results.

Thus the liquidator must first call upon persons on the A list (*see* (c) above). Only if the individual A list member cannot pay the amount due on his shares may the liquidator resort to the person on the B list, if any, in respect of those shares. If the A list member has owned the shares for a year or more, there is then no one to whom the liquidator can resort in respect of those shares.

Having received such A list assets as he can collect, the liquidator applies those assets to *all the debts of the company, pari passu,* in the *order of distribution of assets, irrespective of the date when any particular debt was contracted.* Thus he will dispose of the creditors with fixed charges first, set aside a sum for costs, pay the preferential creditors next, and then the creditors with floating charges. Finally he will reach the unsecured creditors. Let us suppose that at this point he has not enough money to pay them all in full: he will then pay them, *pari passu,* as much as he can, e.g. 50p in £1.

Only then can he resort to the B list, and even when he does so he can only claim from a B list member when the corresponding A list member has been unable to pay. Moreover, he is now restricted by (*b*) above. If all the outstanding debts were contracted *after* the persons on the B list had transferred their shares, he cannot claim contribution from any of them. But let us suppose that there is one debt of £500 contracted *before* six B list members had transferred their shares. There are many other debts amounting to £10,000 in all contracted *after* all the B list members had transferred their shares. The total liability on the shares of the six B list members is £1,000. In such a case the liquidator can demand from them *only £500,* (*b*), and he must apply this £500 *pari passu* towards *all the debts.* It is clear that if he has £500 to apply towards debts of £10,500, each creditor will receive only one-twenty-first of the amount which he is owed. The single B list creditor will therefore receive one-twenty-first of £500; yet there is still a liability on the B list shares of £500.

4. Special rules where an unlimited private company re-registers as limited.

Section 77 lays down special rules which apply where an unlimited private company has re-registered as limited (*see* 2:33) and then goes into liquidation. These rules also apply where an unlimited private company re-registers as a public (and therefore necessarily limited) company. They are as follows:

(*a*) Despite s. 74(2)(*a*) (*see* **2**), (which imposes a time limit of one year on the liability of a past member), a past member who was a member of the company *at the time of re-registration* is liable to contribute to the assets in respect of debts contracted *before* that time if the winding up commences within *three years* from re-registration: s. 77(2).

(*b*) Despite s. 74(2)(*c*) (*see* **2**), (which exonerates past members entirely unless the existing members are unable to meet their obligations), where *all* the existing members have become members *since* the time of re-registration, a person who was a past or present member *at that time* is liable to contribute to the assets in respect of debts contracted *before* that time, even though the existing members have satisfied the contributions required from them: s. 77(3).

This rule is subject to the time limits imposed on liability both by s. 74(2)(*a*) and s. 77(2).

(*c*) Despite s. 74(2)(*d*) and (3) (*see* **2**), (which impose a limit on the liability of a member of a company limited by shares or guarantee), the liability of any person who was a *past or present member* of the company *at the time of re-registration* in respect of debts contracted *before* that time is *unlimited*.

The intention of the section is clearly to ensure that the members of an unlimited company do not escape their obligations by re-registering the company as limited. No provision, however, seems to have been made for *distribution,* and it seems a little hard on the creditors who dealt with an unlimited company that they should receive exactly the same proportion of the distributed assets as those creditors who dealt with the company after it re-registered as limited. This is especially the case where the distributed assets are greatly increased by the rules of *contribution* given above.

Progress test 28

1. Define a contributory. Give the statutory provisions regarding the death and bankruptcy of a contributory. (**1**)

2. Give the statutory provisions regarding the liability of a contributory. What do you understand by the terms 'A list' and 'B list'? (**2**)

29
Voluntary winding up

1. Resolutions for voluntary winding up. Section 84(1) provides that a company may be wound up voluntarily:

(*a*) when the *period*, if any, fixed for its duration by the articles *expires*, or the *event*, if any, *occurs*, on the occurrence of which the articles provide that it is to be dissolved, and the company has passed an *ordinary resolution* to be wound up voluntarily;

(*b*) if the company passes a *special resolution* to be wound up voluntarily;

(*c*) if the company passes an *extraordinary resolution* to the effect that it cannot continue its business *by reason of its liabilities*, and that it is advisable to wind up.

Section 85(1) requires notice of any of the above resolutions to be given by the company within 14 days by advertisement in the *Gazette*.

2. The commencement of voluntary winding up. As in bankruptcy, the *moment of commencement* of the winding up is of great legal importance. Section 86 states that the moment of commencement of a voluntary winding up is the time of the *passing of the resolution*.

3. The consequences of a voluntary winding up. These are:

(*a*) Under s. 87(1), the company ceases to carry on business, except so far as is required for its beneficial winding up.

(*b*) Under s. 87(2), the company's corporate state and powers continue until dissolution.

(*c*) Under s. 88, any transfer of shares without the sanction of the liquidator, and any alteration in the status of members, is void.

(*d*) Under s. 91(2) and s. 103, the powers of the directors cease on the appointment of a liquidator. But in a *members'* voluntary winding up the company in general meeting or the liquidator can sanction their continuance, while in a *creditors'* voluntary winding up the liquidation committee (*see* **11**) or, if there is no such committee, the creditors may do so. If the company has passed the resolution for winding up but no liquidator has yet been appointed, the directors must not, by s. 114, exercise their powers without the sanction of the court except for the limited purposes of disposing of perishable goods and other goods the value of which is likely to diminish if they are not immediately disposed of and of doing all such other things as may be necessary for the protection of the company's assets.

(*e*) If the liquidation occurs because of insolvency, the company's servants are dismissed. The liquidator may continue the employment of the servants, but this will be a *new* contract.

(*f*) By s. 112(1) the liquidator or any contributory or creditor may apply to the court to decide any question arising in the winding up and to exercise any of the powers which the court might exercise in a winding up by the court (*see* 30:**26–29**).

4. The declaration of solvency. Section 89(1) states that where it is proposed to wind up a company voluntarily, the *directors* or, *if more than two, the majority of them*, may at a board meeting make a statutory declaration that they have inquired into the company's affairs and have formed the opinion that it will be able to pay its debts in full within a specified period not exceeding 12 months from the commencement of the winding up.

Section 89(2) states that this declaration is ineffective unless:

(*a*) it is made *within the five weeks preceding* the date of the passing of the resolution for winding up, or on that date but before the passing of the resolution; and

(*b*) it contains a *statement of assets and liabilities* as at the latest practicable date.

Section 89(3) requires the declaration to be delivered to the registrar within 15 days after the passing of the resolution.

Section 89(4) provides that a director who makes this declaration without reasonable grounds for his opinion is liable to imprisonment or a fine or both. Further, s. 89(5) states that if the company is duly wound up but its debts are not paid in full within the specified period, it is presumed (unless the contrary is shown) that the director did not have reasonable grounds for his opinion. This provision puts the burden of proof on the director concerned.

The declaration of solvency is extremely important, for it *determines the nature of the winding up*. Section 90 states that when such a declaration *has been* made as above, the winding up is a *members'* voluntary winding up. When it *has not been* made, the winding up is a *creditors'* voluntary winding up.

Accordingly we must now see first what the Act provides regarding a members' voluntary winding up, and then what it provides regarding a creditors' voluntary winding up.

5. Appointment of liquidator in members' voluntary winding up. Section 91(1) empowers the *company* in general meeting to appoint a liquidator.

Section 92(1) empowers the *company* in general meeting also to fill any casual vacancy in the office of liquidator, subject to any arrangement with its creditors.

6. Liquidator's duty to call meetings in members' voluntary winding up. Section 93(1) and (2) requires the liquidator to summon a general meeting of the company at the end of the first year from the commencement of the winding up, and of each succeeding year, or at the first convenient date within three months from the end of the year or such longer period as the Secretary of State may allow, and to lay before the meeting an account of his acts and dealings and of the conduct of the winding up during the preceding year.

7. Final meeting and dissolution in members' voluntary winding up. Section 94(1) and (2) states that, as soon as the winding up is completed, the liquidator must make up an account of the winding up, showing how it has been conducted and the property disposed of, and must call a general meeting by advertisement in the *Gazette*, stating the time, place and object of the meeting, and published at least one month before the meeting. He must lay the account before this meeting.

Section 94(3) states that within a week after the meeting, he must send a copy of the account to the registrar, and make a return to him of the holding and date of the meeting. If, however, a quorum is not present at the meeting, he must, by s. 94(5), make a return that the meeting was duly called, and that no quorum was present.

The registrar, under s. 711 Companies Act 1985, must publish in the *Gazette* the receipt by him of the return.

By s. 201(2) the registrar, on receiving the account and return under s. 94(3), must immediately register them, and on the expiration of three months from the registration of the return the company is *deemed to be dissolved*. However, by s. 201(3) the court, if applied to by the liquidator or other interested person, may make an order deferring the date of dissolution.

8. Insolvency of company in members' voluntary winding up.

If in a *members'* voluntary winding up the liquidator is at any time of the opinion that the company will not be able to pay its debts in full within the period stated in the declaration of solvency, s. 95 requires him

(*a*) to summon a meeting of creditors for a day not later than the 28th day after the day on which he formed that opinion;

(*b*) to post notices of the meeting to the creditors not less than seven days before the date of the meeting;

(*c*) to cause notices of the meeting to be advertised in the *Gazette* and in two local newspapers;

(*d*) during the period before the meeting, to furnish creditors free of charge with such information concerning the company's affairs as they may reasonably require; and

(*e*) to make out a statement in the prescribed form as to the affairs of the company, lay that statement before the meeting and attend and preside at the meeting.

The statement under (*e*) must show:

(*i*) particulars of the company's assets, debts and liabilities;

(*ii*) the names and addresses of the creditors;

(*iii*) the securities held by each of them;

(*iv*) the dates when these securities were given; and

(*v*) such other information as may be prescribed.

By s. 96 the winding up, as from the day of the creditors' meeting, is in effect converted into a creditors' voluntary winding up, as if no declaration of solvency had been made.

9. Creditors' meeting in a creditors' voluntary winding up. In

a creditors' voluntary winding up s. 98(1) requires the company:

(*a*) to cause a meeting of its creditors to be summoned for a day not later than the 14th day after the day on which there is to be held the company meeting at which the resolution for voluntary winding up is to be proposed;

(*b*) to cause the notices of the creditors' meeting to be posted to the creditors not less than seven days before the date of the meeting; and

(*c*) to cause notice of the creditors meeting to be advertised in the *Gazette* and in two local newspapers.

By s. 98(2) the notice of the creditors' meeting must state *either*:

(*a*) the name and address of a person qualified to act as an insolvency practitioner (*see* 31:**15**) who, during the period before the meeting, will furnish creditors free of charge with such information concerning the company's affairs as they may reasonably require; *or*

(*b*) a place in the locality of the company's principal place of business where, on the two business days immediately before the date of the meeting, a list of the names and addresses of the company's creditors will be available for inspection free of charge.

Section 99 provides that the directors must:

(*a*) make out a statement in the prescribed form as to the company's affairs;

(*b*) cause that statement to be laid before the creditors' meeting; and

(*c*) appoint one of themselves to preside at the meeting;

and that it is the duty of that director to attend the meeting and preside over it. The statement of the company's affairs must show the same information as the statement of affairs required under s. 95 (*see* **8**).

10. Appointment of liquidator in creditors' voluntary winding up. Section 100 states that both the creditors and the company at their respective meetings may nominate a liquidator. If they nominate different persons, the *creditors'* choice prevails. If the creditors do not make a nomination, then the *company's* nominee becomes the liquidator.

If two different persons are nominated so that the creditors' nominee becomes the liquidator, any director, member or creditor may apply to the court within seven days for an order either that the company's nominee shall be the liquidator instead of or together with him, or appointing some other person.

If a vacancy occurs in the office of liquidator, s. 104 states that, unless the liquidator was appointed by the court, the creditors may fill the vacancy.

11. Liquidation committee in creditors' voluntary winding up. Section 101(1) states that the creditors at their first or any subsequent meeting may appoint a committee (the 'liquidation committee') consisting of *not more than five* persons. If they do so, the company may, by s. 101(2), also appoint *not more than five* persons to act as members of the committee.

If, however, the creditors resolve that all or any of the persons appointed by the company ought not to be members, then those persons are not qualified to act unless the court directs otherwise, and the court may appoint other persons to act as members instead of those mentioned in the resolution.

12. Liquidator's duty to call meetings in creditors' voluntary winding up. Section 105(1) and (2) makes the same provision for the holding of general meetings of the company as is made by s. 93(1) and (2) relating to a members' voluntary winding up (*see* **7**), but adds that *creditors' meetings* must also be held at the same times.

13. Final meeting and disssolution in creditors' voluntary winding up. Section 106 makes the same provision for the holding of a final general meeting of the company as is made by s. 94 (*see* **8**), relating to a members' voluntary winding up, but adds that a final *creditors' meeting* must also be held.

Section 711 Companies Act 1985 and s. 201(2) Insolvency Act 1986 also apply in the same way (*see* **8**).

14. Powers of liquidator in voluntary winding up. The remaining sections of the Act dealt with in this chapter apply to either voluntary winding up, whether it is a members' or creditors' winding up.

The powers of the liquidator in a voluntary winding up are to be found in ss. 165 and 166 taken along with the 4th Schedule, which is in three Parts.

Part I of the 4th Schedule sets out the powers which are exercisable *with sanction.* By s. 165(1) the sanction required by the liquidator for the exercise of these powers is in a *members'* voluntary winding up the sanction of an extraordinary resolution of the company, and in a *creditors'* voluntary winding up the sanction of the court or the liquidation committee (or, if there is no such committee, a meeting of the company's creditors).

The powers in Part I of the 4th Schedule are:

(*a*) power to pay any class of creditors in full;

(*b*) power to make any compromise or arrangement with creditors; and

(*c*) power to compromise all calls, debts and liabilities and all claims between the company and a contributory or other debtor and all questions in any way relating to the assets or the winding up of the company.

By s. 165(3) the liquidator in either type of voluntary winding up may *without sanction* exercise either of the powers specified in Part II of the 4th Schedule, which are:

(*a*) the power to bring or defend any action or legal proceeding in the name and on behalf of the company; and

(*b*) the power to carry on the business of the company so far as may be necessary for its beneficial winding up.

Under the same subsection he may also *without sanction* exercise any of the *general* powers specified in Part III of the 4th Schedule. It will be seen in the next chapter that these general powers can be exercised without sanction in a winding up by the court also.

The general powers set out in Part III of the 4th Schedule are:

(*a*) power to sell any of the company's property by public auction or private contract;

(*b*) power to do all acts and execute, in the name and on behalf of the company, all deeds, receipts and other documents and for that purpose to use, when necessary, the company's seal;

(*c*) power to prove, rank and claim in the bankruptcy or insolvency of any contributory;

(*d*) power to draw, accept, make and indorse any bill of exchange or promissory note in the name and on behalf of the company;

(*e*) power to raise on the security of the assets of the company any money which is necessary;

(*f*) power to take out in his official name letters of administration to any deceased contributory, and to do in his official name any other act necessary for obtaining payment of any money due from a contributory which cannot conveniently be done in the name of the company;

(*g*) power to appoint an agent to do any business which he is unable to do himself; and

(*h*) power to do all such other things as may be necessary for winding up the company's affairs and distributing its assets.

By s. 165(4) the liquidator in either type of voluntary winding up may:

(*a*) settle a list of contributories (which is *prima facie* evidence of the liability of the persons named in it to be contributories);

(*b*) make calls; and

(*c*) summon general meetings of the company for the purpose of obtaining its sanction by special or extraordinary resolution or for any other purpose he may think fit.

Section 165(6) provides that where the liquidator in exercising his powers disposes of any of the company's property to a person who is 'connected' with the company, he must notify the liquidation committee, if there is one, of that fact. By s. 249 a person is 'connected' with a company if *either*:

(*a*) he is a director or shadow director of the company or an associate of such director or shadow director; *or*

(*b*) he is an associate of the company.

The term 'associate' for this purpose has a wide and detailed definition set out in s. 435 of the Act. It covers a great variety of family, partnership, employment, trust and corporate relationships.

Section 166 imposes a restriction on the powers of a liquidator in a *creditors'* voluntary winding up during the period after the liquidator has been nominated by the company and before the holding of the creditors' meeting under s. 98, at which a different person may be nominated as liquidator (*see* **11**). The restriction is that the liquidator during that period requires the sanction of the court for the exercise of his powers, except that he may, without sanction:

(*a*) take into his custody or under his control all the property to which the company is or appears to be entitled;

(*b*) dispose of perishable goods and other goods the value of which is likely to diminish if they are not immediately disposed of; and

(*c*) do all such other things as may be necessary for the protection of the company's assets.

It is further provided that the liquidator must attend the creditors' meeting held under s. 98 and report to the meeting on any exercise by him of his powers.

15. Summoning of general meetings of creditors or contributories.

By s. 168(2) the liquidator *may* summon general meetings of the creditors or contributories to ascertain their wishes; and it is his *duty* to summon meetings when the creditors or contributories by resolution direct him to do so or when he is requested in writing to do so by one-tenth in value of the creditors or contributories (as the case may be).

Section 168(2) applies also to the liquidator in a winding up by the court.

16. Court's power to appoint and remove liquidator in voluntary winding up.

Section 108(1) empowers the court to appoint a liquidator in a voluntary winding up if from any cause whatever there is no liquidator acting.

Section 108(2) empowers the court to remove a liquidator *on cause shown* and to appoint another.

The widely worded phrase 'on cause shown' is clearly intended to give the court an unfettered discretion in the matter, and the expression certainly includes insanity, bias, dishonesty, and undesirability on any grounds.

17. Notice by liquidator of his appointment.

Regardless of the manner in which he is appointed, the liquidator is required within 14 days by s. 109 to publish in the *Gazette* and deliver to the registrar a notice of his appointment.

If the appointment is not duly notified and is not shown by the company to have been known at the time to the person concerned then, under s. 42 Companies Act 1985, it cannot be relied on by the company against that person.

18. Removal of liquidator in voluntary winding up otherwise

than by order of court. Section 171(2) provides that, as a general rule, the liquidator in a voluntary winding up may be removed from office only by an order of the court (*see* **16**) or:

(*a*) in a *members'* voluntary winding up, by a general meeting of the company summoned specially for that purpose; or

(*b*) in a *creditors'* voluntary winding up, by a general meeting of the company's creditors summoned specially for that purpose.

By s. 171(3), however, there is this exception: if the liquidator was appointed by the court under s. 108 (*see* **16**), a meeting for replacing him can only be summoned if he thinks fit *or* the court so directs *or* the meeting is requested:

(*a*) in a *members'* voluntary winding up, by members representing at least one half of the total voting rights; or

(*b*) in a *creditors'* voluntary winding up, by at least one half in value of the company's creditors.

19. Vacation of office by liquidator in voluntary winding up. By s. 171(4) a liquidator must vacate office if he ceases to be a person who is qualified to act as an insolvency practitioner in relation to the company.

He must also, by s. 171(6), vacate office after the holding of the final meeting or, in the case of a creditors' voluntary winding up, meetings, as soon as he has complied with the requirement for giving notice to the registrar that the meeting or meetings have been held and of the decisions (if any) of the meeting or meetings.

Section 171(5) provides that a liquidator may, in prescribed circumstances, resign his office by giving notice of his resignation to the registrar.

20. Release of liquidator in voluntary winding up. The release of the liquidator in a voluntary winding up is dealt with in s. 173.

By s. 173(2) a person who has ceased to be a liquidator has his release from the following times:

(*a*) if he has been removed from office by a general meeting of the company or of the company's creditors which has not resolved against his release, or if he has died, the time at which notice is given to the registrar that he has ceased to hold office;

(*b*) if he has been removed from office by a general meeting of creditors which has resolved against his release, or by the court, or if he has vacated office under s. 171(4) (no longer qualified to act as insolvency practitioner), the time fixed by the Secretary of State on an application being made to him by that person;

(*c*) if he has resigned, the time prescribed;

(*d*) if he has vacated office under s. 171(6) (after the holding of the final meeting of the company in a members' voluntary winding up, or the holding of the final meetings of the company and of creditors in a creditors' voluntary winding up), the time at which he vacated office, unless the final meeting of creditors resolved against his release, in which case he must apply to the Secretary of State for a time to be fixed.

The effect of a release is to discharge the liquidator from all liability for his conduct in the winding up, but this does not prevent the exercise of the summary remedy under s. 212 against a liquidator who has misapplied the company's property or been guilty of any misfeasance or breach of any duty in relation to the company: s. 173(4).

21. Power of liquidator to sell the company's property for shares. Usually the liquidator sells the undertaking and all the property of the company for *cash*, which is then distributed in the normal way to creditors and members. But sometimes he sells them for *shares* in another company, so that the members, instead of receiving their capital and any surplus assets in the form of money, become *shareholders in another company*.

In the final chapter we shall consider the various methods of company reconstruction and amalgamation, of which this is one. At this point, however, we must consider the provisions of s. 110 which enable the liquidator to make this arrangement.

Section 110(1)–(3) states that when a company is in *voluntary liquidation*, and the whole or part of its business or property is to be transferred to *another company*, the liquidator may, with the sanction of a *special resolution*, accept in compensation *shares in the transferee company* for distribution among the members of the transferor company.

Section 110(5) states that such an arrangement is binding on the members of the transferor company, but s. 111(1) and (2) protects dissentients. It permits any member who did not vote in favour of the special resolution to dissent in writing to the liquidator at the registered office within seven days of the passing of the resolution, and to require the liquidator *either* to abstain from implementing the arrangement *or* to purchase his shares.

If, as is usually the case, the liquidator decides to purchase his shares, s. 111(3) states that the purchase-money must be paid before the company is dissolved, and that it must be raised by the liquidator in such way as is determined by special resolution.

The provisions of ss. 110 and 111 apply in exactly the same way in a *creditors'* voluntary winding up, except that s. 110(3) prevents the liquidator from exercising his powers without the *sanction of the court or the liquidation committee*.

22. Expenses of voluntary winding up. By s. 115 all expenses properly incurred in the winding up, including the remuneration of the liquidator, are paid out of the company's assets in priority to all other claims.

23. Right of creditor or contributory to winding up by the court. Section 116 states that the fact that a company is in voluntary liquidation does not bar the right of a creditor or contributory to have it wound up *by the court*, if there are proper grounds. If a contributory should apply, however, the court will not make an order for winding up by the court unless it is satisfied that the rights of the contributories will be prejudiced by a voluntary winding up.

Progress test 29

1. When may a company be wound up voluntarily? (**1**)

2. At what moment does a voluntary winding up commence? (**2**)

3. What are the consequences of a voluntary winding up? (**3**)

4. What is the importance of the declaration of solvency? By whom is it made, and to whom is it submitted? (**4**)

5. In a members' voluntary liquidation, who appoints the liquidator? (**5**)

6. Give an account of the liquidator's duty to call meetings in a members' voluntary winding up. (**6, 7**)

7. If, in a members' voluntary winding up, the liquidator suddenly realises that the company is not solvent after all, what should he do?   (**8**)

8. Give the statutory provisions relating to the first meeting of creditors in a creditors' voluntary winding up.   (**9**)

9. In a creditors' voluntary liquidation, who appoints the liquidator?   (**10**)

10. State the rules which apply to the liquidation committee in a creditors' voluntary winding up.   (**11**)

11. Give an account of the liquidator's duty to call meetings in a creditors' voluntary winding up.   (**9, 12, 13**)

12. What are the powers of the liquidator in a voluntary winding up?   (**14**)

13. In what circumstances is it the duty of the liquidator in a voluntary winding up to summon meetings of creditors or contributories at the request of such persons?   (**15**)

14. What are the powers of the court regarding appointment and removal of the liquidator in a voluntary winding up?   (**16**)

15. How may a liquidator in a voluntary winding up be removed otherwise than by an order of the court?   (**18**)

16. When must a liquidator in a voluntary winding up vacate office?   (**19**)

17. How does a liquidator in a voluntary winding up obtain his release?   (**20**)

18. Give an account of the statutory provisions regarding the power of the liquidator to sell the company's business or property for shares in another company instead of for cash.   (**21**)

30
Winding up by the court

1. Circumstances in which a company may be wound up by the court. Section 122(1) Insolvency Act 1986 states that a company may be wound up by the court if:

(*a*) the company has passed a special resolution to that effect;

(*b*) a public company registered as such on its original incorporation has not been issued with a certificate under s. 117 Companies Act 1985 within a year from registration (*see* **5:3**);

(*c*) the company does not commence business within one year from incorporation or suspends business for a whole year;

(*d*) the number of members is reduced below two;

(*e*) the company is unable to pay its debts;

(*f*) the court is of the opinion that it is just and equitable that the company should be wound up.

2. Definition of inability to pay debts. Section 123 explains what is meant by s. 122(*e*), and states that a company is deemed unable to pay its debts if:

(*a*) a creditor for more than £750 has served on the company a demand for the sum due, and the company has for three weeks neglected to pay it or to secure or compound for it to his satisfaction; *or*

(*b*) execution is unsatisfied; *or*

(*c*) it is proved to the court's satisfaction that the company is unable to pay its debts as they fall due; *or*

(*d*) it is proved to the court's satisfaction that the value of the company's assets is less than the amount of its liabilities, taking into account its contingent and prospective liabilities.

3. The meaning of 'just and equitable'. The court's power under s. 122 to wind a company up on the ground that it is just and equitable to do so is purely discretionary. There is therefore no definite number of occasions on which the court will exercise its power, but it has done so in the following cases:

(*a*) Where the substratum or main object has failed: *Re German Date Coffee Co.* (1882) (*see* 2:**19**).

(*b*) Where there was deadlock in the management: *Re Yenidje Tobacco Co. Ltd.* (1916).

(*c*) Where the company was formed for a fraudulent purpose.

(*d*) Where the company was a 'bubble', i.e. it never in fact had any business or property.

(*e*) Where a director had voting control and refused to hold meetings, produce accounts or pay dividends: *Loch* v. *John Blackwood Ltd.* (1924).

(*f*) Where, in a private company which distributed its profits as directors' remuneration and paid no dividends, all three of the members were directors, and one of them was removed from office as director under what is now s. 303 Companies Act 1985 by the other two: *Ebrahimi* v. *Westbourne Galleries Ltd.* (1973).

Here the House of Lords held that the words 'just and equitable' are *general words* of wide application and must not be restricted:

(*i*) to particular instances; nor

(*ii*) by the previous clauses of the section; nor

(*iii*) to cases where *mala fides* can be proved; nor

(*iv*) to circumstances where the petitioner is wronged in his capacity of *shareholder*.

Further, while the concepts of probity, good faith and mutual confidence, and the remedies where these are absent, developed in the law of partnership, they apply in the same way to registered companies, and it is merely confusing to refer to small companies of this kind as 'quasi-partnerships'. Individuals in companies have rights and obligations *inter se* which are not submerged in the company structure, and the 'just and equitable' provision enables the court to subject the exercise of legal rights (such as the right to remove a director under what is now s. 303 Companies Act 1985) to equitable considerations.

The court will not, however, grant an injunction to *prevent* the exercise of legal rights, even though it may give a remedy for the inequitable use of them: *Bentley-Stevens* v. *Jones* (1974).

Where the entitlement to management participation is the basis of the relationship between the members, it appears that exclusion from management will be a ground for winding up whether it arises from the inequitable exercise of legal rights or a repudiation of the legal rights of others: *Re A & B.C. Chewing Gum* (1975).

4. The presentation of the winding-up petition. While s. 122 (*see* **1**) gives the *grounds* on which a company may be wound up by the court, s. 124 gives the *persons* by whom the petition for winding up may be presented.

Under s. 124 there are *the following possible petitioners*:

(*a*) The *company*, after passing a special resolution (*see* **1**).

(*b*) The *directors*.

(*c*) A *creditor*, including a contingent or prospective creditor.

A judgment creditor has a right to a winding-up order even though the company has a disputed claim for a larger sum against him: *Re Douglas Griggs Engineering Co.* (1963).

(*d*) A *contributory*, whether A list or B list. Despite the definition of a contributory in s. 79(1), the term includes for the purposes of s. 124 a holder of *fully-paid shares* (*see* **28:1, 2**).

A contributory, however, may petition only if one of the following conditions is fulfilled:

(*i*) if the membership is reduced below the statutory minimum (*see* **2:34**); *or*

(*ii*) if he is an original allottee; *or*

(*iii*) if he has held his shares for any six out of the previous 18 months; *or*

(*iv*) if the shares devolved on him through the death of a former holder.

The last three provisions are designed to prevent a person from buying shares in a company with the sole intention of qualifying himself to bring a winding-up petition. Section 124(3), however, permits a contributory to bring a winding-up petition under grounds (*e*) or (*f*) where he is liable under s. 76 (*see* **11:36**).

A *personal representative* of a *deceased* contributory, even though he is not registered as a member in respect of the shares, is a contributory for the purposes of s. 124: *Re Bayswater Trading Co. Ltd.* (1970). An *unregistered* allottee of shares is likewise a contributory for the purposes of s. 124 since there is nothing in that section which expressly requires registration: *Re J.N.2 Ltd.* (1978). An unregistered *trustee in bankruptcy* of a *bankrupt* contributory, however, is not: *Re Bolton Engineering Co. Ltd.* (1956).

(*e*) The *Secretary of State*, if the ground of the petition is that specified in s. 122(1)(*b*) or in a case falling within s. 440 Companies Act 1985 (expedient in the public interest, following report of inspectors, etc.) (*see* 22:7).

(*f*) The *official receiver*, where the company is already in voluntary liquidation, and the interests of the creditors or contributories are not adequately protected.

An example of this occurred in *Re Ryder Installations Ltd.* (1966), where the voluntary liquidator's conduct was irregular and his accounts unsatisfactory.

The statutory right to present a winding-up petition in accordance with the section cannot in any way be restricted or excluded by provisions to that effect in the articles.

5. Non-statutory rules concerning petitioners. Apart from the possible petitioners under s. 124, there are decisions establishing that the following persons may present a winding up petition:

(*a*) a secured creditor (who will not lose his security by doing so);

(*b*) a creditor's executor;

(*c*) an assignee of a debt or part of a debt, including an equitable assignee;

(*d*) a holder of bearer debentures;

(*e*) a mortgagee who intends to exercise his power of sale (but he will be restrained from so doing until his petition is heard);

(*f*) a shareholder whose calls are in arrear (but he must first pay the amount of the call into court).

Conversely, the holder of a share warrant cannot present a petition.

6. Powers of court on hearing petition. Section 125(1) empowers the court to dismiss the petition, or adjourn the hearing, or make any order that it thinks fit, but states that it *must not refuse* to make a winding-up order merely because the assets have been fully mortgaged or because there are no assets at all. Despite this provision, however, a fully-paid shareholder is not entitled to a winding-up order unless he can show that he, as a member of the company, will achieve some advantage or avoid or minimize some disadvantage which would accrue to him by virtue of his membership: *Re Chesterfield Catering Co. Ltd.* (1977).

Section 125(2) states that where the petition is presented by members on the ground that it is just and equitable that the company should be wound up, the court must make a winding-up order unless it is of the opinion that the petitioners have some other remedy available to them, and that they are acting unreasonably in failing to pursue it. A good example of this situation occurred in *Charles Forte Investments* v. *Amanda* (1964) (*see* 12:7).

7. Power of court to stay proceedings against the company. Section 126 is a section applying only to the period of time *after* the presentation of the petition and *before* a winding-up order has been made.

It states that during this period the company, or any creditor or contributory, may apply to the appropriate court to stay any proceedings which are pending against the company, and the court may do so.

8. The commencement of winding up by the court. Section 129(1) states that where *before the presentation of a petition* for winding up by the court, the company has passed a resolution for *voluntary* winding up, the winding up is deemed to have commenced *at the time of the passing of the resolution.*

Section 129(2) states that in all other cases (i.e. where the company has *not* previously resolved to wind up voluntarily) a winding up by the court commences *at the time of the presentation of the petition.*

It is helpful at this point to compare s. 86 which deals with the moment of commencement of a voluntary winding up, stating that it is the time of the passing of the resolution to wind up. This explains the provisions of s. 129(1), and the two sections should always be studied together.

9. The consequences of a winding-up order. Once the winding-up order is made, its consequences *date back* to the commencement of the winding up. This is the reason why it is essential to know exactly when the moment of commencement is. Section 129(2), as we have just seen, states that as a rule it is *the time of the presentation of the petition*, so that in the normal case the consequences of the winding-up order will date back to that time.

These consequences are:

(*a*) Under s. 127, any disposition of the company's property, any transfer of shares, and any alteration in the status of members is void, unless the court orders otherwise.

(*b*) Under s. 128(1), any execution against the company's property is void.

(*c*) Under s. 130(1), a copy of the winding-up order must be sent at once by the company to the registrar who, under s. 711 Companies Act 1985, must publish notice of its receipt by him in the *Gazette*.

If its receipt had not been officially notified by the registrar at the material time and if the company cannot show that it was known at that time to the person concerned, then, under s. 42 Companies Act 1985, the company cannot rely on the making of the order against that person.

(*d*) Under s. 130(2), actions against the company are stayed. (This section does not come into operation until the winding-up order is made, and s. 126 no longer applies.)

(*e*) Under s. 136(2) the official receiver automatically becomes the liquidator, unless, under s. 140, the court appoints as liquidator the person who has just ceased to be the administrator of the company under an administration order or the person who has been the supervisor under an approved voluntary arrangement.

(*f*) The powers of the directors cease.

(*g*) The servants of the company are dismissed.

10. The official receiver. The appointment and functions of official receivers are provided for in ss. 399–401. Official receivers are appointed by the Secretary of State for Trade and Industry and are attached to the courts. Their functions extend to individual bankruptcy as well as to the winding up of companies. The Secretary of State may, in order to facilitate the disposal of the business of the official receiver attached to any court, appoint an officer of his own department to act as deputy to that official receiver.

11. The provisional liquidator. Section 135(1) and (2) empowers the court to appoint a provisional liquidator at any time *after* the presentation of the petition and *before* the making of the winding-up order. Either the official receiver or any other fit person may be appointed.

This is a purely *temporary* appointment, for as soon as the winding-up order is made the official receiver automatically becomes the liquidator (*see* 9(*e*)). It is not made in every case, but only where proof by affidavit is given that there are sufficient grounds for the appointment, usually that the assets are in jeopardy.

To secure the appointment, application must be made to the court by a creditor, a contributory, or the company. If the court grants the application, it must notify the official receiver who is usually, though not necessarily, the person appointed.

Section 135(4) and (5) makes it clear that the powers of the provisional liquidator depend on the order appointing him. He is merely a receiver, his function being to protect the assets of the company; thus he cannot sell the assets unless they are perishable.

12. The appointment of the liquidator. Section 136 deals with the functions of the official receiver in relation to the office of liquidator, but it must be remembered that these provisions are subject to s. 140 by which in certain circumstances the court may appoint the administrator or supervisor as the case may be (*see* 9).

Section 136(2), as we have already seen in 9(*e*), states that as soon as the winding-up order is made, the *official receiver* automatically becomes *liquidator* and acts as such until another person is appointed. This occurs in *every* compulsory liquidation and is in no way connected with the appointment of a *provisional* liquidator under s. 135 between the time of the presentation of the petition and the making of the winding-up order.

Section 136(3) provides that the official receiver is, by virtue of his office, the liquidator during any vacancy.

Section 136(4) entitles the official receiver, at any time when he is the liquidator, to summon separate meetings of the creditors and contributories for the purpose of choosing a person to be liquidator in his place. By s. 136(5)(*c*) he *must* summon such meetings if he is at any time requested to do so by one quarter in value of the company's creditors.

By s. 137(1) the official receiver may, at any time when he is the liquidator, apply to the Secretary of State for the appointment of a person as liquidator in his place.

If the official receiver has exercised his power of summoning meetings under s. 136, but no person has been chosen to be liquidator as a result of those meetings, then it is the duty of the official receiver to decide whether to refer the need for an appointment to the Secretary of State: s. 137(2).

On an application under s. 137(1) or a reference under s. 137(2) the Secretary of State may, by s. 137(3), either make or decline to make an appointment. If he makes an appointment, then the liquidator, by s. 137(4), must notify his appointment to the company's creditors.

Section 139 deals with the choice of a liquidator at the meetings of creditors and contributories summoned for that purpose. Each meeting may nominate a person to be liquidator and the creditors' nomination prevails if different persons are nominated, except that a creditor or contributory may, within seven days of the creditors' nomination, apply to the court for an order appointing the contributories' nominee or some other person as liquidator instead of the creditors' nominee.

13. The statement of affairs. Section 131(1) states that where the court has made a winding-up order, a statement of the company's affairs must, unless the court orders otherwise, be made out and *submitted to the official receiver.*

It must be in the prescribed form, verified by affidavit, and show:

(*a*) particulars of assets, debts and liabilities;

(*b*) names and addresses of creditors;

(*c*) securities held by them, and the dates when these were given; and

(*d*) any further information which may be prescribed or which the official receiver may require.

Section 131(3) states that the statement must be submitted and verified by some or all of the following persons, as the official receiver may require:

(*a*) past or present officers of the company;

(*b*) persons who have taken part in its formation within one year before the winding-up order;

(*c*) persons who are, or have been within that year, in the company's 'employment' (widely defined in s. 131(6) as including employment under a contract for services) and who are capable of giving the requir d information;

(*d*) persons who are, or have been within that year, officers or in the employment of another company which is, or has been within that year, an officer of the company now in liquidation.

Section 131(4) requires the statement to be submitted *within 21 days* from the official liquidator's notice requiring it.

14. Investigation by official receiver. Section 132(1) requires the official receiver to investigate:

(*a*) if the company has failed, the causes of its failure; and

(*b*) generally, the promotion, formation, business dealings and affairs of the company;

and to make such report (if any) to the court as he thinks fit.

The official receiver may also, at any time during the winding up, apply to the court for the public examination of officers and others under s. 133 (*see* **35**).

15. Summary of the duties of the official receiver.

(*a*) He may be appointed *provisional liquidator after* the presentation of the petition and *before* the winding-up order is made, under s. 135. He is then merely a receiver and his function is to protect the assets during this intervening period.

(*b*) He becomes the *liquidator* automatically in all cases as soon as the winding-up order is made, under s. 136(2) (unless the court makes an appointment under s. 140). He acts as liquidator until another person is appointed.

(*c*) He may summon separate *meetings* of creditors and contributories, under s. 136(4) for the purpose of choosing a person to be liquidator in his place.

(*d*) He may apply to the *Secretary of State* for the appointment of a liquidator, under s. 137.

(*e*) He is, by virtue of his office, the *liquidator* during any *vacancy* under s. 136(3).

(*f*) He receives and considers the *statement of affairs*, under s. 131.

(*g*) He makes an *investigation* and may *report* to the court, under s. 132.

(*h*) He may apply to the court for the *public examination* of officers and others under s. 133 and take part in that examination.

16. Resignation and vacation of office of liquidator. Section 172(6) provides that a liquidator may, in prescribed circumstances, *resign* his office by giving notice of his resignation to the court.

By s. 172(5) a liquidator or provisional liquidator (other than the official receiver) must *vacate office* if he ceases to be a person who is qualified to act as an insolvency practitioner in relation to the company.

The other case in which a liquidator must *vacate office* comes at the end of the winding up. If it appears to the liquidator that the winding up is for practical purposes complete and if the liquidator is not the official receiver, the liquidator must, by s. 146(1), summon a final general meeting of the creditors to receive his report on the winding up. The liquidator must then, by s. 172(8), vacate office as soon as he has given notice to the court and the registrar of companies that the meeting has been held and of its decisions (if any).

17. Removal of liquidator. Two subsections of s. 172 deal with removal of a liquidator.

Section 172(4) provides that if the liquidator was appointed by the Secretary of State, he may be removed from office by a direction of the Secretary of State.

Section 172(2) covers all other cases: it provides that the liquidator may be removed from office only by an order of the court or by a general meeting of the creditors summoned specially for that purpose, and that a provisional liquidator may be removed from office only by an order of the court.

18. Release of liquidator. The release of the liquidator is dealt with in s. 174.

By s. 174(2) where the official receiver has ceased to be liquidator and a person becomes liquidator in his stead, the official receiver has his release:

(*a*) if the person was nominated by a general meeting of creditors or contributories, or was appointed by the Secretary of State, from the time at which the official receiver gives notice to the court that he has been replaced;

(*b*) if the person is appointed by the court, from the time fixed by the court.

By s. 174(3) if the official receiver while he is a liquidator gives notice to the Secretary of State that the winding up is for practical purposes complete, he has his release from the time fixed by the Secretary of State.

By s. 174(4) a person other than the official receiver who has ceased to be a liquidator has his release from the following times:

(*a*) if he has been removed from office by a general meeting of creditors which has not resolved against his release, or if he has died, the time at which notice is given to the court that he has ceased to hold office;

(*b*) if he has been removed from office by a general meeting of creditors which has resolved against his release, or by the court or the Secretary of State or if he has vacated office under s. 172(5) (no longer qualified to act as insolvency practitioner), the time fixed by the Secretary of State on an application being made to him by that person;

(*c*) if he has resigned, the time prescribed;

(*d*) if he has vacated office under s. 172(8) (on the completion of winding up), the time at which he vacated office unless the final meeting resolved against his release, in which case he must apply to the Secretary of State for a time to be fixed.

By s. 174(5) a person who has ceased to hold office as a provisional liquidator has his release from the time fixed by the court on an application being made by him.

The effect of a release is to discharge the official receiver or a liquidator or provisional liquidator from all liability for his conduct in the winding up, but this does not prevent the exercise of the summary remedy under s. 212 against a liquidator who has misapplied the company's property or been guilty of any misfeasance or breach of any duty in relation to the company: s. 174(6).

19. General functions of liquidator. By s. 143(1) the functions of the liquidator are to secure that the assets of the company are got in, realised and distributed to the creditors and, if there is a surplus, to the persons entitled to it.

By s. 143(2), if the liquidator is not the official receiver, it is his duty:

(*a*) to furnish the official receiver with such information,

(*b*) to produce to the official receiver, and allow him to inspect, such books, papers and other records, and

(*c*) to give him such other assistance,

as the official receiver may reasonably require for the purposes of carrying out his functions in relation to the winding up.

20. The position of the liquidator regarding the company's property. Section 144 states that the liquidator obtains *custody and control* of the company's property. It is important to notice that he does not obtain *title* to it, i.e. *ownership*, unless he applies to the court under s. 145(1) for a *vesting order* to be made and the court makes an order to that effect.

This is one of the ways in which a liquidation differs from a bankruptcy, for in a bankruptcy the property of the debtor (with minor exceptions) vests in the trustee in bankruptcy.

21. Duty to summon final meeting. If it appears to the liquidator that the winding up is for practical purposes complete and if the liquidator is not the official receiver, the liquidator must, by s. 146(1), summon a final general meeting of the creditors to receive his report of the winding up and to decide whether he should have his release under s. 174.

By s. 146(3) it is the duty of the liquidator to retain sufficient sums from the company's property to cover the expenses of summoning and holding this final meeting.

22. Liquidation committee. Section 141 deals with the liquidation committee which may be set up in a winding up by the court.

By s. 141(1), where separate meetings of creditors and contributories have been summoned for the purpose of choosing a person to be liquidator, those meetings may establish the liquidation committee.

Alternatively, by s. 141(2) the liquidator, provided he is not the official receiver, may at any time, if he thinks fit, summon separate general meetings of the creditors and contributories to decide whether such a committee should be established. Further, he *must* summon such a meeting if he is requested to do so by one-tenth in value of the creditors.

If the meetings of creditors and contributories are in disagreement as to whether a committee should be established, a committee must be established unless the court orders otherwise: s. 141(3).

By s. 141(4) the liquidation committee is not able or required to carry out its functions at any time when the official receiver is liquidator; at such a time its functions are vested in the Secretary of State except to the extent that rules made under s. 411 provide otherwise.

Where there is for the time being no liquidation committee, and the liquidator is a person other than the official receiver, the functions of such a committee are vested in the Secretary of State except to the extent that the rules provide otherwise: s. 141(5).

23. The powers of the liquidator. The powers of the liquidator in a winding up by the court are to be found in s. 167 taken along with the 4th Schedule. The form and contents of that Schedule have already been detailed in relation to voluntary winding up (*see* 29:**14**) and may therefore be more briefly treated here.

Section 167(1) provides that in a winding up by the court any of the powers specified in Parts I and II of the 4th Schedule may be exercised by the liquidator with the sanction of the court or the liquidation committee, and that any of the general powers in Part III of that Schedule may be exercised by him with or without sanction.

By s. 167(2) where the liquidator (provided he is not the official receiver) in the exercise of his powers disposes of any of the company's property to a person who is 'connected' with the company or employs a solicitor to assist him in the carrying out of his functions, he must, if there is for the time being a liquidation committee, give notice to the committee of that exercise of his powers. The term 'connected' is defined in s. 249 (*see* 29:**14**).

Section 167(3) provides that the liquidator, in exercising any of the powers conferred by s. 167 and the 4th Schedule, is subject to the control of the court, and empowers any creditor or contributory to apply to the court regarding them.

24. Supplementary powers of liquidator. Section 168(2) empowers the liquidator to call meetings of creditors or contributories in order to ascertain their wishes, and requires him to do so whenever the creditors or contributories *by resolution so direct*, or whenever *requested in writing* to do so by *one-tenth in value* of the creditors or contributories.

Section 168(3) empowers the liquidator to apply to the court for directions in any matter which arises in the winding up, and s. 168(5) enables any person who is aggrieved by an act of the liquidator to apply to the court, which may then make such order as it thinks just.

25. Liability of the liquidator. We have already seen that the ownership of the company's property remains in the company and does not pass to the liquidator on the making of the winding-up order (**20**). He is not, therefore, a *trustee* either for the company or for the creditors or contributories, any more than a director is (*see* 16:**56**).

He is, however, in a *fiduciary relation* towards the company and the creditors, and for *breach of the many statutory duties* imposed on him he will be liable to pay damages to any creditor or contributory who has been injured by the breach. Moreover, if he is *negligent* in his application of the company's assets, he will likewise incur liability to any person who suffers as a result, and proceedings can be taken against him, as against a promoter, director, or any officer of the company under s. 212 for *misfeasance* (*see* 31:**13**).

In *Pulsford* v. *Devenish* (1903), the liquidator advertised in the usual way for creditors to make their claims against the company, but took no further steps to notify a creditor whose debt appeared in the company's books, but who did not know of the liquidation. HELD: The liquidator was liable to compensate him.

26. General powers of the court. The remainder of the sections on compulsory winding up deal with the powers of the court. Some of these powers must be considered in detail, and the rest of this chapter is concerned with them, but others require no explanation, and a short list of them will suffice:

(*a*) Section 147 empowers the court to *stay the winding up proceedings* at any time in a proper case, on the application of the liquidator, the official receiver, any creditor or contributory.

(*b*) Section 148 requires the court to *settle a list of contributories*, and empowers it to *rectify the register of members*. It also requires it to *collect the company's assets and apply them towards its liabilities*. A list of contributories is not necessary where calls need not be made on them.

(*c*) Section 150 empowers the court to *make calls* on the contributories on the list.

(*d*) Section 153 empowers the court to *fix a time within which creditors must prove their debts*, or be excluded from the benefit of any distribution made before proof.

(*e*) Section 155 empowers the court to specify the rights of inspection of the company's books and papers by creditors and contributories.

Under s. 160 the powers of the court conferred by ss. 148, 150 and 153 may be *delegated to the liquidator* as an officer of the court and subject to the control of the court, though he may not, without the special leave of the court, *rectify the register of members*. Nor can he *make a call* without either the special leave of the court or the sanction of the liquidation committee.

27. Extent to which set-off allowed. Section 149(1) empowers the court to order any contributory to pay any money which he owes to the company, exclusive of calls. If, however, the company at the same time owes money to the contributory, s. 149(3) allows the debts to be set off against each other *when all the creditors have been paid in full*.

Further, it has been held that set-off must be allowed when the contributory *becomes bankrupt* after the commencement of the winding up.

28. Court's power of public examination. Section 133(1) provides that the official receiver *may* at any time during the winding up apply to the court for the public examination of any person who is or has been an officer of the company, or has acted as liquidator or administrator or as receiver or manager or has in some other way taken part in the company's promotion, formation or management.

By s. 133(2) the official receiver *must* make such an application, unless the court orders otherwise, if he is requested to do so by:

(*a*) one-half in value of the creditors; or
(*b*) three-quarters in value of the contributories.

If the court directs that a public examination be held, the person concerned must attend on a day appointed by the court and be publicly examined as to the promotion, formation or management of the company or as to the conduct or its business and affairs, or his conduct or dealings in relation to the company; s. 133(3).

Questions concerning these matters may, by s. 133(4), be put by any of the following persons:

(*a*) the official receiver;

(*b*) the liquidator;

(*c*) any person who has been appointed as special manager of the company's property or business (*see* 31:**3**);

(*d*) any creditor who has tendered a proof in the winding up; and

(*e*) any contributory.

29. Court's power to arrest absconding contributory. It has been said that by far the most delightful section in the Companies Act 1948 was s. 271, giving the court power to arrest a contributory. The section, now s. 158 Insolvency Act 1986, states that on proof that a contributory is about to quit the United Kingdom or to abscond or to remove or conceal his property in order to evade payment of calls, the court may have him arrested, and his books, papers and movable personal property seized, and him and them safely kept for such time as the court may order.

NOTE: The meaning is clear, but the language picturesque, conjuring up an image of a disconsolate contributory incarcerated along with and entirely surrounded by his books, papers, and movable personal property, while acres of good arable land (unaffected by the section) lie abandoned.

30. Dissolution. Where a winding up follows its full course, the procedure for the dissolution of the company is governed by s. 205.

By s. 205(1) the registrar of companies will have received *either*:

(*a*) a notice under s. 172(8) from the liquidator (other than the official receiver) that a final meeting of creditors has been held to consider the liquidator's report; *or*

(*b*) a notice from the official receiver that the winding up is complete.

On receiving either notice, the registrar must immediately register it, and at the end of three months after that registration, the company is dissolved: s. 205(2).

This is, however, subject to the exception that the Secretary of State, if applied to by the official receiver or by any other person appearing to be interested, may defer the date of the dissolution for such period as he thinks fit: s. 205(3).

By s. 205(4) an appeal may be made to the court against the Secretary of State's decision, and by s. 205(5) it is the duty of the person who has applied for such a deferment to deliver to the registrar a copy of the Secretary of State's direction within seven days after it has been given.

31. Early dissolution. An alternative to dissolution under s. 205 is the early dissolution procedure provided for by ss. 202–203. Up to a third of the companies which go into compulsory liquidation have few or no assets, and the aim of this alternative procedure is to save the time of the official receiver and the expense of following through the full procedure.

Section 202(2) provides that the early dissolution procedure is available only if the official receiver is the liquidator and if it appears to him:

(*a*) that the realisable assets are insufficient to cover the expenses of the winding up; *and*

(*b*) that the affairs of the company do not require any further investigation.

The application is made by the official receiver to the registrar of companies and, by s. 202(3), the official receiver must give at least 28 days' notice of his intention to make such application to the creditors and contributories and to the administrative receiver (if any). With the giving of that notice the official receiver, by s. 202(4), ceases to be required to perform any duties in relation to the company.

The official receiver's application under s. 202(2) is registered by the registrar and at the end of three months from registration the company is dissolved: s. 202(5).

Section 203(1)–(3) permits an application to be made by the official receiver or any creditor or contributory or the administrative receiver (if any) to the Secretary of State for a direction that the winding up should proceed as if no notice under s. 202(3) had been given, on the ground that:

(*a*) the realisable assets are sufficient to cover the expenses of the winding up; or

(*b*) the affairs of the company do require further investigation; or (*c*) the early dissolution is for any other reason inappropriate.

The Secretary of State may also defer the date of the dissolution beyond the three-months' period.

In s. 203(4) and (5) there are the same provisions as in s. 205(4) and (5), respectively, regarding appeal to court against a Secretary of State's direction and regarding delivery of a copy of his direction to the registrar within seven days.

Progress test 30

1. In what circumstances may a company be wound up by the court? (**1**)

2. Discuss the court's power to wind up a company when it thinks it just and equitable to do so. (**3**)

3. Who may present a winding-up petition? (**4**)

4. At what moment does a winding up by the court commence? (**8**)

5. What are the consequences of a winding-up order? (**9**)

6. Under what circumstances may a provisional liquidator be appointed after the presentation of the winding up petition and before the making of the winding up order? Who may apply for his appointment, and what are his powers? (**11**)

7. Give the statutory provisions on the appointment of a liquidator in a winding up by the court. (**12**)

8. What are the contents of the statement of affairs? Who submits it, and to whom is it submitted? (**13**)

9. Who is the official receiver? What are his duties? (**10, 12–15**)

10. In what manner may a liquidator resign? (**16**)

11. How may a liquidator be removed from office? (**17**)

12. How does the liquidator obtain his release? (**18**)

13. What is the legal position of the liquidator with regard to the company's property? (**20**)

14. What is the procedure for establishing a liquidation committee? (**22**)

15. What are the powers of the liquidator in a winding up by the court? (**23**)

16. When is the liquidator required to call a meeting of creditors or contributories? (**24**)

17. Discuss the liability of the liquidator. (**25**)

18. How far is a set-off allowed between a company and its contributories? (**27**)

19. Give an account of the court's power of public examination. (**28**)

20. What is the procedure for dissolution where a winding up runs its full course? (**30**)

21. In what circumstances is an accelerated dissolution permissible, and what is the procedure for obtaining it? (**31**)

31

Provisions of general application in winding up

1. Proof of debts. Provisions as to the debts which may be proved in a winding up, as to the manner and conditions of proving a debt and as to the manner and expenses of establishing the value of any debt or security are amongst the matters capable of inclusion in rules made by statutory instrument under s. 411 and the 8th Schedule.

2. Preferential debts. Section 175(1) provides that the company's preferential debts, listed in the 6th Schedule, must be paid in priority to all other debts.

By s. 175(2) they rank equally among themselves after the expenses of the winding up and must be paid in full, unless the assets are insufficient to meet them, in which case they abate in equal proportions.

Section 175(2) further provides that preferential debts have priority over the claims of holders of a floating charge created by the company.

There are five categories of preferential debts listed in the 6th Schedule:

(a) debts due to the Inland Revenue, i.e. principally sums deducted by the company as PAYE from remuneration paid during the preceding year;

(b) debts due to Customs and Excise, i.e. principally VAT referable to the preceding six months, any car tax which has become due within the preceding year, and various duties under the Betting and Gaming Duties Act 1981 which have become due within the preceding year;

(c) social security contributions which have become due within the preceding year;

(d) sums owed by the company as contributions to occupational pension schemes and state scheme premiums;

(e) remuneration, including holiday remuneration, owed by the company to employees for the preceding four months, not exceeding a prescribed amount for each employee, with the same preference extended to sums owed by the company to any person (e.g. a bank) who has advanced money to the company to enable it to pay the remuneration.

The relevant date which fixes the period of the preceding year, six months, etc. for the purposes of these debts is, by s. 387:

(a) in the case of a voluntary winding up, the date of the passing of the resolution for winding up; and

(b) in the case of a winding up by the court, the date of the appointment of a provisional liquidator or, if no such appointment was made, the date of the winding-up order, except that if the winding up by the court has followed immediately upon the discharge of an administration order, the relevant date is the date of the making of the administration order.

Section 176(2) states that when a landlord or other person has distrained on the company's property *within three months* before the winding-up order, the preferential debts are a *first charge* on the goods distrained on, or the proceeds of sale, but, by s. 176(3), the landlord or other person will have the *same priority* as the person to whom the payment is made. Thus a landlord must return the goods distrained on, or the proceeds of sale, if he exercised his rights within the previous three months, but he then ranks equally with the other preferential creditors, over whom he would otherwise have an advantage.

3. Appointment of special manager. Section 177(1) provides that, where a company has gone into liquidation or a provisional liquidator has been appointed, the court may appoint any person to be the special manager of the business or property of the company.

The application may be made by the liquidator or provisional liquidator in any case where it appears to him that the nature of the business or property or the interests of the creditors or contributories or members require the appointment: s. 177(2).

It is for the court to decide what powers the special manager has: s. 177(3) and (4).

His remuneration may be provided for in rules under s. 411 and the 8th Schedule.

4. Disclaimer of onerous property. Sections 178 to 182 deal with a liquidator's power to disclaim onerous property. The law on this subject was substantially amended by the Insolvency Act 1985.

The leading provision is in s. 178(2): the liquidator may, by giving the prescribed notice, disclaim any 'onerous property', even although he has taken possession of it, tried to sell it or in some other way exercised rights of ownership in relation to it.

By s. 178(3) the following is 'onerous property':

(*a*) any unprofitable contract; and

(*b*) any other property of the company which is unsaleable or not readily saleable or is such that it may give rise to a liability to pay money or perform any other onerous act.

The effect of the disclaimer is to terminate the company's rights and liabilities in respect of the property, but not the rights and liabilities of other persons: s. 178(4).

Section 178(5) prevents a liquidator from giving a notice of disclaimer if a person interested in the property has first applied in writing to him requiring him to decide within 28 days whether he will disclaim or not and the liquidator has not given notice of disclaimer within that period.

By s. 178(6) any person who sustains loss or damage as a result of a disclaimer is deemed a creditor of the company to the extent of the loss or damage and so may prove for the loss or damage in the winding up.

Section 181(2) and (3) provides that an application may be made to the court by any person who claims an interest in the disclaimed property or by any person who is under any liability in respect of it (other than a liability discharged by the disclaimer) for the court to make an order for the vesting of the disclaimed property in, or for its delivery to, the applicant or a trustee for him. The effect of any such court order must be taken into account in assessing the loss or damage sustained by any person for the purposes of s. 178(6).

Section 179 provides that a disclaimer of *leasehold* property does not take effect unless a copy of the disclaimer has been served on every underlessee or mortgagee whose address is known to the liquidator, and *either*:

(*a*) no application to the court under s. 181 is made within the next 14 days after the notice; *or*

(*b*) where such an application has been made, the court directs that the disclaimer shall take effect.

By s. 182(1) the court must not make an order under s. 181 vesting leasehold property in any underlessee or mortgagee except on terms making that person:

(*a*) subject to the same liabilities as the company was subject to under the lease at the commencement of the winding up; or

(*b*) if the court thinks fit, subject to the same liabilities as that person would be subject to if the lease had been assigned to him at the commencement of the winding up.

Where no underlessee or mortgagee is willing to accept such terms, the court may vest the company's interest in the property in any person who is liable to perform the lessee's covenants in the lease, and the court may vest the interest in such a person freed from all incumbrances created by the company: s. 182(3).

5. Rights of creditors as to execution or attachment. Section 183(1) states that where a creditor has issued execution against the company's goods or land, or has attached any debt due to the company, he may not keep the benefit of the execution or attachment against the liquidator unless he completed it before *the commencement of the winding up*.

However, by s. 183(2), where a creditor has had notice of a meeting at which a resolution for voluntary winding up is to be proposed, he must complete the execution or attachment *before the date on which he had the notice*.

A person who buys under a sale by the sheriff any of the company's goods on which execution has been levied acquires a good title against the liquidator provided he buys in good faith. Further, the court may set aside the liquidator's rights in favour of the creditor if it thinks fit.

Section 183(3) explains what is meant by 'completion'. It states that execution against goods is completed by seizure and sale, or by the making of a charging order under s. 1 of the Charging Orders Act 1979, attachment by receipt of the debt, and execution against land by seizure, by the appointment of a receiver, or by the making of a charging order as above.

6. Duties of sheriff as to goods taken in execution. Section 184(1) and (2) states that where a company's goods are taken in execution, and *before their sale* notice is served on the sheriff that a provisional liquidator has been appointed, a winding-up order made, or a resolution for voluntary winding up passed, he must if required deliver the goods and any money seized or received in part satisfaction of the execution to the liquidator.

The costs of the execution are a first charge on the goods or money, and the liquidator may sell those goods to satisfy that charge.

Section 184(3) states that where under an execution for a sum of more than £250 goods are sold or money paid to avoid sale, the sheriff must deduct the costs of the execution from the proceeds of sale or the money paid, and *hold the balance for 14 days*. By s. 184(4), if within that time notice is served on him of the presentation of a petition for winding up, or a meeting called at which a resolution for voluntary winding up is to be proposed, and then a winding-up order is in fact made, or the resolution for voluntary winding up passed, he *must pay the balance to the liquidator*, who may retain it as against the execution creditor. Notice of a meeting of *creditors*, however, will not defeat the execution creditor. The words of the subsection must be strictly construed, and the execution creditor will only be defeated by notice of a meeting of the *company* to pass a winding-up resolution: *Re T. D. Walton* (1966).

Section 184(5) states again that the court may set aside the liquidator's rights in favour of the creditor if it thinks fit.

7. Rescission of contracts by the court. Section 186(1) permits a person who is, as against the liquidator, entitled to the benefit or subject to the burden of a contract made with the company to apply to the court for the court to make an order rescinding the contract on such terms as to payment by or to either party of damages for non-performance or otherwise as the court thinks just.

By s. 186(2) any damages payable under the order to such a person may be proved by him as a debt in the winding up.

8. Notification of liquidation. Section 188(1) states that where a company is in liquidation, every business document on which the

company's name appears must contain a statement that the company is being wound up.

9. Interest on debts. Interest up to the date of winding up is included in the debt proved by a creditor.

Section 189, which originated in the Insolvency Act 1985, provides for interest in respect of the period for which the debt has been outstanding *since the company went into liquidation.*

Section 189(2) provides that *any surplus remaining after full payment of the debts proved in the winding up,* must be applied in paying interest on those debts.

By s. 189(4) the rate of interest is whichever is the greater of:

(*a*) the rate in s. 17 of the Judgments Act 1838, which is varied from time to time by statutory instrument; and

(*b*) the rate applicable to the debt apart from the winding up.

All interest payable under s. 189 ranks equally, whether or not the debts on which it is payable rank equally.

10. Information as to pending liquidations. If any winding up is not concluded within one year after its commencement, the liquidator must, by s. 192, at prescribed intervals until the winding up is complete, send to the registrar of companies statements containing prescribed particulars concerning the proceedings in, and position of, the liquidation.

11. Meetings to ascertain wishes of creditors or contributories. Section 195(1) provides that the court may have regard to the wishes of creditors or contributories as regards all matters relating to the winding up, and, if it thinks fit, for the purpose of ascertaining those wishes, may direct meetings of creditors or contributories to be held, and may appoint a person to act as chairman and report the result to the court.

By s. 195(2) in the case of creditors regard must be had to the value of each creditor's debt, and by s. 195(3) in the case of contributories regard must be had to the number of votes conferred on each contributory by the Companies Act 1985 or the articles.

12. Offences of fraud, deception, etc. before and during winding up. Sections 206 to 211 specify numerous offences of which a past or present officer of a company in liquidation can be found guilty.

The offences include the following:

(a) concealing any part of the company's property to the value of £120 or more: s. 206(1)(a);

(b) concealing or falsifying books or papers relating to the company's affairs: ss. 206(1)(c) and 209;

(c) pawning, pledging or disposing of any property of the company which has been obtained on credit and has not been paid for (unless such disposal was in the ordinary way of the company's business): s. 206(1)(f);

(d) having made a gift of the company's property within five years before the commencement of winding up: s. 207(1);

(e) failing to hand over to the liquidator company property, books and papers: s. 208(1);

(f) making any material omission from any statement relating to the company's affairs: s. 210(1); and

(g) making a false representation to creditors for the purpose of obtaining their consent to some agreement: s. 211(1).

With regard to most of these offences the Act provides that it is a defence for the person charged to prove that he had no intent to defraud or no intent to conceal the company's state of affairs or to defeat the law. It is important to note that the onus of proving innocence thus lies on the person charged.

13. Misfeasance. Section 212 is an important provision. It states that if it appears in liquidation that any past or present officer, promoter, liquidator, administrator or administrative receiver or person who has otherwise taken part in the management of the company has misapplied or retained any of the company's money or property, or been guilty of any misfeasance, or breach of any fiduciary or other duty towards the company, the court may examine into his conduct on the application of:

(a) the official receiver; or

(b) the liquidator; or

(c) any creditor; or

(d) any contributory, with leave of the court.

The court may then compel him to *restore the money or property*, or to *contribute such sum as the court thinks just* to the company's assets *by way of compensation.*

For the purposes of this section, an auditor is an officer of the company (*see* 19:**19**).

14. Fraudulent and wrongful trading and use of prohibited company names. The court may impose *personal liability* for a company's debts on:

(*a*) persons who have been knowingly parties to the carrying on of the company's business to defraud creditors ('fraudulent trading'): s. 213;

(*b*) directors who ought to have realised that insolvent liquidation was inevitable but failed to take every step to minimize the potential loss to creditors ('wrongful trading'): s. 214; and

(*c*) persons involved in the management of a company which, without the authority of the court, is re-using the name of a company which went into insolvent liquidation within the previous five years: ss. 216 and 217.

These provisions have already been considered in relation to the limited liability clause of the memorandum (*see* 2:**34**).

15. Qualification of liquidator. Section 230 requires a liquidator and a provisional liquidator to be qualified to act as an insolvency practitioner in relation to the company.

Part XIII (i.e. ss. 388–398) deals with insolvency practitioners and their qualification. By s. 388 these provisions cover not only liquidators, provisional liquidators, administrators, administrative receivers and supervisors of voluntary arrangements in relation to companies but also trustees and other persons in relation to individual bankruptcy. They do not, however, apply to the official receiver.

By s. 390(1) only an individual may become qualified to act as an insolvency practitioner. Normally, by s. 390(2), he must be a member of a professional body recognised by the Secretary of State under s. 391. Otherwise he must obtain a special authorization from a competent authority under ss. 392–393, by applying to the Secretary of State or other authority specified by him and furnishing such information (including information as to his education and practical training and experience) as may be required. If the competent authority proposes to refuse authorization or proposes to withdraw it, the person concerned has a right to make representations to the competent authority under s. 395, and if necessary to have his case referred to and decided by the Insolvency Practitioners Tribunal under ss. 396–397. The constitution and procedure of the Tribunal are governed by the 7th Schedule.

There must be security for the proper performance of the liquidator's functions: s. 390(3).

Section 390(4) provides that a person is disqualified from acting as an insolvency practitioner if:

(*a*) he has been adjudged bankrupt and has not yet been discharged;

(*b*) he is subject to a disqualification order under the Company Directors Disqualification Act 1986; or

(*c*) he is a patient under the Mental Health Act 1983.

While, by s. 389(1), it is an offence for a person to act as an insolvency practitioner when he is not qualified to do so, s. 232 provides that the acts of the liquidator are valid notwithstanding any defect in his appointment, nomination or qualifications.

16. Supplies of gas, electricity, water and telephone. Formerly the suppliers of public utilities, though they were not preferential creditors, were, because of their monopoly position, able to compel the liquidator to pay outstanding accounts in full under the threat that otherwise the supplies would be discontinued. The Insolvency Act 1985 altered the law on this matter.

The rights of the suppliers of the public utilities of gas, electricity, water and telephone in a liquidation are now stated in s. 233 Insolvency Act 1986. The supplier, by s. 233(2), *may* impose on the liquidator the condition that he will personally guarantee the payment of the charges for the *continuing* supply, but *must not* impose the condition that any outstanding charges for the *pre-liquidation* supply are paid.

17. Getting in the company's property. Section 234(2) provides that, where *any person* has in his possession or control any property, books, papers or records to which the company appears to be entitled, the court may require that person to hand over the items to the liquidator.

By s. 234(3) and (4), if the liquidator seizes or disposes of property which is not property of the company at a time when he has reasonable grounds for believing that it is company property, he has:

(*a*) no liability for any loss or damage resulting from the seizure or disposal unless it was caused by his own negligence; and

(*b*) a lien on the property (or proceeds of sale) for expenses incurred in the seizure or disposal.

18. Duty to co-operate with liquidator. Section 235 makes it the duty of past and present officers of the company and other persons (including employees) who have had connections with the company during the previous year to give to the liquidator (defined here as including, in a compulsory winding up, the official receiver) such information concerning the company and its affairs as the liquidator may reasonably require and also to attend on him at such times as he may reasonably require.

19. Inquiry by court into company's dealings. Under s. 236 the court may, if applied to by the liquidator (including again the official receiver in a compulsory winding up), summon to appear before it:

(*a*) any officer of the company;

(*b*) any person known or suspected to have in his possession any property of the company or supposed to be indebted to the company; or

(*c*) any person whom the court thinks capable of giving information concerning the company's affairs.

The court has, in this connection, powers to arrest persons and keep them in custody and to seize and hold books, papers, records, money or goods in their possession.

By s. 237 the court has further enforcement powers which may be exercised in the light of evidence obtained from the inquiry under s. 236.

20. Transactions at an undervalue. Section 238(2) and (3) provides that where a company has entered into a transaction with any person *at an undervalue*, the liquidator may, if the transaction falls within a *specified period* before the winding up, apply to the court for an order to restore the position to what it would have been if the company had not entered into the transaction.

By s. 238(4) a company enters into a transaction at an undervalue for the purposes of this provision if:

(a) the company makes a *gift* to the person or receives *no consideration*; or

(b) the value of the consideration is *significantly less* than the value of the consideration provided by the company.

However, by s. 238(5), the court must not make an order under s. 238 if it is satisfied:

(a) that the company entered into the transaction in good faith and for the purpose of carrying on its business; *and*

(b) that at the time when it did so there were reasonable grounds for believing that the transaction would benefit the company.

By s. 240(1) the transaction must have been entered into *within two years* before the commencement of the winding up, and, in addition, by s. 240(2), the company must *either* have been unable to pay its debts at the time of the transaction *or* have become unable to pay its debts as a result of the transaction. However, the requirements of s. 240(2) are presumed to be satisfied unless the contrary is shown, if the transaction is entered into by the company with a person who is 'connected' with the company, as defined in ss. 249 and 435 (*see* 16:**30**).

Section 241(1), without restricting the court's general power to make under s. 238(3) such order as it thinks fit, specifies some particular orders which it may make. For example, the court may:

(a) require any property transferred as part of the transaction to be vested in the company;

(b) require any property to be vested in the company if it represents the application of the proceeds of sale of the property transferred;

(c) release or discharge any security given by the company;

(d) require any person to pay money to the liquidator for benefits received from the company; and

(e) provide for any surety or guarantor whose obligations were released or discharged under the transaction to be under a new or revived obligation.

By s. 241(2), although the court order may affect property of a person other than the person with whom the company entered into the transaction, it must not prejudice any interest in property which was acquired from a person other than the company *and* which was acquired in good faith, for value and without notice of the relevant circumstances, i.e. the circumstances which make an order under s. 238 appropriate.

21. Preferences. The provisions relating to preferences are similar to those relating to transactions at an undervalue. Section 239(2) and (3) provides that where a company has *given a preference* to any person within a *specified period* before the winding up, the liquidator may apply to the court for an order to restore the position to what it would have been if the company had not given the preference.

By s. 239(4) a company gives a preference for the purposes of this provision if:

(*a*) the person is one of the company's creditors or a surety or guarantor for any of the company's debts or liabilities; *and*

(*b*) the company does anything which has the effect of putting that person into a better position, in the event of the company going into insolvent liquidation, than he would have been in if the thing had not been done.

Section 239(5) provides that the court must not make an order unless the company was influenced by a desire to produce the effect stated in s. 239(4)(*b*) above, but s. 239(6) provides that if the preference is given to a person 'connected' with the company (otherwise than by mere employment), the company is presumed, unless the contrary is shown, to have been influenced by such a desire.

By s. 240(1) the specified period relating to preferences is:

(*a*) *two years* before the commencement of winding up if the preference has been given to a person who is 'connected' with the company; and

(*b*) *six months* before the commencement of winding up in any other case.

By s. 240(2) the company must *either* have been unable to pay its debts at the time of the preference *or* have become unable to pay its debts as a result of the preference. The presumption in s. 240(2) relating to transactions at an undervalue with a 'connected' person does not apply to preferences.

In other respects the provisions relating to preferences are the same as those relating to transactions at an undervalue (*see* **20**).

22. Extortionate credit transactions.

Section 244(1) and (2) provides that the court may, if applied to by the liquidator, make an order with regard to a transaction for providing credit to the company, if the transaction:

(*a*) is or was *extortionate*; *and*

(*b*) was entered into in the period of *three months* before the company went into liquidation.

By s. 244(3) a transaction is extortionate for the purposes of this provision if, considering the risk accepted by the person providing the credit:

(*a*) the terms of it are or were such as to require grossly exorbitant payments to be made in return for the provision of the credit; *or*

(*b*) it contravened ordinary principles of fair dealing in some other way.

It is presumed, unless the contrary is proved, that a transaction is or (as the case may be) was extortionate.

By s. 244(4) an order may contain one or more of the following as the court thinks fit:

(*a*) provision setting aside any obligation created by the transaction;

(*b*) provision varying the terms of the transaction in some other way;

(*c*) provision requiring a party to the transaction to pay to the liquidator any sums paid to that person by the company;

(*d*) provision requiring any person to surrender to the liquidator any property held by him as security for the transaction; and

(*e*) provision directing accounts to be taken between any persons.

23. Avoidance of certain floating charges.

The aim of the statutory provisions for the avoidance of certain floating charges, now in s. 245 Insolvency Act 1986, is to prevent a company from selecting one of its existing unsecured creditors and, by giving him a floating charge on its assets, enabling him to claim a priority over the others. It is similar in principle to the rules regarding preferences (*see* **21**).

The provisions were strengthened by the Insolvency Act 1985.

Section 245(2) provides that a floating charge on a company's undertaking or property created at a *specified time* is invalid except to the extent of the total of:

(*a*) the money paid or the value of the goods or services supplied to the company at the same time as, or after, the creation of the charge;

(*b*) the value of the discharge or reduction, at the same time as, or after, the creation of the charge, or any debt of the company; and

(*c*) the amount of interest (if any) payable on (*a*) or (*b*) in accordance with the agreement under which the money was paid, the goods or services supplied or the debt discharged or reduced.

The relevant period of time for this provision is, by s. 245(2), the period of *two years* before the commencement of winding up if the charge is created in favour of a person who is 'connected' with the company, and the period of *12 months* before the commencement of winding up in other cases.

However, s. 245(4) provides that where a company creates a floating charge within the 12 months before the commencement *and* the person in favour of whom the charge is created is not 'connected' with the company, then the floating charge will not be invalid unless:

(*a*) the company is at the date of the creation of the charge unable to pay its debts; *or*

(*b*) the company becomes unable to pay its debts as a result of the transaction under which the charge was created.

24. Unenforceability of liens on books, etc. Section 246(2) provides that a lien or other right to retain possession of any of the books, papers or other records of the company is unenforceable in so far as its enforcement would deny possession of these items to the liquidator.

This provision does not apply to a lien on documents which give a title to property: s. 246(3).

25. Court's power to declare dissolution void. Section 651 Companies Act 1985, which was amended by the Insolvency Act 1985, provides that a dissolved company can be revived if necessary. This process of resurrection is sometimes advisable if the company is subsequently found to have had either unpaid debts or undistributed property.

Section 651(1), as amended, states that, on an application by the liquidator or any other interested person, the court at any time *within 12 years from the date of dissolution* may make an order, on such terms as the court thinks fit, declaring the dissolution to have been *void*.

By section 651(2) such proceedings may then be taken as might have been taken if the company had not been dissolved.

Section 651(3) makes it the duty of the applicant to deliver to the registrar within seven days an office copy of the order.

26. Defunct companies. A company can also be restored to life under ss. 652–653 Companies Act 1985, the main purpose of which is to enable a company which is no longer carrying on business, but which has not been wound up, to be dissolved by removal from the register (*see* 27:**1**).

Section 652(1) states that where the registrar has reasonable cause to believe that a company is not carrying on business, he may send a letter inquiring whether it is doing so.

Section 652(2) states that if *within one month* he does not receive an answer, he must *within the next 14 days* send a registered letter, referring to the first letter, and stating that if an answer is not received within one month a notice will be published in the *Gazette* with a view to striking the company off the register.

Section 652(3) states that if he receives an answer saying that the company is not carrying on business, or does not receive any answer within one month after sending the second letter, he may publish in the *Gazette* and send to the company a notice that *after three months* the name of the company will, unless cause is shown to the contrary, be struck off the register and the company dissolved.

Section 652(4) requires the registrar to publish and send to the company or the liquidator (if any) a notice similar to that specified in s. 652(3) where a company is in *liquidation*, but he has reasonable cause to believe either that no liquidator is acting, or that the affairs of the company have been fully wound up, and the returns required to be made by the liquidator have not been made *for six consecutive months*.

Section 652(5) states that after the specified time the registrar may strike the company's name off the register, and must publish notice of the fact in the *Gazette*, whereupon the company is *dissolved*. This does not affect, however, either the liability, if any, of the directors, officers, or members, or the power of the court to wind up the company: s. 652(6).

Finally, s. 653(2) states that if the company, or any member or creditor, feels aggrieved by the company having been struck off, it or he may apply to the court *within 20 years*. If the court is satisfied that the company was carrying on business when it was struck off, or that it is just to restore it to the register, it may order the company's name to be restored. In order to qualify as an applicant the petitioner must show that he was a member or creditor *at the date of dissolution*. The words 'any member', however, extend to the personal representative of a deceased member, even though he was never on the register of members, since it is not unlikely that in the course of the 20 years a registered member might die: *Re Bayswater Trading Co. Ltd.* (1970).

A copy of the court order must, by s. 653(3), be delivered to the registrar, and the company is then *deemed to have continued to exist as if its name had not been struck off*. The court may place it and other persons in their original position. The effect of this provision is that all acts done by the company during the period between dissolution and restoration are validated, and this period is ignored for the purposes of the Limitation Act.

27. The property of a dissolved company. Section 654 states that where a company is dissolved, all its property, except that which it holds on trust for another person, is deemed to be *bona vacantia*, and accordingly belongs to the Crown. Section 655(1) authorizes the Crown to dispose of such property despite the possibility that an order may be made under s. 651 or 653 reviving the dissolved company. By s. 654(2) if such an order is made, the disposition is not affected but the Crown must pay to the company the amount received for the property or, if none, an amount equal to its value.

Alternatively, s. 656 empowers the Crown to *disclaim* the property by a notice signed by the Treasury Solicitor.

Progress test 31

1. What are preferential debts? (**2**)
2. In what circumstances and by what procedure may a special manager be appointed in liquidation? (**3**)

3. Give an account of the liquidator's right of disclaimer. (**4**)

4. What is the position of a person who suffers loss as a result of the exercise by the liquidator of his right of disclaimer? (**4**)

5. What are the rights of a creditor who has issued execution against a company which is in liquidation? (**5**)

6. What provision is made for the payment of interest on debts between the commencement of winding up and the date of payment? (**9**)

7. State what you understand by misfeasance proceedings. Who may apply to the court in connection with such proceedings? (**13**)

8. For what nature of conduct may the court impose personal liability for the company's debts in a winding up? (**14; 2:34**)

9. Give the statutory provisions regarding the qualification of a liquidator. (**15**)

10. What condition may the suppliers of public utilities impose on a liquidator in return for continuing their services despite outstanding charges? (**16**)

11. Give an account of the court's power to conduct an inquiry into a company's dealings. (**19**)

12. What is meant by a 'transaction at an undervalue' for the purposes of the Insolvency Act 1986? (**20**)

13. State the statutory provisions relating to preferences given by a company before the commencement of winding up. (**21**)

14. What orders may be made by the court where the company has entered into an extortionate credit transaction? (**22**)

15. Under what circumstances will a floating charge on the company's assets be invalid? (**23**)

16. Discuss the court's power to declare a dissolution void. (**25**)

17. Give the statutory provisions regarding the removal from the register of defunct companies. (**26**)

18. Once a defunct company has been removed from the register, who can apply, and within what period of time, for its restoration? (**26**)

19. To whom does any property of a dissolved company belong? (**27**)

32

Arrangements and reconstructions

1. The scope of s. 425. We have already seen in 29:**21** that a company in voluntary liquidation may make an arrangement with its creditors under s. 110 Insolvency Act 1986. A company which is *not* in liquidation, however, cannot proceed under that section. It must instead enter into either a voluntary arrangement under Part I of the Insolvency Act 1986 (*see* 26:**6–8**) or a scheme of arrangement under s. 425 Companies Act 1985, under which almost any type of compromise, arrangement or reorganisation of the company's capital can be effected.

Section 425 has been mentioned before in connection with the alteration of rights attached to shares (*see* 11:**13**). But it has a far wider scope than this. Since, as we shall see below, the consent of the court has to be obtained, the section permits the company to enter into any type of scheme regarding either its creditors or its members which does not conflict with the general law or with any particular statutory provision. Thus the company could not under this section be empowered to do an *ultra vires* act, or to convert its issued share capital into redeemable shares (*see* 11:**24**) but only to do acts which are lawful in themselves.

Moreover, the section does not enable the company to avoid a prescribed statutory procedure where there is one, e.g. for the reduction of capital.

2. Power to compromise with creditors and members. Section 425(1) (as amended by the Insolvency Act 1985) states that where a compromise or arrangement is proposed between a company and its creditors or any class of them, or its members or any class of them, the court may, on the application of the company, or any creditor, or member, or liquidator or administrator, *order a meeting* of the creditors or members, or any class of them, as the case may be.

Section 425(2) states that if a *majority in number* representing *three-quarters in value* of the creditors or members or any class of them, present and voting either in person or by proxy, agree to any compromise or arrangement, it is *binding if sanctioned by the court*.

The court will refuse to sanction the arrangement unless the class meetings are properly constituted. Thus where one of the members was the wholly-owned subsidiary of a company which was to purchase all the shares under the arrangement, Templeman J. held that that member formed a class on its own, separate from the other members, since it had different interests, and accordingly he refused to sanction the arrangement: *Re Hellenic & General Trust Ltd.* (1976).

Section 425(3) states that the court order has no effect until a copy has been delivered to the registrar for registration. Further, a copy of the order must be annexed to every copy of the memorandum subsequently issued.

3. Information to be sent with notice of the meeting. Section 426(2) requires the company to send with the notice of the meeting called under s. 425 a *statement* explaining the *effect of the scheme*, and stating in particular the *material interests of the directors* and the effect of the scheme on them.

If the notice is given by advertisement, such a statement must be included, or a place notified where creditors or members may obtain copies of one: s. 426(3).

Where the scheme affects the rights of debenture-holders, the statement must give a similar explanation with regard to the trustees of any deed for securing the issue as is required with regard to the directors: s. 426(4).

4. Matters for which the court may provide. Section 427(1)–(2) states that where an application is made to the court under s. 425 for the sanction of a scheme, and that scheme is one under which the whole or part of the company's undertaking or property is to be *transferred to another company*, the court may provide for the following matters listed in s. 427(3):

(a) the transfer of the whole or part of the undertaking, property or liabilities of the transferor company to the transferee company;

(b) the allotting or appropriation by the transferee company of shares or debentures in that company;

(c) the continuation by or against the transferee company of legal proceedings which are pending by or against the transferor company;

(d) the dissolution, without winding up, of the transferor company (*see* **27:1**);

(e) dissenting persons;

(f) any other incidental matters.

Section 427(5) requires a copy of the court order to be delivered to the registrar within seven days.

5. Comparison with a reconstruction under s. 110 Insolvency Act 1986. It is clear from s. 427 that it is possible under ss. 425–427 for companies to amalgamate, so that the undertaking and property of one is transferred to another. This may, as is obvious from s. 427(1)(d), involve the dissolution of the transferor company without a winding up (i.e. a 'merger').

In 29:**20** we saw that much the same sort of result can be achieved under s. 110 Insolvency Act 1986, and it is therefore interesting to compare and contrast the two types of reconstruction:

(a) Section 110 Insolvency Act 1986 is a much *narrower* section than s. 425. It permits only one type of reconstruction, by which a company in voluntary liquidation sells its undertaking for shares in another company. Section 425 covers a wide variety of activities, as was mentioned in **1**.

(b) Section 110 Insolvency Act 1986 can be used only by a company in *voluntary liquidation*. Section 425 is frequently used by a company which is a going concern, even though the court may provide, under s. 427, for the dissolution of the transferor company in appropriate circumstances.

(c) Section 110 Insolvency Act 1986 can be used without obtaining the *sanction of the court*, unless the winding up is a *creditors'* voluntary winding up, when either the sanction of the court or of the liquidation committee must be obtained. Section 425 invariably requires the sanction of the court.

(d) A dissentient under s. 110 Insolvency Act 1986 can require the liquidator either to purchase his interest or to abandon the whole scheme. Under s. 425 the scheme will bind all the members once it is sanctioned by the court, though the court may make provision for dissentients under s. 427(1)(*e*).

6. Takeover offers. The statutory provisions relating to 'takeover offers' are contained in Part XIIIA of the Companies Act 1985.

Part XIIIA, consisting of ss. 428–430F of the Act, was added by s. 172 and 12th Schedule Financial Services Act 1986. Section 172 of that Act provides that the new ss. 428–430F Companies Act 1985 are to be substituted for the original ss. 428–430 Companies Act 1985, which were within Part XIII of the Act. The provisions have now been allocated a Part for themselves and the term 'takeover offer', formerly merely a popular term, has now a statutory definition. The major principles have remained unchanged, but the provisions have been amended and their terminology modernized.

By s. 428(1) 'a takeover offer' means an offer to acquire all the shares, or all the shares of any class, in a company (other than shares which at the date of the offer are already held by the offeror), and which is on terms which are the same for all the shares to which the offer relates or for all the shares of each class.

By s. 430E(1) the provision that the takeover offer must extend to 'all the shares' is to be regarded as satisfied where the offer extends to all shares other than those of the offeror's associates (e.g. a company in the same group as the offeror).

It can often happen that the person making a takeover offer wishes to enhance his offer in order to attract further acceptances, and the question of the date when an offer is made must be provided for because of the time factors involved in the statutory provisions. Section 428(7) answers the question by stating that where the terms of an offer make provision for their revision and for acceptances on the previous terms to be treated as acceptances on the revised terms, the revision is not to be regarded as the making of a fresh offer, and so the date of the revised offer is to be taken to be the same as the date of the original offer.

The earlier versions of the takeover provisions referred to the offer as being made by the 'transferee company', while the term 'transferor company' was used of the company which was being taken over. These somewhat clumsy terms have been replaced by the terms 'offeror' and 'the company', respectively. Section 428(8), therefore, defines 'the offeror' as meaning the person making a takeover offer and 'the company' as meaning the company whose shares are the subject of the offer.

With regard to the term 'offeror', it should be noted that it is possible for a takeover offer to be made by two or more persons jointly, and, by s. 430D, there are modifications to the statutory provisions in such a case.

It should also be appreciated that, although the term 'transferee company' has been dropped in favour of the term 'offeror', the person making the offer will in fact usually be another company (an artificial legal person) and not an individual (a natural person).

7. Right of offeror to buy out minority shareholders. Section 429(1) and (2) provides that, if the offeror has received acceptances for at least *nine-tenths* of the shares (or nine-tenths of the class) to which the offer relates, he may give notice to the holder of any shares (or shares of the class) not acquired that *he desires to acquire* those shares.

In order to be able to exercise this right the offeror must, by s. 429(3), have acquired the minimum nine-tenths of shares *before the end of four months from the date of the offer*, and the notice which he gives to the holder under subsection (1) or (2) above must be given *within two months after he has acquired the necessary minimum nine-tenths*.

By s. 429(4) the offeror must send a copy of the notice to the company along with a statutory declaration stating that the conditions for the giving of the notice are satisfied. If the offeror is a company, this statutory declaration must be signed by a director: s. 429(5).

If, while the takeover offer is open, the offeror acquires shares to which the offer relates but does so in some other way than by acceptances of the offer (e.g. he may purchase them in the market), then, provided that the price which he has paid for them does not exceed the price offered in the takeover offer, these shares can be counted towards the nine-tenths necessary for the exercise of the right to buy under s. 429.

The effect of a notice under s. 429 is that the offeror is *entitled and bound to acquire the shares on the terms of the offer:* s. 430(2).

At the end of *six weeks from the date of the notice*, the offeror must, by s. 430(5), pay or transfer *to the company* the consideration for the shares to which the notice relates, and, by s. 430(6), must accompany it by a transfer executed on behalf of the shareholder by a person appointed by the offeror so that the company may register the offeror as the holder of the shares.

The consideration received by the company under s. 430(5) must be held on trust by it for the shareholder concerned: s. 430(9).

8. Right of minority shareholder to be bought out by offeror.
Section 430A(1) and (2) provides that, if a takeover offer results in the offeror obtaining nine-tenths of the shares (or class of shares), counting in shares which he has acquired in some other way than by acceptances, the holder of any shares who has not accepted the offer may write to the offeror *requiring him to acquire his shares*. This enables a shareholder who refused to accept the offer to change his mind, as he may very well wish to do when he finds himself in a helpless minority.

By s. 430A(3) the offeror must give any shareholder who has not accepted the offer notice of the rights which he may exercise under subsections (1) and (2) above. He must do this *within one month* after the time when he acquires the necessary nine-tenths, and if at that point of time the offer is still open for acceptance, the offeror must mention that fact in the notice under s. 430A(3).

By s. 430A(4), however, the shareholder is legally entitled to a longer period for the exercise of his right to be bought out. The notice given to him under s. 430A(3) may specify a period for the exercise of the right, but this period must be *not less than three months after the end of the period within which the offer can be accepted.*

The provisions for notice under s. 430A(3) do not apply if the offeror has given the shareholder a notice under s. 429 that he desires to acquire the shares: s. 430A(5).

The effect of the exercise by a shareholder of his right to be bought out under s. 430A is that the offeror is *entitled and bound to acquire the shares on the terms of the offer or on such other terms as may be agreed:* s. 430B(2).

9. Applications to court. Under s. 430C there are three possible situations in which an application to court may be made in connection with a takeover offer:

(*a*) By s. 430C(1), where a shareholder has received a notice under s. 429 stating that the offeror, having obtained the necessary nine-tenths, desires to acquire his shares also, the court may, if the shareholder applies to it *within six weeks after the giving of the notice,* *either:*

(*i*) order that the offeror shall not be entitled and bound to acquire the shares; *or*

(*ii*) specify terms of acquisition different from those of the offer.

(*b*) By s. 430C(3), where the shareholder exercises his rights under s. 430A to be bought out, the court may, if an application is made to it by him or by the offeror, order that the terms on which the offeror is entitled and bound to acquire the shares shall be such *as the court thinks fit.*

(*c*) By s. 430C(5), where a takeover offer has not been accepted by the necessary nine-tenths, with the result that the offeror is not entitled to give notices under s. 429(1) or (2), the offeror may apply to the court for an order authorizing him to give such notices. The purpose of this provision is to cover the situation where the offeror has not reached his target of nine-tenths because he has been unable to trace all the shareholders. The court must be satisfied:

(*i*) that the offeror has after reasonable enquiry been unable to trace one or more of the shareholders concerned;

(*ii*) that the shares of these shareholders, if added to the shares for which acceptances have been given, would amount to nine-tenths; *and*

(*iii*) that the consideration offered is fair and reasonable.

Further, the court must have regard to the number of shareholders who *have been traced but who have not accepted the offer,* and must not make an order unless it considers that it is just and equitable to do so.

10. View taken by court on application of dissenting shareholder.

Under the former provisions also, an application to court within category (*a*) in **9** above could be made by a dissenting shareholder, and decided cases have established a number of points regarding the view taken by the court on such applications.

The court will normally take the view that since the required majority have approved the scheme, it is up to the dissenting shareholder to show grounds for his disapproval of it. Thus the offer will be treated as *prima facie* a fair one, and the burden of showing otherwise is on the dissentient who seeks relief. In discharging it he must show unfairness to the shareholders *as a body*, so that while the market price of the shares is a relevant factor, the personal circumstances of the dissentient are not: *Re Grierson, Oldham and Adams* (1968).

Where, however, the offer is in reality being made by the same majority shareholders who have accepted it, the burden of proof is *reversed* and it is up to the offeror to *show that the scheme is fair*. This is a perfect example of what is meant by 'lifting the veil' of incorporation, and the facts of *Re Bugle Press Ltd.* (1961), are interesting in this connection.

> B.P. Ltd. had an issued capital of 10,000 £1 shares, of which Jackson held 4,500, Shaw held 4,500, and Treby held 1,000. Jackson and Shaw then incorporated a new company, called Jackson and Shaw (Holdings) Ltd., with an issued capital of 100 shares, of which each of them held 50. This company then made an offer under what is now s. 428 Companies Act 1985 to the shareholders of B.P. Ltd. Jackson and Shaw naturally accepted the offer, but Treby refused it on the grounds that the price was too low. HELD: He was not bound to sell at that price. Where 'as a matter of substance the persons who are putting forward the offer are the majority shareholders', it is up to them to show that the scheme is fair and not to the dissenting shareholder to show that it is unfair.

NOTE: Here the corporate personality of Jackson and Shaw (Holdings) Ltd., has been disregarded. The 'veil' has been lifted to reveal, behind the corporate person, the natural persons of Jackson and Shaw – those same natural persons who are accepting the offer made, in substance, by themselves.

11. The meaning of 'reconstruction' and 'amalgamation'. In his celebrated speech in *Liversidge* v. *Anderson* (1942), Lord Atkin quoted a passage from Lewis Carroll's *Through the Looking-Glass*: '"When I use a word," Humpty Dumpty said, "it means just what I choose it to mean, neither more nor less." "The question is," said Alice, "whether you can make words mean so many different things."'

Unfortunately, you can. And the longer the word, the safer you are, for while people sometimes ask you what you mean by a *short* word, they rarely have the courage to inquire what a *long* word means.

Words such as 'reconstruction' and 'amalgamation' have *no fixed technical legal significance*, but are used loosely to indicate some sort of re-arrangement or re-organisation entered into by companies. Examiners who ask students to explain what these words mean, therefore, are in effect asking for an account of procedures which can be adopted under ss. 425–427 and 428 Companies Act 1985 and 110 Insolvency Act 1986. All that can be said about the *meaning* of the words is that a 'reconstruction' can cover, for instance, a reorganisation of share or loan capital which is purely *internal* affecting *one company only* (s. 425), or the formation of a *new* company to carry on the business of the old one, with the same shareholders (s. 110 Insolvency Act 1986). The word 'amalgamation' necessarily involves *two companies*, but can cover the transfer of the whole undertaking from one company to another under ss. 425–427, or the absorption of one company by another under s. 110 Insolvency Act 1986, or even extend to the *economic*, though not the legal, unity obtainable under s. 428.

Humpty Dumpty clearly had the right idea, but it is very important for examination purposes not to be drawn into prolonged and inconclusive discussion, and instead to show a detailed knowledge of the procedures which can be adopted under the various sections. Too many students take refuge in complexity, no doubt believing with Oscar Wilde that 'to be intelligible is to be found out'. Examiners are not unaware of this, and the best marks will always go to the student who understands what he knows, knows what he means, and means what he says.

Progress test 32

1. Discuss the company's power to enter into a scheme of arrangement with its creditors or members. (**2**)

2. When a meeting of creditors or members is called in connection with a scheme of arrangement, what information must be sent out with the notice of the meeting? (**3**)

3. When application is made to the court to sanction a scheme of arrangement, and the scheme is one under which the whole or part of the company's undertaking is to be transferred to another company, for what matters may the court provide? (**4**)

4. Compare and contrast a reconstruction under s. 110 Insolvency Act 1986 with a reconstruction under ss. 425–427. (**5, 29:20**)

5. What do you understand by a 'takeover offer'? (**6**)

6. Give an account of the statutory provisions which permit a company making an offer for the shares of another company to acquire the shares of a dissenting minority. (**7**)

7. What is the position in a takeover offer of a dissenting shareholder whose shares are not acquired by the company making the offer? (**8**)

8. What applications may be made to the court in connection with a takeover offer? (**9**)

9. Where a dissenting shareholder in a takeover offer applies to the court to prevent his shares being acquired, what principles guide the court in making its decision? (**10**)

10. Discuss the various types of reconstruction and amalgamation which may be effected by companies. (**11**)

Appendix
Examination technique

Revision

1. Introduction. All students have their own methods of revising and you will certainly have yours. It is likely, however, that you will benefit by spending a few minutes reading this short guide to revision.

Your revision should have three main aims:

(*a*) complete understanding of the subject;
(*b*) retention and recall of the subject;
(*c*) the ability to explain and apply the subject.

Understanding is the key to both the learning and use of a subject. Thus it is understanding which is crucial to examination success and your revision should be designed above all to reinforce understanding. No matter how much a subject may interest you when you actually study it, learning it for an examination can at best be tedious and at worst boring. You must try to lessen this effect.

2. Revision programme. Tedium in revision is caused mainly by reading the same original notes over and over again. This is also unproductive. It is far better to adopt a *positive revision* programme, one which uses your time profitably and enables you to teach yourself. Your Handbook is the perfect basis for such a programme.

Revision should be done a chapter at a time. Try adopting the following sequence.

(*a*) *Re-read* the chapter thoroughly.
(*b*) *Make revision notes.* These can consist of no more than the headings in the text with a very brief note about important principles. Take each note in turn and try to recall and explain the subject matter.

If you can, proceed to the next; if you cannot, look in your Handbook. By doing this, you will revise, test your knowledge and spend your time profitably by concentrating your revision on those aspects of the subject with which you are least familiar. In addition, you will have an excellent last-minute revision aid.

(c) Construct a chart for each topic using the headings in your Handbook. Many people respond well to diagrammatic explanations and summaries which provide an extremely quick and efficient means of revision. You need to think how best to construct them and in doing so you teach yourself and better understand the subject.

Two tips: do not try to include too much on each diagram; and do not try to economize on paper. The impact and usefulness of a diagram depends very much on its visual simplicity. The same applies to revision notes.

(d) Prepare concise explanations of key principles that you are likely to need so that during the examination you do not have to think about how to explain something which you probably know well but cannot easily put into words there and then.

(e) Answer the progress tests again. You should find a significant improvement in the number of questions that you can answer immediately. This exercise will primarily test your ability to recall and explain facts.

(f) Plan answers to the specimen examination questions set by the relevant examining body. Planning answers is often a more useful exercise than actually writing the answer out in full. In planning you have in effect answered the question and writing it out is a largely mechanical exercise. If, however, you feel that you need the practice in essay writing, answer some fully.

Read the notes on answering questions (see **3** below) before planning any answers.

The examination

3. Examination technique.

(a) Read the examination instructions carefully.

(b) Read through the questions and provisionally mark which ones to answer. Take care over your choice. An apparently simple question might have a hidden twist – do not get caught out. Similarly, never decide to answer a question which is in two or more parts on the strength of the first part alone. Make sure that you can answer *all* parts.

(c) Make sure you have selected the right number of questions – you get no extra marks for answering more!

(d) Remember that the first 50 per cent of the marks for any question is the easier to earn. Unless you are working in complete ignorance, you will always earn more marks per minute while answering a new question than while continuing to answer one that is more than half done. So you can earn many more marks by half-completing two answers than by completing either one individually.

(e) Concentrate on displaying your knowledge. There is almost always one question that you are not happy about but nevertheless need to attempt. In answer to such a question put down all you *do* know, and then devote the unused time to improving some other answer. Certainly you will not get full marks by doing this, but nor will you if you fill your page with nonsense. By spending the saved time on another answer you will at least be gaining the odd mark or so.

(f) Plan all your answers – this is absolutely vital.

(g) If time is running out put down your answer in the form of notes, making sure that every part of the question has some answer – no matter how short – that summarizes the key elements. Don't worry about shortage of time: it is more often a sign of knowing too much than too little.

(h) Check through your answers. A few minutes doing this can eliminate many minor errors and give a final 'polish' to your answers.

Company law papers

4. Acts and cases. An examiner does not require the numbers of the sections of the Acts to be stated, but if you can do this accurately you will improve the general tone of your paper. The invaluable expression 'The Act provides' can always be used where memory fails.

The names of cases (though not the dates) should be memorized and cited where appropriate, and you should never invent a case. You may give hypothetical facts to explain the workings of a particular legal rule, but you must do this honestly, stating that the facts are imaginary. If you know that there is a decided case on a particular point, but cannot remember its name, you should simply write 'In a decided case it was held that ...'

5. Types of question. Questions on company law fall into four main categories:

(*a*) The *direct* question asking for specific knowledge, phrased in a manner which makes it easily identifiable, for example: By what machinery and in what circumstances can a company (*i*) increase its capital, (*ii*) purchase its own shares?

Here the examiner is being as explicit as possible. He wants to know if the student has learnt the material in 11:**18** and 11:**25–28**.

Questions of this type *should always be attempted*, for it is almost impossible to misunderstand them.

(*b*) The *indirect* question asking for specific knowledge, usually by means of a citation from a judgment, report or textbook, for example: Comment on and explain the following passage from the judgment of Lord Coleridge, C.J. in *Re Perkins* (24 Q.B.D. 613): 'It seems to me extremely important not to throw any doubt on the principle that companies have nothing whatever to do with the relations between trustees and their *cestuis que trust* in respect of the shares of the company'.

The student usually dislikes this type of question unless he has had legal training. He does not understand 24 Q.B.D. 613. He has not read *Re Perkins*. He does not know what happened in *Re Perkins*. What does Lord Coleridge, C.J. (Chief Justice? Charles James?) mean? Why does Lord Coleridge think it so important? And what is it that is so important? Why does he always have an examination on a day when he cannot think clearly?

A moment's reflection will restore confidence. First, unnecessary words must be ignored. 'It seems to me extremely important not to throw any doubt on the principle that ...' adds nothing to the question, so that it can be reduced to:

'Companies have nothing (whatever) to do with the relations between trustees and their *cestuis que trust* in respect of the shares of the company.'

Now it should be clear that the question is on *trusts* of shares. Section

360 is the only section of the Act which concerns trusts. The answer therefore is to be found in 11:**11–14**.

This type of question *should also always be attempted*, for it is easier than it looks.

(*c*) The *problem* question, often consisting of the facts of a decided case which the student may or may not recognise, e.g.: X and Y hold all the issued shares of B Ltd. They also together hold 950 shares in C Ltd. The other shareholder in C Ltd. is Z, who holds the remaining 50 shares in its issued share capital. B Ltd. makes an offer for Z's shares in C Ltd. at a valuation made by the latter company's accountants. Z refuses the offer. What are the respective rights of X and Y on the one hand and Z on the other hand?

Here you may at once recognise the facts as being similar to those in *Re Bugle Press Ltd.* (1961). If so, you will find the question easier to answer than if you have never heard of this case. But you should not let failure to recognise a case prevent you from answering a question. You can still get good marks for knowing the principles of law involved, and the statutory provisions contained in ss. 428–430F (*see* 32:**6–10**).

If you have difficulty in understanding the legal situation described in the question, you should draw a small diagram on a piece of rough paper, e.g.:

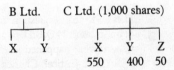

This sort of diagram indicates clearly that *the figures are important* and must be considered, but no diagram should ever be included in a script.

Sometimes a problem question consists of entirely hypothetical facts, and if so, you should first identify it in the way described earlier. You should then discuss the principles and statutory provisions applicable exactly as if the question were a direct one.

(*d*) The 'gossip' question, e.g.: Discuss the aphorism that a company, like a marriage, can be created more easily and cheaply than it can be dissolved. This is by far the most dangerous type of question, for you will realise that with a little luck and a good command of

English you can cover at least a page *without knowing anything at all*. But you should be careful: *the examiner realises this too*. No marks will be given for rhetoric. No marks will be given for an account, however entertaining, of the marriage ceremony or of the grounds for divorce. *This question is in a company law paper*. The examiner wants the candidate to compare the ease and cheapness of company *formation* with the ease and cheapness of *dissolution*. But there are several methods of dissolution: some are easier and cheaper than others. Presumably he requires a discussion of all of them.

The difficulty of this question is now apparent. Some of the material required will be found in Chapters 4 and 26, but clearly a very wide discussion of formation and dissolution is needed and the student must have a comprehensive knowledge to deal well with such a topic.

Finally, however, do not let nervousness turn to despair. Every student should remember that someone has to pass, or the profession will die out!

Index

M&E Handbooks

Law

'A' Level Law/B Jones
Basic Law/L B Curzon
Cases in Banking Law/P A Gheerbrant, D Palfreman
Cases in Company Law/M C Oliver
Cases in Contract Law/W T Major
Commercial and Industrial Law/A R Ruff
Company Law/M C Oliver, E Marshall
Constitutional and Administrative Law/I N Stevens
Consumer Law/M J Leder
Conveyancing Law/P H Kenny, C Bevan
Criminal Law/L B Curzon
English Legal History/L B Curzon
Equity and Trusts/L B Curzon
Family Law/P J Pace
General Principles of English Law/P W D Redmond, J Price, I N Stevens
Jurisprudence/L B Curzon
Labour Law/M Wright, C J Carr
Land Law/L B Curzon
Landlord and Tenant/J M Male
Law of Banking/D Palfreman
Law of Evidence/L B Curzon
Law of Torts/J G M Tyas
Law of Trusts/L B Curzon
Meetings: Their Law and Practice/L Hall, P Lawton, E Rigby
Mercantile Law/P W D Redmond, R G Lawson
Private International Law/A W Scott
Sale of Goods/W T Major
The Law of Contract/W T Major
Town and Country Planning Law/A M Williams